MW00977126

THE ANNUAL DIRECTORY OF AMERICAN
AND CANADIAN BED & BREAKFASTS

New England

Includes

EASTERN CANADA

2000 EDITION • VOLUME I

THE ANNUAL DIRECTORY OF AMERICAN AND CANADIAN BED & BREAKFASTS

New England

Includes

EASTERN CANADA

2000 EDITION • VOLUME I

Tracey Menges, *Compiler*

BARBOUR
PUBLISHING, INC.
Uhrichsville, Ohio

Copyright © 1989, 1990, 1991, 1992, 1993, 1994, 1995, 1996, 1997, 1998, 1999 by Barbour Publishing, Inc.

ISBN 1-57748-771-0

All rights reserved. Written permission must be secured from the publisher to use or reproduce any part of this book, except for brief quotations in critical reviews or articles.

Published by Barbour Publishing, Inc., P.O. Box 719, Uhrichsville, Ohio 44683
http://www.barbourbooks.com

Cover design and book design by Harriette Bateman
Page composition by Roger A. DeLiso, Rutledge Hill Press®

Printed in the United States of America.

1 2 3 4 5 6—02 01 00 99

Contents

Introduction

The 2000 edition of *The Annual Directory of New England Bed & Breakfasts* is one of the most comprehensive directories available today. Whether planning your honeymoon, a family vacation or reunion, or a business trip (many bed and breakfasts provide conference facilities), you will find what you are looking for at a bed and breakfast. They are all here just waiting to be discovered.

Once you know your destination, look for it, or one close by, to see what accommodations are available. Each state has a general map with city locations to help you plan your trip efficiently. There are listings for all New England states and the Canadian Provinces of New Brunswick, Nova Scotia, Prince Edward Island, Quebec. Don't be surprised to find a listing in the remote spot you thought only you knew about. Even if your favorite hideaway isn't listed, you're sure to discover a new one.

How to Use This Guide

The sample listing below is typical of the entries in this directory. Each bed and breakfast is listed alphabetically by city and establishment name. The description provides an overview of the bed and breakfast and may include nearby activities and attractions. *Please note that the descriptions have been provided by the hosts. The publisher has not visited these bed and breakfasts and is not responsible for inaccuracies.*

Following the description are notes that have been designed for easy reference. Looking at the sample, a quick glance tells you that this bed and breakfast has four guest rooms, two with private baths (PB) and two that share a bath (SB). The rates are for two people sharing one room. Tax may or may not be included.

GREAT TOWN

Favorite Bed and Breakfast

123 Main Street, 12345
(800) 555-1234

This quaint bed and breakfast is surrounded by five acres of award-winning landscaping and gardens. There are four guest rooms, each individually decorated with antiques. It is close to antique shops, restaurants, and outdoor activities. Breakfast includes homemade specialties and is served in the formal dining room at guests' leisure. Minimum stay of two nights.

Hosts: Sue and Jim Smith
Rooms: 4 (2 PB; 2 SB) $65-80
Full Breakfast
Credit Cards: A, B
Notes: 2, 5, 8, 10, 11, 12, 13

The specifics of "Credit Cards" and "Notes" are listed at the bottom of each page. For example, the letter A means that MasterCard is accepted. The number 10 means that tennis is available on the premises or within 10 to 15 miles.

In many cases, a bed and breakfast is listed with a reservation service that represents several houses in one area. This service is responsible for bookings and can answer other questions you may have. They also inspect each listing and can help you choose the best place for your needs.

Before You Arrive

Now that you have chosen the bed and breakfast that interests you, there are some things you need to find out. You should always make reservations in advance, and while you are doing so you should ask about the local taxes. City taxes can be an unwelcome surprise. Make sure there are accommodations for your children. If you have dietary needs or prefer nonsmoking rooms, find out if these requirements can be met. Ask about check-in times and cancellation policies. Get specific directions. Most bed and breakfasts are readily accessible, but many are a little out of the way.

When You Arrive

In many instances you are visiting someone's home. Be respectful of their property, their schedules, and their requests. Don't smoke if they ask you not to, and don't show up with pets without prior arrangement. Be tidy in shared bathrooms, and be prompt. Most places have small staffs or may be run single-handedly and cannot easily adjust to surprises.

With a little effort and a sense of adventure you will learn firsthand the advantages of bed and breakfast travel. You will rediscover hospitality in a time when kindness seems to have been pushed aside. With the help of this directory, you will find accommodations that are just as exciting as your traveling plans.

We would like to hear from you about any experiences you have had or any inns you wish to recommend. Please write us at the following address:

Barbour Publishing, Inc.
P.O. Box 719
Uhrichsville, Ohio 44683

THE ANNUAL DIRECTORY OF AMERICAN AND CANADIAN BED & BREAKFASTS

New England

Includes

EASTERN CANADA

2000 EDITION • VOLUME I

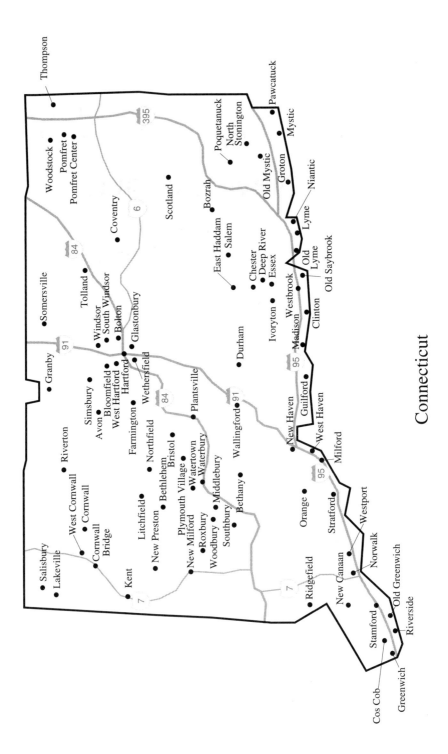

Connecticut

Connecticut

Nutmeg Bed & Breakfast Agency

P.O. Box 1117, West Hartford, 06127-1117
(860) 236-6698; (800) 727-7592
FAX (860) 232-7680
e-mail: nutmegbnb@home.com
www.bnb-link.com

405. This Colonial farmhouse was built in 1850 and sits on three acres bordering the Farmington River. Lovely screened porch and open deck where guests are welcome to relax and enjoy the scenery. The guest room, on the second floor, is furnished with white wicker. The steps, quite steep, are original, adding to the authenticity of the house. The guest room has a double bed, TV, and air conditioning for the warmer weather. There is an additional small room for a child. Continental breakfast. Children welcome. No smoking.

BETHANY

Bed & Breakfast, Ltd.

P.O. Box 216, New Haven, 06513
(203) 469-3260; e-mail: BandB@aol.com
www.bedandbreakfastltd.com

A gracious English country manor built in the 1930s in a lovely bucolic setting. Eclectic furnishings including many interesting antiques. Two rooms with private or semi-private baths. Barbecue available. Great area for hiking, horses, or bicycling. Children welcome. Convenient to Yale University. $95-110.

Nutmeg Bed & Breakfast Agency

P.O. Box 1117, West Hartford, 06127-1117
(860) 236-6698; (800) 727-7592
FAX (860) 232-7680
e-mail: nutmegbnb@home.com
www.bnb-link.com

204. This stately English-style country manor, built in 1937, has a surprisingly contemporary interior. Convenient to New Haven for Yale functions. Exercise equipment available and there are three guest rooms. The second floor room has twin beds, which can be made into a king-size bed, and private bath. Also on the second floor is a room with a futon and a half-bath. These two rooms would be most suitable for families traveling together. On the third floor is a double bed and private bath. Continental breakfast. Children welcome. No smoking.

BETHLEHEM

Nutmeg Bed & Breakfast Agency

P.O. Box 1117, West Hartford, 06127-1117
(860) 236-6698; (800) 727-7592
FAX (860) 232-7680
e-mail: nutmegbnb@home.com
www.bnb-link.com

310. On a very secluded hillside is one of the oldest New England bed and breakfasts. The building dates back to the 1700s and features three sitting rooms, three dining rooms, and four guest rooms. All are tastefully furnished. One guest room has a fireplace, one of four original to the house. Wide-plank floors and lots of rustic charm inside combine with the beauty of the country outside for an unbeatable getaway experience. Full breakfast. Children welcome. No smoking.

BLOOMFIELD

Nutmeg Bed & Breakfast Agency

P.O. Box 1117, West Hartford, 06127-1117
(860) 236-6698; (800) 727-7592
FAX (860) 232-7680
e-mail: nutmegbnb@home.com
www.bnb-link.com

450. Four guest rooms with private and shared baths. One has connecting playroom with TV and telephone. Another is a full suite with fireplace. Convenient to West Hartford and Hartford and across the road from Penwood State Forest for walking, jogging, or cross-country skiing. Full breakfast. Children welcome.

BOLTON

Jared Cone House

25 Hebron Road, 06043
(860) 643-8538; FAX (8660) 643-8538
e-mail: jsmith8046@aol.com

The Jared Cone House is one of the largest and oldest houses in Bolton. Bolton is a rural community with a population of 5,000, and is in the hilly farmland countryside just 10 miles east of

Jared Cone House

Hartford. Accommodations feature spacious bedrooms with queen-size beds, private baths, decorative fireplaces, and scenic views. Full breakfast is served on the weekends, featuring local homemade maple syrup; Continental breakfast served weekdays. Enjoy colonial hospitality year-round. Welcome!

Host: Cinde Smith
Rooms: 2 (PB $55-70
Full or Continental Breakfast
Credit Cards: None
Notes: 2, 5, 7, 8, 9, 10, 11, 12

BOZRAH

Bed & Breakfast, Ltd.

P.O. Box 216, New Haven, 06513
(203) 469-3260; e-mail: BandB@aol.com
www.bedandbreakfastltd.com

On a vineyard, this lovely bed and breakfast offers casual comfort and charm. Each room is replete with private bath, fireplace, and in-room TV and telephone. A wonderful full breakfast is offered daily. Near Mystic and Foxwoods Casino. Take a peek at its third-floor ballroom. Call for reasonable rates.

Nutmeg Bed & Breakfast Agency

P.O. Box 1117, West Hartford, 06127-1117
(860) 236-6698; (800) 727-7592
FAX (860) 232-7680
e-mail: nutmegbnb@home.com
www.bnb-link.com

505. Gambral Home circa 1790. Lovely country setting; host grows berries and makes wine; the berries are served in the country breakfast. Twenty minutes from Mystic and Ledyard. The four guest rooms have private baths, TVs, telephones, gas fireplaces, beautiful furnishings, ceiling fans; one bath has jet tub. Breakfast is served in glass-enclosed sunroom and guests have use of several sitting rooms. Guest room wing has its own private entrance. No children. No smoking.

NOTES: Credit cards accepted: A MasterCard; B Visa; C American Express; D Discover; E Diner's Club; F Other; 2 Personal checks accepted; 3 Lunch available; 4 Dinner available; 5 Open all year; 6 Pets welcome;

BRISTOL

Bed & Breakfast, Ltd.

P.O. Box 216, New Haven, 06513
(203) 469-3260; e-mail: BandB@aol.com
www.bedandbreakfastltd.com

A 32-room English Tudor home, three wings, a dozen baths, and numerous stone and marble fireplaces. Cable TV and telephone available. Suites with bedroom, sitting room, kitchen, and private baths available. $125.

Nutmeg Bed & Breakfast Agency

P.O. Box 1117, West Hartford, 06127-1117
(860) 236-6698; (800) 727-7592
FAX (860) 232-7680
e-mail: nutmegbnb@home.com
www.bnb-link.com

411. Bright and spacious English Tudor mansion has a grand foyer, large den, elegant formal dining room, sunroom, and back patio overlooking Farmington Valley and the fountains in the large yard. The ballroom suite contains a large living room with double sofa bed, a full eat-in kitchen, bedroom with double bed, and bath. Also five suites on second floor, including one with two bedrooms and a kitchen. There is a guest room with a Jacuzzi. All rooms have ceiling fans and TVs. Full breakfast. Smoking in designated areas only. Children welcome.

CHESTER

The Inn at Chester

318 West Main Street, 06412
(860) 526-9541; (800) 949-STAY
FAX (860) 526-4387

Nestled in the Connecticut River valley, the inn is on 12 wooded acres. A full-service inn offers fine dining, a tavern, game room, exercise room, sauna, bikes, and tennis. all the rooms are decorated with Eldred Wheller reproductions.

Two rooms have fireplaces. Each room has telephone, TV, air conditioning, and private bath. The post-and-beam dining room was voted best new restaurant in 1992 in Connecticut and has continued to win awards for its dining.

Host: Leonard Lieberman
Rooms: 42 (PB) $105-215
Continental Breakfast
Credit Cards: A, B, C
Notes: 2, 3, 4, 5, 6, 8, 9, 10, 11, 12, 14, 15

CLINTON

Captain Dibbell House

21 Commerce Street, 06413
(860) 669-1646; (888) 889-6882
FAX (860) 669-2300

This 1866 Victorian, on a historic residential street, is two blocks from the harbor and has a century-old, wisteria-covered iron truss bridge. Rooms are furnished with a comfortable mix of heirlooms, antiques, auction finds, and a growing collection of original art by New England artists. Bicycles are available. The inn is closed January through March. Children 14 and older are welcome.

Hosts: Helen and Ellis Adams
Rooms: 4 (PB) $89-109
Full Breakfast
Credit Cards: A, B, C
Notes: 2, 7, 9, 10, 11, 12, 13, 14

Nutmeg Bed & Breakfast Agency

P.O. Box 1117, West Hartford, 06127-1117
(860) 236-6698; (800) 727-7592
FAX (860) 232-7680
e-mail: nutmegbnb@home.com
www.bnb-link.com

501. This 1865 Victorian sea captain's home is two blocks from the beach and one block from town. It is furnished with family heirlooms, antiques, and other comfortable pieces. A formal dining room and a grand living room featuring a fireplace, player piano, TV, and games, offer opportunities for conversation and relaxation.

---

7 No smoking; 8 Children welcome; 9 Social drinking allowed; 10 Tennis nearby; 11 Swimming nearby; 12 Golf nearby; 13 Skiing nearby; 14 May be booked through a travel agent; 15 Handicapped accessible.

Four guest rooms have private baths and ceiling fans. Bicycles, fresh fruits, flowers, bathrobes, and light refreshments are some of the amenities offered. Full breakfast. Smoking permitted in designated areas only. No children.

CORNWALL

Covered Bridge

69 Maple Avenue, Norfolk, 06058
(860) 542-5944; FAX (860) 542-5690
e-mail: tremblay@esslink.com
www.obs-us.com/chesler/coveredbridge

1C. A spectacular setting overlooking the Housatonic River makes this a very special getaway. There are two cottages, one with twin beds, the other with a queen-size bed. A Continental breakfast is delivered to the door. Flyfishing and canoe rentals are also available. $125-150.

2C. Enjoy warm, quiet hospitality at this custom-designed stone home set on a 64-acre private estate with breathtaking views of the countryside. Hearty full breakfasts are served before the library fireplace or on the terrace. All of the rooms are decorated in antiques. Two guest rooms with private baths. $135.

CORNWALL BRIDGE

Nutmeg Bed & Breakfast Agency

P.O. Box 1117, West Hartford, 06127-1117
(860) 236-6698; (800) 727-7592
FAX (860) 232-7680
e-mail: nutmegbnb@home.com
www.bnb-link.com

344. Recently renovated small inn/motel has five rooms on the second floor of inn; three rooms have private baths, two share and are rented to families or to couples traveling together; also second-floor sitting room with

TV, books, and games. Rooms have TVs. Children allowed (five and under stay free). Smoking permitted. Dog and cat on premises. Pets welcomed. Checkin 2:00 P.M.; checkout 11:00 A.M.

COS COB

Cos Cob Inn

50 River Road, 06807
(203) 661-5845; FAX (203) 661-2054
e-mail: innkeeper@coscobinn.com

Built in the late 1870s, this Federal-style manor was recently updated and redecorated in 1998. Old World nautical charm greets guests with rich detailed mill work, high ceilings, French doors, and a hand-painted compass rose on the oak floored entryway. Private bath, TV, VCR, voice mail, extra data port, ceiling fan, air conditioning, hair dryer, iron and ironing board, refrigerator, coffee maker, and a basket of treats in every room. Suite selections have sitting rooms, private porches, and Jacuzzi. Minutes away from four-star restaurants and shopping.

Hosts: Rick and Cindy Kral
Rooms: 14 (PB) $69-189
Continental Breakfast
Credit Cards: A, B, C, E
Notes: 2, 5, 7, 10, 11, 12, 14

COVENTRY

Bed & Breakfast, Ltd.

P.O. Box 216, New Haven, 06513
(203) 469-3260; e-mail: BandB@aol.com
www.bedandbreakfastltd.com

This Colonial-style farmhouse exudes warmth and seasoned character. To be enjoyed are the working fireplaces in the common room and front parlor. Selections include the Sunshine Room, the Dollhouse Room (complete with furnished dollhouse), and the Peach Room. Guests are invited to use the in-ground pool,

NOTES: Credit cards accepted: A MasterCard; B Visa; C American Express; D Discover; E Diner's Club; F Other; 2 Personal checks accepted; 3 Lunch available; 4 Dinner available; 5 Open all year; 6 Pets welcome;

hot tub in the solarium, screened porch, hammocks, and therapeutic massage (available by appointment). Call for reasonable rates.

Nutmeg Bed & Breakfast Agency

P.O. Box 1117, West Hartford, 06127-1117
(860) 236-6698; (800) 727-7592
FAX (860) 232-7680
e-mail: nutmegbnb@home.com
www.bnb-link.com

457. This Colonial was built in 1731 and operated as a tavern until 1823. It was used as part of the Underground Railroad in the mid-1800s. The two guest rooms have canopied beds, working fireplaces, and a feather mattress for winter warmth. Both have a private bath, and one bath has a Jacuzzi. There is also a cottage with private entrance, sofa bed, private bath, fireplace, and small kitchen. Hostess will prepare a hearth-cooked dinner with advance notice. Full country breakfast on weekends; Continental weekdays. Children 10 and over welcome. No smoking. Cat in residence.

DEEP RIVER

Riverwind Inn

209 Main Street, 06417
(203) 526-2014; FAX (203) 526-0875
www.innformation.com/ct/riverwind

With its eight wonderfully appointed guest rooms, rambling common areas, and informal country atmosphere, Riverwind is more than just a place to stay; it's a destination. Relax, step back in time, and enjoy a stay amid an enchanting collection of New England and southern country antiques. Each morning starts with the inn's complimentary southern buffet breakfast.

Hosts: Barbara Barlow and Bob Bucknall
Rooms: 8 (PB) $105-175
Full Breakfast
Credit Cards: A, B
Notes: 2, 5, 9, 10, 11, 12, 14

DURHAM

Nutmeg Bed & Breakfast Agency

P.O. Box 1117, West Hartford, 06127-1117
(860) 236-6698; (800) 727-7592
FAX (860) 232-7680
e-mail: nutmegbnb@home.com
www.bnb-link.com

509. Georgian Colonial built in 1740 with museum-quality restoration. Furnished with antiques. Two second-floor guest rooms with private baths, one room with twin beds, and one pencil-post double- canopied rope bed. Both bathrooms have beautifully crafted fixtures. Continental breakfast. No smoking. Charming cat on the premises.

EAST HADDAM

Bishopsgate Inn

7 Norwich Road, 06423
(860) 873-1677; FAX (860) 873-3898

This exceptional 1818 Colonial home welcomes guests seeking gracious hospitality in well-appointed accommodations. Six tastefully furnished guest rooms with private baths. Four have open fireplaces and one a sauna. A short walk to the Goodspeed Opera House and shops, the inn's setting offers seclusion even in the middle of town. Known for its exceptional kitchen. Ample breakfasts are included while picnic lunches to go and candlelight dinners served in guests' rooms can be ordered.

Hosts: The Kagel Family—Colin Sr., Jane, Colin Jr., and Lisa
Rooms: 6 (PB) $100-150
Full Breakfast
Credit Cards: A, B
Notes: 2, 3, 4, 5, 7, 9, 12

7 No smoking; 8 Children welcome; 9 Social drinking allowed; 10 Tennis nearby; 11 Swimming nearby; 12 Golf nearby; 13 Skiing nearby; 14 May be booked through a travel agent; 15 Handicapped accessible.

ENFIELD

Nutmeg Bed & Breakfast Agency

P.O. Box 1117, West Hartford, 06127-1117
(860) 236-6698; (800) 727-7592
FAX (860) 232-7680
e-mail: nutmegbnb@home.com
www.bnb-link.com

412. This 1876 large high-style Queen Anne Victorian home has been lovingly restored by new owners who have kept the original double entrance door, leaded glass transoms, stained-glass windows, and five ornamental fireplaces. The third-floor Windsor Suite occupies the entire floor, has French Quarter king-size bed, huge skylight, private bath with Jacuzzi, TV, VCR, and telephone. Continental breakfast may be served in suite or on wraparound porch in pleasant weather. Children welcome (day bed in suite could accommodate one child or adult). No smoking. No resident pets.

ESSEX

The Griswold Inn

36 Main Street, 06426
(860) 767-1776

More than a country hotel. More than a comfortable bed, an extraordinary meal, or a superb drink. It embodies a spirit understood perhaps only as one warms up to its potbellied stove or is hypnotized by the magic of a crackling log in one of its many fireplaces. It is a kaleidoscope of nostalgic images. There are 31 guest rooms, all with air conditioning, private baths, tele-

The Griswold Inn

phones, and piped-in classical music. Some have fireplaces.

Hosts: Gregory, Douglas, and Geoffrey Paul
Rooms: 31 (PB) $90-185
Continental Breakfast
Credit Cards: A, B, C
Notes: 2, 3, 4, 5, 7, 8, 9, 10, 11, 12

Nutmeg Bed & Breakfast Agency

P.O. Box 1117, West Hartford, 06127-1117
(860) 236-6698; (800) 727-7592
FAX (860) 232-7680
e-mail: nutmegbnb@home.com
www.bnb-link.com

508. If guests are boating enthusiasts, this entertaining hostess, whose family shares the passion, would love to trade some sailing stories. This special home, right on the bank of the Connecticut River, is convenient to many attractions of the area, 20 miles from Mystic, and close to Hammonasset public beach in Madison. Theaters and fine restaurants are nearby. Two rooms have private baths. Full breakfast. Children welcome.

FARMINGTON

Nutmeg Bed & Breakfast Agency

P.O. Box 1117, West Hartford, 06127-1117
(860) 236-6698; (800) 727-7592
FAX (860) 232-7680
e-mail: nutmegbnb@home.com
www.bnb-link.com

402. Small inn has traditional country furnishings. Guest rooms each have private bath, TV, VCR, and telephone. The gracious staff can help arrange a dinner or business meeting in-house or nearby. Children under 12 stay free in same room. Continental breakfast served.

406. This elegant estate is now a gracious small inn with beautifully landscaped grounds, tennis court, conference room, and lounge. There are six rooms with TVs, telephones, and private baths. A short drive from Hartford. Perfect for the business traveler. Continental breakfast served. Children welcome.

415. This is a luxurious new inn with suites complete with kitchens, fireplaces, and bathrooms with all the amenities. Enjoy complimentary racquet club privileges with pools and tennis courts. Continental breakfast. Children welcome.

GLASTONBURY

Butternut Farm

1654 Main Street, 06033
(860) 633-7197; FAX (860) 659-1758

An 18th-century architectural jewel is furnished in museum-quality period antiques. Estate setting has ancient trees, herb gardens, prize dairy goats, barnyard chickens, pigeons, ducks, and a goose. Four Abyssinians inhabit the main house. Enjoy a full breakfast of fresh eggs, milk, and cheese. Ten minutes from Hartford. All of Connecticut is within 90 minutes. Two rooms, two suites, and one apartment, all with private baths. Cancellation policy.

Host: Don Reid
Rooms: 5 (PB) $75-95
Full Breakfast
Credit Cards: C
Notes: 2, 5, 7, 8, 9, 10, 11, 12, 13

Butternut Farm

GRANBY

Nutmeg Bed & Breakfast Agency

P.O. Box 1117, West Hartford, 06127-1117
(860) 236-6698; (800) 727-7592
FAX (860) 232-7680
e-mail: nutmegbnb@home.com
www.bnb-link.com

416. Historic colonial summer home of the Edwards family, built in 1812, now a restored bed and breakfast. All four guest rooms have private baths, are well-appointed, and have their own character. Two rooms also have working fireplaces for a romantic country getaway. Minutes from the airport, this is a perfect wedding night location for couples catching a flight the next day. The keeping room and parlor decorated in Victorian-style are for guests' use. Host is a floral designer, so flowers are everywhere. Full breakfast. Children eight and older welcome. No smoking. Small dog in residence.

442. There is a sophisticated country atmosphere to this stone house. The separate guest wing includes a sitting room with TV, and two guest rooms with private baths. Convenient to Bradley International Airport, state parks, historic Old Newgate Prison, and local attractions. Guests enjoy wine, cheese, and crackers in the afternoon. Horses can be boarded for a nominal fee. Continental breakfast. Children welcome. No smoking.

GREENWICH

The Stanton House Inn

76 Maple Avenue, 06830
(203) 869-2110; FAX (203) 629-2116

The Stanton House Inn is a converted mansion that is now a bed and breakfast inn, in the prestigious village of Greenwich. The Stanton House Inn offers elegant surroundings, comfortable rooms, and a satisfying Continental

7 No smoking; 8 Children welcome; 9 Social drinking allowed; 10 Tennis nearby; 11 Swimming nearby; 12 Golf nearby; 13 Skiing nearby; 14 May be booked through a travel agent; 15 Handicapped accessible.

breakfast at rates competitive with area hotels. The rooms are bright and cheery, decorated primarily with Laura Ashley-style fabrics, period antiques, and reproductions. Three rooms with working fireplaces. On-site outdoor swimming pool (seasonal). One whirlpool tub.

Hosts: Tog and Doreen Pearson
Rooms: 22 (PB) $95-179
Continental Breakfast
Credit Cards: A, B, C, D, E
Notes: 5, 7, 9, 10, 11, 12, 14

GRISWOLD

Nutmeg Bed & Breakfast Agency

P.O. Box 1117, West Hartford, 06127-1117
(860) 236-6698; (800) 727-7592
FAX (860) 232-7680
e-mail: nutmegbnb@home.com
www.bnb-link.com

503. Colonial farmhouse built in 1740 has original wide board oak and pine floors, latch hook doors in old colonial style. Apple, pear, peach, and cherry trees as well as a kitchen garden surround the property. The Pear Room has a hand-crafted white oak queen-size bed, cable TV, and private bath. The adjoining room has a twin bed and can be used as sitting room or for a third party. The Wisteria Room has a double bed and bath shared with hosts. House is air conditioned. Continental breakfast. Children welcome. No smoking. Dog on premises.

GROTON

Bluff Point Bed & Breakfast

26 Fort Hill Road, Route 1, 06340
(860) 445-1314
www.visitmystic.com/bluffpoint

A restored Colonial bed and breakfast (early 1990s) on U.S. Route 1 and adjacent to Bluff Point State Park Coastal Preserve. Conveniently four miles from the Mystic Seaport

Museum. Large common area with shared TV is available to guests. The home is equipped with a central fire sprinkler system. No smoking or pets. "We give warm and friendly service to our guests."

Hosts: Walter and Edna Parfitt
Rooms: 3 (PB) $85-95
Continental Breakfast
Credit Cards: A, B, C
Notes: 2, 5, 7, 10, 11, 12

GUILFORD

Bed & Breakfast, Ltd.

P.O. Box 216, New Haven, 06513
(203) 469-3260; e-mail: BandB@aol.com
www.bedandbreakfastltd.com

This log-style mountain lodge is a real treasure. It sits on 3.5 acres of wooded bliss. Three rooms offer a variety of amenities. Front porch for sunning or relaxing, enjoying the deer, perennial gardens, and seasonal view of Long Island Sound. Musical hosts can play viola de gamba and recorders. Near Yale, antique shops, the shoreline, and great outlet malls. $95-125.

Nutmeg Bed & Breakfast Agency

P.O. Box 1117, West Hartford, 06127-1117
(860) 236-6698; (800) 727-7592
FAX (860) 232-7680

510. A contemporary home with lovely grounds awaits the guest who wishes to be near the coast. The two rooms have private baths— one has a king-size bed and the other has twin beds. There is also a private sitting room for guests. Enjoy a short walk to the village green, colonial churches, and shops. Full breakfast. Children welcome. Smoking in designated areas only.

518. This cottage has a private entrance, gardens, and lovely grounds. Inside, guests will find a small sitting room and small dining

NOTES: Credit cards accepted: A MasterCard; B Visa; C American Express; D Discover; E Diner's Club; F Other; 2 Personal checks accepted; 3 Lunch available; 4 Dinner available; 5 Open all year; 6 Pets welcome;

room with refrigerator and microwave. The bedroom has a private bath. The sitting room can accommodate a third person on a pull-out sofa bed. Continental breakfast. Children welcome. No smoking.

523. Breathtaking view of Long Island Sound in front and woodsy gardens in back of this charming house built in style of a mountain lodge. Lots of wood and windows, Scandinavian decor combines elegant antiques with more modern paintings and furnishing. Convenient to Madison and Sound beaches, New Haven, Clinton outlet malls, and trails for hiking out the back door. Spacious living room for guests' use, down comforters on beds. Master bedroom has lovely view of gardens in back and shares bath with twin bedroom if parties are traveling together, otherwise bath will be private. Another guest room has a hall private bath. Continental breakfast. Children 10 and older welcome. No smoking. Cat in residence.

HARTFORD

Nutmeg Bed & Breakfast Agency

P.O. Box 1117, West Hartford, 06127-1117
(860) 236-6698; (800) 727-7592
FAX (860) 232-7680
e-mail: nutmegbnb@home.com
www.bnb-link.com

404. This 1910 Victorian-style home has large front porch, leaded- and stained-glass windows, carved ceilings, large second-floor bedroom with antique double bed, bureau, large closet, private bath with shower, no tub. House is convenient to all downtown businesses and attractions, all schools in area, and one block to public transportation. Two rooms on third floor, one with twin beds, one with double, share bath with claw-foot tub and shower. Continental breakfast. No children. No smoking. Cat in residence.

HARWINTON

Nutmeg Bed & Breakfast Agency

P.O. Box 1117, West Hartford, 06127-1117
(860) 236-6698; (800) 727-7592
FAX (860) 232-7680
e-mail: nutmegbnb@home.com
www.bnb-link.com

313. Historic home in Litchfield County dating to 1783 surrounded by stone walls on lovely country road perfect for strolling; large antique shop attached. Lower level guest suite very cozy with original chestnut beams and planking, oriental rugs, and antique furnishings. Sleigh beds, sitting area, full private bath, TV, VCR, books, separate climate control for heat and air conditioning. Continental breakfast served in great room overlooking orchard. Fax and telephone available. Convenient to Litchfield, antique shops, state parks, Hartford's attractions, many fine restaurants. Children welcome. No smoking. Dogs and cats in residence (not in guest suite).

IVORYTON

The Copper Beech Inn

46 Main Street, 06442
(860) 767-0330; (888) 809-2056
www.copperbeechinn.com

Gracious gardens and rustic woodlands set the stage for this handsome inn. A gallery offers

The Copper Beech Inn

antique oriental porcelain, and the dining room is noted for fine country French cuisine. Beautiful countryside, quaint villages, museums, antique shops, theater, and water sports distinguish the area. Two-night minimum stay for weekends and holidays. Closed Christmas and the first week of January. Children over 10 welcome. Dining rooms and first-floor guest rooms in carriage house are handicapped accessible.

Hosts: Eldon and Sally Senner
Rooms: 13 (PB) $123.20-201.60
Continental Breakfast
Credit Cards: A, B, C, E
Notes: 2, 4, 5, 7, 9, 10, 11, 12

KENT

Nutmeg Bed & Breakfast Agency

P.O. Box 1117, West Hartford, 06127-1117
(860) 236-6698; (800) 727-7592
FAX (860) 232-7680
e-mail: nutmegbnb@home.com
www.bnb-link.com

303. Enjoy the fall foliage from this lovely Colonial, circa 1790. Guests are offered a suite that has a living room, private bath, and air conditioning. There is a cot available for the suite's sitting room for extra family members. Additional room has double bed and private bath. Both have ceiling fans. Continental breakfast served in the guest's room. Children welcome. No smoking. Dog and cat on premises.

322. Friendliness awaits guests at this 1860s Colonial home. Unwind in the romantic rose-stenciled room with beamed ceiling or the country Adirondack room with carved Victorian headboard, both with private baths. There is an adjacent cottage with a sitting area, private bath, and kitchen. Relax by the fireplace in the cozy den or walk the lovely grounds and view St. John's Ledges. After a Continental

breakfast, visit the antique shop. Near hiking, skiing, canoeing, museums, and fine restaurants. Children over 12 welcome. No smoking.

LAKEVILLE

Nutmeg Bed & Breakfast Agency

P.O. Box 1117, West Hartford, 06127-1117
(860) 236-6698; (800) 727-7592
FAX (860) 232-7680
e-mail: nutmegbnb@home.com
www.bnb-link.com

328. Set on lovely private acreage, this 15-room turn-of-the-century bed and breakfast is filled with antiques and charm. Guests may choose rooms with a sleigh or a spool bed, each with its own private bath. After a sumptuous Continental breakfast, enjoy some of the area's many attractions: Lime Rock Park, Music Mountain, and Mohawk ski area. Children over eight are welcome. No smoking.

LITCHFIELD

Nutmeg Bed & Breakfast Agency

P.O. Box 1117, West Hartford, 06127-1117
(860) 236-6698; (800) 727-7592
FAX (860) 232-7680
e-mail: nutmegbnb@home.com
www.bnb-link.com

333. On a quiet country road outside the historic village of Litchfield, this bed and breakfast features two guest rooms with private baths. The house is a pre-Revolutionary Colonial, shaded by century-old sugar maples. Horses and sheep graze in the pasture. Guests may enjoy a delicious full breakfast on the stone terrace or the covered porch in warm weather where they can overlook a view of the wooded brook. Children over 12 welcome.

NOTES: Credit cards accepted: A MasterCard; B Visa; C American Express; D Discover; E Diner's Club; F Other; 2 Personal checks accepted; 3 Lunch available; 4 Dinner available; 5 Open all year; 6 Pets welcome;

LYME

Covered Bridge

69 Maple Avenue, Norfolk, 06058
(860) 542-5944; FAX (860) 542-5690
e-mail: tremblay@esslink.com
www.obs-us.com/chesler/coveredbridge

2LY. European charm and antiques make this Colonial set on 14 acres a very special retreat. Several pieces of furniture have been hand painted by the hostess, reflecting her Swiss heritage. The three queen-bedded guest rooms, each with a private bath, have gorgeous handmade quilts. Full breakfast served. $95-110.

MADISON

Madison Beach Hotel

94 West Wharf Road, P.O. Box 546, 06443
(203) 245-1404

Built in the early 1800s, the Madison Beach Hotel is nestled on a private beach on Long Island Sound, and it is distinctly Victorian in style and decor. Most hotel rooms have private balconies overlooking the water. Antique oak bureaus, wainscoting, wicker and rattan furniture, along with old-fashioned wallpaper, complete the Victorian feeling. The hotel's restaurant serves lunch, dinner with entertainment on weekends, and outdoor dining. Closed January and February.

Hosts: Betty and Henry Cooney; Roben and Kathy
  Bagdasarian
Rooms: 35 (PB) $85-225
Continental Breakfast
Credit Cards: A, B, C, D, E
Notes: 2, 3, 4, 8, 9, 10, 11, 12, 13, 14, 15

Nutmeg Bed & Breakfast Agency

P.O. Box 1117, West Hartford, 06127-1117
(860) 236-6698; (800) 727-7592
FAX (860) 232-7680
e-mail: nutmegbnb@home.com
www.bnb-link.com

520. Tasteful gambrel Colonial with large living room for guests, gracious dining room, pool, large eat-in kitchen, fireplace in family room, pool, patio for breakfast on nice days; about five minutes from beach. Two second-floor guest rooms which share a bath are offered. Continental breakfast is served. No children. No smoking. No resident pets.

Tidewater Inn

949 Boston Post Road, 06443
(203) 245-8457

This shoreline inn offers a cozy, elegant atmosphere and warm hospitality. The area offers beaches, antique and specialty shops, colonial historic districts, craft and fine art galleries. Rooms provide private bath, TV, air conditioning, outgoing telephone. Selected rooms offer canopied beds, fireplaces, refrigerators, VCRs, or Jacuzzi. Enjoy access to the beamed sitting room with fireplace, English garden, menus from area restaurants, literature about the area, beach passes, and refrigerator stocked with cold drinks and snacks.

Hosts: Jean Foy and Rich Evans
Rooms: 9 (PB) $80-170
Full Breakfast
Credit Cards: A, B, C
Notes: 2, 5, 7, 9, 11

MIDDLEBURY

Nutmeg Bed & Breakfast Agency

P.O. Box 1117, West Hartford, 06127-1117
(860) 236-6698; (800) 727-7592
FAX (860) 232-7680
e-mail: nutmegbnb@home.com
www.bnb-link.com

304. This New England Colonial is near the village green and is convenient to Taft School and Westover. There are four guest rooms, two of which share a bath. Enjoy the outdoor activities offered in the area and then relax in this inviting home. Full breakfast. Children welcome. No smoking.

7 No smoking; 8 Children welcome; 9 Social drinking allowed; 10 Tennis nearby; 11 Swimming nearby; 12 Golf nearby; 13 Skiing nearby; 14 May be booked through a travel agent; 15 Handicapped accessible.

Tucker Hill Inn

96 Tucker Hill Road, 06762
(203) 758-8334

Tucker Hill Inn is a large center-hall Colonial just down from the village green in Middlebury. It was built around 1920 and was a restaurant and catering house for almost 40 years. The period rooms are spacious. Nearby are antiques, country drives, music and theater, golf, tennis, water sports, fishing, hiking, and cross-country skiing. Closed Christmas Day.

Hosts: Richard and Susan Cabalenski
Rooms: 4 (2 PB; 2 SB) $80-125
Full Breakfast
Credit Cards: A, B, C
Notes: 2, 7, 8, 9, 10, 11, 12, 14

MILFORD

Nutmeg Bed & Breakfast Agency

P.O. Box 1117, West Hartford, 06127-1117
(860) 236-6698; (800) 727-7592
FAX (860) 232-7680
e-mail: nutmegbnb@home.com
www.bnb-link.com

207. This 1820 colonial is in the historic area of downtown. Lovely English gardens in front, gazebo and lawn swing on banks of Wepawaug River. Three rooms with double beds share a bed with a tub and shower. Near public transportation and convenient to New Haven. Continental breakfast. No smoking.

213. The host calls her home "a seaside bungalow." The house was built in 1910 and overlooks Long Island Sound on a very quiet, peaceful lane. The sunny second-floor guest room with a double bed and an additional room with twin beds share a bath. The room has a water view and a large connecting screened porch for taking in the ocean air. Continental breakfast. Smoking permitted outside only. Cat in residence.

MYSTIC

The Adams House of Mystic

382 Cow Hill Road, 06355
(860) 572-9551

Charming 1750 Colonial home features four rooms with private baths and queen-size beds; one room has a fireplace. Adjacent garden cottage features two rooms, one with sauna; each with private bath, queen-size bed, and private entrance. Hearty candlelight breakfast served daily with tea in the afternoons. Smoke free. Children welcome in cottage. One and one-half miles to downtown Mystic Seaport and aquarium. Open year-round.

Hosts: Mary Lou and Gregory Peck
Rooms: 7 (PB) $95-165
Full Breakfast
Credit Cards: A, B
Notes: 2, 5, 7, 8, 10, 11, 12

The Adams House of Mystic

Comolli's House

36 Bruggeman Place, 06355
(860) 536-8723

Ideal for vacationers touring historic Mystic or the business person who desires a homey respite while traveling. This immaculate home, on a quiet hill overlooking the Mystic Seaport complex, is convenient to Olde Mistick Village and the aquarium. Sightseeing, sporting activities, shopping, and restaurant information are provided by the host. Off-season rates are available.

Host: Dorothy M. Comolli
Rooms: 2 (PB) $75-125
Continental Breakfast
Credit Cards: F
Notes: 2, 10, 11, 12

Covered Bridge

69 Maple Avenue, Norfolk, 06058
(860) 542-5944; FAX (860) 542-5690
e-mail: tremblay@esslink.com
www.obs-us.com/chesler/coveredbridge

1MYCT. This restored 150-year-old Victorian farmhouse is on two acres of lovely landscaped grounds with old stone walls, fruit trees, and an outdoor eating area for the enjoyment of guests. A full breakfast is served in the dining room and a Scottish tea is served in the afternoon. There are six guest rooms, one with fireplace and all with private baths. $125-145.

2MYCT. An 1840s Greek Revival just outside the center of town is beautifully decorated with antiques and offers four exquisitely decorated guest rooms: one with a fireplace and another with a Jacuzzi. A delicious full breakfast is served in the dining room. $95-145.

House of 1833 Bed & Breakfast

72 North Stonington Road, 06355
(860) 536-6325; (800) FOR-1833

This elegant Greek Revival mansion is on three acres just minutes from all Mystic area attractions. The mansion was fully restored in 1994 with romance and comfort in mind. All five guest rooms are elegantly furnished with fireplaces and private baths. Several have canopied beds and whirlpool tubs as well. The estate-like surroundings include a swimming pool and a Har-Tru tennis court. Bicycles are also available for touring the

House of 1833

countryside. A full breakfast is served with piano accompaniment.

Hosts: Matt and Carol Nolan
Rooms: 5 (PB) $95-225
Full Breakfast
Credit Cards: A, B
Notes: 2, 5, 7, 9, 10, 11, 12, 14

Nutmeg Bed & Breakfast Agency

P.O. Box 1117, West Hartford, 06127-1117
(860) 236-6698; (800) 727-7592
FAX (860) 232-7680
e-mail: nutmegbnb@home.com
www.bnb-link.com

513. Built in 1837, this large farmhouse is surrounded by fruit trees and strawberry beds. Eight guest rooms have private baths; all have fireplaces. There is also a spacious dining room and a warm family room. The home-cooked full breakfast, with specialty muffins, is amply satisfying. Children welcome. Cat and dog in residence. No smoking.

515. Take a walk back in time in this historic 1771 house. The keeping room was once used for open hearth cooking—now it is the sitting room. There are five guest rooms, each with a private bath, a fireplace, and a Jacuzzi in the bath. Continental breakfast. No children. No smoking.

7 No smoking; 8 Children welcome; 9 Social drinking allowed; 10 Tennis nearby; 11 Swimming nearby; 12 Golf nearby; 13 Skiing nearby; 14 May be booked through a travel agent; 15 Handicapped accessible.

Red Brook Inn

P.O. Box 237, Old Mystic, 06372
(860) 572-0349

Red Brook Inn offers colonial hospitality in two 18th-century buildings. Near Mystic and Foxwoods Casino on seven acres of woods. Most bedrooms are furnished with antique beds, working fireplaces, or whirlpool tubs. The area is tranquil and serene. A full breakfast is served every morning, and afternoon refreshments are readily available. Three minutes to downtown, the aquarium, and Mystic Seaport Museum.

Host: Ruth Keyes
Rooms: 10 (PB) $95-189
Full Breakfast
Credit Cards: A, B, C, D
Notes: 2, 5, 7, 8, 9, 10, 11, 12

Six Broadway Inn

6 Broadway, 06355
(860) 536-6010 (phone/FAX)
www.visitmystic.com/sixbroadway

Featured on HGTV. The only bed and breakfast in historic downtown Mystic. A luxurious 1854 Victorian Italianate. Each guest room has a private bath, air conditioning, queen-size bed, European antiques, and Fretté Italian linens. Continental plus breakfast, afternoon refreshments, guest refrigerator, fireplaced parlor. Fabulous location! One and one-half blocks to downtown shopping, dining, and Mystic River. Three blocks to Mystic Seaport Museum. Only minutes to casinos and aquarium.

Hosts: Jerry and Joan Sullivan
Rooms: 5 (PB) $90-225
Continental Breakfast
Credit Cards: A, B, C, D
Notes: 2, 5, 7, 9, 10, 11, 12

Steamboat Inn

73 Steamboat Wharf, 06355
(203) 536-8300

On the river, this romantic and luxurious inn is in the heart of downtown Mystic. Ten beautiful rooms, all with antique and custom furnishings, TV, telephones, and individually controlled heat and air conditioning. Six rooms feature wood-burning fireplaces, along with four dock-level demi-suites with double whirlpools. A Continental breakfast is included, featuring home-baked muffins daily. There are many shops, restaurants, and boats all within walking distance.

Host: Diana Stadtmiller
Rooms: 10 (PB) $110-275
Continental Breakfast
Credit Cards: A, B, C, D
Notes: 5, 7, 9, 12, 14, 15

NEW CANAAN

Roger Sherman Inn

195 Oenoke Ridge, 06840
(203) 966-4541; FAX (203) 966-0503
www.rogershermaninn.com

The historic Roger Sherman Inn dates back to the 1700s. It has 17 charming guest rooms and six elegant dining rooms ideal for any occasion including small corporate functions. The Roger Sherman Inn with its quiet, peaceful surroundings combine the tradition at an historic inn and the elegance and perfection of European dining. Two-bedroom suite available. Antiquing nearby.

Rooms: 17 (PB) $110-175
Suite: $300
Continental Breakfast
Credit Cards: A, B, C, D, E
Notes: 2, 3, 4, 5, 7, 8, 9, 12, 14, 15

NEW HAVEN

Bed & Breakfast, Ltd.

P.O. Box 216, New Haven, 06513
(203) 469-3260; e-mail: BandB@aol.com
www.bedandbreakfastltd.com

Bed and Breakfast, Ltd. offers more than 125 listings of bed and breakfasts throughout Connecticut from elegantly simple to simply ele-

gant. The emphasis is on variety of accommodations, gracious hospitality, and very affordable rates. In operation for the 16th year, the
service features Victorian, Federal, Greek
Revival, Tudor, Italianate, and contemporary
homes in every price range. Deluxe and suite
rates are slightly higher. Children are welcome
at some establishments. Inquire about other
amenities listed in notes.

Contact: Jack Argenio
Rooms: 125 plus (80 PB; 45 SB) $65-185
Full and Continental Breakfast
Credit Cards: A, B
Notes: 2, 5, 9, 10, 11, 12, 13

1. This typical Colonial-style home is located
in a professional, residential neighborhood
close to Yale University. Its charm and warmth
are felt in its lovely antique furnishings. Two
rooms are offered…both cozy and cheerful. An
ideal situation and gregarious hostess are perfect for the business or leisure traveller. $65-95

2. This grand Italianate is in the historic area of
the city. It is listed in the National Register of
Historic Places and has been on several house
tours. Its rooms are filled with antique treasures and contemporary pieces. A four-room
suite is offered featuring a private entrance, sit-
ting/breakfast room, huge living room, and
Victorian bedroom. Private bath, of course.
Color cable TV and telephone access adds to
the grandeur of this home. Five minutes to Yale
and downtown. $150.

3. This new inn is the quintessential bed and
breakfast. Its period furnishings and artful
touches are not to be missed. Several rooms
with private baths and sitting areas, Jacuzzis,
and air conditioning are some of the amenities.
Very close to Yale and the New Haven hospitals. Each room boasts its own thematic touch
and privacy. $90-135.

Nutmeg Bed & Breakfast Agency

P.O. Box 1117, West Hartford, 06127-1117
(860) 236-6698; (800) 727-7592

FAX (860) 232-7680
e-mail: nutmegbnb@home.com
www.bnb-link.com

201. This historic mansion was built in the
1840s. It has been newly renovated with period
furniture. The seven guest rooms have queen-
size beds, telephones, cable TV, air conditioning, and private baths. Convenient to downtown
activities. Full breakfast. No smoking.

202. This English colonial home is near public
transportation. The large second-floor guest
room has a double bed, private bath, and spacious area to work. Continental breakfast is
served in large sunroom with fireplace. This
room is also used for the sitting room. Continental breakfast. No smoking. Children 12 and
older welcome. Cat in residence.

203. This 1920 Queen Anne has beamed ceilings, fireplace in parlor, eclectic but charming
furnishings, gracious hosts. First floor has two
rooms that share a bath. Another suite is available on the third floor. Kitchen and breakfast
nook on second floor for convenience of
guests. Five-minute drive to public beach in
West Haven, convenient to Yale, downtown
New Haven, airport. Continental breakfast buffet. Children welcome. No smoking. One cat in
residence.

205. This turn-of-the-century grand, gracious,
large home is in a special residential area. Formal dining room and lovely gardens await visitors. The third floor has a room with a full
walk-through bath shared with a second room.
On the second floor, one room has a full private
bath and may be used with a room with a single bed. Also there is a lovely suite with a private bath with a tub. The shower is down the
hall. First and second floors are air conditioned
and the third floor has a large fan. Continental
breakfast. Children welcome. No smoking.

208. Catch a game at the Yale Bowl or the bus
downtown from this bed and breakfast in the
Westville section. This English Tudor has guest

7 No smoking; 8 Children welcome; 9 Social drinking allowed; 10 Tennis nearby; 11 Swimming nearby;
12 Golf nearby; 13 Skiing nearby; 14 May be booked through a travel agent; 15 Handicapped accessible.

rooms with a shared bath. Guests help themselves to Continental breakfast during the week; full breakfast on weekends. Children welcome. Smoking restricted. Dog in residence.

210. Walk to Yale from this gracious Victorian home set in the residential section of New Haven. A newly decorated third-floor suite consists of a bedroom with a large private bath and a smaller bedroom. A guest room is also available on the second floor. Continental breakfast. Children welcome. Cats in residence.

215. This home near Yale is a 1910 Dutch Colonial with a private garden and deck. Two guest rooms are on the second floor. One has a double bed and the other has twin beds; both share a bath. Baby equipment available. The house is just over one block from the bus. Continental breakfast. Infants traveling with parents welcome. No smoking. Dog in residence.

Three Chimneys Inn at Yale

1201 Chapel Street, 06511
(203) 789-1201; (800) 443-1554 (outside CT)
FAX (203) 776-7363
e-mail: chimneysnh@aol.com
www.threechimneysinn.com

Two blocks from Old Main Gate at Yale University and just steps from the renowned Shubert, Yale Repertory, and Palace Theaters; the Yale Center for British Art; Yale Art Gallery;

Three Chimneys Inn at Yale

and the Peabody Museum of Natural History, in a vibrantly eclectic little area known as Chapel West, reigns this grand "painted lady." Understated elegance in 10 distinctive guest rooms with full private baths. Fireplaces reflect the Georgian and Federal period furnishings and oak-work of days gone by. The inn offers unique venues for both social and business gatherings. Gourmet breakfast; traditional afternoon tea and sweets; honor bar; guest pantry; catering.

Host: Jane Peterson
Rooms: 10 (PB) $160
Full Breakfast
Credit Cards: A, B, C, D
Notes: 3, 4, 5, 7, 9, 10, 11, 12, 14, 15

NEW MILFORD

Covered Bridge

69 Maple Avenue, Norfolk, 06058
(860) 542-5944; FAX (860) 542-5690
e-mail: tremblay@esslink.com
www.obs-us.com/chesler/coveredbridge

1NM. Vista for viewing, woods for walking, hills for cross-country skiing, streams for fishing, flower gardens, and a pool are some of the attractions of this sprawling estate three miles outside of town. First-floor guest room with private bath and an upstairs guest room. $60-95.

Heritage Inn

34 Bridge Street, 06776
(860) 354-8883; FAX (860) 350-5543

The Heritage Inn is a country hotel that combines personal comfort with efficiency in a relaxed atmosphere. Here guests will find welcomed amenities like a 20-inch color TV with bedside remote control, plus air conditioning, private bath, and a telephone in every room. In addition, guests will receive a newspaper every morning and a full breakfast. Enjoy New Milford's traditional New England charm while staying at the Heritage Inn. Picnic on the town green. Shops, boutiques, restaurants, movie theaters, historic attractions, and churches and synagogues are close by.

Host: Ray Barton
Rooms: 20 (PB) $85-100
Full Breakfast
Credit Cards: A, B, C, D
Notes: 2, 5, 6, 8, 10, 11, 12, 13, 14

The Homestead Inn

5 Elm Street, 06776
(860) 354-4080; FAX (860) 354-7046
e-mail: homesteadct.com

Mix friendly conversation with a hearty Continental breakfast while relaxing in the living room or on the front porch of this 145-year-old inn overlooking the village green. Short walks to restaurants, shops, churches, and antiques. Furnished with antiques and older reproductions, private baths, room telephone, color TV, and air conditioning. Open year-round. AAA- and Mobil-approved.

Hosts: Rolf and Peggy Hammer
Rooms: 15 (PB) $80-105
Continental Breakfast
Credit Cards: A, B, C, D, E
Notes: 2, 5, 8, 12, 14

Nutmeg Bed & Breakfast Agency

P.O. Box 1117, West Hartford, 06127-1117
(860) 236-6698; (800) 727-7592
FAX (860) 232-7680
e-mail: nutmegbnb@home.com
www.bnb-link.com

A charming home built with wood from a reverse wood tobacco barn, this bed and breakfast is delightfully landscaped with a pool. First-floor room with separate entrance to deck has twins or king-size bed and private bath. Second-floor room has twin beds and shared bath. One small bedroom on second floor is suitable for a child. Continental breakfast includes home-grown berries, homemade jams, popovers, and muffins prepared by a former chef. Children welcome. Smoking in designated area only. Dog in residence.

319. This 1850s Colonial-style home with more than three acres of glorious grounds, formal dining room, living room with fireplace, front porch, patio. Two newly decorated rooms on the first floor have private baths, air conditioning, and ceiling fans. One room has a TV and VCR; the other room has a TV. One block from public transportation, convenient to many good restaurants and private schools, and antiquing. Full breakfast. Closed Thanksgiving, Christmas, and New Year's. Children 12 and older welcome. No smoking. No pets in residence.

NEW PRESTON

Atha House

Box 2015, 06777
(860) 355-7387 (phone/FAX)
e-mail: athahouse@aol.com

Cozy Cape Cod cottage in the rural Washington area offers year-round beauty and solitude. Two comfortable rooms each with private bath. Tastefully appointed sitting room and living room with fireplace and grand piano. Convenient to historic sites, nature trails, galleries, and antique shops. No smoking. By advance reservations only. Seasonal rates. Continental plus breakfast served.

Host: Ruth Pearl
Rooms: 2 (PB) $90-110
Continental Breakfast
Credit Cards: None
Notes: 2, 5, 6, 7, 8, 11

The Boulders Inn

East Shore Road, Route 45, 06777
(860) 868-0541; (800) 55-BOULD(ers)
FAX (860) 868-1925
e-mail: boulders@bouldersinn.com
www.bouldersinn.com

Built in 1895 as a private residence, the Boulders Inn is nestled at the foot of Pinnacle Mountain in the Litchfield Hills, overlooking

The Boulders Inn

the beautiful Lake Waramaug. This architecturally striking Victorian home combines mansion-like elegance with the warmth of the country. In the 50 years of its existence as an inn, it has established an outstanding reputation, receiving countless kudos from respected national publications such as the *New York Times*, *Travel & Leisure* magazine, the *Wine Spectator*, *Country Inn and Bed & Breakfast* magazine, and so forth. The restaurant has been voted one of the top 10 in Connecticut.

Hosts: Kees and Ulla Adema
Rooms: 17 (PB) $225-345
Full Breakfast
Credit Cards: A, B, C
Notes: 2, 4, 5, 7, 9, 11, 12, 13, 14, 15

NIANTIC

Inn at Harbor Hill Marina

60 Grand Street, 06357
(860) 739-0331; FAX (860) 691-3078
e-mail: info@innharborhill.com
www.innharborhill.com

The only thing this inn overlooks is the water. A delightful waterside bed and breakfast offering eight rooms with panoramic views of the Niantic River and/or Long Island Sound. All rooms have cable TV, air conditioning, and private baths. Relax on wicker seating on the wraparound porch overlooking the marina and flower gardens. Kayaks for guests' use and passes to local beaches. Short drive to casinos and Mystic. Walk to shops, antiques, restaurants, and theaters. AAA-rated three diamonds.

Transient slips for those wishing to come by boat. Exit 74 off I-95.

Rooms: 8 (PB) $85-165
Continental Breakfast
Credit Cards: A, B, C
Notes: 2, 5, 7, 8, 9, 11, 12

Nutmeg Bed & Breakfast Agency

P.O. Box 1117, West Hartford, 06127-1117
(860) 236-6698; (800) 727-7592
FAX (860) 232-7680
e-mail: nutmegbnb@home.com
www.bnb-link.com

522. Wake up on the water in a completely renovated bed and breakfast with sparkling new interior and exterior. Eight bedrooms with water or marina view; two rooms with balcony. All have ceiling fans. Transient boat slips available at marina. Restaurants, shops, theaters within walking distance. Convenient to Mystic, Foxwoods, Harkness Memorial Park, Westbrook and Clinton shopping outlets. Continental breakfast. Children welcome. No smoking. No pets on premises.

NORFOLK

Covered Bridge

69 Maple Avenue, 06058
(860) 542-5944; FAX (860) 542-5690
e-mail: tremblay@esslink.com
www.obs-us.com/chesler/coveredbridge

2N. Romantic 1880 Victorian on 11 acres of woods, gardens, and a brook is just steps from the village green. All have private baths, two with Jacuzzis, two with fireplaces. A full breakfast is served on one of the lovely porches, in the dining room, or in one of the four enchanting guest rooms. $110-145.

Greenwoods Gate
Bed & Breakfast Inn

105 Greenwoods Road East, 06058
(860) 542-5439; www.greenwoodsgate.com

NOTES: Credit cards accepted: A MasterCard; B Visa; C American Express; D Discover; E Diner's Club; F Other; 2 Personal checks accepted; 3 Lunch available; 4 Dinner available; 5 Open all year; 6 Pets welcome;

Warm hospitality greets guests in this beautifully restored 1797 Colonial home. Small and elegant, it has four exquisitely appointed guest suites each with private bath, one with a Jacuzzi. Fine antiques, fireplaces, and sumptuous breakfasts indulge guests. *Yankee* magazine calls this "New England's most romantic Bed and Breakfast." *Country Inns Bed and Breakfast* magazine calls it "a Connecticut Jewel." New in 1996: the Lilian/Rose Suite with country elegance. Afternoon tea, early evening refreshments served. Children over 12 are welcome.

Hosts: George and Marian Schumaker
Suites: 4 (PB) $175-245
Full Breakfast
Credit Cards: None
Notes: 2, 5, 7, 9, 10, 11, 12, 13, 14

Manor House

Manor House

69 Maple Avenue, 06058
(860) 542-5690
www.manorhouse-norfolk.com

Victorian elegance awaits guests at this historic Tudor/Bavarian estate. Antique-decorated guest rooms, several with fireplace; canopies, balconies, a two-person Jacuzzi, and a two-person soaking tub offer a romantic retreat. Enjoy a sumptuous breakfast in the Tiffany-windowed dining rooms or be treated to breakfast in bed. Designated "Connecticut's Most Romantic Hideaway" and included in *Fifty Best Bed and Breakfasts in the USA*. Children over 12 welcome.

Hosts: Hank and Diane Tremblay
Rooms: 9 (PB) $100-250
Full Breakfast
Credit Cards: A, B, C, D
Notes: 2, 5, 7, 9, 10, 11, 12, 13, 14

Nutmeg Bed & Breakfast Agency

P.O. Box 1117, West Hartford, 06127-1117
(860) 236-6698; (800) 727-7592
FAX (860) 232-7680
e-mail: nutmegbnb@home.com
www.bnb-link.com

302. Visit the northwest hills and stay in an 18th-century inn with Victorian furnishings. The seven guest rooms have private baths. The inn serves dinner Wednesday through Sunday in its spacious dining room with a large fireplace. Full breakfast. Children 10 and older welcome. Smoking permitted.

308. This Colonial inn is in the country on 22 acres, complete with a pool and tennis court. The original main building has four guest rooms with private baths. Some have fireplaces and decks. The carriage house has an additional 16 rooms—some with private and some with shared baths. A full breakfast is served in the inn, where guests can also enjoy a fireplace in the parlor. Children welcome. Smoking permitted outside only.

NORTHFIELD

Covered Bridge

69 Maple Avenue, 06058
(860) 542-5944; FAX (860) 542-5690
e-mail: tremblay@esslink.com
www.obs-us.com/chesler/coveredbridge

A 1755 Colonial farmhouse close to the town of Litchfield offers a two-bedroom suite with a sitting area with a TV and a bath. A full breakfast is served in the dining room with a fireplace which is also open to the living room. $95-135.

7 No smoking; 8 Children welcome; 9 Social drinking allowed; 10 Tennis nearby; 11 Swimming nearby; 12 Golf nearby; 13 Skiing nearby; 14 May be booked through a travel agent; 15 Handicapped accessible.

NORTH STONINGTON

Antiques & Accommodations

32 Main Street, 06359
(860) 535-1736; (800) 554-7829
FAX (860) 535-2613

Centered among Mystic, Foxwoods Casino, and superb sandy beaches in an enchanting historic village. Browse through the hosts' collection of fine antiques and enjoy the library. Stroll through the lovingly tended English gardens, relax on the porches and patios. Greet the morning with the multi-course candlelight breakfast replete with gleaming silver and sparkling crystal. Luxuriate in blissful bed chambers where canopied beds, fresh flowers, and fireplaces await guests. *Connecticut Magazine*'s Top Three Bed and Breakfasts in Connecticut, November 1996. Cover of *Country Inns*, April 1995.

Hosts: Ann and Tom Gray
Rooms: 6 (PB) $99-229
Full Breakfast
Credit Cards: A, B
Notes: 2, 5, 7, 9, 10, 11, 12, 14

Nutmeg Bed & Breakfast Agency

P.O. Box 1117, West Hartford, 06127-1117
(860) 236-6698; (800) 727-7592
FAX (860) 232-7680
e-mail: nutmegbnb@home.com
www.bnb-link.com

511. A 1742 Colonial home on 150-acre horse farm has beautiful pasture views of southeast Connecticut. Enjoy Mystic and Foxwoods Casino. Three guest rooms have queen-size beds and the fourth room has a king-size or twin beds. All have private baths. Full breakfast. Children welcome. No smoking. Dogs and horses on premises.

NORWALK

The Silvermine Tavern

194 Perry Avenue, 06850
(203) 847-4558; FAX (203) 847-9171

From its creaky wooden floors and venerable ancestor paintings to its traditional New England Cuisine and antique canopied beds, the Silvermine Tavern is everything a country inn should be: warm, friendly, inviting—and brimming with charm. Stay the night in a cozy antique-furnished guest room and savor award-winning dining, either alfresco over the mill pond in summer or by the crackling fire in winter. Just an hour from New York City and only 10 minutes from I-95.

Hosts: Frank and Marsha Whitman
Room: 11 (PB) $99-125
Suite: $175
Continental Breakfast
Credit Cards: A, B, C, E
Notes: 2, 3, 4, 5, 9, 14

OLD GREENWICH

Harbor House Inn

165 Shore Road, 06870
(203) 637-0145; FAX (203) 698-0943

This lovely bed and breakfast is in a quiet New England village. Shopping, beach, and fine restaurants are nearby. Train station is one mile away. New York City is 45 minutes away. There are bikes for guests' use and kitchen facilities available. Each room is equipped with a refrigerator, coffee maker, TV and VCR, and telephone with voice mail. Lunch and dinner available nearby.

Hosts: Dolly Stuttig and Dawn Browne
Rooms: 23 (17 PB; 6 SB) $89-149
Continental Breakfast
Credit Cards: A, B, C
Notes: 5, 7, 10, 11, 12, 13, 14

NOTES: Credit cards accepted: A MasterCard; B Visa; C American Express; D Discover; E Diner's Club; F Other; 2 Personal checks accepted; 3 Lunch available; 4 Dinner available; 5 Open all year; 6 Pets welcome;

Nutmeg Bed & Breakfast Agency

P.O. Box 1117, West Hartford, 06127-1117
(860) 236-6698; (800) 727-7592
FAX (860) 232-7680
e-mail: nutmegbnb@home.com
www.bnb-link.com

108. This Victorian inn has 23 guest rooms with a large entry/sitting room. Guests are free to use the kitchen for storing or cooking. Seventeen rooms have private baths and six have shared baths. All rooms have TV, VCR, small refrigerator, and coffee maker. Continental breakfast. Children welcome. Smoking permitted outside only.

OLD LYME

Old Lyme Inn

85 Lyme Street, P.O. Box 787, 06371
(860) 434-2600; (800) 434-5352
FAX (860) 434-5352

Outside, wildflowers bloom all summer; inside, fireplaces burn all winter, beckoning guests to enjoy the romance and charm of this 13-room Victorian country inn with an award-winning, three-star *New York Times* dining room. Within easy reach of the state's attractions, it is tucked away in an old New England art colony. Nonsmoking rooms available.

Host: Diana Atwood Johnson
Manager: Debbie Capone
Rooms: 13 (PB) $99-158
Continental Breakfast
Credit Cards: A, B, C, D, E
Notes: 2, 3, 4, 5, 6, 8, 9, 10, 11, 12, 14, 15

Old Lyme Inn

OLD MYSTIC

Covered Bridge

69 Maple Avenue, 06058
(860) 542-5944; FAX (860) 542-5690
e-mail: tremblay@esslink.com
www.obs-us.com/chesler/coveredbridge

1OMCT. This 1800s Colonial offers a quiet retreat only minutes from the center of Mystic. There is a pleasant living room with a fireplace and a large dining room where a full breakfast is served. There are four guest rooms in the main house, three with fireplaces, and four guest rooms in the carriage house, two with whirlpool tubs. All rooms have queen-size beds and private baths. $115-145.

OLD SAYBROOK

Bed & Breakfast, Ltd.

P.O. Box 216, New Haven, 06513
(203) 469-3260; e-mail: BandB@aol.com
www.bedandbreakfastltd.com

This unique home overlooks scenic salt marshes and a navigable inlet off Long Island Sound. Three lovely appointed bedrooms are available featuring private and semi-private baths. Walk to beaches, and enjoy the scenic bike routes and factory outlets. Nearby attractions include the Essex Steamtrain, Gillette Castle, and Mystic Seaport. Come relax, feel at home, and enjoy all that this home has to offer. $85-110.

Deacon Timothy Pratt Bed & Breakfast

325 Main Street, 06475
(860) 395-1229

Step back in time and enjoy the splendor of yesteryear in this circa 1746 national historic register home in the heart of the historic district within walking distance to Main Street

7 No smoking; 8 Children welcome; 9 Social drinking allowed; 10 Tennis nearby; 11 Swimming nearby; 12 Golf nearby; 13 Skiing nearby; 14 May be booked through a travel agent; 15 Handicapped accessible.

Deacon Timothy Pratt

shops, restaurant, theaters, the river. Guest rooms are romantically furnished in period style with private baths, working fireplaces, cable TV, whirlpool, telephone/modem line. Full country breakfast on fine china. Sherry, tea, and snacks always available. Picturesque yard with gardens, hammock, and swing. Wonderful area for walking, biking, boating. One mile to Long Island Sound beaches and Connecticut River cruises. Beach passes, maps, and advice provided.

Host: Shelley Nobile
Rooms: 3 (PB) $95-160
Full Breakfast
Credit Cards: A, B, C
Notes: 2, 5, 7, 8, 9, 10, 11, 12, 13, 14

Nutmeg Bed & Breakfast Agency

P.O. Box 1117, West Hartford, 06127-1117
(860) 236-6698; (800) 727-7592
FAX (860) 232-7680
e-mail: nutmegbnb@home.com
www.bnb-link.com

514. The river and sound meet at this bed and breakfast. The host even has beach passes for her guests. The contemporary home has a lovely deck off the living room facing the Oyster River and two of the three guest rooms have a water view. One room has a private bath. The two additional rooms share a hall bath. Arrangements can be made to have a private bath. Full breakfast. Children welcome. Smoking permitted outside only. Dog in residence.

ORANGE

Nutmeg Bed & Breakfast Agency

P.O. Box 1117, West Hartford, 06127-1117
(860) 236-6698; (800) 727-7592
FAX (860) 232-7680
e-mail: nutmegbnb@home.com
www.bnb-link.com

206. This bright Colonial farmhouse was built in 1725 and has been in the same family for 11 generations. There are two second-floor guest rooms which share a bath. One room has a double bed, the other twin beds. Continental breakfast. Children are welcome. No smoking permitted. Dog, cows, and horses on premises.

PAWCATUCK

Nutmeg Bed & Breakfast Agency

P.O. Box 1117, West Hartford, 06127-1117
(860) 236-6698; (800) 727-7592
FAX (860) 232-7680
e-mail: nutmegbnb@home.com
www.bnb-link.com

506. This unique single-story house has a beautiful addition for guests. The new wing has a king-size bed that can be made into twin beds, a private bath, and private entrance with a small deck. Enjoy a walk down the street to a spectacular water view. This is close to Mystic Seaport and many beaches. Full breakfast. Children welcome. No smoking. Cats in main part of the house only.

PLANTSVILLE

Bed & Breakfast, Ltd.

P.O. Box 216, New Haven, 06513
(203) 469-3260; e-mail: BandB@aol.com
www.bedandbreakfastltd.com

This 1740 Colonial on one acre is nestled in with period homes and near a beginner's ski slope. Guests can enjoy a homey, comfortable atmosphere, an evening snack, and a wonderful, attentive breakfast! Four-poster beds, an

NOTES: Credit cards accepted: A MasterCard; B Visa; C American Express; D Discover; E Diner's Club; F Other; 2 Personal checks accepted; 3 Lunch available; 4 Dinner available; 5 Open all year; 6 Pets welcome;

outdoor pool, nearby tennis courts, and antique shops are some of what this property offers. A gourmet dinner is available upon request. Two rooms available. $75-95.

Nutmeg Bed & Breakfast Agency

P.O. Box 1117, West Hartford, 06127-1117
(860) 236-6698; (800) 727-7592
FAX (860) 232-7680
e-mail: nutmegbnb@home.com
www.bnb-link.com

465. This 11-room central-chimney Colonial, circa 1740, is on a beautifully landscaped acre with a pool and surrounded by centuries-old maple trees. There are four fireplaces and a dutch oven in the great room. The guest room has a king-size bed, private bath, and air conditioning. Full breakfast served. Children welcome. Smoking in designated areas only. Cat and dog on premises.

PLYMOUTH

Nutmeg Bed & Breakfast Agency

P.O. Box 1117, West Hartford, 06127-1117
(860) 236-6698; (800) 727-7592
FAX (860) 232-7680
e-mail: nutmegbnb@home.com
www.bnb-link.com

407. This beautiful 1825 Greek Revival, furnished with antiques, is on three lovely acres enhanced with a perennial garden. There are four guest rooms. They share two baths, and a private bath can be arranged for additional cost. The bed and breakfast is convenient to activities in the northwest hills. Full breakfast. No smoking. No children.

PLYMOUTH VILLAGE

Shelton House Bed & Breakfast

663 Main Street, Route 6, 06782
(860) 283-4616 (phone/FAX)
e-mail: sheltonHBB@prodigy.net

Shelton House

Enjoy a step back in time with a stay in this historic 1825 Greek Revival, elegantly furnished with antiques and period furniture. Separate guest living room with fireplace and TV. Lovely grounds. Full breakfast served. Afternoon tea. Convenient to Route 8 and I-84. Short distance to all attractions in the scenic Litchfield Hills. Four guest rooms with private and semiprivate baths.

Hosts: Pat and Bill Doherty
Rooms: 4 (2 PB; 2 SB) $65-90
Full Breakfast
Credit Cards: None
Notes: 2, 5, 7, 10, 11, 12, 13

POMFRET

Bed & Breakfast, Ltd.

P.O. Box 216, New Haven, 06513
(203) 469-3260; e-mail: BandB@aol.com
www.bedandbreakfastltd.com

This 1885 grand 8,000-square-foot residence features at TV/media room, library, music room, and glorious antiques. Five bedrooms, some with fireplaces. Guests can enjoy the gardens, deck, porch, large book collection, hiking trails, fishing, swimming, museums, and herb gardens. Near the Pomfret School and Sturbridge Village. Evening sherry and sweet cookies complete the picture of this romantic getaway. $95-125.

7 No smoking; 8 Children welcome; 9 Social drinking allowed; 10 Tennis nearby; 11 Swimming nearby; 12 Golf nearby; 13 Skiing nearby; 14 May be booked through a travel agent; 15 Handicapped accessible.

POMFRET CENTER

Nutmeg Bed & Breakfast Agency

P.O. Box 1117, West Hartford, 06127-1117
(860) 236-6698; (800) 727-7592
FAX (860) 232-7680
e-mail: nutmegbnb@home.com
www.bnb-link.com

414. Very private, quiet setting on 10 acres next to 500-acre Audubon Sanctuary for this charming bed and breakfast which is near bike trails and just 10 minutes to the best antique shopping; 35 minutes to Sturbridge. First floor Garden Room has outside entrance, double four-poster canopied bed, private bath, and sleeper-sofa that converts to single bed. Second-floor Countryside Room has three exposures, queen-size bed, and private bath. Down comforters and pillows in each room. Continental breakfast. Children four and older welcome. No smoking. Cats in residence.

421. This Victorian sits on six acres with flower and vegetable gardens. The formal dining room and sitting room have fireplaces. There are two queen-size rooms with private baths, and twin- and queen-size rooms with a shared bath. Full breakfast. No smoking. Children welcome. Dog in residence.

POQUETANUCK

Captain Grant's, 1754

109 Route 2A, 06365
(860) 887-7589; (800) 982-1772
FAX (860) 892-9151
wv./w.bbonline.com/ct/captaingrants

Built in 1754, Captain Grant's is now a national historic home. Colonial ambiance includes canopied beds, fireplaces, a library, keeping room, kitchenette, and three-story deck; all for guests' exclusive use. Modern amenities include all private baths, air conditioning, color cable TV, evening wine, and a full country breakfast. Minutes from Foxwoods

Casino, Mystic, Coast Guard Academy, Naval submarine museum, and much more.

Hosts: Ted and Carol
Rooms: 6 (PB) $80-150
Full Breakfast
Credit Cards: A, B, C, D
Notes: 5, 7, 8, 9, 10, 11, 12, 14

PUTNAM

Nutmeg Bed & Breakfast Agency

P.O. Box 1117, West Hartford, 06127-1117
(860) 236-6698; (800) 727-7592
FAX (860) 232-7680
e-mail: nutmegbnb@home.com
www.bnb-link.com

413. This 1850s Greek Revival-style home has covered porches on both levels. Stone walls, barns, fields, and trees enhance the five acres of this country setting. Convenience to the area's fine antiquing, private schools, and Sturbridge Village, as well as fine restaurants, make this a perfect getaway choice as well as accommodation for the school weekend visits, numerous county fairs, and antique shows. The two guest rooms are on second floor. The suite has queen-size bed with trundle bed in adjoining sitting room (good for family traveling together). Second room has double bed. There is one bath upstairs, but host will book as private unless couples are traveling together. Both rooms have access to second floor porch and view. Continental breakfast. Children 10 and older welcome. No smoking. Cat in residence.

RIDGEFIELD

Nutmeg Bed & Breakfast Agency

P.O. Box 1117, West Hartford, 06127-1117
(860) 236-6698; (800) 727-7592
FAX (860) 232-7680
e-mail: nutmegbnb@home.com
www.bnb-link.com

101. Savor a Finnish sauna in a 1945 Cape-style house. The private lower level suite has a

---

NOTES: Credit cards accepted: A MasterCard; B Visa; C American Express; D Discover; E Diner's Club; F Other; 2 Personal checks accepted; 3 Lunch available; 4 Dinner available; 5 Open all year; 6 Pets welcome;

queen-size bed and a wonderful luxurious bath. The floor is terra cotta tile; furnishings are tastefully European; and a TV is provided so guests might never want to reappear outside the room, except to enjoy their tasty Continental breakfast. Smoking is not permitted. Dog and cats in residence.

102. Originally a private boys' school, this home sits on a hilltop overlooking five pastoral acres with a magnificent view. It is only one hour from Manhattan. Guests enjoy a private suite that includes a large sitting room with fireplace and a private bath. French doors separate the main house from the guest suite. Continental breakfast is served. Smoking is permitted.

West Lane Inn

22 West Lane, Route 35, 06877
(203) 438-7323; FAX (203) 438-7325

The West Lane uniquely combines the graceful charm of an intimate country inn with every convenience of a luxurious large hotel. Amenities abound…spacious, individually appointed and climate controlled rooms, some with fireplaces, all with queen-size beds, private full baths, color remote cable TV, one-day laundry and dry cleaning, modem jacks, voice mail, an irresistible array of award-winning restaurants, museums, boutiques, antique shopping plus the ease of access to year-round activities.

Hosts: M. M. Mayer and Deborah Prieger
Rooms: 18 (PB) $125-170
Continental Breakfast
Credit Cards: A, B, C, E
Notes: 5, 8, 9, 10, 11, 12, 13, 14

RIVERSIDE

Nutmeg Bed & Breakfast Agency

P.O. Box 1117, West Hartford, 06127-1117
(860) 236-6698; (800) 727-7592
FAX (860) 232-7680
e-mail: nutmegbnb@home.com
www.bnb-link.com

105. These active hosts have decided to share this lovely country-style Cape home. Guest room has private bath. New York City is only one hour away. Full breakfast is served. Children are welcome. No smoking.

110. More than 100-years-old, this farmhouse is on three-quarters of an acre. Spacious and bright first-floor room with deck, private bath with shower, contemporary furnishings, TV, small refrigerator, and coffee maker. On weekdays a Continental breakfast served; weekends full breakfast served. House is one-half mile from Riverside Railroad station, close to Greenwich beaches, many antique stores, and other Greenwich attractions. Crib and high chair are available. Smoking is permitted on the deck only.

RIVERTON

Nutmeg Bed & Breakfast Agency

P.O. Box 1117, West Hartford, 06127-1117
(860) 236-6698; (800) 727-7592
FAX (860) 232-7680
e-mail: nutmegbnb@home.com
www.bnb-link.com

305. Close to Lime Rock Park and many of the private schools, this log home is secluded on five acres. Superb place for cross-country skiing, hiking, and stream fishing. Two guest rooms with private baths. The former innkeepers will also prepare a hearty dinner for overnight guests with prior arrangements. Children welcome. Full breakfast. Smoking in designated area only. Cat in residence.

Old Riverton Inn

Route 20, Box 6, 06065
(860) 379-8678; (800) EST-1796
FAX (860) 379-1006

Hospitality for the hungry, thirsty, and sleepy since 1796. Overlooking the designated Wild and Scenic Farmington River and the Hitchcock Chair Factory Store. Listed in the National

Register of Historic Places. Serving lunch and dinner Wednesday through Sunday. Originally a stagecoach stop on the Hartford to Albany route. Pets welcome with prior approval.

Hosts: Mark and Pauline Telford
Rooms: 12 (PB) $85-175
Full Breakfast
Credit Cards: A, B, C, D, E
Notes: 3, 4, 5, 7, 8, 9, 10, 11, 12, 13, 14

ROXBURY

Nutmeg Bed & Breakfast Agency

P.O. Box 1117, West Hartford, 06127-1117
(860) 236-6698; (800) 727-7592
FAX (860) 232-7680
e-mail: nutmegbnb@home.com
www.bnb-link.com

301. The main house, built in 1790, has a private guest wing with private entrance and bath, a canopied waterbed with feather mattress. A sitting area has a pull-out sofa bed for children. Guests may use the main house to relax in front of the wood-burning stove. The Shepaug River and hiking trails beckon guests outdoors. Full breakfast. Children welcome. No smoking. Pets on premises.

SALISBURY

Nutmeg Bed & Breakfast Agency

P.O. Box 1117, West Hartford, 06127-1117
(860) 236-6698; (800) 727-7592
FAX (860) 232-7680
e-mail: nutmegbnb@home.com
www.bnb-link.com

324. Cottage adjacent to large Colonial on lake has one room for bed and breakfast with twin beds or king-size bed, bath shared with host. Convenient to Lime Rock and all private schools in area; about 45 minutes to Tanglewood. Full breakfast. No children. No smoking. Dogs and cat in residence. Couples only.

337. This 1813 Colonial is in the historic district of Salisbury, one of Connecticut's most charming villages. Two guest rooms with private baths. Breakfast is served in the dining room or on the stone terrace. Walk to fine restaurants, shops, and antiques. Convenient to Lime Rock. Children are welcome. No smoking. Pets are on premises.

SCOTLAND

Nutmeg Bed & Breakfast Agency

P.O. Box 1117, West Hartford, 06127-1117
(860) 236-6698; (800) 727-7592
FAX (860) 232-7680
e-mail: nutmegbnb@home.com
www.bnb-link.com

454. A 1797 Colonial-style country inn with a large sitting room for guests, keeping room, and kitchen for breakfast. Also a TV room with fireplace, double bedroom, and queen-size bedroom with fireplace. Both share a bath. Full breakfast. Children over 10 welcome. No smoking. Cat on premises.

SIMSBURY

Merrywood Bed & Breakfast

100 Hartford Road, 06070
(860) 651-1785; FAX (860) 651-8273
e-mail: mfmarti@aol.com

Merrywood provides a five-acre sanctuary which beckons guests to stroll its ground and gardens. The inn is a Colonial Revival furnished with American and Continental antiques, offering amenities of a five-star hotel yet with an Old World atmosphere. The inn is centrally air conditioned and has a large porch, library, and living room with fireplace. Breakfast is prepared in the French manner served by candlelight on handmade linen and antique English porcelain. Afternoon tea can be served with finger sandwiches and sweets. Merry-

Merrywood

wood is convenient to the best hiking trails and views in Connecticut.

Rooms: 3 (PB) $130-155
Full Breakfast
Credit Cards: A, B, C, D, E
Notes: 2, 5, 7, 9, 10, 11, 12, 13

Simsbury 1820 House

731 Hopmeadow Street, Route 10 & 202, 06082
(860) 658-7658

An elegant country inn and restaurant featuring 32 antique appointed guest rooms all with private bath. Our cafe is open Monday through Thursday offering fine cuisine in a casual atmosphere as well as a full bar. Friday and Saturday the restaurant is available for weddings and other special occasions for up to 200 people.

Host: Diane Ropiak, innkeeper
Rooms: 32 (PB) $145-195

Continental Breakfast
Credit Cards: A, B, C, D, E
Notes: 5, 10, 11, 12, 13, 15

SOMERSVILLE

Old Mill Inn Bed & Breakfast

63 Maple Street, 06072
(860) 763-1473 (phone/FAX)

Surrounded by giant maple trees, this spacious old New England home provides romantic lodging and gourmet breakfast. Guests have use of the private beach on the serene Scantic River with hammock, swing, canoe, picnic table, and fishing. Bicycles available for countryside touring and a soothing spa to end a perfect day. Gazebo enhances picturesque settings for intimate weddings, parties, and family reunions.

Rooms: 5 (1 PB; 4 SB) $85-95
Full Breakfast
Credit Cards: None
Notes: 2, 4, 5, 7, 9, 10, 11, 12, 13

SOUTHBURY

Nutmeg Bed & Breakfast Agency

P.O. Box 1117, West Hartford, 06127-1117
(860) 236-6698; (800) 727-7592
FAX (860) 232-7680
e-mail: nutmegbnb@home.com
www.bnb-link.com

320. A Georgian Federal home, circa 1818, has six guest bedrooms, three acres of nicely landscaped grounds with pool, cozy keeping room with fireplace, cable TV, VCR, exercise room. Convenient to antiquing, private schools, horseback riding, hiking, vineyards, fishing, and all outdoor activities. Can be booked for weddings or receptions up to 100 guests. Afternoon high tea. Full breakfast but Continental breakfast is occasionally served with breakfast bar adjacent to guest rooms. Picnic lunches can be arranged. Children 12 and older welcome. No smoking. No pets. Two small dogs in residence.

7 No smoking; 8 Children welcome; 9 Social drinking allowed; 10 Tennis nearby; 11 Swimming nearby; 12 Golf nearby; 13 Skiing nearby; 14 May be booked through a travel agent; 15 Handicapped accessible.

SOUTHPORT

Nutmeg Bed & Breakfast Agency

P.O. Box 1117, West Hartford, 06127-1117
(860) 236-6698; (800) 727-7592
FAX (860) 232-7680
e-mail: nutmegbnb@home.com
www.bnb-link.com

109. Cape Cod style home in lovely wooded setting, with deer, chipmunks, wild turkeys sharing the back acreage. Two second floor guest rooms with twin beds and handworked coverlets. Beds in one room can be put together for a king-size bed. Both rooms can be used for a family with shared full bath, or one for two people with private bath. Enjoy a bountiful full breakfast and the view on the sun porch, or spend a crisp evening by the kitchen hearth or living room fire. Great base for all Fairfield county exploration and activities. Thirty minutes to New York City. Children welcome. No smoking. Cat on premises.

SOUTH WINDSOR

Nutmeg Bed & Breakfast Agency

P.O. Box 1117, West Hartford, 06127-1117
(860) 236-6698; (800) 727-7592
FAX (860) 232-7680
e-mail: nutmegbnb@home.com
www.bnb-link.com

410. All guest rooms in this large Palladian-style mansion, circa 1788, have fireplaces. The original floor plan is intact, and two rooms have original paper. Convenient to Hartford, Springfield, and many historic sites. Close to bus line. Two rooms on first floor with sitting area, desk, outdoor sitting area, private bath, cable TV. All telephones have data lines; rooms ADA handicapped accessible. Space is available for meetings for up to 10 people. Continental breakfast. Children are welcome. No smoking.

STAMFORD

Nutmeg Bed & Breakfast Agency

P.O. Box 1117, West Hartford, 06127-1117
(860) 236-6698; (800) 727-7592
FAX (860) 232-7680
e-mail: nutmegbnb@home.com
www.bnb-link.com

116. This Nantucket Colonial has a water view on a sandy beach. Breakfast is served on the sun porch. Two guest rooms, each with a private bath. Full breakfast served. Children are welcome. No smoking.

STORRS

Storrs Farmhouse

418 Gurleyville Road, 06268
(860) 429-1400

This New England Cape Cod home is within two miles of the University of Connecticut. It is a 10-minute walk to the Nipmuck Walking Trail, trout fishing, antique shop, yet they are close to the Jorgenson Auditorium at the University for its culture programs and plays. One and one-half hours to Boston, two and one-half hours from New York City. There is an apartment also available.

Host: Elaine Kollet
Rooms: 4 (PB) $65
Full Breakfast
Credit Cards: None
Notes: 2, 5, 8, 9, 10, 11, 12, 13, 14

STRATFORD

Covered Bridge

69 Maple Avenue, 06058
(860) 542-5944; FAX (860) 542-5690
e-mail: tremblay@esslink.com
www.obs-us.com/chesler/coveredbridge

This 1843 Federal Greek Revival farmhouse, set on several acres, is listed in the National Register of Historic Places. Antique-decorated parlor, living room with fireplace, and large sun porch are available for guest use. There are four guest rooms, two with private baths and two available as a suite with a bathroom. Full breakfast is served. $100.

THOMPSON

Lord Thompson Manor

Route 200, P.O. Box 428, 06277
(860) 923-3886; FAX (860) 923-9310

Formerly known as the Gladding Estate, built in 1917 by Providence mercantilist John Gladding as a summer home, this stately 30-room manor house has been reborn as the Lord Thompson Manor. From the moment guests step inside, a feeling of comfort will embrace them. The manor, with its unique appointments of gum wood paneling, parquet floors, African marble fireplaces, high ceilings, and rich, warm colors radiate a feeling of privilege to all who enter.

Hosts: Jackie and Andrew Silverston
Rooms: 6 (4 PB; 2 SB) $100-160
Full Breakfast
Credit Cards: A, B, C
Notes: 2, 3, 4, 5, 7, 8, 9, 11, 12, 14, 15

TOLLAND

Nutmeg Bed & Breakfast Agency

P.O. Box 1117, West Hartford, 06127-1117
(860) 236-6698; (800) 727-7592
FAX (860) 232-7680
e-mail: nutmegbnb@home.com
www.bnb-link.com

403. Just east of Hartford is this lovely two-story Colonial, circa 1840, on three acres. The two guest rooms have queen-size beds and private baths. The home a treat to stay in and is beautifully decorated with English country antiques that have been carefully selected. Full breakfast. Children are welcome. Smoking permitted outside only.

The Tolland Inn

The Tolland Inn

63 Tolland Green, 06084-0717
(860) 872-0800; www.tollandinn.com

Built in 1800, the inn stands on Tolland's historic village green, less than one mile north of I-84 exit 68. Seven guest rooms are decorated with antiques and furniture made by the host. Two suites have canopied beds, one with sitting room and fireplace, one with sitting room and hot tub. The first-floor room has a canopied bed, fireplace, and a sunken hot tub. Three beautiful common rooms and a fireplace complete the picture. Convenient to Brimfield Fair, Old Sturbridge, and the University of Connecticut. AAA three-diamond-rated.

Hosts: Susan and Stephen Beeching
Rooms: 7 (PB) $78.40-95.20
Suites: $123.20-145.60
Full Breakfast
Credit Cards: A, B, C, D, E
Notes: 2, 5, 7, 9, 10, 11, 12, 14

WALLINGFORD

Nutmeg Bed & Breakfast Agency

P.O. Box 1117, West Hartford, 06127-1117
(860) 236-6698; (800) 727-7592
FAX (860) 232-7680
e-mail: nutmegbnb@home.com
www.bnb-link.com

209. The original part of this center chimney Colonial was built in 1742 as the family homestead, with an addition in 1995. It rests on two handsome acres with a pond at the end of the property. The two guest rooms are in the original part of the house. One room has a double bed; the other has either a king-size bed or twin beds and each has a private bath. The host is an international traveler and a gourmet cook. Full breakfast. Children welcome. No smoking. Dog and cat in residence.

Addington's

WATERBURY

Nutmeg Bed & Breakfast Agency

P.O. Box 1117, West Hartford, 06127-1117
(860) 236-6698; (800) 727-7592
FAX (860) 232-7680
e-mail: nutmegbnb@home.com
www.bnb-link.com

318. This restored Victorian, in the historic district, is furnished with antiques. It offers three guest rooms on the second floor, two of which share a bath. The other has a private bath. There is also a third-floor suite. A grand city gem, the architecture is the best that New England cities have to offer. Continental breakfast is served. Smoking is not permitted.

WATERTOWN

Addington's Bed & Breakfast

1002 Middlebury Road, 06795
(860) 274-2647

Enjoy the comfortable country charm of this 1840 Colonial farmhouse, where a candle glows in every window as a sign of welcome. The bed and breakfast is nestled in the foothills of Litchfield County. Near area antique shops, historic district, and Main Street. Three country-charm rooms enhanced by dolls, quilts, and country handicrafts made and sold by the owners. Wonderful homemade breads and pastries for guests' enjoyment.

Hosts: Jan Lynn and Eric Addington
Rooms: 3 (1 PB; 2 SB) $85-100

Full and Continental Breakfast
Credit Cards: A, B
Notes: 2, 5, 7, 9, 11, 13

WESTBROOK

Covered Bridge

69 Maple Avenue, 06058
(860) 542-5944; FAX (860) 542-5690
e-mail: tremblay@esslink.com
www.obs-us.com/chesler/coveredbridge

Federal Colonial close to the beach offers five guest rooms, three with private baths, all with air conditioning and a TV. A full breakfast is served and on the grounds there are gas grills and picnic tables for guests' use. $80-115.

Nutmeg Bed & Breakfast Agency

P.O. Box 1117, West Hartford, 06127-1117
(860) 236-6698; (800) 727-7592
FAX (860) 232-7680
e-mail: nutmegbnb@home.com
www.bnb-link.com

516. For the many activities along the Connecticut coast, this house built in 1895 is ideal. There are two guest rooms, each with a private bath. The home is 150 feet from the beach and is furnished with antiques. Full breakfast served. Children are welcome. No smoking.

517. This stately Federal-style house was built in 1880 and is two blocks from the sound. There are three floors and five guest rooms, all with private baths. The rooms all have TVs. Full breakfast served. Children 10 and older welcome. No smoking.

521. For lovers of the Victorian era, this house is ideal. Built in 1876, it is close to the beach and downtown. Four rooms have private baths and five rooms have shared baths. The interior is newly decorated in the Victorian period. Full breakfast is served on Sunday; Continental is served the rest of the time. Children welcome. Smoking permitted.

Welcome Inn Bed & Breakfast

433 Essex Road, 06498
(860) 399-2500

Originally a strawberry farm, the inn was built around 1897 and retains its country charm. Convenient to everything the Connecticut River valley and seashore have to offer. The inn is decorated with antiques, fine reproductions, lace, and heirlooms. Breakfast is served 8:00-9:30 A.M. daily with delicious homemade goodies and special coffee. Relax in the parlor with a crackling fire, a glass of sherry, and a good book, or in the garden. Hosts will be happy to assist guests with arranging restaurant reservations, tours, and other activities.

Hosts: Alison and Robert Bambino
Rooms: 4 (PB) $90-135
Full Breakfast
Credit Cards: A, B
Notes: 2, 5, 7, 9, 10, 11, 12,

WEST CORNWALL

Nutmeg Bed & Breakfast Agency

P.O. Box 1117, West Hartford, 06127-1117
(860) 236-6698; (800) 727-7592
FAX (860) 232-7680
e-mail: nutmegbnb@home.com
www.bnb-link.com

317. A great seasonal getaway spot. Newly renovated streamside studio cottages have working fireplaces, private baths, porches with sitting area, coffee makers in rooms. Hearty Continental breakfast served on porch. Pets accepted. Convenient to Lime Rock, Housatonic River, Kent, and Salisbury, private schools. Fly-fishing guide on premises, canoeing, hiking, kayaking. Good restaurants are nearby. Children are welcome. No smoking.

WEST HARTFORD

Nutmeg Bed & Breakfast Agency

P.O. Box 1117, West Hartford, 06127-1117
(860) 236-6698; (800) 727-7592
FAX (860) 232-7680
e-mail: nutmegbnb@home.com
www.bnb-link.com

441. This single-story home is furnished with a blend of modern, traditional, and antique. One guest room with TV has two twins or king-size bed and private bath. Convenient to Hartford, the University of Connecticut, and the University of Hartford. Hungarian spoken. Continental breakfast. Children are welcome. No smoking.

WEST HAVEN

Nutmeg Bed & Breakfast Agency

P.O. Box 1117, West Hartford, 06127-1117
(860) 236-6698; (800) 727-7592
FAX (860) 232-7680
e-mail: nutmegbnb@home.com
www.bnb-link.com

212. A lovely porch wraps around this 80-year-old Victorian not far from Long Island Sound. The accommodations are on the first floor and include a dining room, kitchen, parlor, private bath, private entrance, and a double bed in the bedroom. On the weekends, a candlelight dinner can be arranged. Continental breakfast is served on weekdays; full breakfast is served on weekends. Children over 10 are welcome. No Smoking.

7 No smoking; 8 Children welcome; 9 Social drinking allowed; 10 Tennis nearby; 11 Swimming nearby; 12 Golf nearby; 13 Skiing nearby; 14 May be booked through a travel agent; 15 Handicapped accessible.

WESTPORT

Nutmeg Bed & Breakfast Agency

P.O. Box 1117, West Hartford, 06127-1117
(860) 236-6698; (800) 727-7592
FAX (860) 232-7680
e-mail: nutmegbnb@home.com
www.bnb-link.com

104. This Georgian Colonial, with pool, has a second-floor guest room with a king-size bed that can be made into twin beds, wicker furnishings, and private bath with shower. Convenient to railroad station. A full breakfast is served. Children are welcome. Smoking is not permitted. Dog in residence.

111. This home combines rural beauty with metropolitan sophistication in a breathtaking setting overlooking Long Island Sound. The private guest wing has its own sitting room, fireplace, and entrance. There are three guest rooms that have either a private or shared bath. Enjoy the beach during summer. Continental breakfast is served. Children are welcome. No smoking. $60.

WETHERSFIELD

Nutmeg Bed & Breakfast Agency

P.O. Box 1117, West Hartford, 06127-1117
(860) 236-6698; (800) 727-7592
FAX (860) 232-7680
e-mail: nutmegbnb@home.com
www.bnb-link.com

408. Nestled in the historic village of Old Wethersfield, this classic Greek Revival brick house has been lovingly restored to provide a warm and gracious New England welcome to all travelers. Built in 1830, it boasts five airy guest rooms furnished with period antiques. Three rooms have private baths; two rooms share a bath. Fresh flowers; cozy living room and parlor. Afternoon tea and elegant full breakfast are served. Children over 11 are welcome.

429. This attractive Colonial home is rich in the history of the town. The hostess, a member of the historical society, offers one guest room with a private bath. A small room suitable for a child is available. Close to a park and safe for walking. Full breakfast is served. Children are welcome. Smoking is permitted in designated areas only.

WINDSOR

Covered Bridge

69 Maple Avenue, 06058
(860) 542-5944; FAX (860) 542-5690
e-mail: tremblay@esslink.com
www.obs-us.com/chesler/coveredbridge

1WINCT. This 1860 Queen Anne Victorian rests in Connecticut's oldest town and is furnished with exquisite period antiques and William Morris wallpapers. Guests are welcome to relax in the living room or music room with a grand piano and a century-old music box. Three guest rooms with private baths offered. One room has a fireplace. $75-100.

Nutmeg Bed & Breakfast Agency

P.O. Box 1117, West Hartford, 06127-1117
(860) 236-6698; (800) 727-7592
FAX (860) 232-7680
e-mail: nutmegbnb@home.com
www.bnb-link.com

469. Charming Victorian home dating to 1860s, renovated with an addition in 1890. Lovely antique furniture; large front porch; three second-floor bedrooms, two with extra-long double beds, one with extra-long twin beds, and all with private baths. Convenient to airport, University of Hartford, and Loomis Chaffee. Full breakfast. Children over 12 welcome. No smoking. Dog on premises.

NOTES: Credit cards accepted: A MasterCard; B Visa; C American Express; D Discover; E Diner's Club; F Other; 2 Personal checks accepted; 3 Lunch available; 4 Dinner available; 5 Open all year; 6 Pets welcome;

WINSTED

Nutmeg Bed & Breakfast Agency

P.O. Box 1117, West Hartford, 06127-1117
(860) 236-6698; (800) 727-7592
FAX (860) 232-7680
e-mail: nutmegbnb@home.com
www.bnb-link.com

306. Bright wall of windows looking out to deck and gardens make a cheerful setting for this spacious bed and breakfast reserved exclusively for guests (host lives in separate house on premises). First floor bedroom is handicapped accessible with private bath with sunken tub and sit-down shower; two second-floor bedrooms share a bath. All rooms are spacious and comfortably furnished. Breakfast is either Continental or full (guests select choices the night before). House is convenient to Norfolk and the Berkshires, Lime Rock, and all private schools in area. TV in living room for guests' use. Children welcome. No smoking. No resident pets.

309. Charming old Victorian home, beautifully restored and filled with antiques has three guest rooms. First floor room has queen-size bed and private bath; two second-floor rooms, share a hall bath. All rooms are spacious and furnished with fine antiques. Full breakfast is served in the formal dining room, and several lovely parlors are for guests' enjoyment.

WOODBURY

Covered Bridge

69 Maple Avenue, 06058
(860) 542-5944; FAX (860) 542-5690
e-mail: tremblay@esslink.com
www.obs-us.com/chesler/coveredbridge

1WOCT. This 1789 Colonial, set on four acres, is in a town which has been described as "the Antique Capital of Connecticut." Many of the original features of the house, such as the large covered porch, wide-oak floorboards, and fireplaces, have been preserved. A grand living room with a fireplace and a library are available for guest's use. There are five lovely bedrooms and suites. A full country breakfast is served. $105-125.

Nutmeg Bed & Breakfast Agency

P.O. Box 1117, West Hartford, 06127-1117
(860) 236-6698; (800) 727-7592
FAX (860) 232-7680
e-mail: nutmegbnb@home.com
www.bnb-link.com

307. Stately red clapboard Garrison Colonial home with patio overlooking perennial gardens has two rooms for bed and breakfast. One newly decorated room shares a bath with another room. If guests prefer, only one room will be booked for an additional price so that bath will be private. Convenient to private schools in area, many fine restaurants, good antiquing, hiking trails, and ski area. Continental breakfast. Children welcome. No smoking. No resident pets.

316. Large, elegant new house on five-acre hilltop is built to savor spectacular views of the surrounding countryside. Great room has glass window wall, and the luxurious bedrooms also look out to the lovely gardens and the pool. Two first-floor rooms share a sumptuous bath. Second-floor suite has living room, bedroom with four-poster bed, and private bath. Air conditioning in bedrooms only, fireplace in living room. Continental breakfast. Children welcome if five feet tall or over because of above ground pool. No smoking. Dog in residence.

345. This 1789 Colonial, on three acres, has been carefully restored and tastefully furnished with antiques. Two guest rooms have double beds and shared bath; combined they make a suite. Remaining three guest rooms all have private baths. They have twin, king-, or queen-size beds. Full breakfast is served. Children

7 No smoking; 8 Children welcome; 9 Social drinking allowed; 10 Tennis nearby; 11 Swimming nearby; 12 Golf nearby; 13 Skiing nearby; 14 May be booked through a travel agent; 15 Handicapped accessible.

five and over are welcome. Smoking is not permitted. Resident cat on the premises.

WOODSTOCK

The Inn at Woodstock Hill

94 Plaine Hill Road, P.O. Box 98, 06267
(860) 928-0528; FAX (860) 928-3236

Nestled atop the hills of Connecticut—far removed from the bustle and glare of city life—lies a hideaway so exquisite, so tranquil, guests might mistake it for Camelot. The Inn at Woodstock Hill offers weary travelers, corporate business people, and fairmaiden brides a choice of 22 spacious and immaculate rooms. Four-poster beds, working fireplaces, private baths, TV/VCRs, and an award-winning restaurant/function room for up to 225 people, await guests. Inquire about smoking privileges.

Hosts: Sheila Becks and Richard Naumann
Rooms: 22 (PB) $90-155
Continental Breakfast
Credit Cards: A, B, D
Notes: 2, 3, 4, 5, 8, 9, 10, 11, 12, 13, 14, 15

Maine

Maple Hill Farm

AUGUSTA

Maple Hill Farm
Bed & Breakfast Inn

Outlet Road, Rural Route 1, Box 1145, Hallowell, 04347
(207) 622-2708; (800) 622-2708
FAX (207) 622-0655; e-mail: info@MapleBB.com
www.MapleBB.com

"Best of Maine 1997...hands down"—*Maine Times*. Unique pampered service for relaxation or business travel combined with this inn's barn-yard menagerie—llamas, pony, goats, sheep, more! On 130 serene acres of unspoiled rural beauty, minutes to turnpike, capitol, national historic district, shopping, eclectic dining, antiquing. Central to coast, lakes, mountains. Adjacent to 550-acre wildlife preserve with pristine pond for canoeing/hiking. Full breakfast featuring eggs from farm. Spacious antique-furnished rooms with air conditioning, telephones, TV. Private whirlpools available. Liquor license. Fully accessible guest room available.

Host: Scott Cowger
Rooms: 7 (PB) $70-145
Full Breakfast
Credit Cards: A, B, C, D, E
Notes: 2, 4, 5, 7, 8, 9, 11, 12, 13, 14, 15

BAILEY ISLAND

Captain York House
Bed & Breakfast

Route 24, P.O. Box 298, 04003
(207) 833-6224; www.iwws.com/captainyork

Enjoy true island atmosphere on scenic Bailey Island, in an unspoiled fishing village accessible by car over the only cribstone bridge in the world. Near Brunswick, Freeport, and Portland. Former sea captain's home tastefully restored to original charm, furnished with antiques. Informal, friendly atmosphere and ocean views from every room. From the deck, enjoy sights of local lobstermen hauling traps and sunsets to remember. Nearby fine dining/summer nature cruise. Ocean-view apartment rental also available. Children over 12 welcome.

Hosts: Alan and Jean Thornton
Rooms: 5 (3 PB; 2 SB) $70-95
Full Breakfast
Credit Cards: A, B
Notes: 2, 5, 7, 12, 14

Captain York House

7 No smoking; 8 Children welcome; 9 Social drinking allowed; 10 Tennis nearby; 11 Swimming nearby; 12 Golf nearby; 13 Skiing nearby; 14 May be booked through a travel agent; 15 Handicapped accessible.

● Greenville

Stratton ●   ● Dexter   Lee ●

16   201

Bangor ●   Machias   Eastport
                      Lamoine   Sullivan   Lubec
Rumford Center   Stockton Springs   Harbor   Gouldsboro
Bethel   Searsport ●Orland
                        Belfast   Cherryfield
2   95   Corea
Waterford   Rockland   Winter Harbor
                       Thomaston Stonington Bar Harbor
Augusta   Waldoboro Camden   Mount Desert Island
              3   Damariscotta
Bridgton   Casco Newcastle
Fryeburg   Wiscasset   Vinalhaven   Isle au Haut
              Naples   Brunswick   Southwest Harbor
Windham   Freeport   Spruce Head
Falmouth
Portland   Friendship
Saco   95
Kennebunk   Chamberlain
Biddeford Pool   New Harbor
Kennebunk Beach   Bailey Island   Newagen
                             Chebeague
Wells   Island   Bath   Georgetown
Eliot
   Kittery   Boothbay
                        Ocean Park   Boothbay Harbor
York,   Kennebunkport
York Beach,   Wells Beach
York Harbor   Ogunquit

Maine

BANGOR

Mann Hill Morgans
Bed & Breakfast

660 Mann Hill Road, Holden, 04429
(207) 843-5657; e-mail: mannhill@mint.net
www.maineguide.com/bangor/mannhill

This lovely and spacious New England Colonial, with private stable, features two beautifully decorated rooms, one with fireplace. Both rooms have private baths. A delightful getaway for those seeking peace and tranquillity. Nestled on a foothill with mountains that surround, it is only two miles from Route 1A. It is the "Maine" route to and from Bar Harbor and Acadia National Park. Ten minutes to Bangor. Fifteen minutes to Bangor International Airport. Forty miles to Bar Harbor.

Hosts: Mary and Larry Winchester
Rooms: 2 (PB) $45-60
Full Breakfast
Credit Cards: A, B, D
Notes: 2, 5, 7, 8, 9, 10, 11, 12, 13

Mann Hill Morgans

BAR HARBOR

Bar Harbor Tides
Bed & Breakfast

119 West Street, 04609
(207) 288-4968; FAX (207) 288-2997
e-mail: info@barharbortides.com
www.barharbortides.com

An 1887 Greek Revival cottage in quiet historic district. One room and three luxurious suites—the suites all have sweeping views of French-

Bar Harbor Tides

man's Bay, king-size beds, and private baths; two have fireplaces. Full gourmet breakfast served on the veranda overlooking the bay, or in the formal dining room with its own grand view of the bay. Very private, nonsmoking.

Hosts: Joe and Judy Losquadro
Rooms: 4 (PB) $150-295
Full Breakfast
Credit Cards: A, B, D
Notes: 5, 7, 10, 12

Black Friar Inn

10 Summer Street, 04609
(207) 288-5091; FAX (207) 288-4197
e-mail: blackfriar@acadia.net
www.blackfriar.com

This comfortably restored and rebuilt Victorian house with antiques is on a quiet side street. Six guest rooms with queen-size beds and private baths, plus a suite with king-size bed, private bath, fireplace, and sofa bed. Rates include delicious full breakfast, late afternoon

Black Friar Inn

NOTES: Credit cards accepted: A MasterCard; B Visa; C American Express; D Discover; E Diner's Club; F Other; 2 Personal checks accepted; 3 Lunch available; 4 Dinner available; 5 Open all year; 6 Pets welcome; 7 No smoking; 8 Children welcome; 9 Social drinking allowed; 10 Tennis nearby; 11 Swimming nearby; 12 Golf nearby; 13 Skiing nearby; 14 May be booked through a travel agent; 15 Handicapped accessible.

refreshments, and rainy day teas. Easy access to Acadia National Park. Short walk to waterfront, shops, and restaurants. Ample parking. Two-night minimum mid-June through mid-October. Sorry, no cots or rollaway beds; the six guest rooms can accommodate one or two people only. Children over 11 welcome.

Hosts: Perry and Sharon Risley and Falke
Rooms: 6 (PB) $90-120
Suite: 1 (PB) $145
Full Breakfast
Credit Cards: A, B, D
Notes: 2, 7, 9, 10, 11, 12

Graycote Inn

Castlemaine Inn

Castlemaine Inn

39 Holland Avenue, 04609
(207) 288-4563; (800) 338-4563

Castlemaine Inn is nestled on a quiet side street in the village of Bar Harbor, which is surrounded by the magnificent Acadia National Park. The rooms are well appointed, with canopied beds and some whirlpool bathtubs, private balconies, and fireplaces. A delightful Continental buffet-style breakfast is served. Air conditioning. Color cable TV with VCR. Open May through October. Children over 13 are welcome.

Hosts: Terence O'Connell and Norah O'Brien
Rooms: 15 (PB) $98-168
Continental Breakfast
Credit Cards: A, B
Notes: 2, 9, 10, 11, 12

Graycote Inn

40 Holland Avenue, 04609
(207) 288-3044; e-mail: graycote@acadia.net
www.graycoteinn.com

This light and airy Victorian house is ideal for a romantic getaway. The day begins with morning coffee placed outside guests' rooms; then enjoy a made-from-scratch breakfast served on a sunny, enclosed porch. The inn is on a large lot with trees, lawns, flower gardens, a croquet court, and hammocks. Relax in wicker chairs on the veranda or walk to shops, art and craft galleries, and restaurants. Five minutes to Acadia National Park.

Hosts: Roger and Pat Samuel
Rooms: 12 (PB) $95-155
Full Breakfast
Credit Cards: A, B, C, D
Notes: 2, 5, 7, 9, 10, 11, 12, 13, 14

Hatfield Bed & Breakfast

20 Roberts Avenue, 04609
(207) 288-9655

Jeff and Sandy Miller invite guests to enjoy quiet country comfort at Hatfield, on a quiet side street just a short walk to the waterfront and town center—a five-minute drive to Acadia National Park or the ferry to Nova Scotia. Previously from rural Pennsylvania, Jeff and Sandy are known for their "country hospitality" and great breakfasts. Smoking is permitted outdoors only and seasonal rates are available. Sorry, no pets.

Hosts: Jeffrey and Sandra Miller
Rooms: 6 (4 PB; 2 SB) $85-110
Full Breakfast
Credit Cards: A, B, D
Notes: 2, 3, 5, 7, 9, 10, 11, 12, 13, 14

Hearthside

7 High Street, 04609
(207) 288-4533; e-mail: hearth@acadia.net

Built at the turn of the century as the residence for Dr. George Hagerthy, Hearthside is now a cozy and comfortable bed and breakfast. Hearthside is on a quiet side street in Bar Harbor. All of the rooms have queen-size beds and private baths; some have private porches, whirlpool tubs, or working fireplaces. All rooms have air conditioning. Each morning a lavish breakfast buffet is served, and lemonade and homemade cookies are offered each afternoon. Off-season rates available.

Hosts: Susan and Barry Schwartz
Rooms: 9 (PB) $90-135
Full Breakfast
Credit Cards: A, B, D
Notes: 2, 5, 7, 9, 10, 11, 12

Hearthside

Heathwood Inn

Heathwood Inn

Rural Route 1, Box 1938, Route 3, 04609
(207) 288-5591; FAX (207) 288-4862
e-mail: heathwoodinn@acadia.net
www.acadia.net/heathwood

This Victorian farmhouse is one of Mount Desert Island's unique country inns. Just minutes from Bar Harbor, Acadia National Park and all island activities. Charming guests accommodations are elegantly decorated with antique furnishings, old family photos, and splendid plasterwork throughout offering a quiet romantic atmosphere for the discrete. Ideal for off-season getaway. Five rooms with luxurious private baths with dual five foot steam showers. Honeymoon suite with a six foot Jacuzzi tub; master suite with fireplace and private deck. The Manderley has a five and one-half foot Finnish dry sauna.

Hosts: Richard and Cynthia Cassey
Rooms: 5 (PB) $92-150
Continental Breakfast
Credit Cards: A, B, D
Notes: 2, 5, 7, 9, 11, 12, 13, 14

The Inn at Bay Ledge

1385 Sand Point Road, 04609
(207) 288-4204; FAX (207) 288-5573

Dramatic and peaceful. Overlooking Frenchmen's Bay. All rooms have ocean views.

7 No smoking; 8 Children welcome; 9 Social drinking allowed; 10 Tennis nearby; 11 Swimming nearby; 12 Golf nearby; 13 Skiing nearby; 14 May be booked through a travel agent; 15 Handicapped accessible.

Picked as one of the 12 most romantic hide-aways on the East Coast for 1998. At top of an 80-foot cliff with steps leading to private beach. On two acres of tall pines. Five miles to town center, two miles to Acadia National Park main entrance. Open May through October. Two-night minimum, June 15 through October 1. Picnic lunches available.

Hosts: Jack and Jeani Ochtera
Rooms: 10 (PB) $150-275
Full Breakfast
Credit Cards: A, B
Notes: 2, 7, 10, 11, 12

Manor House Inn

The Kedge Historic Bed & Breakfast

112 West Street, 04609
(207) 288-5180; (800) 597-8306

The Kedge, built in 1870, has a peaceful beauty that is full of light and comfortable elegance. In town across the street from French-man Bay, this bed and breakfast rests on a double lot and has beautiful gardens. The dream room is 18- x 22-feet, has a king-size brass bed, fireplace, and whirlpool tub. In the historic district. Smoke free. Full breakfast. AAA three-diamond rating. Children seven and older welcome.

Rooms: 3 (PB) $65-160
Full Breakfast
Credit Cards: A, B, C
Notes: 2, 5, 7, 9, 10, 11, 12, 13, 14

Manor House Inn

106 West Street, 04609
(207) 288-3759; (800) 437-0088

This beautiful 1887 Victorian summer cottage is listed in the National Register of Historic Places. Near Acadia National Park. Within walking distance of downtown Bar Harbor and waterfront. Enjoy the acre of landscaped grounds and gardens. Minimum stay July, August, and holidays is two nights. Closed

December through mid-April. Children over 10 welcome.

Host: Mac Noyes
Rooms: 14 (PB) $60-185
Full Breakfast
Credit Cards: A, B, D
Notes: 2, 7, 9, 10, 11, 12, 14

The Maples Inn

16 Roberts Avenue, 04609
(207) 288-3443
e-mail: maplesinn@acadia.net
www.acadia.nj/maples

Built in 1903, this lovely inn is on a quiet tree-lined street, near the downtown area of Bar Harbor and just a short walk to boutiques, intimate restaurants, and the surrounding sea. For the perfect romantic getaway, reserve the

The Maples Inn

NOTES: Credit cards accepted: A MasterCard; B Visa; C American Express; D Discover; E Diner's Club; F Other; 2 Personal checks accepted; 3 Lunch available; 4 Dinner available; 5 Open all year; 6 Pets welcome;

White Birch Suite with wood-burning fireplace. Palates will be treated to host's breakfast recipes, some of which have been featured in *Gourmet* and *Bon Appétit* magazines. Just two miles from Acadia National Park.

Hosts: Tom and Sue Palumbo
Rooms: 6 (PB) $60-150
Full Breakfast
Credit Cards: A, B, D
Notes: 2, 7, 9, 11, 12, 13

Mira Monte Inn & Suites

69 Mount Desert Street, 04609
(800) 553-5109; FAX (207) 288-3115
e-mail: mburns@acadia.net

This 1864 Victorian blends antique furnishings with modern amenities—each room has king- or queen-size bed, cable TV, telephone, air conditioning, and a fireplace, balcony, or both. Two-room suites have a kitchen unit and double whirlpool. On a two-acre village estate with exquisite gardens. Common spaces include the library with a piano, parlor, and the formal dining room as well as the porch and terraces. Four-room housekeeping suite by weekly rental.

Host: Marian Burns
Rooms: 13 (PB) $135-159
Suites: 3 (PB) $190-205
Full Breakfast
Credit Cards: A, B, C, D, E
Notes: 2, 7, 9, 10, 11, 12, 14, 15

The Ridgeway Inn

11 High Street, 04609
(207) 288-9682

Built at the turn of the century, today the Ridgeway Inn offers warm hospitality in a comfortable atmosphere. Set in a quiet in-town location, the inn is just a short walk from the many shops, restaurants, the harbor, and Acadia National Park. The aged stone walls, bright flower-lined yard, and porch with ornamental wrought-iron furniture invites guests inside. Hardwood floors with scatter rugs, fireplaces with ornate mantels, lace curtains set in bay

The Ridgeway Inn

windows, and a sprinkling of antiques, including a working pump organ, provide an intimate and visually pleasing atmosphere. Open year-round with seasonal rates.

Host: Kerry Hartman
Rooms: 5 (PB) $70-150
Full Breakfast
Credit Cards: A, B
Notes: 2, 7, 9, 10, 11, 12

Willows at Atlantic Oakes-by-the-Sea

119 Eden Street, P.O. Box 3, 04609
(800) 33MAINE; www.barharbor.com

The Willows, circa 1913, is on the grounds of Atlantic Oakes-by-the-Sea and was named after the willow trees beside the entrance drive. There are nine guest rooms. All rooms on the

Willows at Atlantic Oakes-by-the-Sea

7 No smoking; 8 Children welcome; 9 Social drinking allowed; 10 Tennis nearby; 11 Swimming nearby; 12 Golf nearby; 13 Skiing nearby; 14 May be booked through a travel agent; 15 Handicapped accessible.

ocean side have ocean views and balconies. Rooms two and three connect via the bath and are rented to one party. Four rooms have king-size beds and the other three rooms have double beds. Continental plus breakfast served in the mansion in season. There are an apartment and penthouse separate from the bed and breakfast available. Not suitable for children. Seasonal rates available. Near Acadia National Park.

Rooms: 9 (7 PB; 2 SB) $73-252
Continental Breakfast
Credit Cards: A, B, C
Notes: 5, 7, 10, 11, 12

BATH

Benjamin F. Packard House

45 Pearl Street, 04530
(207) 443-6069; (800) 516-4578
e-mail: packardhouse@clinic.net
www.mainecoast.com/packardhouse/

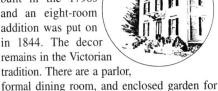

The Packard House is in the heart of Bath's historic district. It was built in the 1790s and an eight-room addition was put on in 1844. The decor remains in the Victorian tradition. There are a parlor, formal dining room, and enclosed garden for guests to enjoy. The midcoast location is perfect for antiquing, historic adventure, oceanfront parks, or shopping in nearby Freeport. Enjoy all of this by making the Packard House one's midcoast home port.

Hosts: Debby and Bill Hayden
Rooms: 3 (PB) $75-95
Full Breakfast
Credit Cards: A, B, C, D
Notes: 2, 5, 7, 9, 10, 11, 12, 14

Fairhaven Inn at Bath

North Bath Road, Rural Route 2, Box 85, 04530
(888) 443-4391; FAX (207) 443-6412
e-mail: fairhvn@gwi.net

Where eagles soar, birds sing, and tidal river meets meadow. This comfortable, quiet 1790 Colonial is renowned for its breakfast and is the perfect midcoast base from which to enjoy all that Maine's coast has to offer. Hiking and cross-country skiing on property. Beaches and Maine Maritime Museum nearby. Smoking restricted to outside only.

Hosts: Susie and Dave Reed
Rooms: 8 (PB and SB) $80-120
Full Breakfast
Credit Cards: A, B, D
Notes: 2, 5, 7, 8, 9, 10, 11, 12, 13, 14

The Galen C. Moses House

1009 Washington Street, 04530
(207) 442-8771; (888) 442-8771
e-mail: galenmoses@clinic.net
www.galenmoses.com

This Italianate structure, built in 1874, has been draped in vivid colors to give it the nickname "the Pink House." The large rooms are reminiscent of 19th-century Victorian style. There are many surprises throughout the house, including a full theater on the third floor. The house also contains a number of assuredly friendly spirits, who make their presence known on a frequent basis. Full gourmet breakfast varies according to the cook's mood. Coffee, juices, and muffins are available for early risers and late sleepers. AAA-rated three diamonds. Close to antique shops, historic house tours, and beaches. Children over 12 welcome. Check website or call for midweek deals.

Hosts: James Haught and Larry Kieft
Rooms: 4 (PB) $79-109
Full and Continental Breakfast
Credit Cards: A, B
Notes: 2, 5, 9, 10, 11, 12

NOTES: Credit cards accepted: A MasterCard; B Visa; C American Express; D Discover; E Diner's Club; F Other; 2 Personal checks accepted; 3 Lunch available; 4 Dinner available; 5 Open all year; 6 Pets welcome;

BELFAST

The Alden House Bed & Breakfast

63 Church Street, 04915
(207) 338-2151; e-mail: info@thealdenhouse
www.bbonline.com/me/alden

USA Today has rated Belfast as "one of the top five culturally cool small towns in America." This midcoastal Maine jewel, which sits on the Penobscot Bay, is home to the Alden House Bed and Breakfast. Featured on the *Oprah Winfrey Show*, the Alden House has been completely renovated for guests' comfort, but retains its Greek Revival beauty of 1840 with imported marble fireplaces and a hand-carved cherry winding staircase. Within minutes one can walk to restaurants, shops, and the waterfront. Guests' stay is ended with a memorable, multi-course breakfast.

Hosts: Jessica Jahnke and Marla Stickle
Rooms: 7 (5 PB; 2 SB) $75-110
Full Breakfast
Credit Cards: A, B, C
Notes: 2, 5, 7, 9, 10, 11, 12, 13, 14

Belhaven Inn Bed & Breakfast

14 John Street, 04915
(207) 338-5435; e-mail: stay@belhaveninn.com

Stay at this circa 1851 Victorian home. A comfortable, family-oriented inn where all children are welcomed. A short walk to harbor, shops, and restaurants. Full country breakfast served on columned veranda or in charming dining room with fantastic leaded-glass cupboard and period mantel. Unwind in one of the two fire-placed common rooms. A circular staircase leads up to four delightful and unique guest rooms. The efficiency guest suite with private entry and sun deck sleeps four. Discounted single, senior, and Canadian rates. "Belhaven—a comfortable haven in Belfast."

Hosts: Anne and Paul Bartels
Rooms: 5 (3 PB; 2 SB) $65-90
Full Breakfast

Credit Cards: A, B
Notes: 2, 5, 6, 7, 8, 9, 10, 11, 12

The Jeweled Turret Inn

The Jeweled Turret Inn

40 Pearl Street, 04915
(207) 338-2304; (800) 696-2304
www.bbonline.com/me/jeweledturret/

Step back into a time when lace, elegant furnishings, and afternoon tea were everyday necessities. The inn is named for the grand staircase that winds up the turret, lighted by stained- and leaded-glass panels with jewel-like embellishments. Lots of antiques, woodwork, fireplaces, public rooms, and two verandas. Gourmet breakfasts and afternoon tea are available in the dining room or, during summer, on the veranda. In the historic district; shops, restaurants, and waterfront nearby. Smoking is permitted in designated areas only.

Hosts: Carl and Cathy Heffentrager
Rooms: 7 (PB) $85-125
Full Breakfast
Credit Cards: A, B
Notes: 2, 5, 9, 10, 11, 12, 13, 14

The Thomas Pitcher House Bed & Breakfast

19 Franklin Street, 04915
(207) 338-6454; (888) 338-6454
e-mail: tpitcher@acadia.net
www.thomaspitcherhouse.com

7 No smoking; 8 Children welcome; 9 Social drinking allowed; 10 Tennis nearby; 11 Swimming nearby; 12 Golf nearby; 13 Skiing nearby; 14 May be booked through a travel agent; 15 Handicapped accessible.

The Thomas Pitcher House

Relax and unwind in the elegant comfort of this handsome, in-town Victorian built in 1873. Spacious guest rooms and inviting common areas feature original Victorian architecture and are distinctively furnished with antiques and reproduction pieces. Fabulous three-course breakfasts are served in the large Chippendale dining room. Host speaks German and some French. Children over 12 welcome. Recommended by Fodor's, the *Boston Herald*, *Jackson Clarion-Ledger*, *Knoxville News-Sentinel*, *Toronto Sun*, and *Allentown Morning Call* newspapers, and *Bride's* magazine.

Hosts: Fran and Ron Kresge
Rooms: 4 (PB) $75-95
Full Breakfast
Credit Cards: A, B
Notes: 2, 5, 7, 9, 10, 11, 12, 13, 14

BETHEL

Abbott House

170 Walker Mills Road, P.O. Box 933, 04217
(207) 824-7600; (800) 240-2377

The Abbott House offers four rooms with three shared baths in an 18th-century Cape Cod on two and one-half acres. In the winter a hot tub is available. Near Sunday River skiway and White Mountains. In summer three rooms with air conditioning and private baths are offered. Perennial gardens, murder mystery weekends, golf, hiking, and multiday packages available. Massage therapists are on staff.

Hosts: Joe Cardell; Penny Bohac and Nestlé
Rooms: 5 (2 PB; 3 SB) $55-90

Full Breakfast
Credit Cards: A, B, C, D
Notes: 2, 4, 5, 7, 9, 10, 11, 12, 13

The Chapman Inn

1 Mill Hill Road, 04217
(207) 824-2657; FAX (207) 824-7152
e-mail: Chapman@nxi.com

Great inn in the center of the historic district. Named "the best family inn in New England" by the New England Travel Guide. Walk to shops, restaurants, championship golf. Outstanding skiing at Sunday River, only five minutes away. Private saunas and game room. Plenty of parking. A 22-bed dorm available—perfect for large groups. Family units available. Owner is a classically trained chef. Lunch and dinner available upon request. Pets welcome by prior arrangements.

Hosts: Fred and Sandra
Rooms: 10 (8 PB; 2 SB) $55-100
Full Breakfast
Credit Cards: A, B, C, D
Notes: 2, 5, 7, 8, 9, 11, 12, 13, 14

BIDDEFORD POOL

The Lodge

19 Yates Street, 04006
(207) 284-7148

Next to the Yacht Club, on Saco Bay at one of the most pristine settings on the Maine coast, Biddeford Pool offers a private beach, rockbound coast, marsh lands, and much more. Guests can choose golf, tennis, boating, sun bathing, or visit many of the fine shops within 10 miles. Stores and restaurants are all nearby. Warm days, 75 degrees, and cool nights, 60 to 70 degrees, are the average temperatures. Smoking permitted outside only. Inquire about accommodations for children.

Host: John Oddy
Rooms: 4 (2 PB; 2 SB) $70-99
Continental Breakfast
Credit Cards: A, B
Notes: 2, 5, 7, 9, 10, 11, 12

NOTES: Credit cards accepted: A MasterCard; B Visa; C American Express; D Discover; E Diner's Club; F Other; 2 Personal checks accepted; 3 Lunch available; 4 Dinner available; 5 Open all year; 6 Pets welcome;

BOOTHBAY

Hodgdon Island Inn

Barter's Island Road, Box 492, 04571
(207) 633-7474
e-mail: info@hodgdonislandinn.com
www.hodgdonislandinn.com

A gracious restored sea captain's home, circa 1810, decorated with wicker and antiques, just a five-minute drive to downtown Boothbay Harbor. Relax on the front porch and watch the sunset over the water. Swim in the heated chlorine-free swimming pool. Six tastefully furnished guest rooms, all with private baths. Full breakfast. Afternoon tea in winter, lemonade in summer. Good old-fashioned Down East hospitality at its best. Children over 12 welcome.

Hosts: Peter Wilson and Peter Moran
Rooms: 6 (PB) $95-125
Full Breakfast
Credit Cards: A, B
Notes: 2, 5, 7, 9, 10, 11, 12

Kenniston Hill Inn

Route 27, P.O. Box 125, 04537-0125
(207) 633-2159 (phone/FAX); (800) 992-2915
e-mail: innkeeper@maine.com

This inn for all seasons is surrounded by large lawns and shady maples. Built in 1786, Kenniston Hill is the most historic inn in Boothbay with 10 antique-filled guest rooms, private baths, and comfy quilts. When there is a chill in the air, seven working fireplaces warm body

Kenniston Hill Inn

and soul. Complimentary full breakfast greets guests. On Route 27, the inn is open all year. Limited handicapped accessibility.

Hosts: Susan and David Straight
Room: 10 (PB) $69-110
Full Breakfast
Credit Cards: A, B, D
Notes: 2, 5, 7, 8, 9, 10, 11, 12, 13, 14, 15

BOOTHBAY HARBOR

Anchor Watch

Anchor Watch Bed & Breakfast

9 Eames Road, 04538
(207) 633-7565

Islands, fir trees, and lobster boats provide the setting for this cozy bed and breakfast on the prettiest shore of the harbor. Country quilts and stenciling set the style inside. Breakfast features a baked cheese omelet or baked orange French toast. Enjoy a table for two or sit with others at an ocean-view window. Watch sunsets from the private pier. Five-minute walk to shops, boat trips, Monhegan ferry, and fine dining. Open year-round.

Hosts: Diane and Bob Campbell
Rooms: 5 (PB) $85-145
Full Breakfast
Credit Cards: A, B, D
Notes: 2, 5, 7, 9, 10, 11, 12

7 No smoking; 8 Children welcome; 9 Social drinking allowed; 10 Tennis nearby; 11 Swimming nearby; 12 Golf nearby; 13 Skiing nearby; 14 May be booked through a travel agent; 15 Handicapped accessible.

The Atlantic Ark Inn

64 Atlantic Avenue, 04538
(207) 633-5690
e-mail: donna@atlanticarkinn.com
www.atlanticarkinn.com

An intimate bed and breakfast inn offers lovely views of the harbor and a five-minute stroll to town. This 100-year-old Maine home offers wraparound porch, balconies, antiques, oriental rugs, floor-length drapes, poster beds, fresh flowers, and private baths—one with Jacuzzi and another with Greek tub. Each morning awaken to a delicious full gourmet breakfast prepared with the freshest and purest of ingredients. Recommended in *Good Housekeeping* as one of the best places to stay in Boothbay Harbor. The Atlantic Ark Inn was featured on the front cover of the 1999 official Maine Tourism publication of *Inns and Bed and Breakfasts for the State*. Smoking permitted outside only. Children over 12 welcome.

Host: Donna Piggott
Rooms: 6 (PB) $95-169
Full Breakfast
Credit Cards: A, B, C
Notes: 2, 7, 9, 10, 11, 12, 14

Bed & Breakfast Reservations North Shore, Greater Boston, Cape Cod

P.O. Box 600035, Newtonville, MA 02460
(617) 964-1606; (800) 832-2632
FAX (617) 332-8572; e-mail: info@bbreserve.com
www.bbreserve.com

67. This cozy 1850 New England Cape is the perfect place to base while taking easy day trips and enjoying one of the most scenic areas of coastal Maine. Antique and fine wood furniture, hand tooled by the host, are featured. The master guest room has a detached full private bath. A two-room guest suite is perfect for families or small groups (up to four) traveling together. A single room in the suite may be taken at private bath rates. A gourmet full breakfast awaits

guests in the morning. Open year-round. Children over 14 welcome. No smoking. $85-95.

1830 Admiral's Quarters Inn

1830 Admiral's Quarters Inn

71 Commercial Street, 04538
(207) 633-2474; FAX (207) 633-5904
e-mail: loon@admiralsquartersinn.com
www.admiralsquartersinn.com

Commanding an unsurpassed view of the harbor, each accommodation has its own deck, separate entrance, and private bath. This 1830 sea captain's home offers charming accommodations, a blend of antiques and white wicker, color-cable TVs and telephones. Hearty homemade buffet breakfast and afternoon refreshments are served in the dining room, the solarium with woodstove, or perhaps on the wraparound porches. Steps away are unique shops and harbor activities. "Way out of the ordinary…but not out of the way." Children 12 and older are welcome.

Hosts: Les and Deb Hallstrom
Rooms: 6 (PB) $75-145
Full Breakfast
Credit Cards: A, B, D
Notes: 2, 7, 9, 10, 11, 12, 13, 14

Five Gables Inn

Murray Hill Road, P.O. Box 335, East Boothbay, 04544
(207) 633-4551; (800) 451-5048

Five Gables Inn is a completely restored Victorian, circa 1890s, on Linekin Bay. All rooms

NOTES: Credit cards accepted: A MasterCard; B Visa; C American Express; D Discover; E Diner's Club; F Other; 2 Personal checks accepted; 3 Lunch available; 4 Dinner available; 5 Open all year; 6 Pets welcome;

Five Gables Inn

have an ocean view and private baths and five have fireplaces. A gourmet breakfast is served in the large common room or on the spacious wraparound veranda. Open mid-May to end of October. Children 12 and older are welcome.

Hosts: Mike and De Kennedy
Rooms: 15 (PB) $100-170
Full Breakfast
Credit Cards: A, B
Notes: 2, 7, 9, 10, 11, 12, 14

Harbour Towne Inn on the Waterfront

71 Townsend Avenue, 04538
(207) 633-4300 (phone/FAX); (800) 722-4240
e-mail: gtme@gwi.net; e-mail: mainco@gwi.net
www.acadia.net/harbourtowneinn

Harbour Towne Inn

"The Finest Bed and Breakfast on the waterfront" commands scenic harbor views from outside decks in a quiet location on Boothbay Harbor. All rooms have private baths in this refurbished Victorian townhouse. Also available is a luxury penthouse that will sleep six in absolute privacy. Walk to shops, art galleries, restaurants, churches, library, dinner theaters, boat trips, and fishing. One- to two-hour drive to skiing. Reservations recommended. Special off-season getaway packages. Continental plus breakfast. Inquire about accommodations for children. Limited handicapped accessibility.

Hosts: The Thomas Family
Rooms: 12 (PB) $59-179
Penthouse: $150-250
Continental Breakfast
Credit Cards: A, B, C, D
Notes: 2, 7, 9, 10, 11, 12, 13, 14

The Howard House

The Howard House Motel Bed & Breakfast

Route 27, 04538
(207) 633-3933; (207) 633-6244
e-mail: howardhs@qwi.net
www.qwi.net/~howardhs

Unique chalet design on 20 wooded acres, quiet setting, beautiful flowers. Each spacious, sparkling, clean room features glass patio door with private balcony, cable TV, and full private bath. Delicious, healthful buffet breakfast. Shopping, sightseeing, boating, island clam bakes, seal and whale watches, and fine

7 No smoking; 8 Children welcome; 9 Social drinking allowed; 10 Tennis nearby; 11 Swimming nearby; 12 Golf nearby; 13 Skiing nearby; 14 May be booked through a travel agent; 15 Handicapped accessible.

restaurants are nearby. AAA three-diamond-and Mobil Travel Guide-approved. Smoking in designated areas only.

Hosts: The Farrins
Rooms: 14 (PB) $69-82
Full Breakfast
Credit Cards: None
Notes: 2, 9, 10, 11, 12, 14, 15

Lion d'Or Bed & Breakfast

106 Townsend Avenue, 04538
(207) 633-7367; (800) 887-7367
e-mail: liondor@gwi.net

Built in 1857, this newly upgraded Victorian inn offers five tastefully decorated rooms with private baths and cable TV. A stay at the Lion d'Or will include a full "wicked" good breakfast. Open all year and in town where guests can enjoy many of the harbor's activities. Reduced rates for stays of three or more nights. Children are welcomed. Every guest is a special guest at the Lion d'Or.

Hosts: Fern Robichaud
Rooms: 5 (PB) $60-90
Full Breakfast
Credit Cards: A, B
Notes: 2, 5, 7, 8, 9, 10, 11, 12, 14, 15

Welch House Inn

56 McKown Street, 04538
(207) 633-3431; (800) 279-7313
e-mail: www.welchhouse@wiscasset.net
www.wiscasset.net/welchhouse

Past and present are happily married in the Welch House, circa 1873. The accommodations are spacious, airy, and smoke free. Guest rooms offer a pleasant mix of the old and new. Most rooms provide a water view and all have private baths. The McKown Hill setting provides an unsurpassed view of the town and Boothbay Harbor. Restaurants, shops, galleries, and all the harbor activities are a two-minute walk down the hill.

Rooms: 16 (PB) $55-145
Full Breakfast
Credit Cards: A, B, C
Notes: 2, 6, 7, 8, 9, 10, 11, 12, 13, 14

BRIDGTON

The Noble House Bed & Breakfast

37 Highland Road, P.O. Box 180, 04009
(207) 647-3733; FAX (207) 647-3733

Stately manor set on a hill across the street from scenic Highland Lake. Secluded lake frontage with canoe, foot-pedal boat, hammock, and barbecue for guests' use. Experience Shaker village, antique and craft shops, museums, and chamber music festival in summer. One hour inland from Portland, and one hour from the White Mountains. Sumptuous full breakfast. Whirlpool baths and family suites. Open June through October. Winter by advance reservation only. Smoking permitted on porches only.

Hosts: Jane Starets
Rooms: 8 (5 PB; 3 SB) $80-129
Full Breakfast
Credit Cards: A, B, C
Notes: 2, 8, 10, 11, 12, 13, 14

The Noble House

NOTES: Credit cards accepted: A MasterCard; B Visa; C American Express; D Discover; E Diner's Club; F Other; 2 Personal checks accepted; 3 Lunch available; 4 Dinner available; 5 Open all year; 6 Pets welcome;

BRUNSWICK

Brunswick Bed & Breakfast

165 Park Row, 04011
(800) 299-4914

The Brunswick Bed and Breakfast is a Greek Revival house overlooking the town green. On the main level, the twin front parlors offer guests the inviting warmth of two fireplaces for wintertime comfort; wraparound front porch for summer leisure. The guest rooms are decorated with antique furnishings, unique accessories, and quilts. Within walking distance of local restaurants, museums, Bowdoin College, and shops. Convenient, allowing guests to easily explore midcoast Maine harbors and coastline.

Hosts: Mercie and Steve Normand
Rooms: 8 (PB) $90-125
Full Breakfast
Credit Cards: A, B
Notes: 2, 5, 7, 9, 10, 11, 12

CAMDEN

Blackberry Inn

82 Elm Street, 04843
(207) 236-6060; (800) 388-6000
FAX (207) 236-9032
e-mail: blkberry@midcoast.com
www.blackberryinn.com

Maine's only "painted lady" Victorian! With elegant parlors, polished parquet floors, Italianate moldings, and carefully painted original tin ceilings, Blackberry Inn is a welcoming getaway to more gracious times. Ten light and resplendent guest rooms—each with private bath. Many offer fireplaces and some feature whirlpool tubs, cable TV, and air conditioning. Only a three-block stroll to Camden's Harbor, shops, and restaurants. Wonderful, scrumptious breakfasts. Perfect year-round escape! Owners are outdoor enthusiasts.

Rooms: 10 (PB) $80-155
Full Breakfast
Credit Cards: A, B, D
Notes: 2, 5, 7, 8, 11, 12, 13, 14

Captain Swift Inn

Captain Swift Inn

72 Elm Street, 04843
(207) 236-8113; (800) 251-0865
FAX (207) 230-0464; www.midcoast.com/~swiftinn

Enjoy the warm atmosphere of yesteryear in this fully restored Federal-period home. Built in 1810, this home retains its wide pine floors, intricate moldings, and 12-over-12 windows still fitted with their original glass. Guests' bed chamber is decorated with period pieces and reproductions, a four-poster bed accented by a handmade quilt, down pillows, and other special touches. At breakfast guests will enjoy inn specialities like crustless sweet pepper quiche served with the inn's baked apple pancake soufflé. Come and relax.

Hosts: Tom and Kathy Filip
Rooms: 4 (PB) $85-115
Full Breakfast
Credit Cards: A, B
Notes: 2, 5, 7, 9, 10, 11, 12, 13, 14, 15

Castleview by the Sea Bed & Breakfast

59 High Street, 04843
(207) 236-2344; (800) 272-VIEW (8439)

Spectacular glass-walled rooms overlooking Camden's only two castles and the sea, right from your bed! Count the stars across the bay and wake up to inspiring Maine views found nowhere else. Bright and airy charm of classical 1856 Cape architecture, wide pumpkin-pine floors, beamed ceilings, claw-foot tubs, skylights, balconies, ceiling fans, and stained glass. Five-minute walk to harbor. Video and reading libraries. Healthy breakfast. Open May through October.

Host: Bill Butler
Rooms: 3 (PB) $75-175
Full or Continental Breakfast
Credit Cards: A, B
Notes: 2, 7, 8, 9, 10, 11, 12, 13, 14

Edgecombe-Coles House

64 High Street, 04843
(207) 236-2336; (800) 528-2336
FAX (207) 236-6227
e-mail: edgecmcol@midcoast.com

Edgecombe-Coles House is a romantic bed and breakfast overlooking the ocean in beautiful Camden. This 200-year-old house sits on a quiet acre well back from traffic. They are open year-round and are in an ideal location to stay for several days, enjoying the many attractions and activities of the Maine coast. In 1997 they were picked as one of the top 20 bed and breakfasts in the country.

Hosts: Terry and Louise Price
Rooms: 6 (PB) $100-195
Full Breakfast
Credit Cards: A, B, C, D
Notes: 2, 5, 7, 9, 10, 11, 12, 13, 14

The Elms Bed & Breakfast

84 Elm Street, 04843
(207) 236-6250; (800) 755-ELMS
FAX (207) 236-7330
e-mail: theelms@midcoast.com
www.midcoast.com/~theelms

"Let us welcome you to the Elms all year." Experience the casual warmth of this circa 1806 home surrounded by beautiful lighthouse artwork and collectibles. Spend the day hiking, sailing, or browsing the many shops and gal-leries within walking distance. Tuck yourself into a spacious bed chamber. Awake to the smells of a delightfully prepared and beautifully presented breakfast. Lighthouse boat tours and quiet season packages. Visit the Elms and leave with the feeling of having been to visit friends. Children over seven welcome.

Hosts: Ted and Jo Panayotoff
Rooms: 6 (PB) $85-105
Full Breakfast
Credit Cards: A, B, D
Notes: 2, 5, 7, 9, 10, 11, 12, 13, 14, 15

The Hartstone Inn

The Hartstone Inn

41 Elm Street, 04843
(207) 236-4259; (800) 788-4823
FAX (207) 236-9575
e-mail: info@hartstoneinn.com
www.hartstoneinn.com

Come fall under the spell of one of Camden's grandest historic homes in the heart of the village. Each guest room is a unique experience in pampered luxury. The beautifully decorated rooms and suites offer a private bath, sitting area, and designer bedding. Elegant china, fine crystal, and the internationally award-winning chef make the hearty breakfast and gourmet candlelit dinner a truly memorable experience. "We look foward to your visit."

Hosts: Mary Jo and Michael Salmon
Rooms: 10 (PB) $75-140
Full Breakfast
Credit Cards: A, B
Notes: 2, 4, 5, 6, 7, 8, 9, 10, 11, 12, 13, 14

NOTES: Credit cards accepted: A MasterCard; B Visa; C American Express; D Discover; E Diner's Club; F Other; 2 Personal checks accepted; 3 Lunch available; 4 Dinner available; 5 Open all year; 6 Pets welcome;

Hawthorn Inn

Hawthorn Inn Bed & Breakfast

9 High Street, 04843
(207) 236-8842

This elegant, turreted Victorian mansion overlooks Camden Harbor with spacious grounds, bright and airy rooms, large deck, lovely antiques throughout, full breakfast, and friendly innkeepers. Stroll through back garden to town amphitheater and harbor park. Near shops and restaurants. Carriage house rooms have full harbor views, private decks, double Jacuzzis, fireplaces, and VCRs. Recommended by *Yankee, Glamour,* and *Outside* magazines. Featured in *Minneapolis Star Tribune* and *Chicago Tribune.* Children over 12 welcome.

Hosts: Patty and Nick Wharton
Rooms: 10 (PB) $95-195
Full Breakfast
Credit Cards: A, B, C
Notes: 2, 5, 7, 9, 10, 12, 13, 14

A Little Dream

60 High Street, 04843
(207) 236-8742

Sweet dreams and little luxuries abound in this lovely white Victorian with wraparound porch. Noted for its lovely breakfast, beautiful rooms, and charming atmosphere. A Little Dream's English country-Victorian decor has been fea-

tured in *Country Inns* magazine, and in *Glamour,* "40 Best Getaways Across the Country." In the historic district just a few minutes from shops and harbor, it is listed in the National Register of Historic Places. Rooms have either a private deck, view, or fireplace. All have special touches, such as imported soaps and chocolates, and a hostess who will do her very best to please.

Hosts: Joanna Ball and Bill Fontana
Rooms: 7 (PB) $95-225
Full Breakfast
Credit Cards: A, B, C
Notes: 2, 7, 10, 11, 12, 13

Maine Stay

Maine Stay

22 High Street, 04843
(207) 236-9636; FAX (207) 236-0621
e-mail: innkeeper@mainestay.com
www.mainestay.com

A comfortable bed, a hearty breakfast, and three friendly innkeepers will be found in this 1802 Colonial home in Camden's historic district. Take a short walk to the harbor, shops, restaurants, and state park. Recommended by the *Bangor Daily News, Miami Herald, Boston Globe, Harper's Bazaar, Country Inns, Glamour, Yankee,* and *Country Living* magazines. Children over eight welcome.

Hosts: Peter and Donny Smith; Diana Robson
Rooms: 8 (PB) $100-150
Full Breakfast
Credit Cards: A, B, C
Notes: 2, 5, 7, 9, 10, 11, 12, 13, 14

7 No smoking; 8 Children welcome; 9 Social drinking allowed; 10 Tennis nearby; 11 Swimming nearby; 12 Golf nearby; 13 Skiing nearby; 14 May be booked through a travel agent; 15 Handicapped accessible.

The Swan House

49 Mountain Street (Route 52), 04843
(207) 236-8275; (800) 207-8275
FAX (207) 236-0906
e-mail: hikeinn@swanhouse.com
www.swanhouse.com

This fine Victorian home dates from 1870 and
has been renovated to offer six spacious guest
rooms. Some offer private sitting areas as well.
A creative and generous full breakfast is
served each morning on the sun porch. Landscaped grounds and a gazebo are available for
guests to relax and enjoy. A hiking trail leading to Camden Hills State Park starts right
behind the inn. Off busy Route 1, Swan House
is a short walk to Camden's beautiful harbor,
shops, and restaurants. Seasonal rates. Children over 12 welcome.

Hosts: Lyn and Ken Kohl
Rooms: 6 (PB) $90-130
Full Breakfast
Credit Cards: A, B
Notes: 2, 5, 7, 9, 10, 11, 12, 13

Maplewood Inn

Hosts: René and Youngok Damen
Rooms: 9 (6 PB; 3 S2B) $45-80
Full Breakfast
Credit Cards: A, B, C, D
Notes: 2, 5, 8, 10, 11, 12, 13

CHAMBERLAIN

Ocean Reefs on Long Cove

376 State Route 32, 04541-3901
(207) 677-2386

Watch the waves break over the reefs, lober-
stermen hauling in traps, or the shoreline
between tides. Hike or bicycle on the roads
along the rocky coast. Pemaquid Beach,
Pemaquid Lighthouse, Fort William Henry,
and the boat to Monhegan Island are all within
five miles. Two-night minimum stay required
during July and August. Closed September 30
through Memorial Day.

Host: John Hahler
Rooms: 4 (PB) $70
Continental Breakfast
Credit Cards: None
Notes: 2, 9, 10, 11, 12

The Swan House

CASCO

Maplewood Inn & Motel

549 Roosevelt Trail (Route 302), 04015
(207) 655-7586; FAX (207) 655-5131
e-mail: rdamen1@maine.rr.com

Cozy family inn in the heart of the lakes region
(Sebago Lake). Nicely renovated 19th-century
house with additional motel units near the outdoor pool. Amenities include cable TV and
miniature golf. One mile from Sebago Lake
State Park and many fine restaurants just minutes away. Inquire about smoking privileges.

CHERRYFIELD

Ricker House

Park Street, Box 256, 04622
(207) 546-2780

Selected as one of the top 50 inns in America.
Comfortable 1802 Federal Colonial, in the

NOTES: Credit cards accepted: A MasterCard; B Visa; C American Express; D Discover; E Diner's Club;
F Other; 2 Personal checks accepted; 3 Lunch available; 4 Dinner available; 5 Open all year; 6 Pets welcome;

Ricker House

National Register of Historic Places, borders the Narraguagus River and offers guests a central place for enjoying the many wonderful activities in Down East Maine, including scenic coastal area, swimming, canoeing, hiking, and fishing. Inquire about accommodations for pets. Cross-country skiing nearby.

Hosts: William and Jean Conway
Rooms: 3 (SB) $53.50-64.20
Full Breakfast
Credit Cards: None
Notes: 2, 7, 10, 11, 12, 13

COREA

The Black Duck on Corea Harbor

Crowley Island Road, P.O. Box 39, 04624
(207) 963-2689; e-mail: bduck@acadia.net
www.blackduck.com

This restored 1890s house, filled with art and antiques, overlooks Down East lobster harbor and open ocean in a tranquil fishing village. Explore the 12 acres and discover hidden salt marshes and a private bay. Curl up in front of a fireplace to read or find a sunny rock outcrop and watch the gulls soar overhead and maybe spot a bald eagle. Rooms and cottages furnished in antiques of various periods. Children under one and over eight are welcome. Low-fat but elegant breakfast in the antique- and art-filled dining room.

Hosts: Barry Canner and Robert Travers
Rooms: 5 (3 PB; 2 SB) $70-145

Suite: 1 (PB) $145
Full Breakfast
Credit Cards: A, B
Notes: 2, 5, 7, 9, 11, 12, 14

DAMARISCOTTA

Brannon-Bunker Inn

349 State Route 129, Walpole, 04573
(207) 563-5941; (800) 563-9225
e-mail: brbnkinn@lincoln.midcoast.com

Intimate, relaxed, country bed and breakfast in an 1820 Cape, 1880 converted barn, and 1900 carriage house. Seven rooms furnished in themes reflecting the charm of yesterday with the comforts of today. Ten minutes to lighthouse, fort, beach, antiques, and craft shopping. Antique shop on the premises.

Hosts: Jeanne and Joe Hovance
Rooms: 7 (5 PB; 2 SB) $69.55-80.25
Continental Breakfast
Credit Cards: A, B, C
Notes: 2, 7, 8, 9, 10, 11, 12, 13, 14, 15

Mill Pond Inn

Route 215, Damariscotta Mills
50 Main Street, Nobleboro, 04555 (mailing)
(207) 563-8014
www.virtualcities.com/me/millpondinn.htm

This 1780 home offers an excellent atmosphere to view the wonders of Maine's wildlife. Complimentary canoes can be paddled from the pond in the back yard directly into Damariscotta Lake. Mountain bikes and guided fishing trips available. Nestled in the little 1800s village of Damariscotta Mills, this inn offers guests a unique experience. Boothbay Harbor, Camden Hills, Pemaquid Lighthouse, Bath-Brunswick area, and the rugged coast of midcoast Maine await.

Hosts: Bobby and Sherry Whear
Rooms: 6 (PB) $80
Full Breakfast
Credit Cards: None
Notes: 2, 5, 10, 11, 12, 13

7 No smoking; 8 Children welcome; 9 Social drinking allowed; 10 Tennis nearby; 11 Swimming nearby; 12 Golf nearby; 13 Skiing nearby; 14 May be booked through a travel agent; 15 Handicapped accessible.

DEXTER

Brewster Inn

37 Zions Hill Road, 04930
(207) 924-3130; FAX (207) 924-9768
e-mail: brewster@nconline.net
www.bbonline.com/me/brewsterinn

Built in the 1930s for Gov. Owen Brewster.
Classic but comfortable elegance furnished
with antiques and family heirlooms, lots of
books, and art. Beautiful gardens. Walk to
downtown shopping and lake. One hour from
coastal Belfast, one hour to Moosehead Lake,
mountains, skiing. On the Maine snowmobile
trails. Take exit 39 from I-95, then 15 miles on
Route 7. Coffee/tea and cookies all day.

Hosts: Ivy and Michael Brooks
Rooms: 7 (PB) $59-89
Full Breakfast
Credit Cards: A, B
Notes: 2, 3, 4, 5, 7, 8, 9, 10, 11, 12, 13, 14, 15

EASTPORT

The Milliken House

29 Washington Street, 04631
(207) 853-2955
e-mail: millikenhouse@eastport-inn.com

Large, gracious 1846 Victorian home just two
blocks from Eastport's waterfront historic dis-

The Milliken House

trict. Will delight Victoriana buffs with its
ornately carved, marble-topped furniture.
Breakfasts are sumptuous and as elegant as the
heavy, carved dining room furniture from
which it is served. Eastport is a small 19th
century island city on Moose Island, connected by causeway to the mainland. Whale
watching, hiking, picnic excursions available.
Ferry to Canada.

Hosts: Joyce and Paul Weber
Rooms: 5 (3 PB; 2 SB) $50-65
Full Breakfast
Credit Cards: A, B, C, D
Notes: 2, 5, 6, 7, 8, 9, 12, 14

Todd House

1 Capen Avenue, Todd's Head, 04631
(207) 853-2328

A full Cape with center chimney circa 1775.
Massive fireplace in common room. Views of
ocean, Passamaquoddy Bay, and its islands.
Large yard with barbecue for cookouts. In
1801, men met here to form a Masonic lodge
and it was later used as a barracks for men who
manned the battery on Todd's Head. Continental plus breakfast served.

Hosts: Ruth M. McInnis
Rooms: 6 (2 PB; 4 SB) $45-80
Continental Breakfast
Credit Cards: A, B
Notes: 2, 5, 6, 7, 8, 9, 15

ELIOT (KITTERY)

The Farmstead Bed & Breakfast

379 Goodwin Road, 03903
(207) 439-5033; (207) 748-3145

Come and step back in time and enjoy the hospitality that Farmstead offers its guests. Awake
to the aroma of coffee, bacon, sausage, and
blueberry pancakes on the griddle. Inspect the
1704 Cape and the "new" floor built in 1896.
Explore the two and one-half acres, swing
under the pear tree, or have an early morning
cup of coffee on the glider after a quiet, restful

NOTES: Credit cards accepted: A MasterCard; B Visa; C American Express; D Discover; E Diner's Club;
F Other; 2 Personal checks accepted; 3 Lunch available; 4 Dinner available; 5 Open all year; 6 Pets welcome;

night. All rooms have private bath, mini-refrigerator, and microwave oven. Picnic facilities and gas grill available.

Hosts: Col. and Mrs. John Lippincott
Rooms: 6 (PB) $54-64
Full Breakfast
Credit Cards: A, B, D
Notes: 2, 5, 6, 7, 8, 9, 10, 12, 14, 15

FALMOUTH

Quaker Tavern Farm

Quaker Tavern Farm Bed & Breakfast

377 Gray Road, Route 26 North, 04105
(207) 797-5540; FAX (207) 797-7599
e-mail: quakerbb@aol.com
www.maineyellowpages.com/quakertavern

Circa 1800. Unblemished country Federal Tavern built by the Quakers. This bed and breakfast has the ambiance only a 200-year-old house can express. Antique double (with trundle for small child) and twin beds, fireplaces in every room, step-out private or shared full bath. Rollaway available. A candlelight, full breakfast served in the dining room. We also offer a reservation service for bed and breakfast guest houses in the state. "One stop shopping" for the tourist. Beautiful spaces and places for people to rest and recreate. Open year-round.

Rooms: 4 (3 PB; 1 SB) $75-90
Full Breakfast
Credit Cards: A, B
Notes: 2, 5, 7, 10, 11, 12, 13

FREEPORT

Anita's Cottage Street Inn Bed & Breakfast

13 Cottage Street, 04032
(207) 865-0932; (800) 392-7121
FAX (207) 865-1344; e-mail: ajwillett@juno.com

A cozy bed and breakfast, nestled in a wonderful wooded area, yet in walking distance to L.L. Bean and 125 village shops. On a dead-end street with cross-country ski trails in the winter and jogging trails in the summer. Rooms are graciously appointed with Laura Ashley linens and decor. A hearty breakfast welcomes guests in the morning. Hiking, swimming, biking, golf, and tennis nearby. Private baths, cable TV, air-conditioned rooms, and smoke free. AAA three-diamond-rated. Efficiency suite also available.

Hosts: Tom and Anita Willett
Rooms: 3 (PB) $65-150
Suite: 1 (PB) $99-199
Full Breakfast
Credit Cards: A, B, C
Notes: 2, 7, 8, 9, 10, 11, 12, 13

The Bagley House

1290 Royalsborough Road, Durham, 04222
(207) 865-6566; (800) 765-1772
FAX (207) 353-5878

Peace, tranquility, and history abound in this magnificent 1772 country home. Six acres of

The Bagley House

7 No smoking; 8 Children welcome; 9 Social drinking allowed; 10 Tennis nearby; 11 Swimming nearby; 12 Golf nearby; 13 Skiing nearby; 14 May be booked through a travel agent; 15 Handicapped accessible.

fields and woods invite nature lovers, hikers, berry pickers, and cross-country skiers. The kitchen's hand-hewn beams and enormous free-standing fireplace with beehive oven inspire mouth-watering breakfasts. A warm welcome awaits guests. Ten minutes from downtown Freeport. Lunch and dinner available by special request.

Hosts: Suzanne O'Connor and Susan Backhouse
Rooms: 7 (PB) $85-125
Suite: $95-135
Full Breakfast
Credit Cards: A, B, C, D, F
Notes: 2, 5, 7, 8, 9, 11, 12, 13, 14, 15

Captain Briggs House Bed & Breakfast

8 Maple Avenue, 04032
(207) 865-1868; (800) 217-2477

Welcome to the Captain Briggs House Bed and Breakfast in the heart of the quaint village of Freeport, just a three-minute walk to L.L. Bean and other fine stores and restaurants. The inn has been lovingly restored with modern amenities tastefully added. The hosts offer comfortable, cheerful guest rooms beautifully decorated with either king-, queen-, full-, or twin-size beds. All rooms have private baths. Relax in the cozy sitting room with cable TV, VCR, and books. A delicious homemade breakfast is served from 8:00 to 9:00 A.M. Non-smoking inn. AAA three-diamond property. Guest telephones.

Hosts: The Frank Family
Rooms: 5 (PB) $67-120
Full Breakfast
Credit Cards: A, B
Notes: 2, 5, 7, 8, 9, 10, 11, 12, 13

Captain Josiah Mitchell House

188 Main Street, 04032
(207) 865-3289

Famous historic ship captain's home, circa 1779. The 1866 miraculous survival-at-sea story of Captain Mitchell of the ship *Hornet* is a classic. Mark Twain, then a young newspaperman, wrote about it. Restored more than 29 years ago by the present owners, the house is filled with antiques. Beautiful grounds and only a five-minute walk to L.L. Bean. Eighteenth year as an inn. Off-season rates available.

Hosts: Alan and Loretta Bradley
Rooms: 6 (PB) $85-95
Full Breakfast
Credit Cards: A, B
Notes: 2, 5, 7, 9, 10, 11, 12, 13, 14

Country at Heart Bed & Breakfast

37 Bow Street, 04032
(207) 865-0512
e-mail: phyllis_stlaurent@onf.com
www.members.aol.com/bedandbrk/web

Enjoy a stay in this cozy 1840 country home, only two blocks from L.L. Bean just off Main

Country at Heart

NOTES: Credit cards accepted: A MasterCard; B Visa; C American Express; D Discover; E Diner's Club; F Other; 2 Personal checks accepted; 3 Lunch available; 4 Dinner available; 5 Open all year; 6 Pets welcome;

Street. Park your car and walk to the restaurants and many outlet stores. Stay in one of three country decorated rooms, the Shaker room, the Quilt room, or the Teddy Bear room, all with double or queen-size beds. The rooms have hand-stenciled borders, handmade crafts, and either antique or reproduction furnishings. Private baths. Full breakfast is served.

Hosts: Terry and Phyllis
Rooms: 3 (PB) $65-150
Full Breakfast
Credit Cards: A, B
Notes: 2, 5, 7, 9, 11, 12, 14

Harraseeket Inn

162 Main Street, 04032
(207) 865-9377; (800) 342-6423
FAX (207) 865-1684

An elegant 84-room country inn two blocks north of L.L. Bean in the village of Freeport. Antiques, 23 fireplaces, Jacuzzi tubs, air conditioning, cable TV, indoor pool, lovely gardens, and two restaurants. Steps from 110 upscale factory outlets; three miles from waterfront. Breakfast and afternoon tea included. AAA four-diamond rating.

Hosts: The Gray Family
Rooms: 84 (PB) $110-235
Full Breakfast
Credit Cards: A, B, C, D, E
Notes: 2, 3, 4, 5, 8, 9, 10, 11, 12, 13, 14, 15

White Cedar Inn

178 Main Street, 04032
(207) 865-9099; (800) 853-1269
www.members.aol.com/bedandbrk/cedar

Historic Victorian home stands just two blocks north of L.L. Bean. Spacious and cozy rooms are antique furnished, with private baths. Full country breakfast served in the sunroom overlooking beautifully landscaped grounds. Air conditioned. AAA three-diamond rating.

White Cedar Inn

Hosts: Phil and Carla Kerber
Rooms: 7 (PB) $70-130
Full Breakfast
Credit Cards: A, B, C, D
Notes: 5, 7, 9, 10, 11, 12, 13, 14

FRIENDSHIP

The Outsiders' Inn Bed & Breakfast

4 Main Street, (Corner of Routes 97 and 220), 04547
(207) 832-5197

The Outsiders' Inn is in the center of the village of Friendship, a short walk from the harbor, the home of historic Friendship sloops and scores of lobster boats. This inn features five comfortable guest rooms with double beds, private and semiprivate baths. Efficiency cottage also available. Full breakfasts served daily. Sea kayak rentals and guided tours available. Sauna on premises. Country furnishings, delicious food, friendly folks. Come enjoy midcoast Maine.

Hosts: Debbie and Bill Michaud
Rooms: 5 (1 PB; 4 SB) $55-70
Full Breakfast
Credit Cards: A, B
Notes: 2, 5, 7, 8, 9, 11, 12

7 No smoking; 8 Children welcome; 9 Social drinking allowed; 10 Tennis nearby; 11 Swimming nearby; 12 Golf nearby; 13 Skiing nearby; 14 May be booked through a travel agent; 15 Handicapped accessible.

FRYEBURG

Acres of Austria

Rural Route 1, Box 177, 04037
(800) 988-4391; FAX (207) 925-6547

View the Old Saco River, White Mountains, or acres of forest from any room. Enjoy the antique billiard table, German/English library, and on-site canoes. Take advantage of the nearby cog railway, antiquing, and outlet shopping. Indulge in Franz's schnitzel, gulash, spinatnock'n, crêpes, and homemade breads and pastries. "Come, sit back, relax, and make yourself at home on our 65 acres."

Hosts: Candice and Franz Redl
Rooms: 6 (PB) $59-165
Full Breakfast
Credit Cards: A, B
Notes: 2, 4, 5, 6, 7, 8, 9, 10, 11, 12, 13, 14, 15

Acres of Austria

Admiral Peary House

9 Elm Street, 04037
(207) 935-3365; (800) 237-8080
e-mail: admpeary@nxi.com

This home, once the residence of Arctic explorer Admiral Robert E. Peary, has been lovingly restored for guests' comfort, with air-conditioned rooms and private bathrooms, country breakfasts, and billiards. The clay tennis court is framed by spacious lawns and perennial gardens. Use one of the bicycles to explore the village and nearby sights. Canoe the Saco River or hike the White Mountains.

Admiral Peary House

Top it off with a leisurely soak in the outdoor spa. Snowshoe rentals and trail in winter.

Hosts: Ed and Nancy Greenberg
Rooms: 6 (PB) $70-128
Full Breakfast
Credit Cards: A, B, C, D
Notes: 2, 5, 7, 8, 9, 10, 11, 12, 13, 14

GEORGETOWN

Coveside Bed & Breakfast

North End Road, 04548
(800) 232-5490; e-mail: coveside@gwi.net
www.gwi.net/coveside

Newly renovated bed and breakfast on five secluded acres in mid-coast Maine. Superb waterfront location with views of Sheepscot Bay from all rooms. All private baths. Walk or canoe to two lobster wharfs; bike to the sandy beach at nearby Reid State park. Fireplace/spa tub suite, two housekeeping suites for longer stays. Canoe and bicycles for guest use. Mem-

Coveside

orable breakfasts served on the patio or airy dining room with view. Open mid-May to mid-October. Special mid-week rates in May, June, September, and October. Children welcome in suites.

Hosts: Carolyn and Tom Church
Rooms: 6 (PB) $95-145
Full Breakfast
Credit Cards: A, B, D
Notes: 2, 7, 9, 10, 11

GOULDSBORO

Sunset House Bed & Breakfast

Route 186, 04607
(800) 233-7156

This late-Victorian home offers guests a choice of six spacious bedrooms spread over three floors with a selection of ocean and freshwater views. The second floor has three bedrooms with private baths. The third floor includes three bedrooms with shared bath and optional kitchen. Perfect accommodations for reunions and traveling couples. A full country breakfast is served.

Hosts: Carl and Kathy Johnson
Rooms: 6 (3 PB; 3 SB) $69-89
Full Breakfast
Credit Cards: A, B, C, D
Notes: 2, 5, 7, 8, 9, 11, 12

GREAT CHEBEAGUE ISLAND

Chebeague Island Inn

Rural Route 1, 492 South Road, 04017
(207) 846-5155; FAX (207) 846-4265
e-mail: ISLEMAN99@aol.com

Step back in time at this circa 1925 bed and breakfast which is the only hotel/restaurant/pub on a 20,000 acre island, eight miles off the coast of Portland. Guests can access the island via two ferries (not bringing cars). Eighteen-acre golf course at front door and litterless beaches abound. No alarm clocks, dress code, tele-

Chebeague Island Inn

phones, or TVs in rooms. Guests can view outstanding sunset on a 150-foot long front porch. Home-cooked food that is reasonably priced. "All-U-Can-Eat" lobster specials. Lovers getaway. Family reunions. Wedding Adventure weekends. Open mid-May through mid-October.

Hosts: The Bowden Family
Rooms: 21 (17 PB; 4 SB) $75-150
Full Breakfast
Credit Cards: A, B, D
Notes: 2, 3, 4, 7, 8, 9, 10, 11, 12

GREENVILLE

Blair Hill Inn

Lily Bay Road; Moosehead Lake, 04441
(207) 695-0224; www.blairhill.com

Breathtaking! Sitting high on a hilltop overlooking magnificent Moosehead Lake and surrounding mountains, the Blair Hill Inn is truly spectacular. Located on one of the most beautiful properties in this pristine northwoods resort area, the inn's 15 acres of gardens, barns, forest, and ponds offer guests a retreat from the ordinary and an opportunity for solitude and spiritual renewal. Luxurious accommodations, fine dining, and warm, personal service make this inn a world-class destination.

Hosts: Dan and Ruth McLaughlin
Rooms: 8 (PB) $175-265
Full Breakfast
Credit Cards: A, B, C, D
Notes: 2, 4, 5, 7, 9, 10, 11, 12, 13

7 No smoking; 8 Children welcome; 9 Social drinking allowed; 10 Tennis nearby; 11 Swimming nearby; 12 Golf nearby; 13 Skiing nearby; 14 May be booked through a travel agent; 15 Handicapped accessible.

The Captain Sawyer House

Lakeview Street, Box 1132, 04441
(207) 695-2369; www.moosehead.net/sawyer

This circa 1849 farm house has four elegant rooms, each with private bath, king- and queen-size beds. A beautiful patio and porch overlook the lake and a comfortable parlor with TV, games, and books is always available for guests. Less than a two-minute walk to village shops, restaurants, and boat marina. Boating, canoeing, fishing, hiking, and snowmobiling are right at the doorstep. Down-hill skiing is 10 minutes away.

Hosts: Ted and Donna Savery
Rooms: 4 (PB) $75-85
Full Breakfast
Credit Cards: A, B
Notes: 2, 5, 8, 9, 11, 12, 13

Greenville Inn

Norris Street, P.O. Box 1194, 04441
(207) 695-2206 (phone/FAX); (888) 695-6000
e-mail: gvlinn@moosehead.net
www.greenvilleinn.com

This 1895 Victorian lumber baron's mansion is on a hill overlooking Moosehead Lake and Squaw Mountain. A large leaded-glass window decorated with a painted spruce tree is the focal point at the landing of the stairway. Gas lights, embossed wall coverings, carved fireplace mantels, and cherry and oak paneling grace the inn. In the elegantly appointed dining rooms, diners may savor fresh Maine seafood, glazed

Greenville Inn

roast duckling, grilled chops, or steaks. Whether relaxing by a cozy fire or sipping cocktails on the veranda at sunset, the evening hours are most enjoyable.

Hosts: The Schnetzers
Rooms: 12 (PB) $105-225
Continental Breakfast
Credit Cards: A, B, D
Notes: 2, 4, 5, 7, 8, 9, 10, 11, 12, 13, 14

ISLE AU HAUT

The Keepers House

P.O. Box 26, 04645
(207) 367-2261

Remote island lighthouse station in the undeveloped wilderness area of Acadia National Park. Guests arrive on the mail boat from Stonington. No telephones, cars, TV, or crowds. Osprey, seal, deer, rugged trails, spectacular scenery, seclusion, and inspiration. Two-night minimum stay June 16 through October 15. Closed November 1 to April 30. Rates include three elegant meals and bikes.

Hosts: Jeff and Judi Burke
Rooms: 5 (SB) $257-294
Credit Cards: None
Notes: 2, 3, 4, 7, 8, 9, 11

KENNEBUNK

Arundel Meadows Inn

P.O. Box 1129, 04043-1129
(207) 985-3770
www.gwi.net/arundel_meadows_inn

This 165-year-old farmhouse, two miles north on Route 1 from the center of town, combines the charm of antiques and art with the comfort of seven individually decorated bedrooms with sitting areas. Two of the rooms are suites, three have fireplaces, some have cable TV, and all have private bathrooms and summer air condi-

Arundel Meadows Inn

tioning. Full homemade breakfasts are prepared by co-owner Mark Bachelder, a professionally trained chef.

Hosts: Mark Bachelder and Murray Yaeger
Rooms: 7 (PB) $75-135
Full Breakfast
Credit Cards: A, B
Notes: 2, 5, 7, 9, 10, 11, 12, 14

The Kennebunk Inn

The Kennebunk Inn

45 Main Street, 04043
(207) 985-3351; FAX (207) 985-8865

The Kennebunk Inn is a historic 200-year-old building in the center of Main Street in downtown Kennebunk. All 28 rooms and suites have private baths and include a hearty Continental breakfast. Each room has a distinctive personality of its own. Antique claw-foot porcelain baths, four-poster beds, hardwood floors, and cozy quilts are just some of the features guests may find in the great variety of rooms. TVs,

and in-room telephones are also available for the person on the go, and don't overlook the several sitting rooms featuring shelves of "good reads" and plenty of games. Skiing one hour away.

Hosts: Kristen and John Martin
Rooms: 28 (PB)
Continental Breakfast
Credit Cards: A, B, C, D
Notes: 2, 4, 5, 6, 7, 8, 9, 10, 11, 12, 14, 15

KENNEBUNK BEACH

The Ocean View

171 Beach Avenue, 04043
(207) 967-2750; FAX (207) 967-5418
e-mail: arena@theoceanview.com
www.theoceanview.com

An intimate oceanfront inn. "The closest you'll find to a bed on the beach." Sights, sounds, and aura of the Atlantic at the doorstep, yet only a scant mile to downtown Kennebunkport. A perfect location! The inn is whimsical and colorful with an eclectic flair. It is a blend of subtle amenities set in an atmosphere of friendliness and helpfulness. It is immaculate and sparkling…a jewel of distinct quality.

Hosts: Carole and Bob Arena
Rooms: 9 (PB) $125-275
Full Breakfast
Credit Cards: A, B, C, D
Notes: 7, 9, 10, 11, 12

KENNEBUNKPORT

Captain Fairfield Inn

8 Pleasant Street, P.O. Box 2690, 04046
(207) 967-4454; (800) 322-1928
FAX (207) 967-8537
e-mail: jrw@captainfairfield.com

A gracious 1813 sea captain's mansion in Kennebunkport's historic district, only steps to the village green and harbor. A delightful walk to sandy beaches, Dock Square Marina, shops, and excellent restaurants. The bedrooms are

7 No smoking; 8 Children welcome; 9 Social drinking allowed; 10 Tennis nearby; 11 Swimming nearby; 12 Golf nearby; 13 Skiing nearby; 14 May be booked through a travel agent; 15 Handicapped accessible.

Captain Fairfield Inn

beautifully decorated with antiques and period furnishings. Several bedrooms have fireplaces, one with a double whirlpool tub. Relax in the living room, study, or enjoy the tree-shaded grounds and gardens. Wake up to birdsong, fresh sea air, and the aroma of gourmet coffee. Cross-country skiing. Children over six welcome.

Rooms: 9 (PB) $110-250
Full Breakfast
Credit Cards: A, B, C, D, E
Notes: 2, 5, 7, 9, 10, 11, 12, 13, 14

Captain's Hideaway

12 Pleasant Street, P.O. Box 2746, 04046-2746
(207) 967-5711; FAX (207) 967-3843
e-mail: hideaway@cybertours.com
www.captainshideaway.com

The Captain's Hideaway is a meticulously restored Federal period home with two luxurious guest rooms in Kennebunkport's lovely historic district. Each room features an antique four-poster canopied bed, gas fireplace, whirlpool tub, private telephone, air conditioning, cable TV with VCR, CD/tape deck stereo systems, and a mini-refrigerator stocked with complimentary non-alcoholic beverages. A custom three-course breakfast is served by candlelight each morning. The Hideaway is but a five-minute walk to Dock Square shops, marinas, galleries, and restaurants.

Hosts: Susan Jackson and Judith Hughes Boulet
Rooms: 2 (PB) $179-279

Full Breakfast
Credit Cards: A, B
Notes: 2, 5, 7, 9, 10, 11, 12, 13, 14

The Captain Jefferds Inn

5 Pearl Street, P.O. Box 691, 04046
(207) 967-2311; (800) 839-6844
FAX (207) 967-0721
e-mail: captjeff@captainjefferdsinn.com

Enjoy the gracious hospitality in this 1804 Federal-style mansion. Each of the inn's 16 guest rooms is named and designed in the spirit of the hosts' favorite places including Assisi, Italy; Adar, Ireland; Charleston, and Chatham. Eight rooms have fireplaces, all have private baths, and are furnished with antiques and period reproductions. Guests are treated to candlelit gourmet breakfasts served on the sunny terrace overlooking the gardens or in front of the warm fire. In the historic district, within easy walking distance of many fine restaurants, shops, and galleries. Pets welcome with prior arrangements. Children eight and older welcome.

Hosts: Pat and Dick Bartholomew
Rooms: 16 (PB) $135-260
Full Breakfast
Credit Cards: A, B, C
Notes: 2, 5, 7, 9, 11, 12, 13, 14

Captain Jefferds Inn

The Captain Lord Mansion

P.O. Box 800, 04046
(207) 967-3141; FAX (207) 967-3172
e-mail: captain@biddeford.com
www.captainlord.com

Enjoy an unforgettable romantic experience at the Captain Lord Mansion, where both your

NOTES: Credit cards accepted: A MasterCard; B Visa; C American Express; D Discover; E Diner's Club; F Other; 2 Personal checks accepted; 3 Lunch available; 4 Dinner available; 5 Open all year; 6 Pets welcome;

Captain Lord Mansion

personal comfort and intimacy are assured by large, beautifully appointed guest rooms, luxurious amenities such as oversized four-poster beds, cozy gas fireplaces, heated marble/tile bathroom floors, several double Jacuzzis, as well as fresh flowers, full breakfasts, afternoon sweets, and personal attention. At the head of a sloping village green overlooking the Kennebunk River, the inn affords a picturesque, quiet, convenient location from which to explore historic Kennebunkport.

Hosts: Bev Davis and Rick Litchfield
Rooms: 16 (PB) $99-399
Full Breakfast
Credit Cards: A, B, D, E
Notes: 2, 5, 7, 9, 10, 11, 12, 14

Charrid House

2 Arlington Avenue, 04046
(207) 967-5695

Built in 1887, this charming cedar-shingled home started life as a gambling casino for the Kennebunkport River Club. It went through incarnations as a tennis clubhouse and a single-family home before becoming Charrid House in 1986. On a residential street, the Charrid House is one block from the stunning scenery of Ocean Avenue and Colony Beach. Several restaurants and shops are within walking distance and the village itself is one mile south.

Host: Ann M. Dubay
Rooms: 2 (2 S1B) $65

Full Breakfast
Credit Cards: None
Notes: 2, 7, 10, 11, 12

Crosstrees

South Street, Box 1333, 04046-1333
(207) 967-2780; (800) 564-1527
FAX (207) 967-2610; e-mail: info@crosstrees.com
www.crosstrees.com

Tucked into a quiet corner of Kennebunkport's historic district is this beautifully restored 1818 Federal-style inn in the National Register of Historic Places. Surrounded by spacious, shaded grounds, lovely perennial gardens, and a sparkling pond, guests relax and feel refreshed. Inside are four guest rooms decorated individually with antiques and period furniture, private baths, three with fireplaces, plus suite with Jacuzzi. Guests enjoy early morning coffee, a full breakfast, and afternoon refreshments. A short walk from shops, galleries, marinas, restaurants, and the ocean. Children over 12 welcome. Cross-country skiing.

Hosts: Dennis Rafferty and Keith Henley
Rooms: 4 (PB) $100-215
Full Breakfast
Credit Cards: A, B
Notes: 2, 5, 7, 9, 10, 11, 12, 13

Elaine's Bed & Breakfast Selections

4987 Kingston Road, Elbridge, NY 13060
(315) 689-2082 (call between 10:30 A.M.–7:00 P.M.)

1. This "Grandma's House" was built in the early 1900s. The rooms are spacious and all have private baths. One large room has a canopied bed and working fireplace. Also available are two suites that can accommodate large parties or families. Full breakfast. There is a separate housekeeping cottage with full bath, fully equipped kitchen, private patio. A full breakfast, served in the main house, is included in rates. Two-night minimum during July and August. Seasonal rates. $90-135.

7 No smoking; 8 Children welcome; 9 Social drinking allowed; 10 Tennis nearby; 11 Swimming nearby; 12 Golf nearby; 13 Skiing nearby; 14 May be booked through a travel agent; 15 Handicapped accessible.

2. This moderately priced bed and breakfast is on a fine old residential street, just a block from Ocean Avenue and a nice walk to downtown Dock Square. There are four guest rooms with private and shared baths. The living room has a fireplace as well as a wood stove and TV. A fully furnished knotty-pine walled guest cottage sits more privately away from the main house and is ideal for a couple or small family. Weekly rental of the cottage is $575. Daily rates may be available during the off-season.

Rooms: 4 (PB) $80-90
Full Breakfast
Credit Cards: A, B
Notes: 2, 5, 7, 8, 9, 10, 11, 12, 14

The Inn on South Street

The Inn on South Street

South Street, P.O. Box 478A, 04046
(207) 967-5151

Now approaching its 200th birthday, this stately Greek Revival house is in the historic district. There are three beautifully decorated guest rooms and one luxury suite. Private baths, fireplaces, a common room, afternoon refreshments, and early morning coffee. A sumptuous breakfast is served in the large country kitchen with views of the river and ocean or, weather permitting, in the garden. On a quiet street within walking distance of restaurants, shops, and the water.

Hosts: Jacques and Eva Downs
Rooms: 3 (PB) $105-155
Suite: 1 (PB) $185-245
Full Breakfast
Credit Cards: A, B
Notes: 2, 7, 10, 11, 12, 13, 14

Kennebunkport Inn

Dock Square, P.O. Box 111, 04046
(207) 967-2621; (800) 248-2621
FAX (207) 967-3705

This large sea captain's home was built in 1899 along the Kennebunk River. Now an inn with a restaurant, known for creative cuisine, classically prepared. Each of the 34 guest rooms offers a private bath, color TV, telephone, and period furnishings. The restaurant lounge with fireplace and swimming pool with patio are popular spots for relaxing. Antique shops, boutiques, galleries, and restaurants are within walking distance. Local theaters, deep sea fishing, golf, and fine beaches are within a short drive. Families welcome. Meeting facilities available. Breakfast and dinner available seasonally.

Hosts: Rick and Martha Griffin
Rooms: 35 (PB) $79.50-279
Full and Continental Breakfast
Credit Cards: A, B, C
Notes: 2, 5, 8, 10, 11, 12, 14, 15

King's Port Inn

Corner of Routes 9 & 35, P.O. Box 1070, 04046
(207) 967-4340; (800) 286-5767
FAX (207) 967-4810
e-mail: info@kingsportinn.com
www.kingsportinn.com

Affordable rates with an attractive location, convenient to Kennebunkport's Dock Square shops, restaurants, area beaches, and attractions. Most guest rooms offer double or queen-size beds, cable TV, telephone, refrigerator, private bath, and air conditioning. Deluxe rooms offer king-size bed, dual shower, and two-person private Jacuzzis. Luxury rooms offer queen-size beds, gas fireplaces, and pri-

NOTES: Credit cards accepted: A MasterCard; B Visa; C American Express; D Discover; E Diner's Club; F Other; 2 Personal checks accepted; 3 Lunch available; 4 Dinner available; 5 Open all year; 6 Pets welcome;

vate Jacuzzis. Other amenities include a Pantry Side-board breakfast buffet offered in the parlor each morning and Surround Sound theater entertainment. Smoking permitted in designated smoking rooms.

Host: Bill Greer
Rooms: 32 (PB) $49-175
Suite: 1 (PB)
Continental Breakfast
Credit Cards: A, B, C, D
Notes: 2, 5, 8, 9, 10, 11, 12, 13, 14, 15

Maine Stay Inn

Lake Brook Bed & Breakfast

P.O. Box 762, (Route 9 Lower Village), 04046
(207) 967-4069
e-mail: carolyn@lakebrookbb.com
www.lakebrookbb.com

Lake Brook Bed and Breakfast is an appealing turn-of-the-century farmhouse on the edge of the salt marsh and tidal brook. Sit on the porch and relax in comfortable rockers and enjoy the flower gardens and ocean breeze. All rooms are individually decorated and offer private baths and ceiling fans. A full gourmet breakfast is served daily. Coffee is ready by 7:00 A.M. Weekends and holidays two- and three-night minimum stay required in season. Reservations suggested. Seasonal rates available. Cross-country skiing nearby.

Rooms: 4 (PB) $90-130
Continental Breakfast
Credit Cards: A, B
Notes: 2, 5, 7, 8, 9, 10, 11, 12, 13, 14

Maine Stay Inn & Cottages

Box 500A, 04046
(207) 967-2117; (800) 950-2117
FAX (207) 967-8757
e-mail: innkeeper@mainestayinn.com
www.mainestayinn.com

A beautiful 1860 Victorian inn distinguished by Queen Anne-period flying staircase, wraparound porch, and bay windows. A variety of accommodations, from charming rooms and suites to delightful one-bedroom cottages, some with fireplaces and double whirlpool tubs. The living room is a comfortable place to sit and meet fellow travelers or enjoy a fire on a cold winter day. The inn is four blocks from the village, allowing guests a leisurely walk to shops, galleries, restaurants, and the harbor.

Hosts: Lindsay and Carol Copeland
Rooms: 17 (PB) $95-225
Full Breakfast
Credit Cards: A, B, C
Notes: 5, 7, 8, 9, 10, 11, 12, 14

Maude's Courtyard Bed & Breakfast

Route 9, Western Avenue, P.O. Box 182, 04046
(207) 967-8433; FAX (207) 967-2858
www.virtualcities.com/ons/me/k/mek8701.htm

Cozy, comfortable, and casual...the perfect place to relax and unwind, just one mile from town, beaches, and golf. Bring own bike. Designed for privacy. Ideal for couples traveling together and families with older children. Two bedrooms upstairs and a first-floor suite. Large sunny rooms furnished with favorite early-attic pieces give a country charm, along with welcoming fresh flowers. Air conditioned. Guests' own fully equipped kitchen. Continental breakfast. Smokers, please step outside.

7 No smoking; 8 Children welcome; 9 Social drinking allowed; 10 Tennis nearby; 11 Swimming nearby; 12 Golf nearby; 13 Skiing nearby; 14 May be booked through a travel agent; 15 Handicapped accessible.

Hosts: Jovanna Kezar and John Paré
Rooms: 3 (1 PB; 2 SB) $55-95
Continental Breakfast
Credit Cards: F
Notes: 2, 7, 8, 9, 10, 11, 12, 14

Old Fort Inn & Resort

Box M-30, 04046
(207) 967-5353; (800) 828-FORT
FAX (207) 967-4547

Discover the hospitality of a luxurious New England inn that combines all of yesterday's charm with today's conveniences—from the daily buffet breakfast to the comfort and privacy of antique-appointed rooms. Includes pool, tennis court, TV, telephones, air conditioning, and a charming antique shop, all in a secluded setting. AAA-rated four diamonds. Closed mid-December through mid-April.

Hosts: David and Sheila Aldrich
Rooms: 16 (PB) $95-325
Full Breakfast
Credit Cards: A, B, C, D
Notes: 2, 7, 9, 10, 11, 12, 14

Old Fort Inn and Resort

The Welby Inn

92 Ocean Avenue, P.O. Box 774, 04046
(207) 967-4655; FAX (207) 967-8654
e-mail: welbyinn@gwi.net
www.welbyinn.com

Built as a spacious Dutch Gambrel home in 1900, the Welby Inn, now in its 14th year, committed to providing its guests all of today's comforts in a setting true to the home's turn-of-the-century origins. Each of the seven rooms has a private bath and one has a working fire-

The Welby Inn

place. A large common room allows ample opportunity for socializing and quiet relaxation. There is a guest pantry with complimentary coffees, teas, and snacks.

Hosts: Allison Rowley and daughter, Merrianne
    Weston
Rooms: 7 (PB) $75-115
Full Breakfast
Credit Cards: A, B, D
Notes: 2, 3, 5, 7

KITTERY

Enchanted Nights Bed & Breakfast

29 Wentworth Street, Route 103, 03904
(207) 439-1489;www.enchanted-nights-bandb.com

An 1890 Princess Anne Gothic Victorian between Boston and Portland. Three minutes to dining and dancing in Portsmouth, historic homes, scenic ocean drives, and the renowned Kittery outlet malls. Convenient day trips to neighboring resorts. For the romantic at heart who delight in the subtle elegance of yesteryear; for those who are soothed by the whimsical charm of a French country inn. Elegant breakfast. Enjoy the suites with whirlpool for two. Cable TV and air conditioning. Pets welcome with restrictions.

NOTES: Credit cards accepted: A MasterCard; B Visa; C American Express; D Discover; E Diner's Club; F Other; 2 Personal checks accepted; 3 Lunch available; 4 Dinner available; 5 Open all year; 6 Pets welcome;

Enchanted Nights

Hosts: Nancy Bogenberger and Peter Lamandia
Rooms: 7 (PB) $47-202
Full Breakfast
Credit Cards: A, B, C, D
Notes: 2, 5, 6, 7, 8, 9, 10, 11, 12, 14, 15

Inn at Portsmouth Harbor

6 Water Street, 03904
(207) 439-4040

Relax in elegant but comfortable surroundings, just a 10-minute stroll across the bridge from historic Portsmouth, New Hampshire, and a short drive to beaches and factory outlets. Brick Victorian with six romantic guest rooms furnished with antiques, each with private bath, most with harbor views. Enjoy widely acclaimed breakfast by the fireplace or on the screened patio. Recommended by the *New York Times*. A no-smoking inn; open year-round.

Hosts: Kim and Terry O'Mahoney
Rooms: 6 (PB) $85-135

Full Breakfast
Credit Cards: A, B, C
Notes: 2, 5, 7, 9, 10, 11, 12, 14

LAMOINE

Capt'n N Eve's Eden

461 Lamoine Beach Road, 04605
(207) 667-3109; e-mail: capteve@aol.com

A beautiful home overlooking Frenchman's Bay. All guest rooms and the sunroom, where a full breakfast is served, enjoy a spectacular view of the bay and Mt. Desert Island.

Rooms: 3 (1 PB; 2 SB) $35-55
Full Breakfast
Credit Cards: None
Notes: 2, 5, 9, 10, 11, 12

LEE

Dunloggin' Bed & Breakfast

P.O. Box 306, 04455
(207) 738-5014 (phone/FAX)
e-mail: dunlogbb@linc-net.net

Quiet, quilts, featherbeds, fishing, hiking, biking, skiing, crafts, and antiques nearby. Beautiful local museum. On Silver Lake on scenic Route 6 to and from New Brunswick. Computer and fax available if needed. Every room redecorated in 1999 in country cozy decor. Lunch and dinner available upon request.

Host: Gail A. Rae
Rooms: 3 (3 SB) $50-75
Full Breakfast
Credit Cards: A, B, D
Notes: 2, 5, 6, 7, 8, 9, 11, 13

LUBEC

Breakers by the Bay

37 Washington, 04652
(207) 733-2487

One of the oldest houses in the 200-year-old town of Lubec, a small fishing village. Three

7 No smoking; 8 Children welcome; 9 Social drinking allowed; 10 Tennis nearby; 11 Swimming nearby; 12 Golf nearby; 13 Skiing nearby; 14 May be booked through a travel agent; 15 Handicapped accessible.

blocks to Campobello Island, the home of Franklin D. Roosevelt. All rooms have refrigerators, TVs, hand-crocheted tablecloths, hand-quilted bedspreads, and private decks for viewing the bay.

Host: E. M. Elg
Rooms: 5 (PB) $53.50-74.90
Full Breakfast
Credit Cards: None
Notes: 2, 7, 10, 12, 14

MACHIAS

Riverside Inn & Restaurant

Route 1, P.O. Box 373, East Machias, 04630
(207) 255-4134

Enjoy Victorian lodging and romantic candlelight dining in a restored sea captain's home on the banks of the East Machias River. Four lovely guest rooms each with private baths. Two are located in the main house and two in the carriage house. All are individually decorated in antique period furnishings. Carriage house rooms offer private balconies overlooking the river. Full breakfast includes fruit, juice, muffins or coffee cake, egg dishes, or the inn's specialty, stuffed blueberry French toast, served in the Captain Elliot dining room overlooking the river. Dinner served by reservation to guests and public. Newly added garden area features water pond, perennials, arbors.

Hosts: Tom and Carol Paul
Rooms: 4 (PB) $68-89
Full Breakfast
Credit Cards: A, B, C
Notes: 2, 4, 5, 7, 11, 12, 13

Riverside Inn

MONHEGAN ISLAND

Monhegan House

1 Main Street, 04852
(207) 594-7983; (800) 599-7983
FAX (207) 596-6472

Enjoy the friendly relaxed atmosphere, inviting front porch, and cozy fireplace of this 1870s island inn. Long a haven for artists, bird watchers, and nature lovers. Whether you come for just overnight or for "the season," the Monhegan House will do their best to make your stay a pleasant and memorable one. Breakfast, lunch, and dinner available at the Monhegan House Cafe. Pets are not permitted.

Host: Zoe A. Zanidakis
Rooms: 33 (33 SB) $90
Credit Cards: A, B, C, D
Notes: 2, 3, 4, 7, 8, 9, 11

MOUNT DESERT

Reibers' Bed & Breakfast

585 Sound Drive, P.O. Box 163, Somesville, 04660
(207) 244-3047; e-mail: reibersbnb@acadia.net
www.acadia.net/reibers

This 150-year-old Colonial homestead, listed in the national register, enjoys meadows and a tidal creek. Full breakfast. Central location. Moderate prices. Open all year.

Hosts: Gail and David Reiber
Rooms: 2 (1 PB; 1 SB) $65-75
Full Breakfast
Credit Cards: A, B
Notes: 2, 5, 7, 9, 10, 11, 12, 13

NAPLES

The Augustus Bove House

Rural Route 1, Box 501, 04055
(207) 693-6365
www.maineguide.com/naples/augustus

Guests are always welcome at the historic 1850 hotel. Originally known as Hotel Naples, it is

The Augustus Bove House

restored for comfort and a relaxed atmosphere at affordable prices. Guest rooms have elegant yet homey furnishings, some with views of Long Lake. An easy walk to the water, shops, and recreation in a four-season area. Open all year, with off-season and midweek discounts. Telephones in each room. Air conditioning, TV, VCR, and hot tub. Coffee or tea anytime.

Hosts: David and Arlene Stetson
Rooms: 11 (7 PB; 2+2 SB) $59-175
Full Breakfast
Credit Cards: A, B, C, D
Notes: 2, 5, 6, 7, 8, 9, 10, 11, 12, 13, 14

Inn at Long Lake

P.O. Box 806, 04055
(207) 693-6226

Enjoy romantic elegance and turn-of-the-century charm at the Inn at Long Lake, nestled amid the pines and waterways of the beautiful Sebago Lakes region. The inn has 16 restored rooms with TVs, air conditioners, and private baths. One minute's walk from the Naples

Inn at Long Lake

Causeway. Four-season activities and fine dining nearby. This three-diamond AAA facility is worth the trip. Midweek discounts available. Named as one of the top 10 bed and breakfasts in the United States in a video competition by Innovations, Inc., of Jersey City, New Jersey. Open April through December.

Hosts: Maynard and Irene Hincks
Rooms: 16 (PB) $69-158
Continental Breakfast
Credit Cards: A, B, D
Notes: 2, 7, 8, 9, 10, 11, 12, 13, 14

Lamb's Mill Inn

Lamb's Mill Inn

Lamb's Mill Road, Box 676, 04055
(207) 693-6253

A charming country inn in the foothills of Maine's western mountain and lake region. Romantic country atmosphere on 20 acres of fields and woods. Five rooms with private baths and a full country breakfast. Hot tub available. Near lakes, antique shops, skiing, and canoeing.

Hosts: Laurel Tinkham and Sandra Long
Rooms: 6 (PB) $85-105
Full Breakfast
Credit Cards: A, B
Notes: 5, 7, 9, 10, 11, 12, 13, 14

NEWAGEN

Newagen Seaside Inn

P.O. Box 29, 04576
(207) 633-5242; (800) 654-5242
e-mail: seaside@wiscasset.net

The Newagen Seaside Inn is one of the few remaining coastal inns that still evoke the spirit of a bygone era. The inn's relaxing, unhurried

7 No smoking; 8 Children welcome; 9 Social drinking allowed; 10 Tennis nearby; 11 Swimming nearby; 12 Golf nearby; 13 Skiing nearby; 14 May be booked through a travel agent; 15 Handicapped accessible.

atmosphere harkens back to its 19th-century roots and makes it an ideal venue for romantic escapes, weekend weddings, family reunions, and artists' workshops. Ideal for families. The inn is on a former nature preserve and is a nature lover's paradise. It sits on 85 acres of forest, lawns, and gardens. Its mile of rocky coastline, with crashing surf and tidal pools, was significant in the life of noted environmental writer Rachel Carson.

Hosts: Heidi and Peter Larsen
Rooms: 26 (PB) $75-200
Full Breakfast
Credit Cards: A, B
Notes: 2, 3, 4, 7, 8, 9, 10, 11, 12, 14, 15

NEWCASTLE

Flying Cloud Bed & Breakfast

River Road, P.O. Box 549, 04553
(207) 563-2484; e-mail: stay@theflyingcloud.com
www.theflyingcloud.com

A lovingly restored 1790 to 1840 sea captain's home which is now a romantic 1990s inn. Full country breakfasts, beautiful water views, great beds, fireplaces, and an extensive library containing books on history and Americana, especially the Civil War. Spacious lawn and decks, 1840s flower garden, open and screened porches. Short walk to Damariscotta Village shops, pubs, and restaurants. Ideal for visiting Boothbay Harbor and the historic Pemaquid

Flying Cloud

area. Day trips to Acadia National Park, Camden, and Freeport.

Hosts: Betty and Ron Howe
Rooms: 5 (PB) $75-95
Full Breakfast
Credit Cards: A, B, C
Notes: 2, 5, 7, 9, 10, 11, 12, 13

NEW HARBOR

Gosnold Arms

146 State Route 32, 04554
(207) 677-3727; www.gosnold.com

On the harbor, the Gosnold Arms Inn and cottages, all with private baths, most with water view. A glassed-in dining room overlooking the water is open for breakfast and dinner. The Gosnold wharf and moorings accommodate cruising boats. Within a 10-mile radius are lakes, beaches, lobster pounds, historic sites, boat trips, golf, antiques, shops, and restaurants. Smoking in designated areas only. Limited handicapped accessibility.

Hosts: The Phinney Family
Rooms: 26 (PB) $79-144
Full Breakfast
Credit Cards: A, B
Notes: 2, 8, 9, 10, 11, 12

OCEAN PARK

Elaine's Bed & Breakfast Selections

4987 Kingston Road, Elbridge, NY 13060
(315) 689-2082 (call between 10:30 A.M.–7:00 P.M.)

A classic 1890, three-story, shingle, ocean shore guest house offers several different accommodations. Choose from rooms that share baths to complete apartments. Continental breakfast served. Walk to Old Orchard Beach Amusement Park. Three-day minimum stay during peak season. No pets. Very moderate rates are available and are based upon the unit, season, and part of the week.

NOTES: Credit cards accepted: A MasterCard; B Visa; C American Express; D Discover; E Diner's Club; F Other; 2 Personal checks accepted; 3 Lunch available; 4 Dinner available; 5 Open all year; 6 Pets welcome;

OGUNQUIT

Chestnut Tree Inn

93 Shore Road, P.O. Box 2201, 03907
(207) 646-4529; (800) 362-0757
www.chestnuttreeinn.com

Guests are encouraged to make themselves at home at this gracious 1870 Victorian inn, the oldest inn in Ogunquit. Relax on the large front porch or in the side yard with gardens and stone water fountain. Enjoy a Continental breakfast in the spacious fireplaced living/dining room. Easy walk to beach, restaurants, and shops—on trolley route. Nonsmoking environment.

Hosts: Cynthia Diana and Ronald St. Laurent
Rooms: 22 (16 PB; 6 SB) $40-125
Continental Breakfast
Credit Cards: A, B, C
Notes: 2, 7, 8, 9, 10, 11, 12, 13, 14

Gorges Grant Hotel

239 Route 1, P.O. Box 2240, 03907
(207) 646-7003; (800) 646-5001
FAX (207) 646-0660
e-mail: gorgesgrant@ogunquit.com
www.ogunquit.com

A modern inn of 81 luxury units, the Gorges Grant is on acres of meticulously manicured grounds in the heart of Ogunquit. Heated indoor/outdoor pools, Jacuzzi, fitness center. Casual, fine dining at Raspberri's, the hotel's own full-service restaurant. Dinner package plans are available. Ogunquit features miles of white-sand beaches, the famous Marginal Way footpath, and picturesque Perkins Cove. Nearby outlet shopping at Kittery and Freeport (L.L. Bean). AAA-rated three diamonds. Reserve on-line.

Hosts: Karen and Bob Hanson
Rooms: 81 (PB) $78-171
Full Breakfast
Credit Cards: A, B, C, D, E
Notes: 4, 7, 8, 9, 10, 11, 12, 15

Holiday Guest House

P.O. Box 2247, 03907
(207) 646-5582; (800) 891-1548
www.holidayguesthouse.com

Fully restored historic 1814 Colonial close to beaches, restaurants, antique shops, outlets, and nature trails. Guest accommodations have private baths and refrigerators.

Hosts: Lou and Rose LePage
Rooms: 2 (PB) $55-95
Continental Breakfast
Credit Cards: A, B, C, D
Notes: 2, 5, 7, 9, 10, 11, 12, 14

Scotch Hill Inn

175 Main Street, P.O. Box 87, 03907
(207) 646-2890; FAX (207) 646-4324
e-mail: scotchhillinn@cybertours.com
www.chickadee.com/scotchhill

The hosts are Donna and Dick Brown who enjoy entertaining, cooking, travel, and good friends. An 1896 Victorian on 1.2 acres featuring a

Scotch Hill Inn

7 No smoking; 8 Children welcome; 9 Social drinking allowed; 10 Tennis nearby; 11 Swimming nearby; 12 Golf nearby; 13 Skiing nearby; 14 May be booked through a travel agent; 15 Handicapped accessible.

charming veranda, pretty flowers, and friendly, gracious atmosphere. Convenient in-town location just five-minute walk to beach. Air conditioned. Inquire about the two carriage houses (breakfast not included). Children welcome in the carriage houses. Bed and breakfast rooms include a full breakfast. Seasonal rates.

Hosts: Donna and Dick Brown
Room: 8 (5 PB; 3 SB) $70-125
Full Breakfast
Credit Cards: A, B
Notes: 7, 9, 10, 11, 12

Terrace By The Sea

11 Wharf Lane, P.O. Box 831, 03907
(207) 646-3232
www.terracebythesea.com

The Terrace By The Sea blends the best of both worlds, with the elegance of a Colonial inn and deluxe motel accommodations, both offering spectacular ocean views in a peaceful, secluded setting across from the beach. All rooms have private baths, air conditioning, telephones, color cable TV, heat, refrigerators; some efficiency kitchens. Easy walking distance to Ogunquit's beautiful sandy beach, Marginal Way, village shops, restaurants, and link to the trolley. Dinner packages available. Outdoor heated pool.

Hosts: John and Daryl Bullard
Rooms: 36 (PB) $110-182
Continental Breakfast
Credit Cards: None
Notes: 2, 4, 7, 10, 11, 12, 14

West Highland Inn

14 Shore Road, 03907
(207) 646-2181

The West Highland Inn is an island of serenity in a New England village setting in the heart of Ogunquit, close to everything it has to offer. The Victorian house, built in 1890, is full of antiques. Hosts offer breakfast each day, with home-baked goodies each afternoon. Ten rooms with private baths. Three efficiencies.

Open from May to November with special holiday weekends from December through April. Pets welcome. Seasonal rates.

Hosts: Linda and Steve Williams Clementine and
   Ferguson, the West Highland terriers
Rooms: 10 (PB) $60-120
Full Breakfast
Credit Cards: A, B
Notes: 2, 6, 7, 9, 10, 11, 12

Yardarm Village Inn

142 Shore Road, 03907
(207) 646-7006; (888) YARDARM
FAX (207) 646-9034
e-mail: L.C.DRURY@worldnet.att.net
www.chickadee.com/yardarm

Yardarm Village Inn is a charming old New England inn is located at 142 Shore Road, just south of the entrance to Perkins Cove, which is the quiet end of town. For your convenience, our inn and efficiency units offer a very diversified and comfortable selection of accommodations. Some with king- or queen-size beds, some with light cooking facilities, all with private baths, air conditioning, and cable TVs plus small refrigerators. The two-bedroom cottages are fully equipped to offer a home away from home for longer vacations. From one you can even walk to the beach. In order to guarantee a relaxed stay for all, we cannot accept pets.

Hosts: Larry and Phyllis Drury
Rooms: 8 (PB)
Continental Breakfast
Credit Cards: None
Notes: 2, 8, 9, 12, 14

ORLAND

Alamosook Lodge

P.O. Box 16, 04472
(207) 469-6393; FAX (207) 469-2528

Welcome to the lodge and the marvelous views of the lake. Enjoy freshwater swimming, canoeing, and fishing. Listen to loons. Experience fall foliage transformed into a blaze of reflecting colors. The winters are magical, with skating,

---

NOTES: Credit cards accepted: A MasterCard; B Visa; C American Express; D Discover; E Diner's Club; F Other; 2 Personal checks accepted; 3 Lunch available; 4 Dinner available; 5 Open all year; 6 Pets welcome;

cross-country skiing, and cozy warmth. Start the day with a sumptuous breakfast, stroll along the water, browse through the gardens, bask in the sun, and soak up the view. The six cheerful rooms with private baths are nonsmoking. Convenient to Bar Harbor, Blue Hill, Castine, and Deer Isle. Three miles off Route 1.

Hosts: Jan and Doug Gibson
Rooms: 6 (PB) $65-98
Full Breakfast
Credit Cards: A, B, C
Notes: 2, 5, 7, 8, 9, 11, 12, 15

The Sign of the Amiable Pig

74 Castine Road, P.O. Box 232, 04472-0232
(207) 469-2561

The bed and breakfast is in Orland village, just off Route 1. The house, named for the delightful weathervane which tops the garage, was built in the 18th century. Furnished with interesting antiques and oriental rugs, it has six working fireplaces, including the large cooking fireplace in the keeping room. Full breakfast is served in the dining room or the keeping room. The remodeled barn is now a guest house available on a weekly or monthly basis with breakfast available by reservation.

Hosts: Charlotte and Wes Pipher
Rooms: 3 (1 PB; 2 SB) $60-75
Guest House: $550; $1,900
Full Breakfast
Credit Cards: F
Notes: 2, 5, 7, 8, 9, 10, 11, 12, 13

The Sign of the Amiable Pig

PORTLAND

Andrews Lodging Bed & Breakfast

417 Auburn Street, 04103
(207) 797-9157; FAX (207) 797-9040
e-mail: andrewsbedandbreakfast@compuserve.com
www.travelguides.com/BB/andrews_lodging

On over an acre of beautifully landscaped grounds on the outskirts of the city of Portland, this 250-year-old Colonial home has been completely renovated for year-round comfort. Hosts offer modern baths, one with whirlpool, a completely applianced guest kitchen, a library, and a solarium overlooking beautiful gardens or pristine snow in the winter. Close to ocean, lakes, golf, skiing, and the mountains.

Hosts: Elizabeth and Douglas Andrews
Rooms: 5 (2 PB; 3 SB) $78-165
Full Breakfast
Credit Cards: A, B
Notes: 2, 5, 6, 7, 9, 12

Andrews Lodging

Bed & Breakfast Reservations North Shore, Greater Boston, Cape Cod

P.O. Box 600035, Newtonville, MA 02460
(617) 964-1606; (800) 832-2632
FAX (617) 332-8572; e-mail: info@bbreserve.com
www.bbreserve.com

133. European-style inn in Portland's historic western promenade district of grand homes

7 No smoking; 8 Children welcome; 9 Social drinking allowed; 10 Tennis nearby; 11 Swimming nearby; 12 Golf nearby; 13 Skiing nearby; 14 May be booked through a travel agent; 15 Handicapped accessible.

has six beautifully decorated guest rooms with private baths, telephones, cable TV, air conditioning, and some fireplaces. A large carriage house, adjacent to the inn, offers two additional accommodations, each with separate entrance. The handicapped accessible, downstairs room has private bath, TV, air conditioning, telephone, and private garden patio. The second-floor suite adds a sitting area. Full gourmet breakfast and complimentary afternoon wine. No smoking. Children over 15 welcome. $165-200.

Inn at St. John

939 Congress Street, 04102
(207) 773-6481; (800) 636-9127
www.maineguide.com/portland/stjohn

A unique 100-year-old inn noted for its European charm and quiet gentility. Just a short walk to the Old Port, waterfront, and arts district. Tastefully decorated rooms with traditional and antique furnishings. Enjoy complimentary Continental breakfast, free parking, and value rates. All rooms offer free local calls and cable TV with HBO. An ideal inn for that off-season getaway. Air-conditioned and nonsmoking rooms available.

Host: Paul Hood
Rooms: 40 (28 PB; 12 SB)
Continental Breakfast
Credit Cards: A, B, C, D, E
Notes: 2, 5, 6, 8, 10, 11, 12, 13, 14, 15

Pomegranate Inn

49 Neal Street, 04102
(207) 772-1006; (800) 356-0408
FAX (207) 773-4426

This 1884 Italianate inn in a historical neighborhood a few minutes' walk to midtown Portland. Eight rooms, all with private bath, some with fireplace, air conditioned, hand-painted walls, antique furnishings, contemporary art. Beautiful garden. Tea offered in the afternoon. One room handicapped accessible.

Host: Isabel Smiles
Rooms: 8 (PB) $95-165
Full Breakfast
Credit Cards: A, B, C, D
Notes: 2, 5, 7, 9, 10, 11, 12, 13, 14

West End Inn

146 Pine Street, 04102
(207) 772-1377

A very special place where the elegance and charm of yesteryear have been preserved and blended with the amenities and convenience of today. All rooms are uniquely decorated and provide new four-poster canopied beds, private baths, cable TV, and telephone access. Breakfast is cooked to order and reflects the quality of this establishment. The staff create an atmosphere of relaxation and enjoyment throughout the guests' stay and are quick to assist with travel tips or dinner reservations.

Hosts: John Leonard and Kelly Gillespie
Rooms: 6 (PB) $89-189
Full Breakfast
Credit Cards: A, B, C
Notes: 2, 5, 7, 8, 9, 10, 11, 12, 13, 14

ROCKLAND

Captain Lindsey House Inn

5 Lindsey Street, 04841
(207) 596-7950; (800) 523-2145
FAX (207) 596-2758
e-mail: kebarnes@midcoast.com
www.midcoast.com/~lindsey/

In the heart of Rockland's historic waterfront district, this in-town inn offers Old World charm with all the modern amenities in a comfortably elegant setting. Antiques and artifacts from around the world grace the spacious guest rooms, cozy lounge, and library. Afternoon refreshments are served fireside and a sumptuous dinner awaits guests in the Waterworks restaurant. Nearby guests will enjoy antiquing, shopping, and windjamming, not to mention stunning coastal scenery and fine Down East hospitality. Seasonal rates. Children 9 and older welcome.

Hosts: Capts. Ken and Ellen Barnes
Rooms: 9 (PB) $65-170
Continental Breakfast
Credit Cards: A, B, C, D
Notes: 3, 4, 5, 7, 9, 10, 11, 12, 13, 14, 15

Lakeshore Inn

184 Lakeview Drive, 04841
(207) 594-4209; (877) 783-7371
FAX (207) 596-6407
e-mail: lakshore@midcoast.com
www.midcoast.com/~lakeshore

The newly renovated Lakeshore Inn, originally built in 1767, is an elegant, smoke-free bed and breakfast inn overlooking the all-season beauty of Lake Chickawaukie. Unwind in front of one of the fireplaces or relax on the deck. Hosts place their emphasis on personalized attention and delicious full gourmet breakfasts. Each of the four tastefully decorated guest rooms has a queen-size bed and its own private bath as well as air conditioning and telephone. Elegant headquarters for schooner cruising, antique hunting, art and artist viewing, summer concerts, or just relaxing in the enclosed outdoor hot tub/spa. Children over 12 welcome.

Hosts: Joseph P. McCluskey and Paula E. Nicols
Room: 4 (PB) $105-125
Full Breakfast
Credit Cards: A, B, C
Notes: 2, 5, 7, 9, 10, 11, 12, 14

RUMFORD CENTER

The Last Resort Bed & Breakfast

P.O. Box 112, 04278-0112
(207) 364-4986

A Colonial Cape in Rumford Corner, nestled in the foothills of western Maine. Country comfort, charm, and good home cooking are a specialty. Skiing within minutes; two state parks and golf courses in the area. Fishing, hunting,

hiking, and boating by the back door. Children are welcome. Plenty of wide-open space for outside activities. Picnic lunch available at additional charge. Smoking permitted in designated areas only.

Host: Joan A. Tucker
Rooms: 3 (SB) $50
Full Breakfast
Credit Cards: None
Notes: 2, 5, 8, 9, 12, 13, 14

SACO

Crown 'n' Anchor Inn

121 North Street, P.O. Box 228, 04072-0228
(207) 282-3829; FAX (207) 282-7495

This Greek Revival two-story house was built during 1827-1828. The ornate Victorian furnishings, double parlors with twin mirrors, and bountiful country breakfast served on bone china by candlelight in the formal dining room afford many pleasant memories for guests. All rooms at the Crown 'n' Anchor Inn are furnished with period antiques, many collectibles, and provide private facilities. The Crown 'n' Anchor Inn provides yesterday's charm, today's comforts, for tomorrow's memories. One room is handicapped accessible.

Rooms: 6 (PB) $60-110
Full Breakfast
Credit Cards: A, B, C
Notes: 2, 5, 6, 7, 8, 9, 10, 11, 12, 13, 14

SEARSPORT

Brass Lantern Inn

81 West Main Street, 04974
(207) 548-0150; (800) 691-0150
FAX (207) 548-0304 (call first)
e-mail: stay@brasslanternmaine.com
www.brasslanternmaine.com

Circa 1850 Victorian sea captain's home conveniently located on the mid-coast of Maine, just a short walk to the town harbor. Guests will be greeted with warm and gracious hospitality.

7 No smoking; 8 Children welcome; 9 Social drinking allowed; 10 Tennis nearby; 11 Swimming nearby; 12 Golf nearby; 13 Skiing nearby; 14 May be booked through a travel agent; 15 Handicapped accessible.

Brass Lantern Inn

Spacious rooms, all with private baths, some with views of Penobscot Bay. Full gourmet breakfast served by candlelight in the elegant dining room. Relax in one of the parlors, or explore the museum, antique shops, flea markets, or take easy day trips to Acadia Park, Camden, or Rockland. Get away from it all, relax and unwind. Children 12 and older welcome.

Hosts: Maggie and Dick Zieg
Rooms: 5 (PB) $75-90
Full Breakfast
Credit Cards: A, B, D
Notes: 2, 5, 7, 9, 10, 11, 12, 13, 14

Homeport Inn

Box 647, East Main Street, Route 1, 04974
(207) 548-2259; (800) 742-5814
FAX (978) 443-6682; e-mail: hportinn@acadia.net
www.bnbcity.com/inns/20015

Homeport, listed in the National Register of Historic Places, is a fine example of a New England sea captain's mansion on beautiful landscaped grounds, with flower gardens extending to the ocean. This elegant home is furnished with family heirlooms and antiques. There are 10 guest rooms, seven with private baths. Victorian cottages are available. A visit offers a rare opportunity to vacation or be an overnight guest in a warm, homey, hospitable atmosphere without the customary travelers' commercialism. Children over three welcome.

Hosts: Edith and George Johnson
Rooms: 10 (7 PB; 3 SB) $55-90
Cottage: $600 per week
Full Breakfast
Credit Cards: A, B, C, D
Notes: 2, 5, 9, 10, 11, 12, 14

Watchtide..."B&B by the Sea"

190 West Main Street, (Atlantic Highway Route 1), 04974
(207) 548-6575; (800) 698-6575
e-mail: stay@watchtide.com
www.watchtide.com

This 18th century inn has been serving up scrumptious breakfasts on the 60-foot sun porch overlooking Penobscot Bay for more than 80 years. On the ocean side of Route 1, the ocean is always in view from the three more than landscaped seaside acres. Ocean view rooms, one with Jacuzzi, available. Walk to beach and park—or browse the Angels to Antiques Shoppe, where guests receive a discount.

Hosts: Nancy-Linn Nellis and Jack Elliott
Rooms: 4 (PB) $80-145
Full Breakfast
Credit Cards: A, B, D
Notes: 2, 5, 7, 8, 9, 10, 11, 12, 13, 14

SOUTHWEST HARBOR

Harbour Cottage Inn

9 Dirigo Road, P.O. Box 258, 04679-0258
(207) 244-5738; FAX (207) 244-7003
e-mail: harbour@downeast.net
www.downeast.net/com/harbour

This quiet and elegant, but informal inn is surrounded by Acadia National Park and welcomes hikers, bicyclers, boaters, and tourists to enjoy the warm, friendly hospitality. Each of the south, harbor-facing guest rooms offers a private full bath with whirlpool or steam bath/shower, hair dryer, individual heat thermostat, ceiling fan, and radio/alarm clock. The ample breakfast is served each morning in the dining room or on the front porch on pleasant days.

NOTES: Credit cards accepted: A MasterCard; B Visa; C American Express; D Discover; E Diner's Club; F Other; 2 Personal checks accepted; 3 Lunch available; 4 Dinner available; 5 Open all year; 6 Pets welcome;

Hosts: Glenda and Mike Sekulich
Rooms: 8 (PB) $65-165
Full Breakfast
Credit Cards: A, B, C, D
Notes: 2, 5, 7, 9, 10, 11, 12, 13, 14

The Island House

Box 1006, 04679
(207) 244-5180

Relax in a gracious, restful seacoast home on the quiet side of the island. Island House favorites, such as blueberry coffeecake and egg Florentine, are served for breakfast. Charming, private loft apartment available. Acadia National Park is just a five-minute drive away. The house is across the street from the harbor with swimming, sailing, biking, and hiking nearby. Children five and older welcome. Cross-country skiing nearby.

Hosts: Charles and Ann Bradford
Rooms: 5 (PB) $65-145
Full Breakfast
Credit Cards: A, B
Notes: 2, 5, 7, 9, 10, 11, 12, 13, 14

The Island House

The Kingsleigh Inn 1904

373 Main Street, Box 1426, 04679
(207) 244-5302; www.kingsleighinn.com

Surrounded by Acadia National Park, on the quiet side of Mount Desert Island. Hosts offer gracious hospitality in a warm, cozy setting. All guest rooms are tastefully decorated, many

The Kingsleigh Inn 1904

having beautiful harbor views, some with private balconies, all with private baths. For that special occasion, try the secluded three-room turret suite with panoramic views of the harbor. A full gourmet breakfast is served. Afternoon refreshments are available on the porch overlooking the harbor or by a crackling fire. AAA three-diamond-approved.

Hosts: Ken and Cyd Collins
Rooms: 8 (PB) $60-190
Full Breakfast
Credit Cards: A, B
Notes: 2, 5, 7, 9, 10, 11, 12, 13, 14

The Lambs Ear Inn

60 Clark Point Road, P.O. Box 30, 04679
(207) 244-9828; www.acadia.net/lambsear

The inn is a stately old Maine house, built in 1857. Comfortable and serene, with a sparkling harbor view. Have sweet dreams on comfortable beds with crisp, fresh linens. Start the day with a memorable breakfast. Spend

The Lambs Ear Inn

7 No smoking; 8 Children welcome; 9 Social drinking allowed; 10 Tennis nearby; 11 Swimming nearby; 12 Golf nearby; 13 Skiing nearby; 14 May be booked through a travel agent; 15 Handicapped accessible.

pleasant days filled with salt air and sunshine. Please visit this special village in the heart of Mount Desert Island surrounded by Acadia National Park. Open May 1 through October 30. Children over eight welcome.

Host: Elizabeth Hoke
Rooms: 6 (PB) $85-165
Full Breakfast
Credit Cards: A, B, C, D
Notes: 2, 7, 9, 10, 11, 12, 14

The Moorings Inn

P.O. Box 744, 04679
(207) 244-5523

Dramatic ocean and mountain views on waterfront. Bicycles, kayaks, canoes, grills, picnic tables free for guests' use. All private baths, cottages, suites, singles. Restaurant on premises. Adjacent to Hinckley Yacht Yard. At entrance of harbor and Somes Sound. View from rooms are a photo opportunity. Nautical motif.

Hosts: Storey and Kandance King
Rooms: 20 (PB) $80-125
Continental Breakfast
Credit Cards: None
Notes: 2, 3, 4, 9, 10, 11, 12

Penury Hall

374 Main Street, Box 68, 04679
(207) 244-7102; FAX (207) 244-5651
e-mail: tstrong@acadia.net
www.acadia.net/penury_n

On the quiet side of Mount Desert, 14 miles from Bar Harbor, is Penury Hall, where guests enjoy a breakfast of eggs Benedict, blueberry pancakes, cinnamon waffles, or popovers. Guests are welcome to use the canoe. The sauna is relaxing after a hard day of hiking or cross-country skiing. Inquire about accommodations for children.

Hosts: Toby and Gretchen
Rooms: 3 (PB) $85
Full Breakfast
Credit Cards: None
Notes: 2, 5, 7, 9, 10, 11, 12, 13, 14

SPRUCE HEAD

Craignair Inn

533 Clark Island Road, 04859
(207) 594-7644; (800) 320-9997
e-mail: craignar@midcoast.com

An oceanside country inn surrounded by natural beauty. A porch overlooks the ocean and garden. Paths lead to the coastline's tidal pools and an off-shore island. Each room is furnished with antiques and lovely homemade quilts. A full-service restaurant is on premises and is known for its outstanding food and spectacular view of the sea, where guests dine surrounded by soft music and candlelight.

Hosts: Neva and Steve Joseph
Rooms: 23 (8 PB; 15 SB) $66-120
Continental Breakfast
Credit Cards: A, B
Notes: 2, 4, 6, 7, 8, 9, 10, 11, 12, 14

STOCKTON SPRINGS

The Hichborn Inn

Church Street, P.O. Box 115, 04981
(800) 346-1522
e-mail: hichborninn@acadia.net
www.members.aol.com/hichborn

This romantic Victorian inn is listed in the National Register of Historic Places. Quiet area just off Route 1. Period furnishings, beds appointed with fine linens and down comforters, sumptuous full breakfasts, which may

Circa 1849

The Hichborn Inn

feature crêpes made with the inn's own raspberries. Penobscot Marine Museum, numerous
antique shops, and fine dining nearby. Advance
reservations recommended.

Hosts: Nancy and Bruce Suppes
Rooms: 4 (2 PB; 2 SB) $60-95
Full Breakfast
Credit Cards: None
Notes: 2, 5, 7, 11, 14

STONINGTON

Burnt Cove Bed & Breakfast

RFD 1, Box 2905, Whitman Road, 04681
(207) 367-2392

Waterfront, quiet on picturesque cove. Relax
on large deck or in interesting cedar-paneled
living room. Views of working lobster
wharves, sail boats, many birds. Small boat
launching available. Near nature conservancy
trails, Stonington Harbor, Isle au Haute mail-
boat, shops, and restaurants. Three guest
rooms, all with water views. Two upstairs
rooms share bath; one has queen-size bed, one
a double and twin beds. Downstairs room with
king-size bed, TV, and private bath. Children
over 12 welcome.

Hosts: Diane Berlew and Bob Williams
Rooms: 3 (1 PB; 2 SB) $65-90
Full Breakfast
Credit Cards: A, B
Notes: 2, 7, 9, 10, 11, 12

STRATTON

The Widow's Walk

171 Main Street, P.O. Box 150, 04982
(207) 246-6901; (800) 943-6995

The Steamboat Gothic architecture of this Vic-
torian home led to a listing in the National
Register of Historic Places. Nearby Bigelow
Mountain, the Appalachian Trail, and Flagstaff
Lake present many opportunities for boating,
fishing, and hiking. In the winter, Sugarloaf
USA, Maine's largest ski resort, offers both

The Widow's Walk

alpine and cross-country skiing, as well as
dogsled rides. Dogs and cats in residence.
Inquire about accommodations for children.

Hosts: Mary and Jerry Hopson
Rooms: 6 (SB) $30-48
Full Breakfast
Credit Cards: A, B
Notes: 2, 5, 7, 9, 11, 12, 13

SULLIVAN HARBOR

Islandview Inn

Route 1, HCR 32, Box 24, 04664
(207) 422-3031

Turn-of-the-century summer cottage is just off
Route 1, 15 minutes from Ellsworth and 35

Island View Inn

---

7 No smoking; 8 Children welcome; 9 Social drinking allowed; 10 Tennis nearby; 11 Swimming nearby;
12 Golf nearby; 13 Skiing nearby; 14 May be booked through a travel agent; 15 Handicapped accessible.

minutes from Bar Harbor. Choose from six guest rooms with private baths. Each room features original furniture, detailed restoration work, and picturesque views of Frenchman's Bay and Mount Desert Island. Private beach, sailing, canoe, and dinghy available. Smoking restricted.

Host: Evelyn Joost
Rooms: 6 (PB) $70-105
Full Breakfast
Credit Cards: A, B, D
Notes: 2, 9, 10, 11, 12

THOMASTON

Cap'n Frost Bed & Breakfast

U.S. Route 1, 241 Main Street, 04861
(207) 354-8217; e-mail: capnfrost@ime.net

This 1840s Cape is furnished with Maine antiques, some of which are for sale. The three guest rooms all have private baths. A full English breakfast is served. The Cap'n is the chef and flips a "mean" pancake. Great restaurants in the area. Many of the guests enjoy a visit to the Farnsworth Museum featuring Monks of the Wyeths. There are schooner day trips to nearby islands, Arcadia National Park is two hours away.

Hosts: Arlene and Harold Frost
Rooms: 3 (PB) $50
Full Breakfast
Credit Cards: None
Notes:2, 7, 9, 10, 11

The Doorway Inn

145 Main Street, 04861
(207) 354-9551; (888) 300-4907
FAX (207) 357-6587; www.doorwayinn.com

This elegant Federal home that has been carefully restored awaits guests' visit to vacation land. The inn has four rooms, all with private baths. Three rooms have queen-size beds and the fourth has twin-size beds. Relax in the personal spa or sit by a cozy fire in the music room. On a hot summer day enjoy a glass of

iced tea on the shady side porch. Thomaston is in mid-coast Maine, just a few minutes south of Rockland. Close to lighthouses, daysailing, hiking, antiquing, golf, fabulous dining, and museums. Free limo service provided within the area. Smoking not permitted on premises.

Hosts: Bruce and Carol Sue Greenleaf
Rooms: 4 (PB) $125-150
Full Breakfast
Credit Cards: A, B
Notes: 2, 5, 7, 8, 9, 10, 11, 12, 13

VINALHAVEN

Fox Island Inn

Carver Street, P.O. Box 451, 04863
(207) 863-2122; e-mail: gailrei@juno.com

Discover the unspoiled coastal Maine island of Vinalhaven. This comfortable, affordable bed and breakfast is in the quaint fishing village nestled around picturesque Carver's Harbor. Enjoy swimming in the abandoned granite quarries and exploring seaside nature preserves by foot or bicycle. State-operated car ferry from Rockland runs six times daily. Island activities include flea markets, church suppers, and wonderful local restaurants.

Host: Gail Reinertsen
Rooms: 6 (SB) $45-75
Continental Breakfast
Credit Cards: A, B, C, D
Notes: 2, 7, 9, 11

WALDOBORO

Elaine's Bed & Breakfast Selections

4987 Kingston Road, Elbridge, NY 13060
(315) 689-2082 (call between 10:30 A.M.–7:00 P.M.)

A nonsmoking 1905 Victorian offers four guest rooms with private and shared baths. Full breakfast served—please advise of special dietary needs. Convenient to all mid-coast activities. Open year-round. $70-80.

NOTES: Credit cards accepted: A MasterCard; B Visa; C American Express; D Discover; E Diner's Club; F Other; 2 Personal checks accepted; 3 Lunch available; 4 Dinner available; 5 Open all year; 6 Pets welcome;

The Roaring Lion

995 East Main Street, 04572
(207) 832-4038

A 1905 Victorian home with tin ceilings and elegant woodwork throughout. The Roaring Lion accommodates special and vegetarian diets on request. Sourdough breakfast and pancakes a specialty, also homemade jams and jellies. Hosts are well traveled and lived in Africa for two years. Their interests include books, gardening, art, and cooking.

Hosts: Bill and Robin Branigan
Rooms: 4 (1 PB; 3 SB) $64.20-74.90
Full Breakfast
Credit Cards: None
Notes: 2, 5, 7, 8, 10, 11, 12, 13, 14

WATERFORD

The Waterford Inne

Chadbourne Road, Box 149, 04088
(207) 583-4037

Escape to country quiet in an inn offering the elegance of a fine country home. Nine uniquely decorated guest rooms and carefully furnished common rooms provide a fine setting for four-star dining in historic Waterford. Near mountains and coastline; water and woodland activities nearby. Closed April. Pets permitted with fee.

Host: Barbara Vanderzanden
Rooms: 9 (7 PB; 2 SB) $75-100
Full Breakfast
Credit Cards: C
Notes: 2, 4, 6, 8, 9, 10, 11, 12, 13

WELLS

Country Peddlar Shop & Inn

51 Harbor Road, Box 804, 04090
(207) 646-6576; (781) 246-0730 (winter)
e-mail: CPedShpInn@aol.com
www.amyscollectibles.com/countrypeddlar.htm

Welcome to this country shop and inn. The Greek Revival-style home, built in 1837, just off Route 1 between Kennebunkport and Ogunquit. Short walk along salt marsh and tidal pools to Wells Harbor. Fish off pier; relax and enjoy the sights and sounds of the harbor. Within walking distance of casual and fine dining, antique shops, or enjoy browsing through the on-premises gift shop featuring their own handcrafted gifts. The guest rooms are large, each decorated with lots of country charm and includes in-room refrigerator, air conditioning, color cable TV, and a full country breakfast. Sited on three-fourths an acre, enjoy lawn games, wandering through the whimsical country gardens or taking a lazy nap in the hammock.

Hosts: Norm and Sandi Johnson
Rooms: 2 (SB) $50-70
Full Breakfast
Credit Cards: None
Notes: 2, 8, 10, 11, 12

WELLS BEACH

Rest Awhile By the Sea Bed & Breakfast

249 Webhannet Drive, 04090
(877) 646-4034 (phone/FAX)
e-mail: restawhile@chamberworks.com

An informal cozy setting overlooking the sea, this renovated barn has been in family since early 1930s. Children are welcome. Beach access just 20 feet from the door. Lifeguards on duty. Enjoy the lovely sandy beach. Plenty of room to stretch out on the decks. Refrigerators, coffee pots, cable TV, barbecue grills and picnic tables. Close to many fine restaurants, antique shops galore.

Hosts: Norm and Priscilla Fournier
Rooms: 4 (2 PB; 2 SB) $59-120
Continental Breakfast
Credit Cards: A, B
Notes: 5, 7, 8, 9, 11, 14

7 No smoking; 8 Children welcome; 9 Social drinking allowed; 10 Tennis nearby; 11 Swimming nearby; 12 Golf nearby; 13 Skiing nearby; 14 May be booked through a travel agent; 15 Handicapped accessible.

Sunrise, Sunset

Sunrise, Sunset, Bed & Breakfast Inn

P.O. Box 353, Moody, 04054-0353
(207) 646-7811; (941) 493-2032 (winter)

Traditional Cape Cod house with views of the ocean and beautiful white sandy beach. Spacious guest rooms with one private bath and two shared baths. Cable TV, stereo, books, games, piano, and fireplace are available for guests' enjoyment. Large yard for sun bathing or lunch at the picnic table. Down East breakfast with the specialty of the day. Near Wells Beach with its fine restaurants, antiques, golf, fishing, summer theater, and trolley line. Rachel Carson Wildlife Refuge for the nature lover. Children welcome.

Host: June Graves
Rooms: 3 (1 PB; 2 SB)
Full Breakfast
Credit Cards: None
Notes: 2, 8, 9, 10, 11, 12, 13, 14

WINDHAM

Sebago Lake Lodge & Cottages

661 White's Bridge Road, P.O. Box 110, 04062
(207) 892-2698; FAX (207) 892-0792

Sebago Lake Lodge and Cottages has 12 rooms and 12 cottages. Most rooms have private baths, kitchenettes, and screened porches with lake views. Rates include Continental breakfast and canoe, rowboat, and kayak usage. Cottages rent from Saturday to Saturday ($550-975) with canoes, rowboats, and kayaks included. Deluxe cottages available at $1,400 per week. Off-season rates available. Boat and seadoo rentals, swim area, cruise boat, bait/gift shop, outdoor fireplace, and horseshoes available.

Hosts: Chip and Debra Lougee
Rooms: 12 (10 PB; 2 SB) $68-200
Cottages: 12 (PB)
Continental Breakfast
Credit Cards: A, B, C
Notes: 7, 8, 9, 11, 12, 14, 15

WINTER HARBOR

Main Stay Inn & Cottages

P.O. Box 459, 04693
(207) 963-5561; (207) 963-2601
www.awa-web.com/stayinn

Restored Victorian home overlooks Henry's Cove. Housekeeping units with fireplaces. Walk to restaurants and post office. A quiet village within a mile of Acadia. Guests may enjoy hiking, biking, and local activities.

Hosts: Pearl and Roger Barto
Rooms: 3 plus 2 units (PB) $45
Credit Cards: A, B
Notes: 2, 5, 7, 8, 9, 11, 12

WISCASSET

The Squire Tarbox Inn

1181 Main Road, Westport Island, 04578
(207) 882-7693; FAX (207) 882-7107
e-mail: squiretarbox@ime.net
www.squiretarboxinn.com

Clean, casual, comfortable, and all country, this is a historic Colonial farmhouse on a back road near midcoast Maine harbors, beaches, antique shops, museums, and lobster shacks. Part of a working farm with a purebred goat dairy, the inn offers a balance

Squires Tarbox

of history, quiet country, good food, and relaxation. Delicious fresh goat cheese served by the fire before dinner. Known primarily for rural privacy and five-course dinners. Children over 14 welcome.

Hosts: Karen and Bill Mitman
Rooms: 11 (PB) $90-179
Full Breakfast
Credit Cards: A, B, C, D
Notes: 2, 4, 7, 9, 14

YORK

The Cape Neddick House

1300 Route 1, P.O. Box 70, Cape Neddick, 03902
(207) 363-2500; FAX (207) 363-4499

In the historic coastal community of York, this 1800s Victorian farmhouse is central to beaches, boutiques, antique shops, wildlife sanctuaries, boat cruises, factory outlets, and historical and cultural opportunities. Sleeping on antique high-back beds, snuggled under handmade quilts, guests are assured of pleasant dreams. No alarm clock needed, as the fragrant smells of cinnamon popovers, apple almond tortes, or ham and apple biscuits gently wake guests. All private baths. Two-room suite with fireplace available. Inquire about

availability of dinner. Smoking restricted. Cross-country skiing nearby.

Hosts: John and Dianne Goodwin
Rooms: 5 (PB) $95-120
Full Breakfast
Credit Cards: None
Notes: 2, 5, 9, 10, 11, 12, 13

YORK BEACH

Dockside Guest Quarters

Harris Island Road, P.O. Box 205, York, 03909
(207) 363-2868; www.docksidegq.com

The Dockside Guest Quarters is a small resort on a private peninsula in York Harbor. Panorama of ocean and harbor activities. Spa-

Dockside Guest Quarters

---

7 No smoking; 8 Children welcome; 9 Social drinking allowed; 10 Tennis nearby; 11 Swimming nearby; 12 Golf nearby; 13 Skiing nearby; 14 May be booked through a travel agent; 15 Handicapped accessible.

cious grounds with privacy and relaxing atmosphere. Beaches, outlet shopping, and numerous scenic walks nearby. Accommodations are in a seacoast inn and multiunit cottages. Full service marina, wedding facilities, and restaurant on-site. Packages and off-season rates are available. AAA-rated three diamonds.

Hosts: The Lusty Family
Rooms: 21 (19 PB; 2 SB) $60-145
Continental Breakfast
Credit Cards: A, B, D
Notes: 2, 3, 4, 5, 7, 8, 9, 10, 11, 12, 14, 15

Homestead Inn

Homestead Inn Bed & Breakfast

5 Long Beach Avenue (Route 1A), 03910
(207) 363-8952 (phone/FAX)
e-mail: HomstedBB@aol.com
www.members.aol.com/homstedBB

A converted 1905 summer boarding house, the inn is at Short Sands Beach. Individually decorated rooms have ocean views; each room has its own sink. Walk to beach, enjoy sunsets, or visit local Nubble Lighthouse. Historic landmarks; fine restaurants. Relax, be pampered, and let the seashore entertain. Continental plus breakfast served outside with an ocean view.

Hosts: Dan and Danielle Duffy
Rooms: 4 (S2B) $55-65

Continental Breakfast
Credit Cards: None
Notes: 2, 7, 9, 10, 11, 12

York Harbor Inn

Route 1A, P.O. Box 573, 03911
(207) 363-5119; (800) 343-3869
www.yorkharborinn.com

Coastal country inn overlooks beautiful York Harbor in an exclusive residential neighborhood. There are 33 air-conditioned rooms with antiques, ocean views, and seven working fireplaces; some rooms have Jacuzzi tubs and ocean-view decks. Fine dining year-round. An English pub on the premises with entertainment. The beach is within walking distance; boating, fishing, antique shops are all nearby. Banquet and meeting facilities available.

Hosts: Joe, Jean, Garry, and Nancy Dominguez
Rooms: 33 (PB) $89-239
Continental Breakfast
Credit Cards: A, B, C, E, F
Notes: 2, 3, 4, 5, 7, 8, 9, 11, 12, 14

YORK HARBOR

Bell Buoy Bed & Breakfast

570 York Street, 03911
(207) 363-7264; FAX (207) 363-5719

At the Bell Buoy, there are no strangers, only friends who have not met. Open year-round and minutes from US 95, Route 1, and the Kittery outlet malls. Only a short walk to sandy beaches, or guests may relax on the large porch or in the guests-only living room with fireplace. A full homemade breakfast will be served in the dining room or on the porch, as desired.

Hosts: Wes and Kathie Cook
Rooms: 4 (PB) $70-95
Full Breakfast
Credit Cards: None
Notes: 2, 5, 7, 8, 9, 11, 12

NOTES: Credit cards accepted: A MasterCard; B Visa; C American Express; D Discover; E Diner's Club; F Other; 2 Personal checks accepted; 3 Lunch available; 4 Dinner available; 5 Open all year; 6 Pets welcome;

Stage Neck Inn

Stage Neck Inn

22 Stage Neck Road, P.O. Box 70, 03911-0070
(207) 363-3850; (800) 222-3238
e-mail: reserve@stageneck.com
www.stageneck.com

A small, European-style resort on a peninsula offering a unique combination of the sparkling ocean, scenic harbor, massive rocky shoreline, and a fine sandy beach. For more than 20 years, Stage Neck Inn has earned AAA's coveted four diamond award for superior comfort and service. Resort amenities include an indoor atrium pool, oceanside pool, clay tennis courts, 18-hole golf, fitness room, two restaurants, and conference and wedding facilities. Packages with full breakfast and gourmet dinner are available year-round.

Host: Phoebe Apgar-Pressey
Rooms: 58 (PB) $185-324
Full Breakfast
Credit Cards: A, B, D
Notes: 3, 4, 5, 7, 8, 9, 10, 11, 12, 15

7 No smoking; 8 Children welcome; 9 Social drinking allowed; 10 Tennis nearby; 11 Swimming nearby; 12 Golf nearby; 13 Skiing nearby; 14 May be booked through a travel agent; 15 Handicapped accessible.

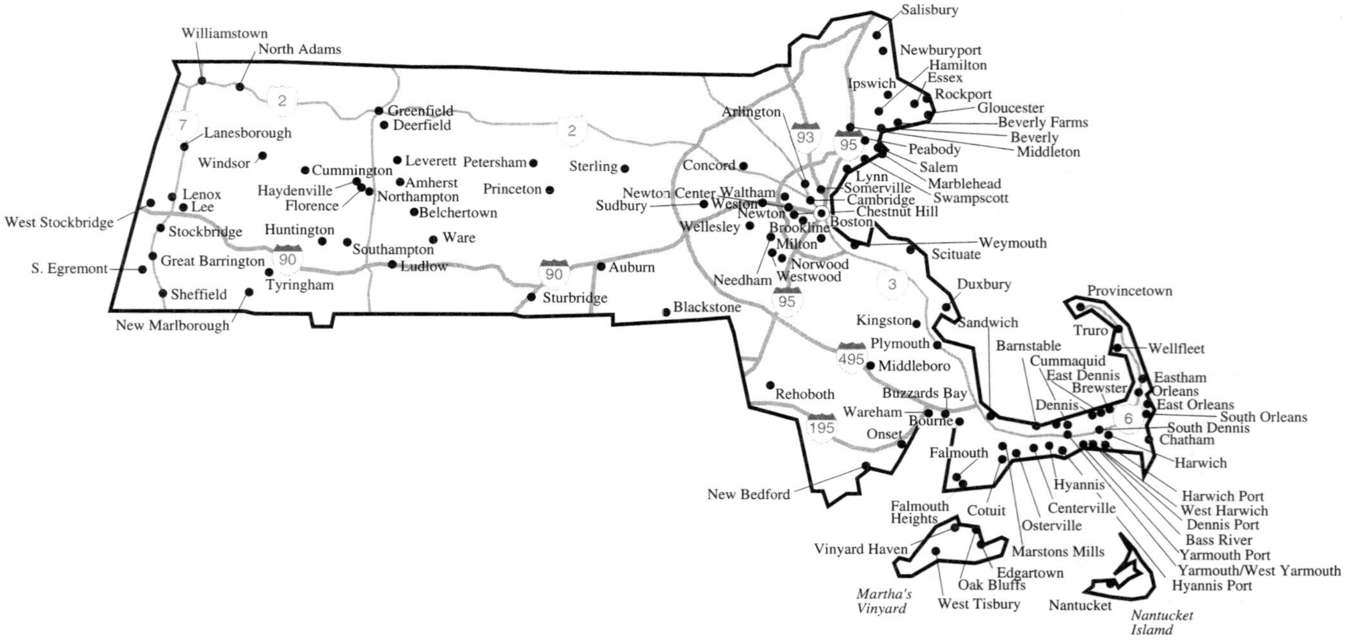

Massachusetts

Salisbury
Newburyport
Hamilton
Essex
Rockport
Gloucester
Beverly Farms
Beverly
Middleton
Peabody
Marblehead
Swampscott
Salem
Lynn
Somerville
Cambridge
Chestnut Hill
Boston
Ipswich
Weymouth
Scituate
Duxbury

Provincetown
Truro
Wellfleet
Eastham
Orleans
East Orleans
South Orleans
Harwich Port
West Harwich
Dennis Port
Bass River
Yarmouth Port
Yarmouth/West Yarmouth
Hyannis Port
Nantucket Island
Cummaquid
East Dennis
Brewster
Dennis
Chatham
Harwich
Hyannis
Centerville
Osterville
Barnstable
Marstons Mills
Sandwich
Cotuit
Nantucket
Plymouth
Kingston
Middleboro
Buzzards Bay
Wareham
Bourne
Onset
Falmouth
Edgartown
Oak Bluffs
West Tisbury
Falmouth Heights
Vineyard Haven
Martha's Vineyard
Rehoboth
New Bedford

Arlington
Milton
Brookline
Newton
Concord
Newton Center
Waltham
Weston
Wellesley
Sudbury
Needham
Norwood
Westwood
Blackstone
Auburn
Sterling
Petersham
Princeton
Leverett
Greenfield
Deerfield
Amherst
Northampton
Belchertown
Ware
Southampton
Ludlow
Cummington
Haydenville
Florence
Huntington
Southampton
Tyringham
Sturbridge

Williamstown
North Adams
Windsor
Lanesborough
Lenox
Lee
Stockbridge
Great Barrington
Sheffield
West Stockbridge
S. Egremont
New Marlborough

95
93
3
6
2
90
7
495
195

Massachusetts

Allen House

AMHERST

Allen House Victorian Bed & Breakfast Inn

599 Main Street, 01002
(413) 253-5000; www.allenhouse.com

Authentic 1886 Stick-style Victorian on three acres opposite the Emily Dickinson homestead. Spacious bed chambers with telephones, modems, and central air conditioning. Antiques, art, and wall decor are historically and artistically featured. Within walking distance of Amherst College, University of Massachusetts, fine galleries, museums, theaters, shops, and restaurants. Free transportation throughout five college area. Full five-course breakfast served. Afternoon and evening tea and refreshments. Winner 1991 Historic Preservation Award. AAA three-diamond-rated. *Bon Appétit's* Historic Christmas Inn. *Boston* magazine's "Best Victorian in New England."

Hosts: Alan and Ann Zieminski
Rooms: 7 (PB) $55-135
Full Breakfast

Credit Cards: A, B, D, E
Notes: 2, 5, 7, 9, 10, 11, 12, 13

ARLINGTON

Bed & Breakfast Reservations North Shore, Greater Boston, Cape Cod

P.O. Box 600035, Newtonville, 02460
(617) 964-1606; (800) 832-2632
FAX (617) 332-8572; e-mail: info@bbreserve.com
www.bbreserve.com

120. Arlington Victorian Manor. Elegance, luxury, romance, and comfort await guests in this glorious accommodation between Cambridge and Lexington. Seven miles from Boston, two from Harvard Square, with excellent public transportation nearby. Restored 1887 Queen Anne-style home retains much of its original architecture and superb detail: magnificent staircase, grand living room with hand-carved cherry mantel, solarium, dining room. Guest rooms have private baths, designer bed linens, ceiling fans. Continental plus breakfast featuring home-baked goods. Afternoon tea in solarium. Nonsmoking. Open year-round. $155-225.

AUBURN

Captain Samuel Eddy House

609 Oxford Street South, 01501
(508) 832-7282

The center-chimney Colonial home, circa 1765, has been restored and handsomely decorated in

NOTES: Credit cards accepted: A MasterCard; B Visa; C American Express; D Discover; E Diner's Club; F Other; 2 Personal checks accepted; 3 Lunch available; 4 Dinner available; 5 Open all year; 6 Pets welcome; 7 No smoking; 8 Children welcome; 9 Social drinking allowed; 10 Tennis nearby; 11 Swimming nearby; 12 Golf nearby; 13 Skiing nearby; 14 May be booked through a travel agent; 15 Handicapped accessible.

period style by the owners. In addition to the large keeping room where guests gather for breakfast, there are three common areas for guests to relax in. Each parlor has a fireplace, and the plant-filled sunroom allows guests to enjoy the country setting with views of Eddy Pond, the surrounding woods, and gardens. Children over five are welcome.

Hosts: Diedre and Michael Meddaugh
Rooms: 3 (PB) $75-95
Full Breakfast
Credit Cards: None
Notes: 2, 5, 7, 9, 12, 13, 14

BARNSTABLE (CAPE COD) _____

Ashley Manor

3660 Old Kings Highway, Box 856, 02630
(508) 888-2246; FAX (508) 362-9927
e-mail: ashleymn@capecod.net
www.capecod.net/ashelymn

Ashley Manor is a very special place, a gracious 1699 mansion on a two-acre estate in Cape Cod's historic district. Romantic rooms and suites feature private baths, whirlpools, and fireplaces. Elegant public rooms with antiques and oriental rugs. Delicious full breakfast in formal dining room or on terrace overlooking parklike grounds and new tennis court. Walk to the beach and village. Prices subject to change. Children over 12 welcome.

Host: Donald Bain
Rooms: 6 (PB) $130-185
Full Breakfast
Credit Cards: A, B, D, F
Notes: 2, 5, 7, 9, 10, 11, 12, 14

Ashley Manor

Bed & Breakfast Cape Cod

P.O. Box 1312, Orleans, 02653
(508) 255-3824; (800) 541-6226
fax (508) 240-0599
e-mail: info@BedandBreakfastCapeCod.com
www.BedandBreakfastCapeCod.com

BAR 01. Built as a residence and tavern in 1790, this lovely old house, now in the National Register of Historic Places, was restored into a charming, historic, and comfortable bed and breakfast. There are three air-conditioned guest rooms. Two are on the second floor, each has an adjoining room with one twin bed and a private bath. The first-floor queen-size bedroom has a fireplace and private bath. The lovely grounds with trees and flowers make a charming setting. Walk five minutes to shops, restaurants, and the whale watching boats from Barnstable Harbor. Hyannis and the ferry to the islands are three miles away. Continental breakfast. $105-125.

Bed & Breakfast Reservations North Shore, Greater Boston, Cape Cod

P.O. Box 600035, Newtonville, 02460
(617) 964-1606; (800) 832-2632
FAX (617) 332-8572; e-mail: info@bbreserve.com
www.bbreserve.com

112. Barnstable Colonial Guest House. Federal Colonial house dates back to 1800. Walk through beautiful gardens and spacious grounds. Stroll along a rambling brook or take a morning walk to the ocean's edge. Relax on the porch and terrace. Large sitting room with fireplace. Short walk to village center with great restaurants and picturesque beach nearby. Guest kitchen for light use. Full gourmet breakfast served in formal dining room or on spacious sun porch with views of grounds. Two suites with private baths, plus first-floor queen-size room with oversized shower in en suite bath and working fireplace. Thirty-five dollars for each additional person. No smoking. $105-125.

Beechwood

2839 Main Street, 02630
(508) 362-6618; (800) 609-6618
FAX (508) 362-0298
www.beechwoodinn.com

Experience the romance of this romantic Victorian inn, with six large guest rooms, some with fireplaces or water views. All rooms are furnished with beautiful period antiques and have private baths. Gourmet breakfasts are served in the paneled dining room, and afternoon tea by the parlor fireplace in winter. In summer, iced tea and lemonade are served on the veranda that overlooks one and one-half acres of beautifully landscaped lawns and gardens. *Cape Cod Life* magazine rated Beechwood as "Best Mid-Cape Bed and Breakfast."

Hosts: Debbie and Ken Traugot
Rooms: 6 (PB) $90-170
Full Breakfast
Credit Cards: A, B, C, D
Notes: 2, 5, 7, 9, 10, 11, 12, 14

Beechwood

Honeysuckle Hill Bed & Breakfast

591 Old Kings Highway, Route 6A, 02668
(508) 362-8418; (800) 441-8418
FAX (508) 362-8386
e-mail: stay@honeysucklehill.com
www.honeysucklehill.com

On the edge of the small village of West Barnstable, the Honeysuckle Hill Bed and Breakfast has been welcoming guests for generations. Listed in the National Register of Historic Places, circa 1810, this enchanting seaside cot-

Honeysuckle Hill

tage offers comfortably elegant rooms and graciously served breakfasts. Built in the Queen Anne style, the inn is surrounded by lush, green lawns and colorful gardens. The five sparkling rooms are furnished in antiques and white wicker, along with featherbeds and Battenburg lace. The baths are outfitted in marble and brass and feature big fluffy towels and English toiletries. A full breakfast is included in the rates and is served in the sunny dining room. Children over 12 welcome.

Hosts: Bill and Mary Kilburn
Rooms: 5 (PB) $95-185
Full Breakfast
Credit Cards: A, B, C, D
Notes: 2, 5, 7, 9, 10, 11, 12

Lamb & Lion Inn

2504 Main Street (Route 6A), P.O. Box 511, 02630
(508) 362-6823; FAX (508) 362-0227
e-mail: lamblion@capecod.net
www.lambandlion.com

The Lamb and Lion Inn combines a classic Cape Cod Inn with the spirit of a small luxury hotel. Ten units create an atrium with a central courtyard overlooking the swimming pool. The spacious accommodations all boast in-room private baths. Six of the suites have well-equipped kitchenettes and two of these units enjoy working fireplaces. The "Barn-stable" and the "Cottage" have multiple sleeping areas. The Lamb and Lion Inn is one of Cape Cod's secret treasures—unique and captivating—truly "The Peaceful Kingdom."

Host: Alice Pitcher
Rooms: 10 (PB) $85-225

7 No smoking; 8 Children welcome; 9 Social drinking allowed; 10 Tennis nearby; 11 Swimming nearby; 12 Golf nearby; 13 Skiing nearby; 14 May be booked through a travel agent; 15 Handicapped accessible.

Continental Breakfast
Credit Cards: A, B
Notes: 2, 5, 6, 8, 10, 11, 12, 14

BASS RIVER (CAPE COD)

The Anchorage

122 South Shore Drive, 02664
(508) 398-8265
e-mail: anchbb@masscot.com

The Anchorage is an ideal place to spend a holiday if people enjoy Cape Cod's broad sandy beaches and warm water. The ocean is just a few steps away. There are theaters, restaurants, hiking, fishing, boating, and all activities to complete your holiday. "Join us for a quiet, relaxing visit where the gentle sea breezes help you to leave all your cares behind."

Host: Ruth T. Masciarotte
Rooms: 3 (PB) $35-60
Continental Breakfast
Credit Cards: None
Notes: 2, 5, 9, 10, 11,12

The Anchorage

BELCHERTOWN

Ingate Farms Bed & Breakfast

60 Lamson Avenue @ South Amherst/Belchertown Line, 01007
(413) 253-0440 (phone/FAX); (888) INGATE-B

Natural country environment amid 400 acres in Holyoke Mountain Range, yet within minutes to the culture and charms of the "Five Colleges Region" in the western Massachusetts Pioneer Valley. Ingate Farms—formerly a bobbin factory, tavern, and then a home—is decorated in Early American antiques and provides comfort, charm, and care via experienced hosts. Swim and ride on the property. Hike the horse trails, fish or bird watch, or boat on the famous Quabbin Reservoir nearby. Excellent restaurants abound. Extended stay, multiple room, and corporate discounts available. Continental plus breakfast served. Children 12 and older welcome.

Hosts: Virginia Kier and Bill McCormick
Rooms: 5 (3 PB; 2 SB) $55-85
Continental Breakfast
Credit Cards: A, B, C
Notes: 2, 5, 7, 9, 10, 11, 12, 13

BEVERLY

Bed & Breakfast Reservations North Shore, Greater Boston, Cape Cod

P.O. Box 600035, Newtonville, 02460
(617) 964-1606; (800) 832-2632
FAX (617) 332-8572; e-mail: info@bbreserve.com
www.bbreserve.com

13. The Inn Next Door Inn. A beautifully decorated, cozy Colonial-style home, offering three attractive guest rooms, a queen-size room with private hall bath on first floor, and two second-floor rooms (which can sleep up to four each) share a bath. In hot weather, common areas have air conditioning. Guest rooms have fans. Guests enjoy the use of kitchen facilities for fixing light snacks, color TV in living room, enclosed sun porch, telephone, and off-street parking. Continental breakfast provided each morning. Complimentary train pick up at Beverly Depot. Children over 12 welcome. No smoking. Whole house may be rented to families/small groups (up to nine). $85-95.

Beverly Farms Bed & Breakfast at the Jon Larcom House

28 Hart Street, 01915
(978) 922-6074

NOTES: Credit cards accepted: A MasterCard; B Visa; C American Express; D Discover; E Diner's Club; F Other; 2 Personal checks accepted; 3 Lunch available; 4 Dinner available; 5 Open all year; 6 Pets welcome;

Beverly Farms

Charming old Colonial with beams, Indian shutters, and fireplaces on the historic and picturesque North Shore. Three bedrooms are available, two with fireplaces, shared and private baths. Within walking distance of the village train and lovely beach. Gourmet Continental breakfast is served in the dining room in the smoke-free home. Children over 12 are welcome.

Hosts: Steve and Peg Powers
Rooms: 3 (2 PB; 1 SB) $85-110
Continental Breakfast
Credit Cards: None
Notes: 2, 5, 7, 11, 12, 13

Bunny's Bed & Breakfast

17 Kernwood Heights, 01915
(978) 922-2392

This Dutch Colonial inn is on a scenic route leading along the state's northeastern coast. The Continental plus breakfast in the dining room feature made-from-scratch breads, muffins, and coffeecakes. Every effort is made to meet special dietary needs if notified in advance. Twenty miles north of Boston and one-half mile from Salem. Close to Gordon College, Endicott College, and Montserrat College of Art.

Hosts: Bunny and Joe Stacey
Rooms: 3 (1 PB; 2 SB) $65-90

Continental Breakfast
Credit Cards: None
Notes: 2, 5, 7, 9, 11, 14

BEVERLY FARMS

Bed & Breakfast Reservations North Shore, Greater Boston, Cape Cod

P.O. Box 600035, Newtonville, 02460
(617) 964-1606; (800) 832-2632
FAX (617) 332-8572; e-mail: info@bbreserve.com
www.bbreserve.com

141. Country Gardens. This former turn-of-the-century equestrian estate has been transformed into a unique bed and breakfast inn. It's idyllic and very private setting features expansive grounds with beautiful perennial gardens and central courtyard with swimming pool. Rooms have private en suite baths. Also available is a two-room suite. A full gourmet breakfast is served. Renovations are in process to provide two additional rooms in the old barn. The inn is centrally positioned on the North Shore, and about 30 minutes to Boston's Logan Airport. Children over 16 welcome. No smoking. Two resident cats. Open year-round. $120-225.

BLACKSTONE

The Fieldstone Victorian

40 Edgewater Drive, 01504
(508) 883-4647

The 1905 Victorian waterfront home on a landscaped acre is minutes from Providence, Rhode Island, and Boston and Worcester, Massachusetts. Antiques enhance the intricately carved woodwork in the common rooms and fireplaced dining room. The two guest rooms have private baths, queen-size beds, water views, cable TV, and homemade cookies. Candlelight gourmet breakfasts are served on antique family china, and include homemade

7 No smoking; 8 Children welcome; 9 Social drinking allowed; 10 Tennis nearby; 11 Swimming nearby; 12 Golf nearby; 13 Skiing nearby; 14 May be booked through a travel agent; 15 Handicapped accessible.

The Fieldstone Victorian

breads, jams, and fruit syrups. Near many genealogical resources, museums, and Blackstone River canoe launches.

Hosts: Joe and Donna Emidy
Rooms: 2 (PB) $75
Full Breakfast
Credit Cards: A, B
Notes: 2, 5, 7, 8, 9, 11, 12

Morin's Victorian Hideaway Bed & Breakfast

48 Mendon Street, 01504
(508) 883-7045

A unique bed and breakfast, nestled on three and one-half acres, overlooking the scenic Blackstone River. The hosts provide a warm and cozy atmosphere for their guests with a fully stocked kitchen, where guests can help themselves to snacks or libations at any time. Sleeping accommodations for the weary traveler include three spacious and charming

Morin's Victorian Hideaway

rooms. Billiard room, exercise room, and in-ground pool and yard games are available. Walking distance to restaurants, shops, stores, and churches.

Hosts: Chip and Lynn Morin
Rooms: 3 (1 PB; 2 SB) $65-75
Continental Breakfast
Credit Cards: None
Notes: 2, 5, 7, 8, 9, 10, 11, 12, 13, 14

BOSTON

Beacon Hill

Beacon Hill Bed & Breakfast

27 Brimmer Street, 02108
(617) 523-7376; e-mail: bhillbb@aol.com

Three spacious rooms with private baths in this elegant 1869 brick row house in Boston's most exclusive neighborhood. Extremely centrally located, historically preserved, easy walk to restaurants, shops, tourist sites, subway. Garage parking nearby. All rooms have interesting architectural details and antiques, two have queen-size beds plus a sofa bed; one converts to studio apartment for weekly stays, no hotel tax (now 13 percent).

Host: Susan Butterworth
Rooms: 3 (PB) $160-240
Full Breakfast
Credit Cards: None
Notes: 5, 7, 8, 9, 14

NOTES: Credit cards accepted: A MasterCard; B Visa; C American Express; D Discover; E Diner's Club; F Other; 2 Personal checks accepted; 3 Lunch available; 4 Dinner available; 5 Open all year; 6 Pets welcome;

Beacon Inns & Guesthouses

248 Newbury Street, 02116
(617) 266-7142; FAX (617) 266-7276

These renovated townhouses offer an affordable alternative to the costly hotel accommodations in Boston's historic Back Bay. All of the guest rooms include a kitchenette, refrigerator, free local telephone service, and air conditioning. Please note that there are no TVs or elevators and that maid service and meals are not provided.

Host: Steven Handler
Rooms: 14 (PB) $99
Credit Cards: A, B
Notes: 2, 5, 7, 11, 12, 13, 14

A Bed & Breakfast Agency of Boston & Boston Harbor Bed & Breakfast

47 Commercial Wharf, 02110
(617) 720-3540; (800) 248-9262
0 800 89 5128 (free phone from U.K.)
FAX (617) 523-5761; e-mail: BOSBNB@aol.com
www.boston-bnbagency.com

Downtown Boston's largest selection of guest rooms in historic bed and breakfast homes including Federal and Victorian townhouses and beautifully restored 1840s waterfront lofts. Also a lovely selection of furnished private studio, or one- and two-bedroom condominiums that are great for families. Exclusive locations include waterfront, Faneuil Hall and Quincy Market, North End, Back Bay, Beacon Hill, Copley Square, Cambridge, Cape Cod, and the Islands. Yachts and houseboats are also available. Credit cards and personal checks accepted. Children welcome. No smoking. May be booked through a travel agent. $70-160.

Bed & Breakfast Associates Bay Colony, Ltd.

P.O. Box 57166, Babson Park, Boston, 02457-0166
(781) 449-5302; (888) 429-7591
FAX (781) 449-5958; e-mail: info@bnbboston.com
www.bnbboston.com

M138. The Hancock. In Boston's Back Bay, in the heart of Copley Square, this fully updated 64 room inn offers modern amenities, a gracious lobby and a perfect location for business or pleasure. All rooms have private bath, telephone, and individual climate control. This inn has a 24-hour cancellation policy. One night's room rate will be charged for cancellations with less than 24-hours. Private bath, TV, telephone, air conditioning. Handicapped accessibility. Pastry buffet in lobby. Discount on-site parking. $140-155.

M140. Bed and Breakfast afloat. Something special for the nautically inclined. This delightful 40-foot Chris Craft is docked in Boston Harbor. Aft bedroom with private deck. Main salon with sleeper sofa. Complete galley. Private bath, TV, telephone, and air conditioning. Smoke-free. Breakfast foods provided. Weekly rates available. $145-170.

M151. City View Bed and Breakfast. This spirited and congenial hostess offers one guest room in her stylish apartment in a Victorian brownstone. Just one block from the Hynes Convention Center in teh Back Bay, this short, quiet street has a European charm. The master guest room is elegant with its four-poster bed and English-country decor. TV, telephone, air conditioning. Adjacent bath—which is shared only with the hostess. Smoke-free. Self-serve Continental breakfast. $120-140.

M158. Courtyard Apartment. This totally delightful one-bedroom apartment offers romance, charm, and style in an historic Beacon Hill townhouse. Entrance through private courtyard garden. Bedroom, full kitchen, living room with sleeper-sofa, beamed ceiling, pine floors, and huge fireplace. Private bath, TV, VCR, private telephone line. Smoke-free. Breakfast foods provided. $150-200.

M162. Century House. This turn-of-the century Romanesque-style inn offers eight finely appointed suites on four floors. It is near

7 No smoking; 8 Children welcome; 9 Social drinking allowed; 10 Tennis nearby; 11 Swimming nearby; 12 Golf nearby; 13 Skiing nearby; 14 May be booked through a travel agent; 15 Handicapped accessible.

Bed & Breakfast Associates Bay Colony, Ltd. (cont.)

Boston's famed Back Bay, Copley Square, Fenway Park, Longwood Medical area, as well as Boston University and MIT. Attention to detail is evident throughout the inn, from the magnificent parlor to the individual decor of each gracious suite. Guest comfort is always a priority. Each suite offers a fireplace, air conditioning, comfortable work area, two-line telephone, voice mail, fax/data line, wet bar, refrigerator, and entertainment center with large TV. Two guest suites are offered on the ground level with few stairs. Private bath. Smoke-free. Continental buffet breakfast.Free off-street parking. $169-279.

M163. Kenmore Inn. Set on a quiet, tree-lined street adjacent to Kenmore Square and Boston University, this elegant four-story brownstone was built in 1896. The property has been lovingly maintained as a private residence and all original architectural details have been preserved. Along with major restoration work in 1998, private baths have been added for all guest rooms. Traditional decor. TV, telephone, and air conditioning. Smoke-free. Continental Breakfast. $120-170.

M225. Whittlesey House. This South End Victorian has been impeccably restored and offers two floors of exquisite guest space including two well-appointed guest rooms, two full baths, a sitting room and kitchen with private entrance and parking ($15). This can be rented as one unit or to two separate parties. The hostess serves a delightful breakfast daily in the elegant dining room she has reserved for exclusive use by her bed and breakfast guests. Private bath, TV, VCR, telephone, and air conditioning. Smoke-free. $99-230.

M228. Back Bay Studio. A garden level suite for those who want the very finest. This grand Victorian townhouse in Boston's desirable Back Bay has been impeccably restored, and a separate entry suite was created to provide deluxe, private accommodations. Features include: a new kitchenette and bath, designer built-ins, TV, telephone, and French doors to a brick patio. Private bath, fireplace, TV, and air conditioning. Smoke-free. Breakfast foods provided. Off-street parking $15. $125-150.

M245. Yvonne's Retreat. On the Fenway, near the Museum of Fine Arts, this delightful one-bedroom apartment provides all the comforts of home. In the heart of the city, guests enjoy a serene setting in this charming, light-filled apartment with a terrific view of the Victory Gardens. The apartment has a full kitchen, separate bedroom , and sleeper-sofa in the living room. Private bath, TV, telephone, and air conditioning in bedroom. Smoke-free. Limited breakfast foods provided. $150-200.

M246. The Artiste. Overlooking the Fenway, this classic Boston apartment building is just a five-minute walk to the Boston Museum of Fine Arts, Fenway Park, and the Isabella Stewart Gardner Museum. Those visiting the Longwood Medical area, Berklee College of Music, Symphony Hall, or the Hynes Convention Center will also find this location very convenient. The guest room is in a condo hosted by a delightful woman. She offers a sunny, immaculate room with glorious views of the surrounding park. The bath is shared with the hostess. TV and air conditioning. Two cats and a golden retriever in residence. Self-serve Continental breakfast. $89-100.

M300. Herbst House. Appleton Street, one of Boston's prettiest residential streets, is just two blocks from historic Copley Square. The hostess offers two beautifully decorated quiet rooms, each with a private en suite bath. A Continental plus breakfast is elegantly served in the dining room. Private bath, TV, air conditioning, and telephone. Smoke-free. $135-165.

M303. On the Park. This bed and breakfast host couple offers a wealth of knowledge about

Boston along with their kind attention to guest needs. They have two pleasant fourth-floor guest rooms which share a bath in the hall. Near Copley Square, the brownstone townhouse is convenient to Boston's tourist and Convention Centers. TV in guest parlor and air conditioning. Smoke-free. Continental breakfast. Two Scotties in residence. $87-105.

M304. Inn on West Newton. This 1868 Victorian brick townhouse is in the historic South End. The inn offers three large, graciously appointed guest rooms. Each room has private en suite bath with shower and tub, central air conditioning, and private telephone with free local calling. One guest room has a fireplace. A comfortable parlor is provided for guests' enjoyment and relaxation. A Continental plus breakfast is offered to guests. TV and VCR. Smoke-free, Free off-street parking. $130-180.

M306. Appleton Studio. In a 19th-century South End townhouse, three blocks from Copley Square, enjoy the privacy and convenience of this small, pleasantly decorated studio apartment with Murphy bed, futon couch, and cooking nook. On one of Boston's prettiest residential streets. Private bath, TV, telephone, and air conditioning. Breakfast foods provided. $99-120.

M323. The Victorian. This historic 1869 brick townhouse is near the Hynes Convention Center and Copley Square. Two pretty second floor guest rooms, each with a decorative fireplace, delightful antiques, and a sitting area where breakfast will be served. Shared bath in hall. TV and air conditioning. Smoke-free. Off-street parking $12. $95-105.

M355. The Aerie. On a quiet street, this South End Victorian townhouse is home to a young, active family who have been lovingly renovating it over the past eight years. On the top floor, they offer a very pleasant guest room with lots of privacy and a private bath in hall. Air conditioning and TV. Smoke-free. Dog and

cat in residence. Continental breakfast served. French spoken. $110-130.

M362. The Apartment Retreat. This private entry suite offers a comfortable home away from home in the South End area near Tremont Street's Restaurant Row. The spacious two-room suite with 11-foot ceilings includes a kitchenette, a private bath, a large living room with a bay window, TV/VCR, air conditioning. Smoke-free. Limited breakfast foods provided. $135-155.

M365. Braddock Suite. This host couple offers two apartment units on the ground level of their Victorian townhouse in the South End area near Copley Square. Immaculate, quiet, and convenient for walking around Boston. One studio apartment and a one-bedroom apartment are both available at discounted weekly and monthly rates. Private bath, TV/VCR, air conditioned, private telephone line. Smoke-free. Breakfast foods provided. $137-165.

M366. My Flat on Braddock. A one-bedroom apartment on a quiet street in the South End area near Copley Square. Guests will feel at home in this spotless unit with thoughtful amenities. Large living room and full kitchen. Please inquire about this home's perfume- and chemical-free policy. Private bath, TV/VCR, air conditioning, private telephone line. Smoke-free. Breakfast foods provided. $137-160.

M368. Park View. It is just a short walk to Copley Place from this circa 1864 South End Victorian brownstone set on Montgomery Park, Boston's secret oasis. This pleasant home is a welcome retreat and the warm, relaxed atmosphere is the deliberate creation of this delightful couple. One guest room with view of park and private bath with antique tub and handheld shower. Small front room available for third guest in party ($50). TV and air conditioning. Smoke-free, Cats in residence. Continental breakfast served. $85-105.

7 No smoking; 8 Children welcome; 9 Social drinking allowed; 10 Tennis nearby; 11 Swimming nearby; 12 Golf nearby; 13 Skiing nearby; 14 May be booked through a travel agent; 15 Handicapped accessible.

M370. Ballet Slippers. This hostess, a former instructor with the Boston Ballet, enjoys telling her guests all about her South End neighborhood with its many great restaurants. Her immaculate condo in a Victorian townhouse features collectibles from her worldwide travels along with an appealing mix of antiques, from Early American through Victorian. Bedroom with delightful private parlor (where she will set out guests' breakfast) and private bath in the hall outside the guest room. Set on private, serene Montgomery Park. TV/VCR in parlor, air conditioning, and telephone. Smoke-free. Continental breakfast. $97-107.

M371. Park Suite. These two talented gentlemen have recently created this stylish new space on the garden level of their South End townhouse. A large studio apartment with its own entry through a private neighborhood park features a sitting room, private bath with large soaking tub, kitchen area and a bed in the alcove. Here, designer contemporary decor mixes with antiques. TV, air conditioning, private telephone line. Smoke-free. Limited breakfast foods provided. $140-175.

M460. Bunker Hill View Apartment. This first-floor one-bedroom apartment is in historic Charlestown. It offers a bedroom, full kitchen, dining room, and parlor with working fireplace and a sleeper sofa. The private deck off of the dining room has view of the hostess's lovely summer gardens. Private bath, TV, private telephone line, and air conditioning. Smoke-free. Cats in residence but not in guests' apartment. Breakfast foods provided. Limited on-street parking. Weekly and monthly rates offered. $110-140.

M466. Monument House Apartment. This delightful, ground-level apartment, in Charlestown, offers privacy and space in an 1870s Victorian townhouse near the base of the famed Bunker Hill Monument. This fully furnished apartment offers private entry, an antique bed, a Pullman kitchen, and a cozy living room with sleeper sofa and TV. Private bath, TV, and private telephone line. Smoke-free. Continental breakfast delivered daily. Cat in residence but not in apartment. Weekly and monthly rates offered. $100-130.

M482. The Cupola. The second-floor guest room, with small balcony, is in an 1847 Greek Revival townhouse, in historic Charlestown set on Boston's famed Freedom Trail. The traditionally furnished room has a bed, private entrance, and private en suite bath. TV, telephone, air conditioning. Smoke-free. Continental breakfast served. Cat and dog in residence but not in guest's room. On-street parking. $100-130.

M483. Boston View. In Jamacia Plain, on the west side of Boston, this new townhouse condo has a spotless two-room guest suite with an entertainment center, private bath, bed and sleeper sofa. Five blocks to trolley into downtown. TV, VCR, air conditioning. Smoke-free. Continental breakfast served. Driveway parking. $80-110.

M490. Captain's House Apartment. In East Boston, adjacent to Logan International Airport, this property is in the row of 1844 Victorian Townhouses originally known as "The Captain's Houses." The private suite overlooks the city skyline and Boston Harbor. This clean but modest third-floor accommodation includes a bed, a sitting area with TV and writing desk, a full kitchen and an en suite bath. Nearby public transit. TV, VCR, private telephone line. Smoke-free. Breakfast foods provided. On-street parking. Monthly rates available. $80-110.

Bed & Breakfast Reservations North Shore, Greater Boston, Cape Cod

P.O. Box 600035, Newtonville, 02460
(617) 964-1606; (800) 832-2632
FAX (617) 332-8572; e-mail: info@bbreserve.com
www.bbreserve.com

NOTES: Credit cards accepted: A MasterCard; B Visa; C American Express; D Discover; E Diner's Club; F Other; 2 Personal checks accepted; 3 Lunch available; 4 Dinner available; 5 Open all year; 6 Pets welcome;

46. Bed and Breakfast Afloat. For the adventurous bed and breakfast guest, a 40-foot Chris Craft docked in the heart of downtown Boston's waterfront on Lewis Wharf. Cozy and comfortable with separate bedroom, boat-shower private bath, living room with double futon, TV, VCR, air conditioning, telephone, table/chairs, and galley kitchen. Ample supply of self-serve breakfast foods. Host will cater for special occasions by advanced arrangement. Available May 1 through October 15. No smoking. Thirty-five dollars for each additional person. $145.

68. Garden Bed Breakfast Suite. In Boston's South End neighborhood, designated as a landmark, preserved historic district. Victorian brick row house built in 1860 and owned by an artist has a separate private entrance leading to double Victorian parlor with beautiful painted ceilings, artwork, and antiques. Bedroom, TV, VCR, telephone, private bath, and fully equipped efficiency kitchen, self-serve breakfast, private bath. Twenty dollars for third person on rollaway. No smoking. Children over 12 welcome. $125-140.

93. Beacon Hill Townhouse. Historic brownstone townhouse in the heart of one of Boston's most requested neighborhoods, Beacon Hill. Three guest rooms include a king-size and two twin-size beds, sharing a bath, plus an oversized suite featuring king-size bed, sitting area with double sleeper sofa, TV, and private en suite bath. Rooms have air conditioning. Continental breakfast put out buffet style in fourth-floor sitting room. Walk to everything. Twenty dollars for each additional person in suite. No smoking. $85-120.

113. The Townhouse. A stately Boston Victorian-era brownstone on a lovely tree-lined street. Beautifully appointed and aesthetically decorated by artist host. One lovely guest room with double bed and private bath on second floor. Daytime use of large parlor. Continental breakfast in contemporary kitchen with access to outside deck. Walk to Copley and many tourist sites. No smoking. $115-125.

128. Park Suite. In the heart of Boston's South End/Back Bay neighborhood. Garden level of restored brick row townhouse, private terrace overlooking private park, furnished with antiques and modern classics. Separate bedroom with queen-size bed, private full bath, living room, and well-equipped kitchen. Cable TV, air conditioning, telephone. Self-serve breakfast. Under 10 minute's walk to Copley Place. Twenty dollars for third person on rollaway. Off-season and extended rates. No smoking. Children over 12 welcome. $135-165.

140. Commonwealth Manor. This stately Back Bay building, originally constructed by a prominent Boston family more than 100 years ago during the Victorian era. The elegance and grace of this accommodation reflects the charm of its historic origins. All of the original architectural details remain intact. Commonwealth Manor is perfect for one person, whether here for business or pleasure. Guests are steps to shopping, restaurants, the Hynes Convention Center, and Copley Place. The accommodations feature a small room with beautiful, large detached private bath. Continental breakfast is provided. $120.

148. Kenmore House. An authentic 19th century building, combined with luxurious contemporary amenities. Each over-sized suite is uniquely decorated with large private bath, fireplace, air conditioning, and comfortable sitting area with TV, VCR, CD player. Work areas have direct two-line telephones with voice mail and fax/data capabilities. Other amenities include wet bar, refrigerator. Suites either have city views or views of the Charles River. The accommodations are located in Back Bay, within easy walking distance to shopping and fine restaurants. Continental breakfast is served. No smoking. Rates quoted do not include tax. $169-279.

7 No smoking; 8 Children welcome; 9 Social drinking allowed; 10 Tennis nearby; 11 Swimming nearby; 12 Golf nearby; 13 Skiing nearby; 14 May be booked through a travel agent; 15 Handicapped accessible.

157. Seaport Yacht Bed and Breakfast. Romance and luxurious accommodations await guests on this 58-foot Chris Craft motor yacht in Boston's newly developed Seaport district. Deluxe accommodations feature a master state-room with queen-size bed, private bath and Jacuzzi; plus two additional twin-size rooms which share a bath. The Seaport can be rented as a private bed and breakfast for groups up to six people or guests can select one of the rooms and expect to share the space with other bed and breakfast guests. Inquire about other special amenities available. No smoking. $110-175.

159. Boston Brownstone. This Brownstone Victorian home is in the Back Bay section of Boston, conveniently around the corner from the Charles River, Boston University, and Kenmore Square. It is a five-story brick building with many decorative fireplaces, magnificent original wood flooring, wall paneling and a grand staircase leading to each floor. While the original details and architectural features have been preserved, recent renovations include the addition of modern tile baths. All rooms are nicely appointed with private baths, TV, air conditioning, and in-room telephones. Continental breakfast. No smoking. Open year-round. $120-150.

162. Beacon Hill Inn. At the foot of Beacon Hill, this newly renovated turn-of-the-century building has 46 charming rooms, ranging from single cozy rooms to deluxe two-room suites. All rooms are nicely appointed and all feature private bath, telephones, TV, and air conditioning. Kitchenettes are available in most rooms. Continental breakfast. Within walking distance to many tourist sites, restaurants, small shops, and area hospitals. The Red Line T-stop to Cambridge is just a few minutes away. Reduced rate parking nearby. No smoking. Open year-round. Children over 16 welcome. Seasonal rates. $82-150.

164. East Fens Bed and Breakfast. This bed and breakfast is a brick Victorian brownstone

on a tree-lined street in Boston, close to public transportation and many tourist sites. Walking distance to Symphony Hall, Northeastern, the Prudential Center, Newbury Street, and the Museum of Fine Arts. Many small shops, stores, cafes, and restaurants are in the neighborhood. Guest rooms are immaculate and tastefully decorated with guest comfort and convenience in mind. Each room has TV, air conditioning, and private bath. Continental breakfast. Twenty-five dollars for each additional person. $125.

Host Homes of Boston

P.O. Box 117, Waban Branch, 02468-0001
(617) 244-1308; (800) 600-1308
FAX (617) 244-5156

Ailanthus House. Reminiscent of Victorian days, this brownstone in the historic district is named for its huge shade tree. Friendly host offers two large second-floor guest rooms, each with en suite bath. Two resident cats. Central location, three blocks to Prudential Center, subway, Hynes Convention Center, Copley Square, Back Bay Amtrak. Great neighborhood restaurants. No smoking. Private bath, telephone, and TV. $125.

Back Bay House. Host offers full first floor in 1868 French Academic-style townhouse on quiet street near the Public Garden and Copley Square. Spacious quarters include bedroom with queen-size bed, mirrored hall, comfortable parlor with fireplace, sofa bed, balcony, cable TV, VCR, and kitchen stocked for basic Continental breakfast. Great central location. Walk to Newbury Street cafés and boutiques, Copley Square conference hotels, Hynes Convention Center. No more than two guests at one time and six-night limited stay. No smoking. Private bath, air conditioning, telephone. $160.

Braddock Close. This 1860 Victorian townhouse is on a quiet street. Two light-filled street-level apartments have separate entrances. The one-bedroom apartment has a large living

NOTES: Credit cards accepted: A MasterCard; B Visa; C American Express; D Discover; E Diner's Club; F Other; 2 Personal checks accepted; 3 Lunch available; 4 Dinner available; 5 Open all year; 6 Pets welcome;

room with sofa bed. The other is a spacious studio apartment. Each has a full bath, equipped kitchen stocked for breakfast, air conditioning, TV/VCR, and telephone. Three blocks to Hynes Convention Center, fine shops, subway. Four blocks to Copley Square, Back Bay Amtrak. Walk to Symphony Hall, restaurants. $145.

Bunker Hill House. Uphill from the Mystic River on a narrow street with a coastal Continental feeling, the hosts offer a tasteful bed and breakfast inspired by a prized historic quilt. Two second-floor guest rooms: king-size bed with en suite bath and twin beds with private hall bath. Spacious guest parlor, fireplaced dining room, patio with river view. Quiet, except for tolling church chimes. Children welcome. One mile to central Boston. One block to bus. A resident cat. No smoking. Air conditioning, cable TV, crib, parking. $108.

Coach House. Converted to a private home in 1890, the original structure housed 12 coaches and staff. Here, on a quiet gas-lit street, this host family offers two well-appointed guest rooms with private baths. Resident cat. Near Freedom Trail, hotels, restaurants, Massachusetts General Hospital, and MIT. No smoking. TV. Air conditioned. $160-185.

Copley Close. An 1870 brownstone in quiet area. Guest apartment has large, bright bedroom with garden view. Full bath. Comfortable living room with cable TV/VCR, air conditioning, telephone. Kitchen stocked for breakfast. Street-level entrance. Note: guests must maintain chemical-free environment—no smoking, strong perfumes, or sprays. Three blocks from Hynes Convention Center and Prudential Center, Copley Place, Back Bay, Amtrak, subway. $145.

1829 Federal. Brick townhouse with fan doorway. Recent renovation combines modern conveniences with early charm. Spacious third-floor guest suite with bath, sofa bed, and

view. Two fourth-floor rooms share bath and TV room. Near Boston Common, Faneuil Hall, antique shops, MIT, and subway. Air conditioned. TV. No smoking. $90-135.

Near Faneuil Hall. Boston's past and present meet in this colorful Faneuil Hall and Quincy Market area. Host's fifth- and sixth-floor walkup has brick-and-beam decor and balcony. Spacious guest room with double bed, skylights, and private bath. Subway two blocks away. Walk to harbor hotels, Freedom Trail, financial center, and restaurants. TV. Air conditioned. No smoking. $94.

On the Avenue. Boston Common, Copley Place, convention hotels, and the subway are steps away from 19th-century ambiance in private professional club. Dining room; guest parlor. Three spacious doubles have telephone and private bath. Four small singles share two baths. Rollaway: $25. Air conditioning, TV, elevator. $130.

On the Park. This 1865 Victorian bowfront in a historic district features antiques and authentic decor. Two fourth-floor guest rooms share a bath. Resident dogs. Four blocks to Copley Square, Hynes Convention Center, Back Bay Orange Line, and Amtrak. No smoking. Air-conditioned. $87.

Two Fountains. Amid the Victorian brownstones (circa 1859) facing a central mall, this home retains the 19th-century decor of spacious rooms, molded ornamental ceilings, and wood detail. Three guest rooms; two at street-level share hall bath. The third room shares host's bath. Guests welcome in parlor and garden. Great restaurants around the corner. Back Bay, Copley Square, Amtrak, subway six blocks away. Air conditioned. TV. Telephone. No smoking. $95.

Victorian Bowfront. Brick townhouse, circa 1869, in historic neighborhood boasts the era's high ceilings, carved wood detail, and marble

7 No smoking; 8 Children welcome; 9 Social drinking allowed; 10 Tennis nearby; 11 Swimming nearby; 12 Golf nearby; 13 Skiing nearby; 14 May be booked through a travel agent; 15 Handicapped accessible.

fireplaces. Two second-floor guest rooms share a bath. City Room has TV. Country Room has striking wall mural and basin. Breakfast is served in rooms. Resident dog and cat. Central location. Walk three blocks to convention center and subway. No smoking. Air conditioned. Telephone. $95.

Oasis Guest House

22 Edgerly Road, 02115
(617) 267-2262; FAX (617) 267-1920
e-mail: oasisgh@tiac.net
www.oasisgh.com

Two renovated Back Bay townhouses with color TV, telephones, central air, and private baths. Within walking distance of restaurants, museums, and points of interest. This is a great in-town location near the Hynes Convention Center. Enjoy the outside decks. Parking. Fine lodging accommodations, since 1982, in the heart of the city for a price much less than at major hotels. Most of the guests are repeats and referrals. Call, fax, or e-mail for more information. Discounted winter rates.

Rooms: 16 (11 PB; 5 SB) $69-109
Continental Breakfast
Credit Cards: A, B, C
Notes: 5, 7, 9, 14

BOURNE

Bed & Breakfast Cape Cod

P.O. Box 1312, Orleans, 02653
(508) 255-3824; (800) 541-6226
FAX (508) 240-0599
e-mail: info@BedandBreakfastCapeCod.com
www.BedandBreakfastCapeCod.com

BOU 01. Built in 1900, in keeping with the Victorian tradition, this home sits on high ground overlooking the Cape Cod Canal. Watch the ships going through the canal from the bedroom. There are two bedrooms both with double beds and a shared bath. The rooms are rented to only one party at a time to ensure a private bath. There are activities galore within easy reach to this home: the famous Cape Cod Canal bike trail, fine beaches, Falmouth and the island ferries, Sandwich and the Heritage Plantation. This is a charming and lovingly restored home. Seasonal rates. $75-120.

BREWSTER (CAPE COD)

Bed & Breakfast Cape Cod

P.O. Box 1312, Orleans, 02653
(508) 255-3824; (800) 541-6226
FAX (508) 240-0599
e-mail: info@BedandBreakfastCapeCod.com
www.BedandBreakfastCapeCod.com

BRE 01. A most extraordinary house in the Captain's town of Brewster. This Cape contemporary home is nestled among the pines in the heart of Brewster. This home offers a decor of vivid antique collections from around the world. There are two very private guest rooms each with a spacious private bath. Both rooms have sliding doors that open onto private patios. Enter this amazing home with own private entrance or use the main entrance. One and one-third miles to a Cape Cod Bay Beach, one mile to Route 6A, the Captain's Highway, one-fourth of a mile to the Cape Cod Bike trail. Very romantic. Seasonal rates. $85-115.

The Bramble Inn & Restaurant

2019 Main Street, 02631
(508) 896-7644

Two antique buildings in the heart of the historic district lovingly restored to reflect a bygone era. All eight rooms have private baths and air conditioning. Chef-owned nationally acclaimed restaurant with five intimate dining rooms, candlelight, antiques, and fresh flowers. Prix fixe four-course dinners by reservation. House specialties include rack of lamb and native seafoods presented with an innovative air. "Dining at its innovative best"—*New York Times*, 1997. Children eight and older welcome.

The Bramble Inn

Hosts: Cliff and Ruth Manchester
Rooms: 8 (PB) $105-135
Full Breakfast
Credit Cards: A, B, C, D
Notes: 2, 4, 7, 9, 10, 11, 12, 14

Candleberry Inn on Cape Cod

1882 Main Street, 02631
(508) 896-3300

Gracious 250-year-old sea captain's home on two acres of gardens and towering trees in the heart of Brewster's historic district. Walk to fine dining, antique shops, and beach. Nine romantic, spacious guest rooms, all with private baths, some with working fireplaces or Jacuzzi, amid antiques, art, and oriental carpets. Guests are pampered with every amenity, including terry-cloth robes in the rooms, and a full gourmet served breakfast.

Candleberry Inn

Hosts: Gini and David Donnelly
Rooms: 9 (PB) $80-195
Full Breakfast
Credit Cards: A, B, C, D
Notes: 2, 5, 7, 9, 10, 11, 12

Old Sea Pines Inn

2553 Main Street, 02631
(508) 896-6114

Lovely turn-of-the-century mansion, once the Sea Pines School of Charm and Personality for Young Women, now a newly renovated and redecorated country inn. Furnished with antiques, some of the rooms have working fireplaces. On three and one-half acres of land, with a wraparound porch looking out over the lawn, trees, and flowers. Complimentary beverage on arrival. Dinner theater on Sunday evening, June, July, August, and September. Children over eight welcome.

Hosts: Stephen and Michele Rowan
Rooms: 18 (PB) $65-125
Full Breakfast
Credit Cards: A, B, C, D, E
Notes: 2, 5, 7, 9, 10, 11, 12, 14, 15

Old Sea Pines Inn

BROOKLINE

Bed & Breakfast Associates Bay Colony, Ltd.

P.O. Box 57166, Babson Park, Boston, 02457-0166
(781) 449-5302; (888) 429-7591
FAX (781) 449-5958; e-mail: info@bnbboston.com
www.bnbboston.com

M646. Longwood Suite. Next to the Longwood Medical Area (Children's, Brigham and

---

Women's and Dana Farber Hospitals), this small suite with double bed is especially suited to stays of one week or longer. You will enjoy the convenience of a kitchenette and private bath on the first floor of this grand Victorian home. Weekly and monthly rates available. $94-104.

Bed & Breakfast Reservations North Shore, Greater Boston, Cape Cod

P.O. Box 600035, Newtonville, 02460
(617) 964-1606; (800) 832-2632
FAX (617) 332-8572; e-mail: info@bbreserve.com
www.bbreserve.com

104. The Tree House. Brick townhouse on a lovely tree-lined street in Brookline, with short walk to public transportation. Easy access to Boston. Off-street parking included. Bright and sunny living room, dining area with access to outside deck. Great Continental plus breakfast. Three guest rooms with TV, air conditioning. One room with private bath and two rooms sharing a bath. Two resident Siamese cats. No smoking. $65-90.

154. Babcock Place. An elegant Queen Anne Victorian era home, built in 1897. A short walking distance to the Commonwealth Avenue, Green Line (B Train) for an easy commute to Boston. Also within walking distance to Coolidge Corner, with its wide variety of ethnically-diverse restaurants, small shops, major bookstores, and a wonderful movie house. Every room of this stately home welcomes guests with a charm and grace that only vintage homes can provide. Three elegantly furnished guest rooms: all have private en suite baths, TV, telephones, and decorative fireplaces. The suite has two rooms and a separate sitting room. Continental breakfast. $115-140.

166. The Inn at Coolidge Corner. A four-story brick brownstone, on a quiet side street in the Coolidge Corner section of Brookline, offers deluxe accommodations at affordable prices,

with easy access to Boston, area colleges, and medical centers. Guest rooms are spacious and feature air conditioning, TV, telephones. Most rooms have private baths; some have kitchenettes. Continental breakfast. Families with children are welcome. The inn has Port-a-cribs for infants. Fifteen dollars per additional person in room. Off-street parking is provided at $5 per night. Premium rates apply during special events. No smoking. $99-139.

The Bertram Inn

The Bertram Inn

92 Sewall Avenue, 02446
(617) 566-2234; (800) 295-3822
FAX (617) 277-1887; www.bertraminn.com

Come home to Victorian elegance at a 90-year-old house in a quiet neighborhood only 10 minutes by subway from central Boston. Freshly restored to its original splendor using period furniture and antiques, the inn boasts working fireplaces, a large front porch, rose garden, and a commons breakfast room with complimentary Continental plus breakfast and afternoon tea. Each of the 14 unique rooms includes cable TV, telephone, and air conditioning. A variety of shops and fine restaurants is only a stroll's distance away. Off-street parking included. Children over seven-years-old are welcome.

Host: Bryan Austin
Rooms: 14 (PB) $84-219
Continental Breakfast
Credit Cards: A, B, C
Notes: 5, 6, 7, 9, 14

NOTES: Credit cards accepted: A MasterCard; B Visa; C American Express; D Discover; E Diner's Club; F Other; 2 Personal checks accepted; 3 Lunch available; 4 Dinner available; 5 Open all year; 6 Pets welcome;

Host Homes of Boston

P.O. Box 117, Waban Branch, Boston, 02468-0001
(617) 244-1308; (800) 600-1308
FAX (617) 244-5156

Beacon Street Victorian. An 1890 restored Victorian townhouse. Second-floor guest room (two-person limit) with private bath. Breakfast in spacious dining room with fireplace, comfortable sitting area. Green Line-C trolley outside door. Fifteen minute ride direct to Back Bay, Hynes Convention Center, Copley Square, Boston University, and Boston Common. Walk to restaurants. No smoking. TV. Air conditioning. Parking available. $95.

Gardener's Cottage. Serenity, convenience, and comfort in this two story apartment. Enter through a spotless, fully equipped kitchen into the living room with broad windows facing the garden. Upstairs is bedroom with queen-size bed, study nook, and full private bath. Hosts provide food for Continental breakfast. Near Boston College, Longwood medical area, shops, restaurants. Green Line-D into the Back Bay four to five blocks away. No smoking. Air conditioning, TV, parking, and telephone. $135.

Studio Apartment. Colonial home (1620 Salem house replica) on quiet cul-de-sac offers above-ground basement room with sofa, galley kitchen, patio, private bath, and private entrance. Choice of breakfast on tray or self-serve. Five blocks to Green Line-C. Ten minutes to Copley Square. TV. Air conditioning. No smoking. $81-90.

BROOKLINE HILLS

Host Homes of Boston

P.O. Box 117, Waban Branch, Boston, 02468-0001
(617) 244-1308; (800) 600-1308
FAX (617) 244-5156

The Tree House. Meg's modern townhouse with traditional decor has a sweeping view from the glass-walled living room and deck. Three second-floor guest rooms share a bath. Also a queen room with air conditioning and private bath. Two Siamese cats. Near Back Bay, Boston College, and Boston University. Ten minutes to Hynes Convention Center via Green Line-C and D (three blocks). Private bath. TV. No smoking. $75-90.

BUZZARDS BAY

Salt Winds Bed & Breakfast

4 Little Bay Lane, 02532
(508) 743-4665

Salt Winds Bed and Breakfast is in a small private home, one mile from the Bourne Bridge and Cape Cod Canal. The quiet side street on a beautifully landscaped lot borders on cranberry bogs, with a wide variety of birds and other wildlife. Just minutes away from all the points of interest that make Cape Cod such a special place to visit. Two tastefully decorated rooms share a bath and in-ground pool provides relaxation and enjoyment.

Hosts: Richard and JoAnn Jensen
Rooms: 2 (SB) $75-85
Full Breakfast
Credit Cards: None
Notes: 2, 5, 7, 10, 11, 12

CAMBRIDGE

Bed & Breakfast Associates Bay Colony, Ltd.

P.O. Box 57166, Babson Park, Boston, 02457-0166
(781) 449-5302; (888) 429-7591
FAX (781) 449-5958; e-mail: info@bnbboston.com
www.bnbboston.com

M800. L'il Abner House. This circa 1910 stucco home belonged to *L'il Abner* cartoonist Al Capp in the 1960s. This comfortable, antiques-filled bed and breakfast on a quiet residential street in Cambridge offers two spacious rooms on the third floor, each with five

---

7 No smoking; 8 Children welcome; 9 Social drinking allowed; 10 Tennis nearby; 11 Swimming nearby; 12 Golf nearby; 13 Skiing nearby; 14 May be booked through a travel agent; 15 Handicapped accessible.

windows. The Studio is furnished with antique brass beds. The second room has a working fireplace. Both have comfortable sitting areas with a sofa and TV. Both share a modern bath, with a marble sink and shower/tub combination. Parking is available, either on the street with visitor permit, or in the garage. Continental breakfast. $100.

M806. University House. Walk to MIT or pick up the Central Square Red Line to Harvard University. This immaculate little house is managed by the hostess, who lives nearby. She maintains two guest rooms, kitchen, dining area, and spacious living room with fireplace for her bed and breakfast guests. This lovely house can be rented by the room or the whole house. Additional futon available. Parking in driveway. $95-120.

M835. The Writer's Corner. A pleasant apartment with one guest room just outside Harvard Square across from the Charles River shoreline. The delightful hostess will share her third-floor apartment with visitors to Harvard and other Cambridge locations. Excellent quality, firm sofa bed, shared bath. $99-120.

A Bed & Breakfast in Cambridge

1657 Cambridge Street, 02138-4316
(617) 868-7082; (800) 795-7122
FAX (617) 876-8991
e-mail: DoanePerry@compuserve.com
www.cambridgebnb.com

Affordable elegance in 1897 house, great beds, fresh flowers, home-baked specialties, homemade jams, afternoon tea, off-street parking, cable TV, telephones in rooms, air conditioning. Hospitable hosts speak French and German. A full fancy Continental plus breakfast served.

Rooms: 3 (SB) $75-190
Continental Breakfast
Credit Cards: A, B, C
Notes: 2, 5, 7, 11, 14

Harding House

288 Harvard Street, 02139
(617) 876-2888; FAX (617) 497-0953
e-mail: reserve@irvinghouse.com
www.irvinghouse.com

Guests will like the style and grace of this 1860s Victorian. Spacious guest rooms include a queen-size bed and private bath, TV, telephone, and air conditioning. Enjoy the Continental plus breakfast in the sunny dining room. Harding House is large enough to let guests be and small enough to make guests feel at home. In mid-Cambridge, guests will find Harvard Square, MIT, or Boston easy to get to by foot or by T. Limited parking available.

Host: Jane Jones
Rooms: 14 (PB) $85-195
Continental Breakfast
Credit Cards: A, B, C, D, E
Notes: 2, 5, 7, 8, 15

Host Homes of Boston

P.O. Box 117, Waban Branch, Boston, 02468-0001
(617) 244-1308; (800) 600-1308
FAX (617) 244-5156

Blue Hawthorne. This 100-year-old Victorian home off Brattle Street is a quiet oasis near bustling Harvard Square. The host offers one first-floor guest room with twin beds, private bath, telephone, and TV. Shady side garden. Three blocks to the square, Red Line, Charles Hotel, restaurants, and shops. Air conditioning. TV. No smoking. $95.

Cambridge Suite. This large home, circa 1855, is on a quiet road only three blocks from bustling Harvard Square. The first-floor guest suite has a sitting room with sofa and desk and private bath. Breakfast served in the dining room. Near William James Hall and law school. Red Line three blocks. TV. Telephone with answering machine. Parking available. Air conditioning. No smoking. $115.

Near Harvard Square. Just a seven-minute walk to the square, Harvard Yard, Brattle

NOTES: Credit cards accepted: A MasterCard; B Visa; C American Express; D Discover; E Diner's Club; F Other; 2 Personal checks accepted; 3 Lunch available; 4 Dinner available; 5 Open all year; 6 Pets welcome;

Street, and Red Line. Quiet, shady location. European decor. Coffee ground fresh for breakfast. Private first-floor guest room with shared bath. Air conditioning. TV. $89.

True Victorian. Host's Victorian jewel sits on a quiet hill near Massachusetts Avenue between Harvard and Porter Squares. Three second-floor guest rooms. Guest rooms are air conditioned. Only four guests at a time, except families. Hearty breakfast in sunny kitchen, often self-serve on weekdays. Red Line and train at Porter Square two blocks. TV. No smoking. $79-89.

Wit and Wisdom. Tucked between Harvard and Porter Square near the Radcliffe Quad, this bright bed and breakfast is ideal for visiting academics. Guest room has large desk over-looking the courtyard and one twin-size bed. Guest shares host's bathroom. Five-minute walk to subway, observatory, law school. Near restaurants and shops. No smoking. Air conditioning. Permit parking. Single occupancy. $75.

Prospect Place

112 Prospect Street, 02139
(617) 864-7500; (800) 769-5303
FAX (617) 576-1159

An elegant Italianate bed and breakfast built in 1866 and in the center of Cambridge near Harvard and MIT, just across the river from Boston. Owned by the same family for over 100 years until 1994. Period details abound, from classic archways to marble fireplaces and cut-glass windows. Eclectically furnished in wonderful antiques; two grand pianos grace the spacious parlor. Complete breakfast served in the Victorian dining room. Early American history, a variety of museums, world-class universities, and musical concerts are all within a few minutes of the front door.

Hosts: Eric and Judy Huenneke
Rooms: 3 (1 PB; 2 SB) $80-125
Full Breakfast
Credit Cards: B
Notes: 2, 5, 7, 8, 14

CENTERVILLE

Adam's Terrace Gardens Inn

539 Main Street, 02632
(508) 775-4707 (phone/FAX)

Beautiful historic captain's home, circa 1835. Entirely renovated, the eight bedrooms are very nice and airy, all equipped with cable TV. Breakfasts are served outside on the screened porch or in the dining room. Specialties are quiches and crêpes served with fresh fruits. Fresh flowers. One-half mile to the beach on Cape Cod. Mobil- and AAA-approved. Seasonal rates.

Rooms: 8 (5 PB; 3 SB) $85-110
Full Breakfast
Credit Cards: A, B, D
Notes: 2, 5, 8, 9, 11, 12, 14

Bed & Breakfast Cape Cod

P.O. Box 1312, Orleans, 02653
(508) 255-3824; (800) 541-6226
FAX (508) 240-0599
e-mail: info@BedandBreakfastCapeCod.com
www.BedandBreakfastCapeCod.com

CEN 03. In the center of olde Centerville sits a lovely Victorian Colonial built in 1850 that has been a bed and breakfast for more than 65 years. Very close to famous Craigville Beach on the warm waters of Nantucket Sound and two blocks to the best homemade ice cream on Cape Cod. There are five rooms and a guest suite with a parlor for guests on the first floor and a suite for families. Rooms are decorated with antiques, wicker, and canopied beds. A lovely bed and breakfast with lots of history. Weekly rates available for one apartment. $90-110.

The Long Dell Inn

436 South Main Street, 02632
(508) 775-2750; (800) THE DELL
e-mail: thelongdellinn@hotmail.com
www.longdellinn.com

Nestled in the heart of "olde" Centerville sits, a lovely Victorian inn built in 1850. This inn has

7 No smoking; 8 Children welcome; 9 Social drinking allowed; 10 Tennis nearby; 11 Swimming nearby; 12 Golf nearby; 13 Skiing nearby; 14 May be booked through a travel agent; 15 Handicapped accessible.

been a guest house for more than 65 years. There are six rooms all with private baths, along with a romantic suite tucked away in our carriage house. Famous Craigville Beach, on the warm waters of Nantucket Sound is just a short stroll away. Two blocks away is the best homemade ice cream on Cape Cod. A quaint inn with lots of history. Continental plus breakfast. Children over 10 welcome.

Hosts: Sandy Jones and Sean Fitzgerald
Rooms: 7 (PB) $99-139
Continental Breakfast
Credit Cards: A, B
Notes: 2, 5, 7, 9, 10, 11, 12

On the Pond Bed & Breakfast

160 Huckins Neck Road, 02632
(508) 775-0417; (401) 454-0246 (off season)
e-mail: onthepondb@aol.com
www.allcapecod.com/onthepond

"Come to our lakefront mid-Cape Cod inn for an unforgettable vacation." Boat, swim, fish, enjoy the deck or sauna or "veg out" watching the latest movies on cable TV/VCR. Suite with living room, refrigerator, and one or two bedrooms (queen- or twin-size beds). All-you-can-eat gourmet breakfast served on sun deck or in glass-walled dining room with great

On the Pond

views of lake. Close to beaches, tennis, golf, shopping, movies, and ferries to Nantucket and Martha's Vineyard.

Hosts: Dotty and Don Horowitz
Rooms: 2 (PB) $60-125
Full Breakfast
Credit Cards: A, B
Notes: 2, 5, 7, 8, 9, 10, 11, 12, 14

CHATHAM (CAPE COD)

Bed & Breakfast Cape Cod

P.O. Box 1312, Orleans, 02653
(508) 255-3824; (800) 541-6226
FAX (508) 240-0599
e-mail: info@BedandBreakfastCapeCod.com
www.BedandBreakfastCapeCod.com

CHA 02. Just around the corner from the Chatham Lighthouse and short walk to one of the Cape's most beautiful beaches this lovely restored antique home represents Cape Cod of yesteryear. There are three guest bedrooms with private baths on the second floor. Relax in an old-fashioned parlor or on a beautiful screened-in porch overlooking meticulous gardens while smelling the salt air. $95.

The Bradford of Chatham

26 Cross Street, P.O. Box 750, 02633
(508) 945-1030; (800) 562-4667
FAX (508) 945-9652
e-mail: info@bradfordinn.com
www.bradfordinn.com

Set like a jewel in the center of town, the Bradford captures the essence of Chatham. This lovely, two-acre retreat of gardens and tranquility offers a variety of accommodations in its collection of nine historic houses, creating a "village within a village." Newly renovated, all rooms have private bath, air conditioning, TV/VCR, telephone, and many offer fireplaces and whirlpools. Begin the days of exploration and relaxation with a complimentary Continental breakfast served in the cozy breakfast room overlooking the outdoor heated swimming pool. Steps away from the shops, gal-

NOTES: Credit cards accepted: A MasterCard; B Visa; C American Express; D Discover; E Diner's Club; F Other; 2 Personal checks accepted; 3 Lunch available; 4 Dinner available; 5 Open all year; 6 Pets welcome;

leries, restaurants, theater, golf, and, of course, the beautiful beaches.

Host: Sharon Loeffler
Rooms: 34 (PB) $95-285
Continental Breakfast
Credit Cards: A, B, C, D
Notes: 7, 9, 10, 11, 12, 14

Carriage House

Carriage House Inn

407 Old Harbor Road, 02633
(508) 945-4688; (800) 355-8868
FAX (508) 945-8909
e-mail: carriageh@capecod.net
www.capecodtravel.com/carriagehouse

Charming traditional cape home tastefully decorated and furnished with antiques and family pieces. Six bright and airy guest rooms feature private baths and air conditioning. Carriage house rooms offer fireplaces, private entrances, and outside sitting areas. Fireplaced living room with piano, spacious grounds, lovely flowers. Home-baked full breakfast served. Guest pantry stocked with beverages and homemade cookies. Easy walk to village attractions. Beach towels and chairs available.

Hosts: Patty and Dennis O'Neill
Rooms: 6 (PB) $95-180
Full Breakfast
Credit Cards: A, B, C, D
Notes: 2, 5, 7, 9, 10, 11,12, 14

Chatham Wayside Inn

512 Main Street, P.O. Box 685, 02633
(508) 945-5550; (800) 391-5734
FAX (508) 945-3407; e-mail: info@waysideinn.com
www.waysideinn.com

Beautifully appointed guest rooms, all with private bath, air conditioning, TV/VCR, and telephone; many offering fireplaces, whirlpool tubs, private balconies, and terraces. Heated outdoor pool, full-service restaurant and pub, with fireside and patio dining. Adjacent golf, a stroll to the sea. Families welcomed. In the heart of Chatham's picturesque district historic district, the Inn continues to be a perfect starting point for all the varied activities on the Cape. Quiet, comfortable elegance, and classic hospitality await. Come begin an old tradition.

Host: Jennifer Butler
Rooms: 56 (PB) $95-350
Full and Continental Breakfast
Credit Cards: A, B, C, D
Notes: 3, 4, 5, 7, 8, 9, 10, 11, 12, 14, 15

The Cyrus Kent House Inn

63 Cross Street, 02633
(800) 338-5368

Comfortably elegant, the inn is an award-winning restoration of a 19th-century sea captain's mansion. Rooms are large, bright, and airy, furnished with antiques. Private baths, telephone, and TV. On a quiet lane in the quaint seaside village of Chatham, a historic district. Excellent restaurants and beaches are within steps. Children over 10 are welcome.

Host: Sharon Mitchell Swan
Rooms: 10 (PB) $80-175
Continental Breakfast
Credit Cards: A, B, C
Notes: 2, 5, 7, 9, 10, 11, 12, 14

The Cyrus Kent House Inn

7 No smoking; 8 Children welcome; 9 Social drinking allowed; 10 Tennis nearby; 11 Swimming nearby; 12 Golf nearby; 13 Skiing nearby; 14 May be booked through a travel agent; 15 Handicapped accessible.

Elaine's Bed & Breakfast Selections

4987 Kingston Road, Elbridge, NY 13060
(315) 689-2082 (call between 10:30 A.M.–7:00 P.M.)

A perfectly lovely 1930s house with eight guest rooms. All rooms have full modern private baths, air conditioning, and TV. Some rooms have VCRs. Walk around the corner to shops. The ocean is a two-minute drive. Gourmet Continental breakfast. Open year-round. Smoke-free. Children 14 and older welcome. Seasonal rates.

Moses Nickerson House Inn

364 Old Harbor Road, 02633
(508) 945-5859; (800) 628-6972
FAX (508) 945-7087; e-mail: tmnhi@capecod.net
www.capecodtravel.com/mosesnickersonhouse

Quiet, elegant, romantic. Built in 1839 by whaling captain Moses Nickerson, this small inn has seven individually decorated guest rooms featuring canopied beds, fireplaces, oriental rugs, private baths, and air conditioning. TV, telephones. Glass-enclosed breakfast room. Walk to the quaint village of Chatham with its fine shops, galleries, and restaurants, or turn right at the end of the driveway and walk to the beach or fishing pier. AAA-rated. Children over 12 welcome.

Hosts: George and Linda Watts
Rooms: 7 (PB) $95-189
Full Breakfast
Credit Cards: A, B, C, D
Notes: 2, 5, 7, 9, 10, 11, 12, 14

Moses Nickerson House Inn

The Old Harbor Inn

The Old Harbor Inn

22 Old Harbor Road, 02633
(508) 945-4434; (800) 942-4434
FAX (508) 945-7665; e-mail: brazohi@capecod.net

Casual elegance invites guests to stay. Eight guest rooms decorated in English country style with designer fabric and linen are a perfect setting to relax. Each room has twins, queen- or king-size bed with full private bath in each room. Some rooms have fireplaces, TVs, and more. A short walk to historic seaside village of Chatham. Explore…Discover…be Pampered! Children 14 and older welcome. Inquire about special off-season pricing.

Hosts: Judy and Ray Braz
Rooms: 8 (PB) $109-229
Continental Breakfast
Credit Cards: A, B
Notes: 2, 5, 7, 10, 11, 12, 14

Port Fortune Inn

201 Main Street, 02633
(800) 750-0792; FAX (508) 945-0792
e-mail: porfor@capecod.net
www.capecod.net/portfortune

Two beautifully restored historic buildings 100 yards from ocean in Old Village near lighthouse. Fourteen elegantly decorated rooms, some with ocean views, all with queen-size beds, private baths, air conditioning, telephones. Many antiques, four-poster beds. Delicious breakfast in ocean-view dining room. Two graciously appointed common rooms, breezy patio surrounded by colorful

Port Fortune Inn

gardens. Open all year. Children 10 and older welcome.

Rooms: 14 (PB) $90-170
Continental Breakfast
Credit Cards: A, B, C
Notes: 5, 7, 9, 10, 11, 12, 14

CHESTNUT HILL

Bed & Breakfast Reservations North Shore, Greater Boston, Cape Cod

P.O. Box 600035, Newtonville, 02460
(617) 964-1606; (800) 832-2632
FAX (617) 332-8572; e-mail: info@bbreserve.com
www.bbreserve.com

7. The Suite at Chestnut Hill. Within Boston's city limits, about eight miles outside the downtown area. This is a private separate suite nestled in a neighborhood of elegant homes. Just a seven-minute walk to public transportation for easy access to Boston. Suite is very tastefully decorated, with many extras, including skylights, dining area, efficiency kitchen, TV, air conditioning, telephone, sitting area, daily maid service. Host provides self-serve breakfast. Queen-size bed with couches converting to two singles to comfortably sleep four. Parking included. Twenty dollars for each additional person in room. No smoking. $100-115.

CONCORD

Bed & Breakfast Reservations North Shore, Greater Boston, Cape Cod

P.O. Box 600035, Newtonville, 02460
(617) 964-1606; (800) 832-2632
FAX (617) 332-8572; e-mail: info@bbreserve.com
www.bbreserve.com

20. The 1775 Colonial Inn. In historic Concord, just 20 miles west of Boston, with easy access from main highways. This is a meticulously restored colonial inn with five guest rooms, all with private baths, color TV, air conditioning, and telephones. Continental buffet breakfast is included. Afternoon tea or sherry is served by the fireplace, in the 200-year-old sitting room. Business support services are available nearby for business travelers. Children over 12 welcome. No smoking. Reduced rates for weekly and monthly stays. $100-115.

Colonel Roger Brown House

1694 Main Street, 01742
(978) 369-9119; (800) 292-1369

This 1775 Colonial home is on the historic register and close to the Concord and Lexington historic districts, 18 miles west of Boston and Cambridge. Five rooms with air conditioning, private baths, cable TV, and telephones. Complimentary beverages at all times. Complimentary use of Concord Fitness Club adjacent to the inn in the restored Damon Mill. Comfortable and cozy atmosphere. Two-bedroom suite with full kitchen and sitting room is also available. Inquire about accommodations for children. Hearty Continental plus buffet breakfast.

Host: Lauri Berlied
Rooms: 5 (PB) $80-120
Suite: $120-160
Continental Breakfast
Credit Cards: A, B, C
Notes: 2, 5, 7, 9, 10, 11, 12, 13, 14

7 No smoking; 8 Children welcome; 9 Social drinking allowed; 10 Tennis nearby; 11 Swimming nearby; 12 Golf nearby; 13 Skiing nearby; 14 May be booked through a travel agent; 15 Handicapped accessible.

Hawthorne Inn

Hawthorne Inn

462 Lexington Road, 01742
(978) 369-5610; FAX (978) 287-4949
www.concord.mass.com

Built circa 1870 on land once owned by Emerson, Hawthorne, and the Alcotts. Alongside the "battle road" of 1775 and within walking distance of authors' homes, battle sites, and Walden Pond. Furnished with antiques, handmade quilts, original artwork, Japanese prints, and sculpture.

Hosts: G. Burch and M. Mudry
Rooms: 7 (PB) $110-215
Continental Breakfast
Credit Cards: A, B, C, D
Notes: 2, 5, 7, 8, 9, 10, 11, 12, 13, 14

COTUIT

Bed & Breakfast Cape Cod

P.O. Box 1312, Orleans, 02653
(508) 255-3824; (800) 541-6226
FAX (508) 240-0599
e-mail: info@BedandBreakfastCapeCod.com
www.BedandBreakfastCapeCod.com

COT 01. The year was 1796 when a wealthy English businessman started construction of this wonderful house. Large rooms, wideboard floors, and a grandeur that is enchanting

are some of its characteristics. Restored several years ago, it is now a welcoming accommodation done in professional style. An inviting parlor with TV, VCR, decks for outside relaxing, and style are apparent as guests walk through the wide halls and rooms. A classic property and beautifully decorated. Seasonal rates. $75-115.

CUMMAQUID (CAPE COD)

The Acworth Inn

4352 Old Kings Highway, P.O. Box 256, 02637
(508) 362-3330; (800) 362-6363

The Acworth Inn sits among the trees along the Old Kings Highway that winds through the historic, unspoiled north side of Cape Cod. The inn offers an opportunity to experience the gracious lifestyle of a bygone era. Built in 1860, it is a classic Cape house, completely renovated and outfitted with charming hand-painted pieces and colorful fabrics. From its central location near Barnstable Harbor one can easily reach all points on the cape, Martha's Vineyard, and Nantucket.

Hosts: Jack and Cheryl Ferrell
Rooms: 5 (PB) $95-185
Full Breakfast
Credit Cards: A, B, C, D
Notes: 2, 5, 7, 9, 10, 11, 12, 14

The Acworth Inn

CUMMINGTON

Cumworth Farm

472 West Cummington Road, 01026
(413) 634-5529

A 200-year-old house with a sugar house and blueberry and raspberry fields on the premises. Pick berries in season. The farm raises sheep and is close to Tanglewood, Smith College, the William Cullen Bryant Homestead, cross-country skiing, and hiking trails. Hot tub. Closed from November 1 to May 1. Lower rate midweek.

Host: Ed McColgan
Rooms: 6 (SB) $75
Full Breakfast
Credit Cards: None
Notes: 2, 7, 8, 9, 10, 11, 12

DENNIS

Bed & Breakfast Cape Cod

P.O. Box 1312, Orleans, 02653
(508) 255-3824; (800) 541-6226
FAX (508) 240-0599
e-mail: info@BedandBreakfastCapeCod.com
www.BedandBreakfastCapeCod.com

DEN 01. This Cape Cod-style house built in 1994 is a short walk to two beaches on Cape Cod Bay, each of which is great for a swim or fishing. The house has two bedrooms, each with private baths, four-poster beds, and cable TV. The decor is beautifully traditional. The rooms are air conditioned for guests' comfort. The Cape Playhouse, several fine restaurants, and shopping are a walk of 10 minutes. There is a suite offering private bath and kitchenette. A weekly rate is available. Seasonal rates. $75-115.

Captain Nickerson Inn

333 Main Street, 02660
(508) 398-5966; (800) 282-1619

Delightful Victorian sea captain's home on a bike path in historic section of Dennis. Comfort-

Captain Nickerson Inn

able front porch is lined with white wicker rockers. Five guest rooms are decorated in period four-poster or white iron queen-size beds and oriental or hand-woven rugs. Cozy terry robes and air conditioning available in all rooms. Breakfast is served in fireplaced dining room. Walk to Indian Lands Trail and the Bass River. Only one-half mile from Cape Cod Bike Trail (22+ miles). Close to shops and good restaurants. No smoking. Children are welcome.

Hosts: Pat and Dave York
Rooms: 5 (3 PB; 2 SB) $65-95
Full Breakfast
Credit Cards: A, B, D
Notes: 2, 7, 8, 9, 10, 11, 12, 14

Isaiah Hall Bed & Breakfast Inn

P.O. Box 1007, 152 Whig Street, 02638
(508) 385-9928; (800) 736-0160
www.isaiahhallinn.com

Enjoy country ambiance and hospitality in the heart of Cape Cod. This lovely 1857 farmhouse is tucked away on a quiet historic side street. Within walking distance of the beach

Isaiah Hall

7 No smoking; 8 Children welcome; 9 Social drinking allowed; 10 Tennis nearby; 11 Swimming nearby; 12 Golf nearby; 13 Skiing nearby; 14 May be booked through a travel agent; 15 Handicapped accessible.

and village shops, restaurants, museums, cinema, and playhouse. Nearby bike trails, tennis, and golf. Comfortably appointed with antiques and orientals. Guest rooms have air conditioning and cable TV. Excellent central location for day trips. Continental plus breakfast is served. Closed mid-October through late April. Children over seven welcome.

Host: Marie Brophy
Rooms: 10 (PB) $95-134
Suite: 1–$156
Continental Breakfast
Credit Cards: A, B, C
Notes: 2, 7, 9, 10, 11, 12, 14

Scargo Manor Bed & Breakfast

909 Main Street, Route 6A, 02638
(508) 385-5534; (800) 595-0034

Elegance on historic Scargo Lake. Beautifully updated 1895 sea captain's home on two and one-half meticulously landscaped acres. Large rooms and suites with king- or queen-size canopied beds and private baths. Large common area with fireplace, TV, and telephone. Continental plus breakfast served in dining room with fireplace or on sun-filled enclosed porch. Nearby beaches, golf, tennis, bike trails, historic sites, restaurants, and the famous Cape Playhouse. Access to all points on Cape Cod. Open April 1 to December 31.

Hosts: Jane and Chuck MacMillin
Rooms: 6 (PB) $80-160
Continental Breakfast
Credit Cards: A, B, C, D
Notes: 2, 7, 10, 11, 12

DENNIS PORT

Bed & Breakfast Cape Cod

P.O. Box 1312, Orleans, 02653
(508) 255-3824; (800) 541-6226
FAX (508) 240-0599
e-mail: info@BedandBreakfastCapeCod.com
www.BedandBreakfastCapeCod.com

DEN 05. Nantucket Sound is just 500 giant steps from this lovely antique Cape Cod home.

Three gracious rooms with private baths and two with fireplaces. Enjoy breakfast and moments after returning from the beach on the flowered-filled patio. $90-150.

"By the Sea"

"By the Sea" Guests

P.O. Box 507, 02639-0006
(508) 398-8685; (800) 447-9202
FAX (508) 398-0334; e-mail: bythesea@capecod.net

A delightful oceanfront bed and breakfast on private beach. Rooms with private baths, color cable TVs, and refrigerators. Continental plus breakfast served on 100-foot glass-screened veranda overlooking Nantucket Sound. Come let the salt air rejuvenate you. Experience the tranquility of a sunset or midnight stroll on the beach, or unwind by a crackling fire. "We offer sea, sand, comfort, and convenience to your heart's content! Won't you be our guest?" Inquire about accommodations for children.

Hosts: Helen and Dino Kossifos
Rooms: 12 (PB) $60-142
Continental Breakfast
Credit Cards: A, B, C, E
Notes: 7, 9, 10, 11, 12

Elaine's Bed & Breakfast Selections

4987 Kingston Road, Elbridge, NY 13060
(315) 689-2082 (call between 10:30 A.M.–7:00 P.M.)

NOTES: Credit cards accepted: A MasterCard; B Visa; C American Express; D Discover; E Diner's Club; F Other; 2 Personal checks accepted; 3 Lunch available; 4 Dinner available; 5 Open all year; 6 Pets welcome;

Right in the center of the south shore of Cape Cod. A very basic air-conditioned private cottage with two twin beds and private shower bath. Table and chairs, refrigerator in Florida room. TV. Outside shower to rinse off sand. Lawn chairs, barbecue, and patio. Private beach access. Excellent biking and recreational area. Great golf nearby as well as all Cape activities. Modest rates—good place for several days' stay.

The Rose Petal Bed & Breakfast

152 Sea Street, Box 974, 02639
(508) 398-8470; e-mail: rosepetl@capecod.net
www.virtualcapecod.com/market/rosepetal/

Picket-fenced gardens surround traditional 1872 New England home in a delightful seaside resort neighborhood. Stroll past century-old houses to a sandy Nantucket Sound beach. Home-baked pastries highlight a full breakfast. A comfortable parlor offers TV, piano, reading. Enjoy queen-size brass beds, antiques, hand-stitched quilts; spacious and bright baths, and air conditioning. Between Hyannis and Chatham, it is convenient to all Cape Cod attractions. AAA three-diamond rating.

Hosts: Dan and Gayle Kelly
Rooms: 3 (2 PB; 1 SB) $59-98
Full Breakfast
Credit Cards: A, B, C
Notes: 5, 7, 8, 9, 10, 11, 12, 14

The Rose Petal

DUXBURY

1803 Windsor House Inn

The 1803 Winsor House Inn

390 Washington Street, 02332
(781) 934-0991; FAX (781) 934-5955
e-mail: winsorhouse@dreamcom.net

Built in 1803 by sea captain Nathaniel Winsor, this charming antique-filled inn is 35 miles south of Boston in the quaint seaside village of Duxbury. The four cozy sunlit bedrooms (two are suites) are complete with private baths, some with canopied beds. Enjoy a casual dinner in the pub, a gourmet dinner in the flower-filled Carriage House, or a romantic evening in the candlelit dining room. Rates do not include tax and are subject to change.

Hosts: David and Patricia O'Connell
Rooms: 4 (PB) $130-210
Full Breakfast
Credit Cards: A, B, C, D
Notes: 2, 4, 5, 7, 8, 9, 10, 11, 12, 14

EASTHAM

Bed & Breakfast Cape Cod

P.O. Box 1312, Orleans, 02653
(508) 255-3824; (800) 541-6226
FAX (508) 240-0599
e-mail: info@BedandBreakfastCapeCod.com
www.BedandBreakfastCapeCod.com

EAS 01. This light-filled attractive guest wing has a high outlook over the marsh with unimpeded view of Cape Cod Bay. Guests' own entrance, private bath, refrigerator, and sitting

7 No smoking; 8 Children welcome; 9 Social drinking allowed; 10 Tennis nearby; 11 Swimming nearby; 12 Golf nearby; 13 Skiing nearby; 14 May be booked through a travel agent; 15 Handicapped accessible.

area with TV and air conditioning. In addition, guests have a deck on which to sit and observe spectacular sunsets. Breakfast is served in the greenhouse or on the deck overlooking the Bay. Three-night minimum. Fifteen dollars for extra person. $115.

The Whalewalk Inn

The Whalewalk Inn

220 Bridge Road, 02642
(508) 255-0617

The welcoming hosts promise an unspoiled environment on outer Cape Cod—one of the country's most beautiful areas. Only minutes by car or bike to beaches, bike trails, or Orleans village. This 1830s home has been restored and creatively decorated with handsome antiques. The 11 guest rooms and five large suites with wet bars are furnished with country antiques, fine linens, and local art. All are air conditioned, have private baths; some have fireplaces. Breakfast and afternoon hors d'oeuvres.

Hosts: Carolyn and Richard Smith
Rooms: 16 (PB) $160-260
Full Breakfast
Credit Cards: A, B, C
Notes: 2, 7, 9, 10, 11, 12, 14

EAST ORLEANS_____

Bed & Breakfast Cape Cod

P.O. Box 1312, Orleans, 02653
(508) 255-3824; (800) 541-6226
FAX (508) 240-0599
e-mail: info@BedandBreakfastCapeCod.com
www.BedandBreakfastCapeCod.com

ORL 06. Experience spectacular views of the Atlantic Ocean and Nauset Beach. Four new, bright and airy guest rooms on the second floor of this splendid home which sits high on a knoll overlooking Nauset Beach. Awaken to a spectacular panoramic view from the window of the surf pounding along the shore or perhaps a passing fishing or sail boat. The rooms offer large private attached baths with tub/shower combination. Large picture windows, cable TV, ceiling fans, and individually controlled heat. A guest living room with refrigerator and two private entrances to guests' quarters. Continental breakfast is offered.

The Farmhouse at Nauset Beach

163 Beach Road, Orleans, 02653
(508) 255-6654

This bed and breakfast is an 1870 Greek Revival historic farmhouse which was once part of a duck farm in East Orleans. One-half mile to beautiful sand dunes and surf of the Atlantic Ocean. Quiet, residential area, 1.6 acres, 90 feet from road. Ocean-view rooms. Gift certificates available. The Standish children, Clark and Florence, are 11th generation descendants of Myles Standish. "Be our guests."

Hosts: The Standishes
Rooms: 8 (PB) $42-110
Continental Breakfast
Credit Cards: A, B
Notes: 2, 5, 8, 9, 10, 11, 12, 14

The Farmhouse

NOTES: Credit cards accepted: A MasterCard; B Visa; C American Express; D Discover; E Diner's Club; F Other; 2 Personal checks accepted; 3 Lunch available; 4 Dinner available; 5 Open all year; 6 Pets welcome;

Ivy Lodge (Guest House)

194 Main Street, Box 1195, 02643-1195
(508) 255-0119

A guest house since 1910, this smoke-free 1864 Greek Revival home is graced with family photos and antiques. A morning wake-up breakfast basket is found outside each guest room door to be enjoyed in the privacy of guest room or under shade trees on the spacious grounds. Midway between ocean and bay beaches in beautiful, historic Orleans on Cape Cod. Shops, restaurants, beaches, and other amenities close by. A two-bedroom detached apartment with nightly and weekly rates is also available. Children welcome in the apartment only.

Hosts: Barbara and David McCormack
Rooms: 3 (PB) $75-85
Continental Breakfast
Credit Cards: None
Notes: 2, 5, 7, 9, 10, 11, 12

Ivy Lodge

Nauset House Inn

143 Beach Road, Box 774, 02643
(508) 255-2195; e-mail: jvessell@capecod.net
www.nausethouseinn.com

The Nauset House Inn is a place where the gentle amenities of life are still observed, a place where sea and shore, orchard and field all combine to create a perfect setting for tranquil relaxation. The Nauset House Inn is ideally near one of the world's great ocean beaches, yet is close to antique and craft shops, restaurants, art galleries, scenic paths, and remote

Nauset House Inn

places for sunning, swimming, and picnicking. Closed November 1 through March 31.

Hosts: Diane and Al Johnson;
Cindy and John Vessella
Rooms: 14 (8 PB; 6 SB) $75-135
Full Breakfast
Credit Cards: A, B, D
Notes: 2, 7, 9, 10, 11, 12

Ship's Knees Inn

186 Beach Road, P.O. Box 756, 02643
(508) 255-1312; FAX (508) 240-1351

A 170-year-old restored sea captain's home; rooms individually appointed with their own Colonial color schemes and authentic antiques. Only a three-minute walk to popular sand-duned Nauset Beach. Swimming pool and tennis on premises. Also available three miles away, overlooking Orleans Cove, are an efficiency and two heated cottages where children of all ages are welcome and smoking is permitted. Children over 12 are welcome at the inn.

Rooms: 22 (11 PB; 11 SB) $45-120
Continental Breakfast
Credit Cards: A, B
Notes: 2, 5, 7, 9, 10, 11, 12, 14

Ship's Knees Inn

7 No smoking; 8 Children welcome; 9 Social drinking allowed; 10 Tennis nearby; 11 Swimming nearby; 12 Golf nearby; 13 Skiing nearby; 14 May be booked through a travel agent; 15 Handicapped accessible.

EDGARTOWN (MARTHA'S VINEYARD)

The Arbor

222 Upper Main Street, P.O. Box 1228, 02539
(508) 627-8137

This turn-of-the-century home was originally built on the adjoining island of Chappaquiddick and was moved by barge to its present location. A short stroll to village shops, fine restaurants, and the bustling activity of Edgartown Harbor, the Arbor is filled with the fragrance of fresh flowers. Peggy will gladly direct visitors to the walking trails, unspoiled beaches, fishing, and all the delights of Martha's Vineyard. Smoking in designated areas only. Children over 12 welcome. Seasonal rates available.

Host: Peggy Hall
Rooms: 10 (8 PB; 2 SB) $120-165
Continental Breakfast
Credit Cards: A, B
Notes: 2, 9, 10, 11, 12

The Arbor

Captain Dexter House of Edgartown

35 Pease's Point Way, P.O. Box 2798, 02539
(508) 627-7289; FAX (508) 627-3328

This historic inn offers both charm and hospitality. Enjoy beautiful gardens. Savor a home-baked Continental plus breakfast and evening apéritif. Relax in a four-poster, lace-canopied bed in a room with a working fireplace. Stroll

Captain Dexter House

to the harbor, town, and restaurants. Bicycle or walk to the beach. Let the innkeepers make a vacation special!

Host: Birdie
Rooms: 11 (PB) $95-300
Continental Breakfast
Credit Cards: A, B, C
Notes: 2, 7, 8, 9, 10, 11, 12, 14

The Edgartown Inn

56 North Water Street, 02539
(508) 627-4794

Historic inn built in 1798 as the home for a whaling captain. Early guests included Daniel Webster, Nathaniel Hawthorne, and Charles Summer. Later, John Kennedy stayed here as a young senator. Completely restored over the

NOTES: Credit cards accepted: A MasterCard; B Visa; C American Express; D Discover; E Diner's Club; F Other; 2 Personal checks accepted; 3 Lunch available; 4 Dinner available; 5 Open all year; 6 Pets welcome;

last 150 years, today it is filled with antiques. Convenient to beaches, harbor, and restaurants. Famous for breakfast, including homemade breads and cakes. Member of the National Trust for Historic Preservation.

Host: Earle Radford
Rooms: 20 (16 PB; 4 SB) $95-195
Full and Continental Breakfast
Credit Cards: None
Notes: 2, 9, 10, 11, 12

Jonathan Munroe House

100 Main Street, P.O. Box 5084, 02539
(508) 627-5536

With its lovely wraparound, columned front porch, the Jonathan Munroe House stands out from the other inns and captain's homes on this stretch of Main Street. Inside the formal parlor has been transformed into a comfortable gathering room with a European flair. Guest rooms are immaculate antique-filled, and dotted with clever details. Many rooms have fireplaces perfect for curling up with an antiquarian book (provided) or match wits over a game of chess (also provided). Breakfast is a gourmet feast served on an outdoor garden patio. "Whatever your needs may be you can be assured that Chip or Sandy will make certain your stay at the Jonathan Munroe House will be relaxing and memorable one."

Host: Sandy Berube
Rooms: 7 (PB)
Full Breakfast
Credit Cards: A, B, C
Notes: 5, 7, 9, 10, 11, 12, 14

Shiverick Inn

5 Pease Point Way, 02539-0640
(508) 627-8441; (800) 723-4292
e-mail: shiverickinn@vineyard.net

In the heart of historic Edgartown on Martha's Vineyard. An elegant and gracious bed and breakfast. This 1840 mansion has fireplaced rooms, air conditioning, private parking, wraparound terrace, private courtyard, afternoon

refreshments. Guests can walk to all activities. If travelling by auto, call (508) 477-8600 for reservations.

Hosts: Marty and Denny Turmelle
Rooms: 10 (PB) $140-325
Continental Breakfast
Credit Cards: A, B, C, D
Notes: 2, 5, 7, 9, 10, 11, 12, 14

ESSEX

Bed & Breakfast Reservations North Shore, Greater Boston, Cape Cod

P.O. Box 600035, Newtonville, 02460
(617) 964-1606; (800) 832-2632
FAX (617) 332-8572; e-mail: info@bbreserve.com
www.bbreserve.com

56. Essex River Inn. Historic 1830 Federal-style inn retaining many of its original features; folding Indian shutters, working fireplaces, and wood carvings. Several porches and balconies overlook salt marsh and Essex River. Seven charming guest rooms, all with private bath, air conditioning, color cable TV, telephone. Spacious penthouse suite features fireplace, efficiency kitchen area, private deck. Walk to restaurants, antique shops, and Woodman's famous "lobster-in-the-rough." Full gourmet breakfast. No smoking. Children 16 and older welcome. Resident cat in common areas. $125-155.

FALMOUTH (CAPE COD)

Bed & Breakfast Cape Cod

P.O. Box 1312, Orleans, 02653
(508) 255-3824; (800) 541-6226
FAX (508) 240-0599
e-mail: info@BedandBreakfastCapeCod.com
www.BedandBreakfastCapeCod.com

FAL 05. Enjoy Cape Cod and take the ferry to Martha's Vineyard from this graceful 100-year-old carriage house and renovated barn.

7 No smoking; 8 Children welcome; 9 Social drinking allowed; 10 Tennis nearby; 11 Swimming nearby; 12 Golf nearby; 13 Skiing nearby; 14 May be booked through a travel agent; 15 Handicapped accessible.

Spacious grounds, surrounded by old shade trees, raspberries, and blueberries. This host home has five beautifully appointed bedrooms with private baths. Spectacular gardens welcome relaxation after a busy day of seaside activities. On a cool night, enjoy a book by the fireplace in the living room library. Seasonal rates. $85-145.

Bed & Breakfast Reservations North Shore, Greater Boston, Cape Cod

P.O. Box 600035, Newtonville, 02460
(617) 964-1606; (800) 832-2632
FAX (617) 332-8572; e-mail: info@bbreserve.com
www.bbreserve.com

84. Falmouth Heights Bed and Breakfast. A short walk to the Martha's Vineyard ferry, pristine beaches, and seaside restaurants. This contemporary bed and breakfast has a large deck and in-ground pool. Each of seven guest rooms, all with private baths, is a colorful work of art, with hand-crafted New England-made furnishings. Comfortable sitting room with fireplace. A delicious breakfast buffet is served in café-style kitchen overlooking deck and pool. $139-159.

Capt. Tom Lawrence House

75 Locust Street, 02540
(508) 540-1445; (800) 266-8139
FAX (508) 457-1790
www.sunsol.com/captaintom/

Beautiful 1861 Victorian, former whaling captain's residence in the historic village of Falmouth. Central air conditioning throughout the whole facility. Comfortable, spacious, corner guest rooms with TVs and refrigerators. Firm beds—some with canopies. Steinway piano and working fireplace. One completely furnished apartment sleeps four. Gourmet breakfast consists of fresh fruit, breads, pancakes made from freshly ground organic grain, and a variety of other delicious specialties. German spoken. Two-night minimum stay.

Capt. Tom Lawrence House

Rooms: 6 (PB) $95-220
Full Breakfast
Credit Cards: A, B
Notes: 2, 9. 10, 11, 12, 14

Grafton Inn

261 Grand Avenue South, 02540
(508) 540-8688; (800) 642-4069
FAX (508) 540-1861; www.graftoninn.com

Cape Cod oceanfront Queen Anne Victorian. Thirty steps to sandy beach. Breathtaking views of Martha's Vineyard. Full gourmet breakfast served at private tables overlooking Nantucket Sound. Complimentary evening wine and cheese. Immaculate accommodations. Thoughtful amenities. Homemade chocolates, fresh flowers, sand chairs, beach

Grafton Inn

NOTES: Credit cards accepted: A MasterCard; B Visa; C American Express; D Discover; E Diner's Club; F Other; 2 Personal checks accepted; 3 Lunch available; 4 Dinner available; 5 Open all year; 6 Pets welcome;

towels. Individual air conditioning and heat. Cable color TV. On bike path. Year-round golf, tennis, deep-sea fishing minutes away. Walk to restaurants, shops, and island ferry. AAA and Mobil three-star rated.

Hosts: Liz and Rudy Cvitan
Rooms: 11 (PB) $95-189
Full Breakfast
Credit Cards: A, B, C
Notes: 7, 9, 10, 11, 12, 14

Hewins House Bed & Breakfast

20 Hewins Street, 02540
(508) 457-4363; (800) 555-4366

At the Hewins House Bed and Breakfast it is the hostess's pleasure to share one of Falmouth's historic homes with guests. Through the years this home has been lovingly preserved. Step back in time and enjoy comfortable elegance and delicious homemade breakfasts. Walk to restaurants, shopping, island ferries, beaches, and bus station from the convenient location. Once guests have stayed at the Hewins House, they will want to return again and again.

Host: Virginia Price
Rooms: 3 (PB) $85-105
Full Breakfast
Credit Cards: A, B, C, D
Notes: 2, 7, 9, 10, 11

The Inn at One Main Street

One Main Street, 02540
(508) 540-7469; (888) 281-6246
e-mail: innat1main@aol.com

This elegant 1892 Victorian is in Falmouth's historic district, where the road to Woods Hole begins. The inn is within walking distance to beaches, bike path, restaurants, shops, and ferry shuttle. Enjoy a romantic getaway in one of six freshly decorated rooms, each with private bath. Whatever wishes guests may have, the hosts will do their very best to ensure an enjoyable stay and send guests home feeling fully refreshed.

The Inn at One Main Street

Hosts: Ilona Cleveland and Jeanne Dahl
Rooms: 6 (PB) $95-130
Full Breakfast
Credit Cards: A, B, C, D
Notes: 2, 5, 7, 8, 9, 10, 11, 12, 14

Mostly Hall Bed & Breakfast Inn

27 Main Street, 02540
(508) 548-3786; (800) 682-0565
FAX (508) 457-1572; e-mail: mostlyhl@cape.com
www.mostlyhall.com

Romantic 1849 southern plantation-style Cape Cod home with wraparound veranda and widow's walk. Set back from the road on an acre of beautiful gardens with a gazebo. Close to restaurants, shops, beaches, and island ferries. Spacious corner rooms with queen-size canopied beds, central air conditioning,

Mostly Hall

7 No smoking; 8 Children welcome; 9 Social drinking allowed; 10 Tennis nearby; 11 Swimming nearby; 12 Golf nearby; 13 Skiing nearby; 14 May be booked through a travel agent; 15 Handicapped accessible.

gourmet breakfast, bicycles, and private baths. Minimum stay Memorial Day through Columbus Day is two nights. Closed January through mid-February.

Hosts: Caroline and Jim Lloyd
Rooms: 6 (PB) $95-145
Full Breakfast
Credit Cards: A, B, C, D
Notes: 2, 7, 9, 10, 11, 12

Village Green Inn

40 Main Street, 02540
(508) 548-5621; (800) 237-1119
FAX (508) 457-5057; e-mail: vgi40@aol.com
www.villagegreeninn.com

Gracious old Victorian, ideally situated on historic village green. Walk to fine shops and restaurants, bike to beaches, tennis, and the picturesque bike path to Woods Hole. Enjoy 19th-century charm and warm hospitality in elegant surroundings. Four lovely guest rooms and one romantic suite all have private baths. Also bicycles, seasonal beverages, and working fireplaces. Personal checks accepted as deposit only. Children 12 and older welcome. Open year-round.

Hosts: Diane and Don Crosby
Rooms: 5 (PB) $85-160
Full Breakfast
Credit Cards: A, B, C
Notes: 5, 7, 9, 10, 11, 12, 14

Village Green Inn

The Wildflower Inn

The Wildflower Inn

167 Palmer Avenue, 02540
(508) 548-9524 (phone/FAX); (800) 294-5459
e-mail: wldflr167@aol.com
www.wildflower-inn.com

Built before the turn of the century, this award-winning inn is in the heart of Falmouth's historic district and a five-minute walk to Falmouth village. Each upstairs guest rooms has its own personality; all have private bath, some with whirlpool. A loft cottage, with private entrance, kitchen, living room, and spiral staircase leading to a romantic loft bedroom also available. A gourmet breakfast, as seen on PBS *Country Inn Cooking*, is served in the gathering room or on the wraparound porch. Complimentary refreshments available 24 hours. Air conditioning throughout. Bicycles. Voted "Best Bed and Breakfast". *Cape Cod Life* 1999. "Home of the Edible Flower Breakfast."

Hosts: Donna and Phil Stone
Rooms: 6 (PB) $85-185
Full Breakfast
Credit Cards: A, B, C
Notes: 5, 7, 8, 9, 10, 11, 12, 14

Woods Hole Passage Bed & Breakfast Inn

186 Woods Hole Road, 02540
(508) 548-9575; (800) 790-8976
FAX (508) 540-4771
e-mail: inn@woodsholepassage.com
www.woodsholepassage.com

NOTES: Credit cards accepted: A MasterCard; B Visa; C American Express; D Discover; E Diner's Club; F Other; 2 Personal checks accepted; 3 Lunch available; 4 Dinner available; 5 Open all year; 6 Pets welcome;

This 100-year-old carriage house sits on spacious grounds adorned by shade trees and berry bushes. The inn is close to the bike path, Martha's Vineyard, Nobska Lighthouse, the Woods Hole Oceanographic Institution, and the many beaches of the cape. Rooms have private baths and are graciously appointed in a comfortable, clean, airy atmosphere. A full gourmet breakfast is served by a huge multipaned window on the patio overlooking the grounds or in the secret garden.

Host: Deb Pruitt
Rooms: 5 (PB) $85-135
Full Breakfast
Credit Cards: A, B, C, D, E
Notes: 2, 5, 7, 8, 9, 10, 11, 12, 14

The Moorings Lodge

FALMOUTH HEIGHTS

Inn on the Sound

313 Grand Avenue, 02540
(508) 457-9666; (800) 564-9668
www.innonthesound.com

The oceanfront Inn on the Sound boasts a million-dollar view of Martha's Vineyard, Vineyard Sound, and miles of shoreline. The inn is across the street from the beach and a short walk to the Martha's Vineyard ferry, bicycle rental, the harbor, restaurants, and shops. Spacious, upscale, casual, beach-house-style guest rooms provide queen-size beds, private baths, lounge seating, and a panoramic view. Included is a sumptuous gourmet breakfast.

Hosts: Renée Ross and David Ross
Rooms: 10 (PB) $95-160
Full Breakfast
Credit Cards: A, B, C, D
Notes: 2, 5, 7, 9, 10, 11, 12, 14

The Moorings Lodge

207 Grand Avenue South, 02540
(508) 540-2370

Enjoy homemade breads for buffet breakfast served on a large glassed-in porch with lovely ocean view. This charming old sea captain's home with spacious, airy rooms overlooks Vineyard Sound and Martha's Vineyard. Just opposite a safe and clean family beach and within a short walking distance of good restaurants and the island ferry. Afternoon refreshment served. Fifteen dollars for extra adult in room.

Hosts: Ernie and Shirley Benard
Rooms: 8 (PB) $85-139
Full Breakfast
Credit Cards: A, B, D
Notes: 2, 7, 8, 9, 10, 11, 12, 14

GLOUCESTER

Bed & Breakfast Reservations North Shore, Greater Boston, Cape Cod

P.O. Box 600035, Newtonville, 02460
(617) 964-1606; (800) 832-2632
FAX (617) 332-8572; e-mail: info@bbreserve.com
www.bbreserve.com

1. Riverview Bed and Breakfast. Turn-of-the-century waterfront home high above the Annisquam River. Enjoy fabulous panoramic views of river and small-boating activity from 100-foot wraparound porch or from own private waterfront deck. Gorgeous terraced gardens and landscaped grounds lead to private dock at water's edge. Guest rooms are beautifully decorated and share two full baths. Private decks. Third person in room is an additional $15-20. Children welcome when

7 No smoking; 8 Children welcome; 9 Social drinking allowed; 10 Tennis nearby; 11 Swimming nearby; 12 Golf nearby; 13 Skiing nearby; 14 May be booked through a travel agent; 15 Handicapped accessible.

124   Gloucester, MA

whole house is rented by same family. No smoking. $80-90.

79. Oceanside Cottage. Small one-bedroom cottage, with breathtaking setting on grounds that slope right to the rugged coastline and ocean's edge. Enjoy spectacular sunsets right at the front door. Cottage has double bed, small living room with TV, shower bath, and galley kitchen stocked with self-serve breakfast foods. Sleeps two. Weekly rates available. Smoking permitted outside only. Open Memorial weekend through September. Three-night minimum stay. Weekly rates available. $90.

105. The Inn at Gloucester Harbor. Charming three-story Colonial directly across from America's oldest harbor, and just a short walk to beaches, restaurants, and waterfront park. All six designer-decorated guest rooms have private baths. Some have direct ocean views and fireplaces. Relax on the front terrace or back yard garden deck and enjoy the ocean breezes and harbor activity. Children seven and older welcome. No smoking. Open year-round. $89-149.

163. William Stevens House Suites. Historic inn overlooking Glocester Harbor, across the boulevard from the famous Gloucester Fisherman statue. Walking distance to beaches, parks, museums, galleries, shops, and restaurants. There are two nicely appointed suites, with more under construction. Each can sleep up to four, and each has private bath, TV, air conditioning, telephones, and breakfast area with refrigerator, microwave, toaster, and coffee maker. Breakfast foods are self-served by guests. Building amenities include a coin-op laundry, off-street parking, and secluded garden area out back. This is a smoke-free environment. Open year-round. families with children welcome. $135-175.

Gray Manor Bed & Breakfast

14 Atlantic Road, 01930
(978) 283-5409; (407) 784-8766 (winter)
www.cape-ann.com/graymanor

Gray Manor Bed and Breakfast is 30 miles north of Boston on picturesque Cape Ann, which has 25 miles of coastline including America's oldest and most historic fishing port. Gray Manor is only a three-minute walk to a beautiful white sandy beach. Private baths, air conditioning, cable TV, refrigerators, decks, kitchenettes, outdoor gas-fired barbecue grills, patio and porches for relaxation. TV in lounge plays movies at night. Enjoy Continental breakfast and socializing on the glassed-in veranda. Open May 1 through October 31. Seasonal rates and kitchenettes available.

Host: Madeline Gray
Rooms: 9 (PB) $50-70
Continental Breakfast
Credit Cards: A, B
Notes: 8, 9, 10, 11

GREAT BARRINGTON

American Country Collection

1353 Union Street, Schenectady, NY 12308
(518) 370-4948; (800) 810-4948
FAX (518) 393-1634 (call first)
e-mail: Carolbnbres@msn.com
www.bandbreservations.com

138. This 1700s Victorian rural farm is on 500 acres of rolling hills, woods, and fields. It is furnished with antiques and oriental rugs. There are four guest rooms, two with private baths. Tanglewood, Norman Rockwell Museum, Berkshire Festival, and skiing are all within 15 minutes. There is an in-ground pool available for guest use. Full breakfast. Smoking outdoors. Resident dog. Children over 10 welcome. $75-100.

Baldwin Hill Farm Bed & Breakfast

121 Baldwin Hill Road N/S (located in Egemont), 01230
(413) 528-4092; (888) 528-4092
FAX (413) 528-6365; e-mail: rpburds@aol.com

A Victorian farm home atop Baldwin Hill has 450 acres available for casual hiking, bird

NOTES: Credit cards accepted: A MasterCard; B Visa; C American Express; D Discover; E Diner's Club; F Other; 2 Personal checks accepted; 3 Lunch available; 4 Dinner available; 5 Open all year; 6 Pets welcome;

Baldwin Hill Farm

watching, and nature walks. Spectacular panoramic 360-degree views of the Berkshires. Country breakfasts from menu. Fieldstone fireplace, living rooms, screened porch, heated pool, gardens. Near concerts, theater, museums, dance, galleries, historic places, and alpine skiing. Shops, antiques, and fine restaurants nearby, with Appalachian Trail botanical and natural preserves. Children over 10 welcome. Inquire about off-site accommodations for pets.

Hosts: Richard and Priscilla Burdsall
Rooms: 4 (3 PB; 1 SB) $82-110
Full Breakfast
Credit Cards: A, B, C, D, E
Notes: 2, 5, 7, 9, 10, 11, 12, 13, 14

Coffing-Bostwick House

98 Division Street, 01230
(413) 528-4511

Unique, historic Greek Revival home (1825). Spacious, well-appointed guest rooms. Cozy parlor with TV; commodious library-living room; elegant mahogany-paneled dining room; all with fireplaces. Lavish homemade full breakfasts with fresh produce and fruits. Relaxed, informal atmosphere. Four acres with lovely river to stroll. Convenient to Tanglewood, Jacob's Pillow, theaters, ski areas, museums, art galleries, antique shops, and fine dining. Midweek discounts; special weekly packages. No smoking is preferred.

Hosts: Diana and William Harwood
Rooms: 6 (2 PB; 4 SB) $60-95

Full Breakfast
Credit Cards: None
Notes: 2, 5, 7, 8, 9, 10, 11, 12, 13

Elaine's Bed & Breakfast Selections

4987 Kingston Road, Elbridge, NY 13060
(315) 689-2082 (11 A.M. to 7 P.M.)

1. Very nice newer nonsmoking Colonial offers two guest rooms. The spacious master bedroom has a color remote-controlled TV, guest refrigerator, and large private bath with deep whirlpool tub. The second guest room shares a bath with the hostess. Continental breakfast. Entire house can be rented for larger groups. $95-125.

2. Very attractive contemporary ranch set far back from the street, overlooks the Housatonic River. Hot tub on deck. Living room-size suite has a sitting area, wood stove, color remote-controlled TV, three walls of windows, cathedral ceiling, and ceiling fan. There is a separate entrance that leads outdoors. The bath is shared with the owner. Resident cat. No smoking. No guest pets. Continental breakfast.

The Turning Point Inn

3 Lake Buel Road, 01230
(413) 528-4777

An 18th-century former stagecoach inn. Full, delicious breakfast. Featured in the *New York Times, Boston Globe,* and *Los Angeles Times.* Adjacent to Butternut Ski Basin; near Tanglewood and all Berkshire attractions. Hiking and

The Turning Point Inn

7 No smoking; 8 Children welcome; 9 Social drinking allowed; 10 Tennis nearby; 11 Swimming nearby; 12 Golf nearby; 13 Skiing nearby; 14 May be booked through a travel agent; 15 Handicapped accessible.

cross-country ski trails. Sitting rooms with fireplaces, cable TV. Groups and families welcome. Two-bedroom cottage with kitchen and living room available for $220 per night.

Hosts: The O'Rurkes—Dennis, Rachel, Teva
Rooms: 8 (6 PB; 2 SB) $85-220
Cottage: 1
Full Breakfast
Credit Cards: None
Notes: 2, 4, 5, 7, 8, 9, 10, 11, 12, 13

GREENFIELD

The Brandt House Country Inn

29 Highland Avenue, 01301-3605
(413) 774-3329; (800) 235-3329
FAX (413) 772-2908
e-mail: info@brandthouse.com
www.brandthouse.com

High on a hill just five minutes from historic Deerfield, and a five-minute walk to town, this 16-room estate offers privacy, elegance, and comfort. Private baths, wraparound porches, a clay tennis court, fireplaces, pool table, feather beds, antiques, glowing hardwood floors, fresh flowers, and cozy bathrobes await guests. A sumptuous home-cooked breakfast is included. Inquire about accommodations for pets. Corporate rates available.

Owner/Innkeeper: Phoebe Compton
Rooms: 9 (PB) $105-175
Credit Cards: A, B, C, D
Notes: 2, 5, 7, 8, 9, 10, 11, 12, 13, 14

HAMILTON

Bed & Breakfast Reservations North Shore, Greater Boston, Cape Cod

P.O. Box 600035, Newtonville, 02460
(617) 964-1606; (800) 832-2632
FAX (617) 332-8572; e-mail: info@bbreserve.com
www.bbreserve.com

30. The Elms Bed and Breakfast. Surrounded by tall elms, this very cozy and immaculate

bed and breakfast invites guests to relax and enjoy its secluded patio and gardens. Location is central to many tourist attractions. Short walk to village center and Boston commuter rail. Two rooms share a bath. Breakfast with homemade goodies. No smoking. $75-80.

HARWICH (CAPE COD)

Bed & Breakfast Cape Cod

P.O. Box 1312, Orleans, 02653
(508) 255-3824; (800) 541-6226
FAX (508) 240-0599
e-mail: info@BedandBreakfastCapeCod.com
www.BedandBreakfastCapeCod.com

HAR 04. Imagine only .3 of a mile to the warm waters of Nantucket Sound. Guests have their own private entrance into a lovely queen-size bedroom with private bath and a sitting area with TV, and guest refrigerator. This is a Cape Cod-style ranch house that sits on very lovely grounds that invites relaxation after a day at the beach. A lovely breakfast is served in the Florida Room. Close to fine restaurants and the ferry to Nantucket. $85.

HARWICH PORT (CAPE COD)

Augustus Snow House

528 Main Street, 02646
(508) 430-0528; (800) 320-0528
www.augustussnow.com

"For the ultimate splurge...The Augustus Snow House has few rivals in all of New England." Romantic Victorian mansion built in 1901; the Augustus Snow House remains one of Cape Cod's most breathtaking examples of Queen Anne Victorian architecture. Today, this turn-of-the-century home with its gabled dormers and wraparound veranda is one of the Cape's most elegant and exclusive inns. Five exquisite guest rooms, each with queen- or king-size beds, fireplaces, private baths (some with Jacuzzis), TVs, air conditioning, tele-

NOTES: Credit cards accepted: A MasterCard; B Visa; C American Express; D Discover; E Diner's Club; F Other; 2 Personal checks accepted; 3 Lunch available; 4 Dinner available; 5 Open all year; 6 Pets welcome;

phones, and full gourmet breakfast. The private beach is just a three-minute stroll away.

Hosts: Joyce and Steve Roth
Rooms: 5 (PB) $105-180
Full Breakfast
Credit Cards: A, B, C, D
Notes: 2, 5, 7, 9, 10, 11, 12, 14

Bed & Breakfast Cape Cod

P.O. Box 1312, Orleans, 02653
(508) 255-3824; (800) 541-6226
FAX (508) 240-0599
e-mail: info@BedandBreakfastCapeCod.com
www.BedandBreakfastCapeCod.com

HRP 04. Only 500 feet from the warm waters of Nantucket Sound is a Cape Cod-style home built in 1730 and restored in 1977. The charming accommodation is decorated in the period with Colonial and Shaker designs. The full gourmet breakfast served in the dining room is a feast. From the private decks in each room, one can see the beach and the ocean. Walk to all the village points of interest including shops, restaurants, and tennis or golf. A great location and a wonderful host and setting. Available June 1 through Labor Day. $150-165.

Bed & Breakfast Reservations North Shore, Greater Boston, Cape Cod

P.O. Box 600035, Newtonville, 02460
(617) 964-1606; (800) 832-2632
FAX (617) 332-8572; e-mail: info@bbreserve.com
www.bbreserve.com

25. Inn by the Sea. Less than 500 feet from a private mile-long beach on Nantucket Sound. Guests will enjoy the casual elegance of this inn in quiet setting, with great mid-cape location. Nine decorator-designed guest rooms, en suite baths, some with private entrances, fireplaces, and Jacuzzis. Full country breakfast in formal dining room. Living room with fireplace and spacious sun porch overlooking grounds. Cottage with canopied bed, fireplace, kitchen, sleeps three to four. $205 per night for cottage plus $35 of each additional person. No smoking. $180-250.

102. Queen Anne Victorian. Grand turn-of-the century inn, with gabled dormers and wraparound veranda on lovely grounds. Short walk to a beautiful sandy beach on Nantucket Sound. Five elegant and beautifully decorated guest rooms feature private baths (some with Jacuzzis), TV, and working fireplaces, each encased in hand-carved mantels and wood surrounds to match the existing decor. Memorable, multi-course gourmet breakfast, private individual tables in formal dining room. Location close to Harwich Port ferries to Nantucket. No smoking. $145-170.

Captain's Quarters

85 Bank Street, 02642
(800) 992-6550
www.virtualcapecod.com/market/ captainsquarters

A romantic 1850s Victorian with a classic wraparound porch, nostalgic gingerbread trim, and a graceful curving front stairway. Guest rooms have private baths, queen-size brass beds with eyelet-lace-trimmed sheets, lace curtains, color cable TVs, and comfortable reading chairs. Just a three-minute walk into town and to a lovely ocean beach. Experience Cape Cod in a relaxed and friendly atmosphere.

Hosts: Ed and Susan Kenney
Rooms: 5 (PB) $89-109
Continental Breakfast
Credit Cards: A, B, C, D
Notes: 2, 7, 9, 10, 11, 12, 14

Captain's Quarters

7 No smoking; 8 Children welcome; 9 Social drinking allowed; 10 Tennis nearby; 11 Swimming nearby; 12 Golf nearby; 13 Skiing nearby; 14 May be booked through a travel agent; 15 Handicapped accessible.

Dunscroft by the Sea

24 Pilgrim Road, 02646
(508) 432-0810; (800) 432-4345
FAX (508) 432-5134; e-mail: dunscroft@capecod.ne
www.dunscroftbythesea.comt

Exclusive location! Private, mile-long beach. Romantic and quiet. King- and queen-size canopied beds, four-poster beds, Jacuzzis, and fireplaces. In-town to restaurants, shops, galleries. Full country breakfast—Mmmm. VIP suite with Jacuzzi, fireplace, kitchenette, TV/VCR, king-size canopied bed. Limited handicapped accessibility.

Hosts: Alyce and Wally Cunningham
Rooms: 9 (PB) $125-240
Full Breakfast
Credit Cards: A, B, C
Notes: 2, 5, 9, 10, 11, 12, 14

HAYDENVILLE

Bed & Breakfast, Ltd.

P.O. Box 216, New Haven, CT 06513
(203) 469-3260; e-mail: BandB@aol.com
www.bedandbreakfastltd.com

A western Massachusetts dream come true. Near Smith College, fine restaurants, museums and galleries, and downtown diverse Northampton. Set on a 40-acre hillside, this home offers a spectacular mountain view. Separate and private guest quarters include a separate kitchen for guest use. A perfect choice for those guests seeking a relaxed, friendly, tranquil setting. $95-125.

HUNTINGTON

Carmelwood

8 Montgomery Road, 01050
(413) 667-5786

Beautiful Victorian home on bluff above Westfield River. Three double rooms share two baths off upstairs foyer. Grand piano in gracious parlor. Fireplace. Sunny dining room. Full country breakfasts feature home-grown organic fruits and berries. Extensive gardens. Children over 12 welcome.

Host: Katheryn Corrigan
Rooms: 3 (S2B) $75
Full Breakfast
Credit Cards: C
Notes: 2, 5, 7, 9, 11, 12, 13

HYANNIS

The Inn on Sea Street

358 Sea Street, 02601
(508) 775-8030; FAX (508) 771-0878
e-mail: innonsea@capecod.net

This elegant Victorian inn, with nine romantic guest rooms plus a white wicker cottage is just steps from the beach. Antiques, Persian carpets, canopied beds, TVs, and air conditioning are features of this friendly, unpretentious inn. Refrigerators, telephones, beach chairs and towels are available for guests' use. A full hot gourmet breakfast of homemade delights is served at individual tables set with sterling silver, china, crystal, and fresh flowers. One-night stays welcome.

Hosts: Sylvia and Fred LaSelva
Rooms: 10 (8 PB; 2 SB) $85-135
Full Breakfast
Credit Cards: A, B, C, D
Notes: 2, 7, 9, 10, 11, 12, 14

The Inn on Sea Street

NOTES: Credit cards accepted: A MasterCard; B Visa; C American Express; D Discover; E Diner's Club; F Other; 2 Personal checks accepted; 3 Lunch available; 4 Dinner available; 5 Open all year; 6 Pets welcome;

Mansfield House

Mansfield House

70 Gosnold Street, 02601
(508) 771-9455

This charming New England Bed and Breakfast is set in a quiet residential neighborhood, yet within walking distance of three public beaches and the boats to Nantucket and Martha's Vineyard. This 100-year-old English-style farm house has been totally renovated without losing its 19th-century ambiance. Guest rooms include private bath, king-size or twin beds, cable TV, VCRs. Enjoy a full gourmet breakfast in the charming dining room or on the adjacent porch. Open May through October.

Host: Donald Patrell
Rooms: 4 (PB) $80-95
Full Breakfast
Credit Cards: A, B, C
Notes: 2, 7, 8, 9, 10, 11, 12, 14

Salt Winds Guest House Bed & Breakfast

319 Sea Street, 02601
(508) 775-2038

The hosts Ginny and Craig Conroy will help make your stay on Cape Cod a memorable one. Salt Winds has been a lodging establishment for more than 50 years. Rooms and apartments are fully equipped with private baths, private entrances, TV, and air conditioning. A full breakfast, in-ground heated pool, and free transportation to island ferries is provided. The apartment and efficiency can sleep from two to six people comfortably. A full breakfast is included in the price for the efficiency and apartment.

Hosts: Ginny and Craig Conroy
Rooms: 8 (PB) $95-105
Full Breakfast
Credit Cards: A, B, C, D
Notes: 2, 7, 8, 9, 10, 11, 12, 14

Sea Beach Inn

388 Sea Street, P.O. Box 2428, 02601
(508) 775-4612
www.capecodtravel.com/seabeach

A charming restored 1860 sea captain's house and carriage barn in the heart of Cape Cod. Sea Beach Inn is noted for its warm hospitality and comfortable, air conditioned rooms with private baths. Family units are available in the rustic carriage barn. Just 200 yards from Sea Street Beach. An easy walk to Hyannis Main Street with its unique shops and ferries to Nantucket and Martha's Vineyard. From Hyannis it is an easy trip to Provincetown, Falmouth, and other cape towns. Bus, plane, and train pick-up available.

Hosts: Neil and Elizabeth Carr
Rooms: 9 (7 PB; 2 SB) $85
Continental Breakfast
Credit Cards: A, B, C
Notes: 2, 8, 10, 11, 12

Sea Breeze Inn

397 Sea Street, 02601
(508) 771-7213; FAX (508) 862-0663
e-mail: seabreeze@capecod.net
www.capecod.net/seabreeze/

A Victorian bed and breakfast—closest to the beach, five-minute drive to the boats for the islands, restaurants, shopping, and the Kennedy compound. All of the rooms have private baths and air conditioning. A Continental plus breakfast of cereals, homemade muffins, and scones is served each morning in

7 No smoking; 8 Children welcome; 9 Social drinking allowed; 10 Tennis nearby; 11 Swimming nearby; 12 Golf nearby; 13 Skiing nearby; 14 May be booked through a travel agent; 15 Handicapped accessible.

the dining room. Personal checks accepted on advanced reservations only.

Host: Patricia Gibney
Rooms: 14 (PB) $55-130
Continental Breakfast
Credit Cards: A, B, C, D
Notes: 5, 8, 9, 10, 11, 12, 14

HYANNISPORT

Bed & Breakfast Cape Cod

P.O. Box 1312, Orleans, 02653
(508) 255-3824; (800) 541-6226
FAX (508) 240-0599
e-mail: info@BedandBreakfastCapeCod.com
www.BedandBreakfastCapeCod.com

HYP 02. A lovely Cape Gambrel built in 1913 sits on a lovely quiet lane on the ninth fairway of Hyannisport Golf Course. Walk to a small private association beach. This home invites Cape Cod living. The small beach has a dock, and it is perfect for canoeing in the warm waters of Nantucket Sound. There is a king-size bedroom on the second floor with a sitting area and private hall bath. There is also a double bedroom on the first floor with a private hall bath. A large living room with TV invites relaxation. Only one mile to famous Craigville Beach. Wade to a lovely beach on Squaw Island. Convenient to the island ferries. Host will pick up at bus or boat. Seasonal rates. $80-110.

IPSWICH

Bed & Breakfast Reservations North Shore, Greater Boston, Cape Cod

P.O. Box 600035, Newtonville, 02460
(617) 964-1606; (800) 832-2632
FAX (617) 332-8572; e-mail: info@bbreserve.com
www.bbreserve.com

106. Hillside Cottage. Perfect summer getaway. Wonderful two-bedroom cottage with beautiful views of ocean, private landscaped grounds. Fully equipped, modern kitchen. Dining area with ocean view, sitting area with cable TV, and large screened porch. Picnic table, lawn furniture, and barbecue for guest use. Walk to beach. Families welcome. Sleeps four. No smoking. Seasonal from $975.

116. The Inn at Ipswich Center. This 1850 Colonial inn in historic district, overlooking Ipswich Center. Central to all towns of the North Shore and just minutes from the world-famous Crane Beach. Walk to wonderful shops, restaurants, and the commuter rail. Eleven guest rooms, most with private baths. Air conditioning. Sun room with TV. Breakfast included. Restricted smoking. Children 16 and older welcome. $75-150.

Town Hill Bed & Breakfast

16 North Main Street, 01938
(978) 356-8000; (800) 457-7799
www.townhill.com

A 1945 Greek Revival. Eleven comfortable rooms individually decorated. Walking distance to restaurants, shops, train to Boston. Historic homes and beautiful Crane Beach.

Hosts: Chere and Bob
Rooms: 11 (9 PB; 2 SB) $75-150
Full Breakfast
Credit Cards: A, B, C
Notes: 5, 11, 12, 14

KINGSTON

1760 Peabody Bradford Homestead

6 River Street, 02364
(617) 585-2646

The original Peabody Bradford House, also known as "The Landing," was built circa 1760 by the great grandson of William Bradford and was greatly enlarged around 1900. It is in a rural area with a commanding view of the tidal Jones River, named after Captain Jones of the Mayflower. A short walk gives access to

---

NOTES: Credit cards accepted: A MasterCard; B Visa; C American Express; D Discover; E Diner's Club; F Other; 2 Personal checks accepted; 3 Lunch available; 4 Dinner available; 5 Open all year; 6 Pets welcome;

1760 Peabody Bradford Homestead

Kingston and Plymouth Bays. Three twin-bedded bedrooms, each with its own private bath, are available to guests. There is a sitting room for conversation, reading, or TV. A Continental breakfast is served each morning in the dining room.

Rooms: 3 (PB) $70-90
Continental Breakfast
Credit Cards: None
Notes: 2, 5, 7

LANESBOROUGH

Bascom Lodge/Applachian Mountain Club

P.O. Box 1800, 01237
(413) 443-0011

The lodge is at the summit of the highest mountain in Massachusetts (3,491 feet) in the Berkshires and constructed of native stone and timbers in the 1930s. This hiker- and sightseer-friendly setting is uniquely suited for small gatherings who want incredible 100-mile views. Dinner and trail lunches are also available with vegetarian alternatives. The lodge is in the 14,000-acre Greylock State Reservation with its 50-plus miles of hiking trails. Open

Bascom Lodge

mid-May through mid-October. Private rooms and bunkrooms.

Hosts: Appalachian Mountain Club—Glenn Oswald, manager
Rooms: 8 (8 SB) $56-77
Full Breakfast
Credit Cards: A, B
Notes: 2, 3, 4, 7, 8, 11, 12, 13, 15

LEE

American Country Collection

1353 Union Street, Schenectady, NY 12308
(518) 370-4948; (800) 810-4948
FAX (518) 393-1634 (call first)
e-mail: Carolbnbres@msn.com
www.bandbreservations.com

202. This 250-year-old farmhouse stands on a hillside overlooking the first Shaker settlement in the Berkshires. Tanglewood, Stockbridge, and the Norman Rockwell Museum are within nine miles. One of two common rooms has couches, chairs, a TV, and a fireplace. Air conditioned. Shared baths. Intimate dinners are available for an additional charge Thursdays through Saturday in late spring, summer, and early fall. Full breakfast served. Smoking outside only. $75-90.

Applegate

279 West Park Street, 01238
(413) 243-4451; (800) 691-9012
www.applegateinn.com

A circular driveway leads to this pillared Georgian Colonial home set on six peaceful acres. Applegate is special in every way, with canopied beds, antiques, fireplaces, pool, and manicured gardens. Its mood is warm, hospitable, and relaxed. Enjoy complimentary wine and cheese in the living room, complete with a baby grand piano. Candlelight Continental plus breakfast is served. New TV room with VCR and a small video library. Near Norman Rockwell Museum and Tanglewood in the heart of the Berkshires. Children over 12 are welcome.

7 No smoking; 8 Children welcome; 9 Social drinking allowed; 10 Tennis nearby; 11 Swimming nearby; 12 Golf nearby; 13 Skiing nearby; 14 May be booked through a travel agent; 15 Handicapped accessible.

Applegate

Hosts: Gloria and Len Friedman
Rooms: 6 (PB) $95-230
Continental Breakfast
Credit Cards: A, B
Notes: 2, 5, 7, 9, 10, 11, 12, 13

Ashley Inn Bed & Breakfast

182 West Park Street, 01238
(413) 243-2746; FAX (413) 243-2489
e-mail: innkeeper@ashleyinn.com

New England hospitality in a classic Revival home. Guest rooms with antiques, private baths. Enjoy hosts' antique clock collection in the parlor, TV room, and dining room. Sit down to a delicious homemade breakfast. Afternoon tea served in the parlor or on the marble veranda. Minutes to Tanglewood and all Berkshire attractions. Walk to a public golf course or tennis court. Fine dining nearby.

Hosts: Dawn and Paul Borst
Rooms: 4 (PB) $55-120
Full Breakfast
Credit Cards: A, B, C, D
Notes: 2, 5, 7, 9, 10, 11, 12, 13

Chambéry Inn

199 Main Street, 01238
(413) 243-2221; (800) 537-4321
FAX (413) 243-3600

Restful, romantic, and rejuvenating, this school house teaches guests the three Rs of travel. Come visit the Berkshires' 1885 *petite*

chateau. All 400- to 500-square-foot schoolhouse suites are individually decorated. Standard features include 13-foot ceilings, 8-foot windows, sitting areas with fireplaces, private baths with whirlpools, air conditioning, telephones, and color TV. Choose a king-size canopied or two queen-size beds, or a guest room with a Jacuzzi for two. Room-delivered Continental plus breakfast included. Hospitality and facilities—par excellence!

Hosts: Joseph and Lynn Toole
Rooms: 9 (PB) $85-275
Continental Breakfast
Credit Cards: A, B, C, D
Notes: 2, 3, 4, 5, 7, 9, 10, 11, 12, 13, 15

Devonfield

85 Stockbridge Road, 01238
(413) 243-3298; (800) 664-0880
FAX (413) 243-1360
e-mail: innkeeper@devonfield.com
www.devonfield.com

Historic country estate offering the charm of yesterday and the amenities of today. Set on 40 acres of lawn and fields yet near all Berkshire attractions—Tanglewood, etc. King- or queen-size beds, some suites, fireplaces in four bedrooms, heated pool, tennis court, bicycles, and golf course nearby. Pets welcome in cottage only. Smoking permitted outside only. Children welcome except in July and August.

Hosts: Sally and Ben Schenck
Rooms: 10 (PB) $70-260
Full Breakfast
Credit Cards: A, B, C, D
Notes: 2, 5, 7, 9, 10, 11, 12, 13, 14

Devonfield

NOTES: Credit cards accepted: A MasterCard; B Visa; C American Express; D Discover; E Diner's Club; F Other; 2 Personal checks accepted; 3 Lunch available; 4 Dinner available; 5 Open all year; 6 Pets welcome;

The Parsonage on the Green

20 Park Place, 01238
(413) 243-4364
www.bbhost.com/parsonageonthegreen

An 1851 Colonial inn set back on a quiet corner of the town common. Tastefully decorated with family antiques. Piano, fireplace in parlor, games in library. Thoughtful touches in guest rooms. Afternoon tea. Full breakfast by candlelight on an elegant table setting. Perfect for a romantic getaway. Museums, outlets, restaurants, and skiing nearby. Lunch and dinner available upon request.

Hosts: Donald and Barbara Mahony
Rooms: 4 (2 PB; 2 SB) $65-150
Full Breakfast
Credit Cards: None
Notes: 2, 5, 7, 10, 11, 12, 13

LENOX

Amadeus House

15 Cliffwood Street, 01240
(800) 205-4770; FAX (413) 637-4770
e-mail: info@amadeushouse.com

Amadeus House is a restored Victorian set on a quiet residential street of grand homes in the center of historic Lenox village. Fine restaurants, shops, and art galleries are a short walk away. Each of the eight comfortable guest rooms is named after a favorite composer.

Amadeus House

Most rooms have queen-size beds and private baths. Enjoy the classic wraparound porch or, during chillier weather, savor afternoon tea by the fireplace in the living room.

Hosts: Martha Gottron and John Felton
Rooms: 8 (6 PB; 2 SB) $65-185
Full Breakfast
Credit Cards: A, B, C, D
Notes: 2, 5, 7, 9, 10, 11, 12, 13

Birchwood Inn

Birchwood Inn

7 Hubbard Street, 01240
(413) 637-2600; (800) 524-1646
e-mail: innkeeper@birchwood-inn.com

Drive through the village of Lenox, and at the top of the hill stands the historic Birchwood Inn. The first town meeting was held here in 1767. Elegant and beautifully restored, the inn is known throughout the region for its hospitality. Enjoy antiques, fireplaces, library, and wonderful porch. Cultural activities include the Boston Symphony at Tanglewood and performing arts. There is marvelous fall foliage, hiking, and biking. Full breakfast and tea. Handicapped accessible for the hearing impaired.

Host: Ellen Gutman Chenaux
Rooms: 12 (10 PB; 2 SB) $60-225
Full Breakfast
Credit Cards: A, B, C, D, E
Notes: 2, 5, 7, 9, 10, 11, 12, 13, 14

7 No smoking; 8 Children welcome; 9 Social drinking allowed; 10 Tennis nearby; 11 Swimming nearby; 12 Golf nearby; 13 Skiing nearby; 14 May be booked through a travel agent; 15 Handicapped accessible.

Blantyre

Blantyre

16 Blantyre Road, P.O. Box 995, 01240
(413) 637-3556

A gracious country house/hotel surrounded by
85 acres of grounds. The hotel has a European
atmosphere and exceptional cuisine. Offers
tennis, croquet, and swimming as its leisure
activities. Open May through November.

Host: Roderick Anderson
Rooms: 23 (PB) $270-685
Full or Continental Breakfast
Credit Cards: A, B, C
Notes: 2, 3, 4, 10, 11, 12, 14

Brook Farm Inn

15 Hawthorne Street, 01240
(413) 637-3013

There is poetry here. A lovely century-old Victorian home, nestled in a wooded glen amid
gardens and a pool. There is a large library

Brook Farm Inn

with fireplace, and several guest rooms feature
fireplaces and canopied or brass beds. Poetry
readings with tea and scones are offered each
Saturday. Near Tanglewood, theater, ballet, and
museums. Enjoy hiking, biking, and wonderful
fall foliage. In winter, cross-country and downhill skiing are nearby. Relax and enjoy. Afternoon tea served. Children over 15 welcome.
Smoking permitted in designated areas only.

Hosts: Joe and Anne Miller
Rooms: 12 (PB) $80-200
Full Breakfast
Credit Cards: A, B, D
Notes: 2, 5, 9, 10, 11, 12, 13

The Gables Inn

The Gables Inn

81 Walker Street, 01240
(413) 637-3416; (800) 382-9401

Former home of novelist Edith Wharton.
Queen Anne-style with period furnishings,
pool, tennis, fireplaces, and theme rooms.

NOTES: Credit cards accepted: A MasterCard; B Visa; C American Express; D Discover; E Diner's Club;
F Other; 2 Personal checks accepted; 3 Lunch available; 4 Dinner available; 5 Open all year; 6 Pets welcome;

Host: Frank Newton
Rooms: 18 (PB) $80-210
Full Breakfast
Credit Cards: A, B, D
Notes: 2, 5, 9, 10, 11, 12, 13

Garden Gables Inn

141 Main Street, P.O. Box 52, 01240
(413) 637-0193; FAX (413) 637-4554

A charming 18-room, 200-year-old gabled inn
in the historic center of Lenox on five wooded
acres dotted with gardens, maples, and fruit
trees. A 72-foot outdoor swimming pool, fireplaces, and whirlpool tubs. Fully air conditioned. Minutes from Tanglewood and other
attractions. Good skiing in winter. In-room
telephones. Breakfast included.

Hosts: Mario and Lynn Mekinda
Rooms: 18 (PB) $95-225
Full Breakfast
Credit Cards: A, B, C, D
Notes: 2, 5, 7, 9, 10, 12, 13

The Kemble Inn

The Kemble Inn

2 Kemble Street, 01240
(800) 353-4113; www.kembleinn.com

Nestled in the beautiful Berkshire Hills and
perched on the edge of historic Lenox village
stands the Kemble Inn. With its distant
panoramic mountain views to the west and its
spacious Georgian elegance, the Kemble Inn has
15 rooms and central air. Each room has a color
TV and a telephone, and some rooms have a

fireplace and Jacuzzi. Nearby is Jacob's Pillow
Dance Festival, the Berkshire Theatre Festival,
Tanglewood, and the Chesterwood and Norman
Rockwell Museums. Cross-country and down-
hill skiing nearby. Children over 12 welcome.

Hosts: Richard and Linda Reardon
Rooms: 15 (PB) $85-275
Continental Breakfast
Credit Cards: A, B
Notes: 2, 5, 7, 9, 10, 11, 12, 13, 14, 15

The Rookwood Inn

11 Old Stockbridge Road, P.O. Box 1717, 01240-
1717
(413) 637-4589 (guest line for incoming calls)
(800) 223-9750 (info and reservations)
FAX (413) 637-1352
e-mail: stay@rookwoodinn.com
www.rookwoodinn.com

"Quiet charm nestled in the heart of Lenox."
Modern amenities with Victorian charm. Bountiful heart-healthy breakfasts, afternoon refreshments, and gracious hospitality in comfortable,
family friendly inn. Peaceful setting near town,
a short distance to Tanglewood and other cultural attractions, shops, and restaurants. Twenty
antique-decorated, air-conditioned rooms. Each
has a private bathroom. Some have private
porches, canopied or four-poster beds, sitting
areas, and fireplaces. The full breakfast is served
buffet style. Experience a Rookwood getaway
complete with rest, romance, and renewal.

Hosts: Amy and Stephen Lindner-Lesser
        (owners/innkeepers)
Rooms: 20 (PB) $75-285
Full Breakfast
Credit Cards: A, B, C, D, E
Notes: 2, 5, 7, 8, 9, 10, 11, 12, 13, 14

Summer Hill Farm

950 East Street, 01240
(413) 442-2057; (800) 442-2059
e-mail: innkeeper@summerhillfarm.com
www.summerhillfarm.com

Comfortable 200-year-old farmhouse and con-
verted-barn guest cottage on 20-acre horse

7 No smoking; 8 Children welcome; 9 Social drinking allowed; 10 Tennis nearby; 11 Swimming nearby;
12 Golf nearby; 13 Skiing nearby; 14 May be booked through a travel agent; 15 Handicapped accessible.

Summer Hill Farm

farm are tastefully furnished with genuine English antiques and oriental rugs. The satisfying country breakfast is served in the dining room or on the sun porch looking out over the gardens and view. The atmosphere is peaceful, relaxed, friendly, and unpretentious. Close to Tanglewood, Jacob's Pillow Dance Festival, museums, galleries, theaters, Hancock Shaker Village, good restaurants, and shops. There is also a three-bedroom, two-bath farmhouse available to rent by the week or month. Inquire about accommodations for children. Cottage is handicapped accessible.

Hosts: Michael and Sonya Chassell Wessel
Rooms: 7 (PB) $55-160
Full or Continental Breakfast
Credit Cards: A, B, C
Notes: 2, 5, 7, 9, 10, 11, 12, 13, 14

Whistler's Inn

5 Greenwood Street, 01240
(413) 637-0975; FAX (413) 637-2190
e-mail: rmears3246@aol.com
www.whistlersinnoftheberkshires.com

Old World elegance and modern comfort in an antique-filled Tudor mansion on seven acres of

Whistler's Inn

gardens and woodlands. Eleven rooms with private baths, air conditioning; eight rooms with fireplaces; library; French music room. Sun porch overlooking gardens.

Rooms: 14 (PB) $100-225
Full Breakfast
Credit Cards: A, B, C, D
Notes: 2, 5, 7, 8, 9, 10, 11, 12, 13, 14

LEVERETT

Hannah Dudley House Inn

Hannah Dudley House Inn

114 Dudleyville Road, 01054
(413) 367-2323

This elegant country inn is on 82 tranquil, rural acres and is the ideal getaway. The 200-year-old house has been romantically restored with spacious guest rooms, private baths, fireplaces throughout, and attention to detail. Each room is meticulously and individually decorated with its own theme and comfortably furnished in Colonial style. Common rooms, patios, and an array of benches and hammocks offer a variety of relaxation options both inside and out. The inn's intimate setting also includes a swimming pool, hiking trails, scenic picnic spots, ponds, and special places just waiting to be discovered.

Hosts: Erni and Daryl Johnson
Rooms: 4 (PB) $125-185
Full Breakfast
Credit Cards: A, B
Notes: 2, 5, 7, 9, 10, 12, 13

NOTES: Credit cards accepted: A MasterCard; B Visa; C American Express; D Discover; E Diner's Club; F Other; 2 Personal checks accepted; 3 Lunch available; 4 Dinner available; 5 Open all year; 6 Pets welcome;

LUDLOW

Misty Meadows, Ltd.

467 Fuller Street, 01056
(413) 583-8103

One of Ludlow's oldest, this 200-year-old house has 85 acres on which to wander. A country scenic atmosphere on a working farm that raises Scottish Highlanders. A scenic patio overlooks the Minechoag Mountain Range. Screened cabana with in-ground pool. Brook fishing nearby. An area with a lot of history and many historical sites less than one-half hour away.

Host: Donnabelle Haluch
Rooms: 2 (SB) $30-50
Continental Breakfast
Credit Cards: None
Notes: 2, 5, 6, 8, 9, 10, 11, 12, 13

LYNN

Diamond District Breakfast Inn

142 Ocean Street, 01902-2007
(781) 599-4470; (800) 666-3076
FAX (781) 599-4470
www.diamonddistrictinn.com

Architect-designed Georgian mansion in historic "Diamond District" built in 1911. Features include foyer and grand staircase, spacious fireplace, living and dining room with ocean view, and French doors leading to veranda overlooking the gardens. Guest rooms

Diamond District Breakfast Inn

contain antiques, individual decor, air conditioning, TVs, telephones, down comforters, some fireplaces, whirlpool, deck, ocean views, and private baths. Outdoor heated spa. Candlelight breakfast served outside or by the fire in the formal dining room. King suites with TV, VCR, CD player. Sandy beach for swimming, walking, and jogging jsut steps away. Walk to restaurants. Home-cooked breakfast; vegetarian, low-fat available.

Hosts: Sandra and Jerry Caron
Rooms: 11 (7 PB; 4 SB) $120-250
Full Breakfast
Credit Cards: A, B, C, D, E
Notes: 2, 5, 7, 8, 10, 11, 12, 14

MARBLEHEAD

Bed & Breakfast Reservations North Shore, Greater Boston, Cape Cod

P.O. Box 600035, Newtonville, 02460
(617) 964-1606; (800) 832-2632
FAX (617) 332-8572; e-mail: info@bbreserve.com
www.bbreserve.com

73. Oceanside Tudor. Grand oceanside Tudor with spectacular panoramic views. Luxury, romance, privacy, personal attention. Seven rooms with en suite baths, several with working fireplaces. Ground-level guest room features private oceanfront patio. Large common area with kitchen facilities and fireplace. Continental breakfast at own private table by oceanside picture windows. Private courtyard and gardens. $180-210.

Buena Vista Bed & Breakfast

13 Buena Vista Road, 01945
(781) 631-4766

A bed and breakfast near the sea in historic Marblehead. Guests' own private entrance and deck afford splendid views of Salem Harbor from a country setting on Marblehead's west shore. Awake refreshed and enjoy Mrs.

Buena Vista

Brown's wonderful breakfast which includes home-baked goodies and fresh fruit in season. Rates are per room, per night.

Hosts: Emerson and Betty J. Brown
Rooms: 2 (2 SB) $65
Continental Breakfast
Credit Cards: F
Notes: 2, 7, 11

Compass Rose

36 Gregory Street, 01945
(781) 631-7599

Studio-by-the-Sea. Garden entrance studio overlooking Marblehead Harbor. Queen-size bed, kitchenette stocked with Continental breakfast, private bath—all in a nautical theme.

Cottage on the Avenue. Charming, newly renovated one-bedroom cottage, furnished with new and antique treasures. Queen-size bed, kitchen stocked with Continental breakfast, private patio, garden. Walk to beaches, historical sights, etc.

Hosts: Carol and Bob Swift
Rooms: 2 (PB) $95-125
Continental Breakfast
Credit Cards: A, B
Notes: 2, 5, 7, 8, 9, 10, 11

The Harbor Light Inn

58 Washington Street, 01945
(781) 631-2186

Premier inn one block from the harbor with rooms featuring air conditioning, TV, private baths, and working fireplaces. Four rooms have double Jacuzzis and sun decks. Beautiful 18th-century-period mahogany furniture. Recent acquisition of an adjacent Federalist manor provides more room and amenities, including a conference room and swimming pool. Continental plus breakfast served.

Hosts: Peter and Suzanne Conway
Rooms: 20 (PB) $95-155
Suites: (PB) $165-245
Continental Breakfast
Credit Cards: A, B, C
Notes: 2, 5, 9, 10, 11, 12, 14

The Harbor Light Inn

Harborside House

23 Gregory Street, 01945-3241
(781) 631-1032; e-mail: swliving@shore.net
www.shore.net/~swliving/

This handsome 1850 home in the historic district overlooks Marblehead Harbor. Enjoy water views from a fireplaced parlor, period dining room, third-story sun deck, and summer breakfast porch where guests may sample home-baked breads and muffins. Walk to historic sights, excellent restaurants, and unique shops. Hostess is a professional dressmaker

Harborside House

and nationally ranked competitive swimmer. Enjoy quiet comfort and convenience. Children over 10 welcome.

Host: Susan Livingston
Rooms: 2 (SB) $75-90
Continental Breakfast
Credit Cards: None
Notes: 2, 5, 7, 10, 11, 14

The Marblehead Inn

264 Pleasant Street, 01945
(781) 639-9999; (800) 399-5843
FAX (781) 639-9996; www.marbleheadinn.com

In historic Marblehead, this newly renovated Victorian home was built in 1872. The suite-style inn is a fine example of classic Victorian architecture at Marblehead. The inn offers 10 two-room suites. Each suite has a full kitchenette, TV, private bathroom, and several other amenities. The inn is 15 miles north of Boston and convenient to beaches, restaurants, harbor, shops, and historical points of interest.

Host: David Fallon
Rooms: 10 (PB) $139-189

The Marblehead Inn

Continental Breakfast
Credit Cards: A, B, C
Notes: 2, 5, 7, 8, 10, 11, 12, 14, 15

The Nesting Place

16 Village Street, 01945
(781) 631-6655; (877) 855-5656 (toll-free)
e-mail: louisehir@aol.com
www.thenestingplace.com

This charming 19th-century home is in historic Marblehead and within walking distance of the renowned harbor, beaches, historic homes, galleries, eateries, shops, and parks. A relaxing, refreshing home away from home. Two comfortably furnished guest rooms feature a homemade breakfast, outdoor hot tub, and a smoke-free environment. One-half hour from Boston, or one hour from New Hampshire. Bike trails and public transportation to Boston. Massage and facials available by appointment. Seasonal and weekly rates.

Host: Louise Hirshberg
Rooms: 2 (SB) $65-75
Continental Breakfast
Credit Cards: A, B
Notes: 2, 5, 7, 8, 9, 10, 11, 12, 14

Seagull Inn

106 Harbor Avenue, 01945
(781) 631-1893; FAX (781) 631-3535
e-mail: host@seagullinn.com
www.seagullinn.com

Sun-drenched and comfort-filled suites with flexible occupancy offer TVs, VCR, telephones, and private baths. Glorious gardens in the summer and spectacular views from the decks throughout the year make every season special at the Seagull. Take a short walk to a beach or lighthouse. Watch sailboat races or fishing fleets. Enjoy sunrises or sunsets from the porch or decks. Business travelers are welcomed; meeting space is available.

Hosts: Skip and Ruth Sigler
Rooms: 3 (PB) $100-200
Continental Breakfast
Credit Cards: A, B
Notes: 2, 5, 6, 7, 8, 9, 10, 11, 14

7 No smoking; 8 Children welcome; 9 Social drinking allowed; 10 Tennis nearby; 11 Swimming nearby; 12 Golf nearby; 13 Skiing nearby; 14 May be booked through a travel agent; 15 Handicapped accessible.

MARSTONS MILLS

Bed & Breakfast Cape Cod

P.O. Box 1312, Orleans, 02653
(508) 255-3824; (800) 541-6226
FAX (508) 240-0599
e-mail: info@BedandBreakfastCapeCod.com
www.BedandBreakfastCapeCod.com

MAR 02. Listen to the babbling brook and surround yourself with gardens from this romantic cottage. Antiques, queen-size bed, full kitchen, and patio are just some of the amenities. Private, quiet, and close to saltwater beaches. Pet friendly. Weekly rates available. Season rates. $80-125.

MARTHA'S VINEYARD (EDGARTOWN)

Colonial Inn of Martha's Vineyard

38 North Water Street, P.O. Box 68, Edgartown, 02539
(508) 627-4711; (800) 627-4701

In the heart of historic Edgartown overlooking the harbor sits the Colonial Inn. It offers 43 newly renovated and lovingly refurbished rooms, all with heat, air conditioning, color TVs, telephones, and private baths. Continental breakfast is served daily in the solarium and garden courtyard. Affordable luxury. Closed December through March.

COLONIAL INN

Host: Linda Malcouronne
Rooms: 43 (PB) $90-225
Continental Breakfast
Credit Cards: A, B, C
Notes: 4, 8, 9, 10, 11, 12, 14, 15

MIDDLEBORO

On Cranberry Pond Bed & Breakfast

43 Fuller Street, 02346
(508) 946-0768

Snuggled away among the hills and bogs of northeastern Middleboro is a haven from the daily routine that offers a restful, cozy, country escape with all the modern amenities and more. Three working fireplaces, two common rooms, flower room, corporate meeting room, and dining room. Bass fishing, canoeing, mountain biking, and lots of walking trails are nearby. Thirty minutes from Plymouth, 45 minutes from Boston, Fall River, and New Bedford, and 40 minutes to Cape Cod. Children over seven welcome.

Hosts: Jeannine and Tim LaBossiere
Rooms: 6 (3 PB; 3 SB) $85-140
Full Breakfast
Credit Cards: A, B, C, D, E, F
Notes: 5, 7, 9, 10, 11, 12, 13, 14

MIDDLETON

Bed & Breakfast Reservations North Shore, Greater Boston, Cape Cod

P.O. Box 600035, Newtonville, 02460
(617) 964-1606; (800) 832-2632
FAX (617) 332-8572; e-mail: info@bbreserve.com
www.bbreserve.com

3. Blue Door Bed and Breakfast. The original parts of this now 10-room historic home date back to 1698. Location neighbors Salem/Marblehead area and is just 35 minutes from Boston. Two spacious and luxurious guest rooms have private baths. Large enclosed sunroom overlooks two acres of private grounds with goldfish pond, gazebo, and perennial gardens. In-room amenities include working fireplace in the Victorian Room, and whirlpool tub in Twenties Room. Twenties Room has adjoining room for third person. Host is gourmet cook who will arrange romantic dinners by advanced arrangement at additional charge. No smoking. Special occasion small gatherings can be catered by host. Thirty-five dollars for extra person. $125-140.

NANTUCKET

Cobblestone Inn

Captains Corners

Captains Corners

89 Easton Street, P.O. Box 628, 02554
(508) 228-1692; (800) 319-9990
FAX (978) 948-8192
e-mail: captainscorners@nii.net
www.captainscorner.com

This gracious captain's home offers 15 rooms with mostly private baths. Central residential area near beaches, shops, and restaurants. Nantucket Island welcomes guests with 88 miles of beaches, manicured yards, and gracefully maintained history in its homes.

Host: Barbara Bowman
Rooms: 15 (11 PB; 4 SB) $99-160
Continental Breakfast
Credit Cards: A, B, C
Notes: 2, 7, 8, 9, 10, 11, 12, 14

Cobblestone Inn

5 Ash Street, 02554
(508) 228-1987

Built in 1725, renovated in 1997, the centuries blend walking the two blocks from Steamship Wharf to this quiet cobblestone side street in the heart of historic Nantucket Town. The large rooms have queen-size beds and the third floor is a two-room suite with harbor views. Each room has a private bath with stall shower, central air, telephone, TV, guest pantry, plus a coupon for each guest for a full breakfast at guest's choice of two fine restaurants.

Resident Innkeeper: Robin Hammer-Yankow, owner
Rooms: 7 (PB) $75-290
Full Breakfast
Credit Cards: A, B
Notes: 2, 5, 7

House of Seven Gables

32 Cliff Road, 02554
(508) 228-4706

A quiet Victorian with bright sunny rooms in the historic district of Nantucket. A Continental breakfast is served to the guest room each morning. Walk to museums, beaches, restaurants, and shops.

7 No smoking; 8 Children welcome; 9 Social drinking allowed; 10 Tennis nearby; 11 Swimming nearby; 12 Golf nearby; 13 Skiing nearby; 14 May be booked through a travel agent; 15 Handicapped accessible.

House of Seven Gables

lovely 1883 Victorian home in the historic district on elm-shaded and cobblestoned Main Street. The host is dedicated to guests enjoyment of the island and looks forward to accommodating their needs. All rooms and areas are nonsmoking. A delicious homemade Continental breakfast buffet is included. Children welcome in the annex.

Host: Shirley Peters
Rooms: 18 (PB) $135-160
Continental Breakfast
Credit Cards: A, B, C, D
Notes: 2, 7, 9, 10, 11, 12, 14

Stumble Inne

109 Orange Street, 02254
(508) 228-4482

The Stumble Inne, built in colonial times, is the perfect place to enjoy a Nantucket vacation. The "inne" has seven spacious guest rooms which are tastefully furnished with antiques and reproductions. A variety of accommodations is available, most with queen-size bed, air conditioning, color cable TV, and private bath. Tucked away on the spacious lawn is the inn's Garden Cottage containing two comfortable bedrooms, a full bath, fully equipped kitchen, spacious living room, and private deck. Rates available for cottage upon request.

Hosts: Jeanne and George Todor
Rooms: 8 (7 PB; 1 SB) $125-270
Continental Breakfast
Credit Cards: A, B, C
Notes: 2, 5, 7

Host: Suzanne Walton
Rooms: 10 (8 PB; 2 SB) $95-185
Continental Breakfast
Credit Cards: A, B, C
Notes: 2, 7, 9, 10, 11, 12

Hussey House 1795

15 North Water Street, 02554
(508) 228-0747

In the heart of the historical district—just a three-minute walk from the steamer landing, Main Street, and the nearest beach. Large, airy rooms, each one with a fireplace, private bath, and beautiful antiques. Double, twin, and queen-size canopied beds and family accommodations available. Comfortable sitting room and spacious grounds with gardens, bicycle racks, and private parking.

Hosts: The Johnson Family
Rooms: 5 (PB) $125-185
Continental Breakfast
Credit Cards: None
Notes: 2, 7, 8, 9, 10, 11, 12

The White House

48 Centre Street, 02554
(508) 228-4677; FAX (508) 228-1934

Ideally in the old historic district. Adjacent to the lovely Jared Coffin Garden and within easy walking distance of ferry terminals as well as fine dining, museums, entertainment, shops, and galleries. Afternoon wine and cheese in season. Also available is an apartment accommodating two to four persons renting by the week.

76 Main Street

76 Main Street, 02554
(508) 228-2533

All the quiet and subtle beauty of Nantucket is here for guests to explore in comfort from this

NOTES: Credit cards accepted: A MasterCard; B Visa; C American Express; D Discover; E Diner's Club; F Other; 2 Personal checks accepted; 3 Lunch available; 4 Dinner available; 5 Open all year; 6 Pets welcome;

Rooms: 3 (PB) $75-135
Continental Breakfast
Credit Cards: A, B, C
Notes: 2, 5, 7, 8, 10, 11, 12

The Woodbox Inn

29 Fair Street, 02554
(508) 228-0587

Nantucket's oldest inn, built in 1709, is one-and-a-half blocks from the center of town. The Woodbox offers three queen-size rooms and six suites with working fireplaces, all with private baths. A full breakfast is available along with candlelight gourmet dinners. Voted Wine Spectator Award of Excellence, Nantucket's Most Romantic Dining Room, and rated Nantucket's Finest Dining. Closed January 2 through June 1.

Host: Dexter Tutein
Rooms: 9 (PB) $160-270
Full Breakfast
Credit Cards: None
Notes: 2, 4, 7, 8, 9, 10, 11, 12

The Woodbox Inn

NANTUCKET ISLAND

Safe Harbor

2 Harborview Way, 02554
(508) 228-3222 (phone/FAX)
e-mail: sharbor@nantucket.net

Safe Harbor is a spacious and finely appointed guest house set on wide lawns, on Nantucket Harbor at Children's Beach, in Nantucket town's old historic district. All of the rooms have a water view over the harbor and the yacht basin. Nantucket's celebrated restaurants and shops are within a five-minute walk, as are the churches, galleries, museums, and historic buildings that draw people to this special island. Of course, Nantucket also offers 54 miles of the world's most beautiful beaches. Seasonal rates available.

Host: Sylvia Griggs
Rooms: 5 (PB) $160-190
Continental Breakfast
Credit Cards: A, B
Notes: 2, 5, 6, 8, 9, 10, 11, 12

NEEDHAM

Bed & Breakfast Associates Bay Colony, Ltd.

P.O. Box 57166, Babson Park, Boston, 02457-0166
(781) 449-5302; (888) 429-7591
FAX (781) 449-5958; e-mail: info@bnbboston.com
www.bnbboston.com

IW635. Home Away. Immaculate Cape-style home near Needham Center. Available hosted or unhosted. Two guest rooms with full baths. Very pleasant, traditional decor. Available unhosted by the week or the month. Monthly rate available. Nightly rates are $150-200 for the whole house or per room at $85-105.

Host Homes of Boston

P.O. Box 117, Waban Branch, Boston, 02468-0001
(617) 244-1308; (800) 600-1308
FAX (617) 244-5156

Hilltop House. Quiet, sylvan setting with Boston skyline view in winter. Host offers a large second-floor guest room and en suite bath in Colonial home. Relax on screened porch or shady lawn. Ten minutes to Boston. Near Boston Common, Pine Manor, Wellesley, and Route 128 businesses. Half-mile to commuter train. TV. Air conditioned. Parking. No smoking. $87.

7 No smoking; 8 Children welcome; 9 Social drinking allowed; 10 Tennis nearby; 11 Swimming nearby; 12 Golf nearby; 13 Skiing nearby; 14 May be booked through a travel agent; 15 Handicapped accessible.

NEW BEDFORD

1875 House

367 Seventh Street, 02740
(508) 997-6433; FAX (508) 984-1696

The 1875 House is a wooden house built in the early Victorian era. The home has undergone thoughtful restoration which is reflected in the tasteful decor throughout. Close to the newly designated Whaling National Historic Park, two blocks from the Rotch-Jones-Duff Museum, in the historic area of New Bedford, and in a neighborhood which figured prominently in the Underground Railroad. Also convenient to Cape Cod, Newport, Providence, and Boston—all within an hour's drive. Pets welcome with prior arrangements.

Rooms: 3 (PB) $55-70
Continental Breakfast
Credit Cards: None
Notes: 2, 5, 7, 8, 9, 11, 12

1875 House

NEWBURYPORT

Bed & Breakfast Reservations North Shore, Greater Boston, Cape Cod

P.O. Box 600035, Newtonville, 02460
(617) 964-1606; (800) 832-2632

FAX (617) 332-8572; e-mail: info@bbreserve.com
www.bbreserve.com

125. The Old Salts Bed and Breakfast. Minutes from Newburyport, Plum Island, and gorgeous beaches of the Massachusetts and New Hampshire shores, this Greek Revival farmhouse has been lovingly restored. A glass-enclosed sunroom overlooks three acres of secluded gardens. A sumptuous full country breakfast is served. Three beautiful rooms with private baths. Resident dog. $100-115.

The Windsor House

The Windsor House in Newburyport

38 Federal Street, 01950
(978) 462-3778; (888) TRELAWNY
FAX (978) 465-3443; e-mail: tintagel@greennet.net
www.bbhost.com/windsorhouse

Built as a wedding present, this 18th- century Federal mansion offers a rare blend of Yankee hospitality and the English tradition of bed and breakfast. Designed as a residence/ship's chandlery, the inn recalls the spirit of an English country house. In a historic seaport near a wildlife refuge. Whale watching, museums, theater, and antiques. Rates include afternoon tea, English cooked breakfast, tax, and service.

Hosts: Judith and John Harris
Rooms: 4 (PB) $135
Full Breakfast
Credit Cards: A, B, C, D
Notes: 2, 5, 6, 7, 8, 10, 11, 12, 13, 14

NOTES: Credit cards accepted: A MasterCard; B Visa; C American Express; D Discover; E Diner's Club; F Other; 2 Personal checks accepted; 3 Lunch available; 4 Dinner available; 5 Open all year; 6 Pets welcome;

NEW MARLBOROUGH

Old Inn on the Green & Gedney Farm

Route 57, 01230
(413) 229-3131; (800) 286-3139
FAX (413) 229-8236; e-mail: brad@oldinn
www.oldinn.com

A 1760 inn with period guest rooms and private baths. Three-star (*Boston Globe*) restaurant with candlelight, fireplaces, and alfresco dining. Gedney Farm is a turn-of-the-century renovated barn with deluxe guest rooms and suites with granite fireplaces and whirlpool. Banquet facilities available. Superb wedding site. Lunch is available seasonally.

Host: Brad Wagstaff
Rooms: 26 (PB) $135-325
Continental Breakfast
Credit Cards: A, B, C
Notes: 2, 4, 5, 8, 9, 10, 11, 12, 13, 14

NEWTON

Bed & Breakfast Associates Bay Colony, Ltd.

P.O. Box 57166, Babson Park, Boston, 02457-0166
(781) 449-5302; (888) 429-7591
FAX (781) 449-5958; e-mail: info@bnbboston.com
www.bnbboston.com

IW255. Robin's Nest. This stately Victorian home, in a neighborhood of grand 19th-century homes, has a private two-room guest suite with a charming sitting room, a dazzling new private bath, and facilities available for light cooking. Leave the car in the driveway and walk to the express bus for a 10-minute trip to Boston. Amenities include cable TV, VCR, telephone, small refrigerator, microwave, sandwich bar, and Victorian desk and sofa. $95-110.

Host Homes of Boston

P.O. Box 117, Waban Branch, Boston, 02468-0001
(617) 244-1308; (800) 600-1308
FAX (617) 244-5156

Alderwood. Guests migrate to the gourmet kitchen in this 1930 Colonial. Second-floor guest room has twin beds. Pumpkin the cat lives here. Children welcome. Quiet road near Boston College law campus. One mile to Green Line-D. Ten-minute drive to Boston. Private bath. TV. Air conditioned. $87.

Briarwood. Historic Chestnut Hill landmark home (1875) combines Early American antiques with modern amenities. Exceptional guest wing with private entrance and bath, featuring queen-size bed, two twin beds that double as sofas, skylights, air conditioning, TV, an alcove with dining table, picture window, and light-cooking facilities. Guests prepare own breakfast, food provided. Near restaurants and elegant mall, four blocks to public transit (Green Line-D), one block to Boston College. Boston, three miles. No smoking. $110.

Norumbega. Near the Marriott Hotel, site of the old Norumbega Park on the Charles River, is this bright and impeccable modern Victorian home. First floor guest room with adjacent private hall bath. Walk to village, commuter train. Short drive to subway. Near Massachusetts Pike, I-95. No smoking. TV. Air conditioning. Parking. $87.

Rockledge. Stately 1882 Victorian in prime location where guests return again and again. Cordial hosts offer bright, spacious rooms, antiques, and gardens. Three second-floor guest rooms, parlor with TV. Queen-size and twin rooms share hall bath. Double room with bath en suite. Ceiling fans. Chloe the cat in residence. Two blocks to lake, village restaurants, shops, and Green Line-D. Fifteen minutes to Back Bay, Copley Square. No smoking. $81-95.

7 No smoking; 8 Children welcome; 9 Social drinking allowed; 10 Tennis nearby; 11 Swimming nearby; 12 Golf nearby; 13 Skiing nearby; 14 May be booked through a travel agent; 15 Handicapped accessible.

NEWTON CENTER

Host Homes of Boston

P.O. Box 117, Waban Branch, Boston, 02468-0001
(617) 244-1308; (800) 600-1308
FAX (617) 244-5156

Park Lane. This large Baronial-style stucco (1911) on quiet street has a Victorian motif. Friendly host offers two third-floor guest rooms, one with double bed and the other with trundle bed; second floor has queen-size bed, private bath Jacuzzi, air conditioning, cable TV. First-floor guest parlor with fireplace. Village, public transit (Green Line-D), restaurants all within 10-minute walk. Five miles from Boston. No smoking. Children welcome. $68-95.

NORTH ADAMS

Blackinton Manor

1391 Massachusetts Avenue, 01247
(413) 663-5795; (800) 795-8613
FAX (413) 663-3121; e-mail: epsteind@bcn.net

An Italianate Federal mansion set in the heart of the scenic and cultural Berkshires just a few moments from Williams College. Meticulously restored and furnished with beautiful antiques, Blackinton Manor serves a gourmet breakfast. All rooms enjoy private baths (one with Jacuzzi) and air conditioning. In-ground swimming pool and beautiful gardens complete the picture. Hosts Dan and Betsey Epstein are pro-

Blackinton Manor

fessional classical musicians, so there is often live music for the guests. Children seven and older welcome.

Hosts: Dan and Betsey Epstein
Rooms: 5 (PB) $105-125
Full Breakfast
Credit Cards: A, B
Notes: 2, 5, 7, 9, 10, 11, 12, 13

NORTHAMPTON

American Country Collection

1353 Union Street, Schenectady, NY 12308
(518) 370-4948; (800) 810-4948
FAX (518) 393-1634 (call first)
e-mail: Carolbnbres@msn.com
www.bandbreservations.com

239. Step out onto a huge deck and see Mount Tom in the view. Enjoy watching the sheep and goats fenced in the 40 acres of pastures just minutes from downtown Northampton. This trilevel homestay bed and breakfast offers guests a unique open floor plan. The second-floor suite and third-floor rooms share a dining area, living room, and private baths. Near colleges and historic Deerfield. Great park nearby for golf, swimming, tennis, hiking, and cross-country skiing. $75-110.

Shingle Hill Bed & Breakfast

7 Mountain Street, P.O. Box 212, Haydenville, 01039
(413) 268-8320

Goat herd and guard llama roam past spectacular mountain view on this 40-acre hillside retreat just 10 minutes from downtown Northampton in the Berkshire foothills. Guests have the use of a living room, dining area, and kitchen that are completely separate from hosts' quarters. Enjoy a leisurely country breakfast—Continental breakfast weekdays; full breakfast weekends—on the enclosed deck overlooking the front pasture. Convenient to I-91, Massachusetts Turnpike, and the Five College (Northampton/Amherst) area.

Host: Sara Sullivan
Rooms: 5 (3 PB; 2 SB) $60-85
Full and Continental Breakfast
Credit Cards: None
Notes: 2, 5, 7, 8, 9, 10, 11, 12, 13

NORTHAMPTON (FLORENCE)

The Knoll

230 North Main Street, 01062-1221
(413) 584-8164; www.crocker.com/~theknoll

The Knoll can be found on 17 acres overlooking farmland and forest. It is in town and yet in a rural setting, with an acre of lawn and a large circular driveway. This is the five-college area of western Massachusetts: Smith, Amherst, Mount Holyoke, and Hampshire Colleges, and the University of Massachusetts.

Host: Mrs. Lee Lesko
Rooms: 3 (SB) $50-60
Full Breakfast
Credit Cards: None
Notes: 2, 5, 7, 10, 12, 13

The Knoll

Lupine House

185 North Main Street, P.O. Box 60483, Florence,
  01062-0483
(413) 586-9766; (800) 890-9766
www.westmass.com/lupinehouse

Lupine House Bed and Breakfast, a recently remodeled circa 1870 home, is three miles from downtown Northampton in the village of Florence. Three tastefully decorated guest rooms have private baths. Bike trail abuts hosts' property. Homemade breakfast includes

fresh breads, fruit, granola, juices, and hot beverages. Special dietary needs are easily accommodated. A short drive to Smith, Amherst, Hampshire, and Mount Holyoke Colleges, University of Massachusetts, Deerfield Academy, and the Williston Northampton School. Open mid-September through early June.

Hosts: Gil and Evelyn Billings
Rooms: 3 (PB) $70
Continental Breakfast
Credit Cards: A, B
Notes: 2, 7, 9, 12, 13

NORWOOD

Bed & Breakfast Associates Bay Colony, Ltd.

P.O. Box 57166, Babson Park, Boston, 02457-0166
(781) 449-5302; (888) 429-7591
FAX (781) 449-5958; e-mail: info@bnbboston.com
www.bnbboston.com

IW560. Lyman Smith House. Just a short walk to the commuter rail, this delightful four-bedroom inn was built in 1850. It is authentically furnished with antiques and reproduction pieces. Each room has a private bath, TV, and telephone. $82-95.

OAK BLUFFS (MARTHA'S VINEYARD)

Tivoli Inn—Martha's Vineyard

125 Circuit Avenue, 02557
(508) 693-7928; e-mail: tivoli@xpres.net
www.mvy.com/tivoli

Tivoli Inn is a newly renovated Oak Bluffs Victorian gingerbread house which has the island charm and exudes a clean and friendly atmosphere. Built during the age of the great sailing ships, the house is replete with a flowery balcony and wraparound latticed porch for setting and rocking. Just beyond the top of Circuit Avenue, the Tivoli Inn is within walking distance of town beaches, ferries, and Main Street

7 No smoking; 8 Children welcome; 9 Social drinking allowed; 10 Tennis nearby; 11 Swimming nearby;
12 Golf nearby; 13 Skiing nearby; 14 May be booked through a travel agent; 15 Handicapped accessible.

Tivoli Inn

shops, and night life. Complimentary Continental plus breakfast served May through October.

Rooms: 6 (3 PB; 3 SB)
Credit Cards: None
Notes: 5, 6, 9, 10, 11, 12, 14

ONSET

The Henderson-Berford Inn

2 Fairway Drive, Buzzards Bay, 02532
(508) 759-8860

Master bedroom with walk-in closet/dressing room, private bath, king-size bed, and guest dining room. The home is at the gateway to Cape Cod near clean and beautiful beaches, the Cape Cod Canal, deep-sea fishing, whale watching, golf, museums, Hyannis, shopping malls, outlets. Fifteen minutes to Falmouth ferry to Martha's Vineyard. Plymouth is 22 miles north, offering a view of historic Plymouth Rock and Cranberry World Visitors Center. One-hour drive to Boston, 45 minutes to Rhode Island. Open May through October. Lunch and dinner available at an extra charge.

Hosts: Mr. and Mrs. Henderson
Rooms: 1 (PB) $65-75
Continental Breakfast
Credit Cards: None
Notes: 7, 9, 11, 12

ORLEANS

Academy Place Bed & Breakfast

8 Academy Place, P.O. Box 1407, 02653
(508) 255-3181; FAX (508) 247-9812

This 1790s sea captain's home, on the village green, is at the edge of Orleans's shopping district. Many fine shops and restaurants are a short walk away. Accompanied by candlelight, Sandy serves a Continental plus breakfast of homemade muffins and breads with chilled juices and fresh fruit, freshly brewed coffee, teas, or hot chocolate. The entire house is air conditioned. Beaches and fishing, two and one-half miles; Cape Cod National Seashore visitor center, four miles; bike trail, one-third mile. Children six and older welcome.

Hosts: Sandy and Charles Terrell
Rooms: 5 (3 PB; 2 SB) $75-95
Continental Breakfast
Credit Cards: A, B
Notes: 2, 7, 9, 10, 11, 12, 14

Academy Place

Bed & Breakfast Cape Cod

P.O. Box 1312, 02653
(508) 255-3824; (800) 541-6226
FAX (508) 240-0599
e-mail: info@bedandbreakfastcapecod.com
www.bedandbreakfastcapecod.com

ORL 01. On one and one-half acres by Cape Cod Bay, this English-style bed and breakfast cottage is the perfect haven for a sea side vacation. Two bedrooms, one with canopied bed, the other has a brass bed, attached private baths, living room, TV, air conditioning, porches, and decks all invite comfort and relaxation. A short distance from Skaket Beach and bike trail. There is also a lovely studio apartment with a spectacular view of the marsh and Cape Cod Bay with guaranteed sunsets. No children. Inquire about rates for cottage. $95-98.

Winterwood at Petersham

OSTERVILLE

Bed & Breakfast Cape Cod

P.O. Box 1312, Orleans, 02653
(508) 255-3824; (800) 541-6226
FAX (508) 240-0599
e-mail: info@bedandbreakfastcapecod.com
www.bedandbreakfastcapecod.com

OST 02. What can be more Cape Cod but being directly on a cranberry bog? A lovely suite with two queen-size bedrooms, a living room, kitchen, and patio all overlooking the bog. This is the perfect spot for a family or two couples traveling together. Convenient to the island ferries, beaches, and all that is wonderful on Cape Cod. Twenty dollars for each extra person. $115.

PETERSHAM

Winterwood at Petersham

19 North Main Street, 01366
(978) 724-8885

An elegant 16-room Greek Revival mansion built in 1842, just off the common of a classic New England town. The inn boasts numerous fireplaces and several porches for relaxing. Cocktails available. In the National Register of Historic Places.

Hosts: Jean and Robert Day
Rooms: 6 (PB) $73.99-95.13

Continental Breakfast
Credit Cards: A, B, C, D
Notes: 2, 5, 7, 8, 9, 12, 13, 14

PLYMOUTH

Another Place Inn

240 Sandwich Street, 02360
(508) 746-0126

At Another Place guests will experience the reality of another time in Plymouth. Guests will be surrounded by warm, comfortable, antique furnishings, in a 200-year-old half-Cape. The host, an experienced gourmet cook, can surprise one's palate with authentic 1620 foods or hearty New England cuisine. Conveniently positioned, Another Place is minutes from shopping, historic sites, or beach areas.

Host: Carol Barnes
Rooms: 3 (PB) $75-105
Full Breakfast
Credit Cards: None
Notes: 2, 5, 7, 10, 11, 12

Bed & Breakfast Cape Cod

P.O. Box 1312, Orleans, 02653
(508) 255-3824; (800) 541-6226
FAX (508) 240-0599
e-mail: info@bedandbreakfastcapecod.com
www.bedandbreakfastcapecod.com

PLY 03. Enjoy spaciousness and splendid ocean views from this stately Colonial home. Sitting

7 No smoking; 8 Children welcome; 9 Social drinking allowed; 10 Tennis nearby; 11 Swimming nearby; 12 Golf nearby; 13 Skiing nearby; 14 May be booked through a travel agent; 15 Handicapped accessible.

on 11 acres of pastures there is a private beach and a private pond. All rooms have baths en suite. Chock full of antiques and treasures, this is a special place and convenient to all that is special on Massachusetts South Shore. $95-125.

Bed & Breakfast Reservations North Shore, Greater Boston, Cape Cod

P.O. Box 600035, Newtonville, 02460
(617) 964-1606; (800) 832-2632
FAX (617) 332-8572; e-mail: info@bbreserve.com
www.bbreserve.com

119. The 1820 English Cottage. A beautifully restored Cape-style bed and breakfast on 40 acres of pastures and wonderful grounds with breathtaking views. Large outside deck where breakfast is served in warmer weather. Three elegantly decorated guest rooms, en suite private baths, working fireplaces, and air conditioning. Large common room with fireplace, TV/VCR. Close to all historic sites. Great location for easy day trips to Boston, Cape Cod, Newport, Rhode Island. Full breakfast. $95-115.

155. Harbor House. This exquisitely designed Nantucket barn house has magnificent views of the harbor, ocean, and pond. This peaceful and secluded setting is perfect for a romantic getaway. Guests may feel like they are miles away from it all, yet this is a fabulous central location for visiting Cape Cod and Boston. Guests are just 15 minutes to historic Plymouth Center, five minutes to Cape Cod, and one hour from Boston and Newport, Rhode Island. All rooms are decorator-designed, with water views, private baths, sun decks, and cable TV. Complimentary wine and cheese. Beach chairs and towels provided. Full breakfast. Families with children three and older welcome. Open year-round. $95-135.

169. Sea Cliff Bed and Breakfast. This bed and breakfast is perched on a cliff high above the ocean, with stairs leading down to a private sandy beach. The ocean views are spectacular.

Explore historic Plymouth, visit Cape Cod, or take wonderful day trips to Boston and Newport, Rhode Island. Return at day's end to the secluded and peaceful setting. There are two guest rooms with private baths upstairs, and a family suite, with small kitchen, downstairs which can sleep up to four comfortably, sharing one bath. Full breakfast. Smoking permitted on outside deck and porch. Families with children of all ages welcome. $100-125.

Foxglove Cottage

101 Sandwich Road, 02360
(508) 747-6576; (800) 479-4746
FAX (508) 747-7622
e-mail: tranquility@foxglove-cottage.com
www.foxglove-cottage.com

Nestled in the heart of historic Plymouth, Foxglove Cottage (circa 1820) is a fully restored, authentic Cape farmhouse furnished with American and Victorian antiques. Its rooms all have en suite private baths, air conditioning/heat, working fireplaces, and reading and sitting areas. Enjoy the common room with its large comfortable sitting area and cable TV/VCR. Minutes from Plimoth Plantation and other historic sites and activities. Open year-round so that guests may enjoy not only the seasons, but the ambiance and warm New England hospitality. Children over 12 welcome.

Hosts: Mr. and Mrs. Charles K. Cowan
Rooms: 3 (PB) $80-95
Full Breakfast
Credit Cards: None
Notes: 2, 5, 7, 9, 10, 11, 12, 14

Plymouth Bay Manor Bed & Breakfast

259 Court Street, 02360
(508) 830-0426; (800) 492-1828
e-mail: info@plymouthbaymanor.com
www.plymouthbaymanor.com

Spectacular ocean views from each of the antique-furnished, beautifully decorated guest rooms. Gaze upon lighthouses, islands, sail boats, and gardens while enjoying a hearty breakfast in the aerial sunroom. The perfect hub for one's New England stay. Walking distance from historic Plymouth sites and attractions and a lovely, quiet beach. Forty-five minutes to Boston, 20 minutes to the Cape, 55 minutes to Newport mansions, and 50 minutes to island ferries. A quaint, artists colony, great shopping, golfing, antiquing, whale watches, and dining town.

Hosts: Cindi and Larry Hamlin
Rooms: 3 (PB) $85-125
Full Breakfast
Credit Cards: A, B
Notes: 2, 7, 9, 10, 11, 12, 14

Remembrance

265 Sandwich Street, 02360
(508) 746-5160

Remembrance is an old cedar-shingled Cape-style home in a lovely residential neighborhood one mile from historic Plymouth, Plimoth Plantation, and the expressway; two blocks from the ocean. It is delightfully decorated with antiques, wicker, original art, plants, and flowers. Delicious full breakfasts served at guests' convenience in the greenhouse overlooking the garden and bird feeders. Tea time. No smoking. Gentle resident pets.

Host: Beverly Bainbridge
Rooms: 2 (SB) $70-85
Full Breakfast
Credit Cards: None
Notes: 2, 5, 7, 9, 10, 11, 12, 14

PRINCETON

Fernside Bed & Breakfast

162 Mountain Road, P.O. Box 303, 01541
(978) 464-2741; (800) 545-2741
FAX (978) 464-2065

An elegant Federal mansion with a breathtaking view of Boston on the eastern slope of Mount Wachusett in central Massachusetts. This gracious home has been carefully restored

Fernside

and exquisitely furnished in antiques and period reproductions. The eight fireplaces, numerous porches, and sitting rooms offer guests the opportunity to renew themselves, enjoy a romantic retreat, or just escape and relax. The Wachusett region provides opportunities for hiking, bird watching, snow shoeing, cross-country and downhill skiing.

Hosts: Jocelyn and Richard Morrison
Rooms: 6 (PB) $115-165
Full Breakfast
Credit Cards: A, B, C, D, E, F
Notes: 2, 5, 7, 9, 10, 11, 12, 13, 14, 15

PROVINCETOWN

The Captain's House

350A Commercial Street, 02657
(508) 487-9353; (800) 457-8885

Open year-round, the house in the center of town is within walking distance to shopping, restaurants, and night life. Reasonable rates and immaculate accommodations. Continental breakfast with home-baked pastries. Private and shared baths with cable TV and a pleasant common room with VCR and music for guests' pleasure. A private patio for sunbathing is also provided. Major credit cards accepted. Off-season rates available. Smoking permitted in designated areas only.

Hosts: Bob Carvalho and David Brennan
Rooms: 11 (3 PB; 8 SB) $55-95
Continental Breakfast
Credit Cards: A, B, C, D
Notes: 2, 5, 9, 10, 11, 12

7 No smoking; 8 Children welcome; 9 Social drinking allowed; 10 Tennis nearby; 11 Swimming nearby; 12 Golf nearby; 13 Skiing nearby; 14 May be booked through a travel agent; 15 Handicapped accessible.

Gabriel's Apartments & Guest Rooms

104 Bradford Street, 02657
(508) 487-3232; (800) 969-2643
FAX (508) 487-1605
e-mail: gabriels@provincetown.com
www.provincetown.com/gabriels

Since 1979 Gabriel's has welcomed friends to two beautiful homes graced by antique furnishings, patios, and gardens. Each guest room and suite, decorated differently, is distinguished by its own personality. Amenities include Continental plus breakfast in the large skylit common room, fireplaces, exercise equipment, hot tubs, a steam room, cable TV, VCRs, in-room telephones, air conditioning, fully equipped kitchens, a sauna, business services; a book and video library, bikes, and private parking. Personal checks are accepted for deposits only. Inquire about accommodations for pets.

Host: Gabriel Brooke
Rooms: 20 (PB) $65-200
Continental Breakfast
Credit Cards: A, B, C, D
Notes: 5, 7, 8, 9, 10, 11, 12, 14

Land's End Inn

22 Commercial Street, 02657
(508) 487-0706; (800) 276-7088

At the very tip of Cape Cod, perched high atop Gull Hill, Land's End Inn commands a panoramic view of Provincetown and all of Cape Cod Bay. Large, airy, comfortably furnished living rooms, a large front porch, and lovely antique-filled bedrooms provide relaxation and visual pleasure to guests. Seasonal rates available.

Host: Anthony Arakelian
Rooms: 16 (PB) $87-285
Continental Breakfast
Credit Cards: A, B
Notes: 2, 5, 7, 9, 11

Watership Inn

Watership Inn

7 Winthrop Street, 02657
(508) 487-0094

Rustic 1820 sea captain's home, with Colonial rooms, private baths, and spacious lobby. Open year-round, serving Continental breakfast daily. Parking is available, and a five-minute walk gets visitors to the beach or to the center of town.

Host: Jim Foss
Rooms: 15 (PB) $36-200
Continental Breakfast
Credit Cards: A, B, C, D
Notes: 5, 9, 10, 11, 12, 14

White Wind Inn

174 Commercial Street, 02657
(508) 487-1526; (888) 449-WIND
www.provincetown.com/whitewindinn

The White Wind Inn is a gracious Victorian mansion built in 1845. Guests enjoy the White Wind's well-appointed accommodations that feature high ceilings, antiques, chandeliers, four-poster and brass beds. All rooms have private baths, TV, VCR, air conditioning or ceiling fans, telephones, and refrigerators. Several rooms have private decks, some with water views. Fireplace rooms provide that extra romantic touch for visits throughout the year. The inn also features the best porch in town. Inquire about accommodations for pets.

Innkeepers: Michael Valenti and Robert Tosner
Rooms: 11 (PB) $85-200
Continental Breakfast
Credit Cards: A, B
Notes: 5, 7, 9, 10, 11

NOTES: Credit cards accepted: A MasterCard; B Visa; C American Express; D Discover; E Diner's Club; F Other; 2 Personal checks accepted; 3 Lunch available; 4 Dinner available; 5 Open all year; 6 Pets welcome;

REHOBOTH

Five Bridge Farm Inn Bed & Breakfast

154 Pine Street, P.O. Box 462, 02769
(508) 252-3190; e-mail: fivbrgin@ici.net
http: //home.ici.net/~fivbrgin/

Five Bridge Farm is a unique property near
Providence, Newport, Cape Cod, and Boston.
Enjoy hiking, cross-country skiing, tennis,
swimming, or quiet time in the library, gazebo,
on 60 acres. Guests are treated to old-fashioned
hospitality and delicious home-cooked breakfasts. Horseback riding, golf, fine restaurants,
beaches, and antiquing are all nearby. Inquire
about accommodations for children.

Hosts: Harold and Ann Messenger
Rooms: 5 (3 PB; 2 SB) $75-105
Full Breakfast
Credit Cards: A, B, D
Notes: 2, 5, 6, 7, 8, 9, 10, 11, 12

Gilbert's Tree Farm Bed & Breakfast

30 Spring Street, 02769
(508) 252-6416

A 150-year-old New England Cape home with
authentic hardware, wood floors, and windows
is on a 17-acre tree farm only 12 miles east of
Providence. Guests may enjoy in-ground pool,
hiking, and pony cart rides. Delicious full

Gilbert's Tree Farm

country breakfasts. Within one hour of Boston,
Plymouth, Newport, and Mystic. An additional
$20 to stable horses.

Host: Jeanne Gilbert
Rooms: 4 (1 PB; 3SB) $60-80
Full Breakfast
Credit Cards: None
Notes: 2, 5, 6, 7, 8, 9, 10, 11, 12, 14

Perryville Inn

Perryville Inn

157 Perryville Road, 02769
(508) 252-9239

This 19th-century restored Victorian in the
National Register of Historic Places is on four
and one-half wooded acres with a quiet brook,
mill pond, stone walls, and shaded paths and is
overlooking an 18-hole public golf course.
Bicycles available for guests, including a tan-
dem. Nearby are antique stores, museums,
Great Woods Performing Arts Center, fine
seafood restaurants, and an old-fashioned New
England clambake. Arrange for a horse-drawn
hayride or a hot-air balloon ride. Within 15
minutes of Providence; one hour of Boston,
Plymouth, Newport, and Mystic. Central air
conditioning.

Hosts: Tom and Betsy Charnecki
Rooms: 4 (PB) $65-95
Continental Breakfast
Credit Cards: A, B, C, D
Notes: 2, 7, 8, 9, 12, 14

7 No smoking; 8 Children welcome; 9 Social drinking allowed; 10 Tennis nearby; 11 Swimming nearby;
12 Golf nearby; 13 Skiing nearby; 14 May be booked through a travel agent; 15 Handicapped accessible.

ROCKPORT

Addison Choate Inn

49 Broadway, 01966
(978) 546-7543; (800) 245-7543
www.cape-ann.com/addison-choate

An 1851 Greek Revival residence with six bright and cheerful rooms and a stable house with two one-bedroom apartments. All have original wide-pine floors, quilts, rag rugs, white wicker chairs, antique and reproduction furniture, private baths. Living room with fireplace; TV room; suites. Private-blend coffee, home-baked cakes, breads. Afternoon tea. Air conditioning. Perennial gardens, pool, parking, porches, friendly cat. Walk to galleries, shops, restaurants, beaches, Boston trains.

Hosts: Knox and Shirley Johnson
Rooms: 8 (PB) $95-150
Continental Breakfast
Credit Cards: A, B, D
Notes: 2, 5, 7, 11, 12, 14

Addison Choate Inn

Bed & Breakfast Reservations North Shore, Greater Boston, Cape Cod

P.O. Box 600035, Newtonville, 02460
(617) 964-1606; (800) 832-2632
FAX (617) 332-8572; e-mail: info@bbreserve.com
www.bbreserve.com

98. The Inn at Mill Pond. A stately 1840 Victorian inn with 14 tastefully decorated guest rooms with private baths. Some larger suites and efficiencies available. Relax on grounds with beautiful flowering gardens and picnic tables. Short walk to sandy beach and town center with quaint shops, many restaurants, and scenic harbor. Commuter rail station nearby for day trip into Boston. Families with children welcome in the annex rooms and carriage house. No smoking. Delicious home-baked Continental breakfast. Twenty dollars for third person in room. $99-125.

167. The Inn at Rockport Center. Historic inn just steps away from the quaint shops, galleries, and restaurants of world-famous Rockport Village. The grounds are quiet and private with an enclosed swimming pool, surrounded by lush perennial gardens. A short walk down a path just beyond the pool, brings guests to a beautiful sandy beach. The inn offers guests a variety of tastefully decorated rooms with TV, air conditioning. Weekly rentals: a two-room suite with small, full kitchen, and more spacious cottage, which overlooks the pool. Both can sleep up to four. Children over 12 welcome. Continental breakfast. No smoking. Inquire about weekly rates. $80-125.

Emerson Inn By the Sea

1 Cathedral Avenue, 01966
(978) 546-6321; (800) 964-5550
e-mail: info@emersoninnbythesea.com
www.emersoninnbythesea.com

Much like an old friend, the Emerson Inn has changed and moved forward, yet it still remains a classic treasure. Ideal for weddings and conferences. Awaiting guests' arrival are 34 air-conditioned, smoke-free guest rooms and suites with private baths, many with magnificent ocean vistas. To relax there is the option of the Day Spa for a facial or massage. Or perhaps a dip in the swimming pool followed by a visit to the whirlpool and sauna.

Hosts: Bruce and Michele Coates
Rooms: 34 (PB) $125-235
Continental Breakfast
Credit Cards: A, B, C, D
Notes: 4, 7, 8, 9, 10, 11, 12, 14

NOTES: Credit cards accepted: A MasterCard; B Visa; C American Express; D Discover; E Diner's Club; F Other; 2 Personal checks accepted; 3 Lunch available; 4 Dinner available; 5 Open all year; 6 Pets welcome;

The Inn on Cove Hill

37 Mount Pleasant Street, 01966
(508) 546-2701; (888) 546-2701
www.cape-ann.com/covehill

Offering a friendly atmosphere with the option of privacy, this lovingly restored 200-year-old Federal home is just two blocks from the harbor and shops. Meticulously appointed cozy bedrooms are furnished with antiques, and some have canopied beds. Wake up to the delicious aroma of hot muffins, and enjoy a Continental breakfast at the umbrella tables in the Pump Garden. The fresh sea air is preserved in the nonsmoking facility.

Hosts: John and Marjorie Pratt
Rooms: 11 (9 PB; 2 SB) $50-125
Continental Breakfast
Credit Cards: A, B
Notes: 2, 7, 9, 11, 12

Linden Tree Inn

26 King Street, 01966
(978) 546-2494; (800) 865-2122
FAX (978) 546-3297; e-mail: ltree@shore.net

The inn is a friendly haven offering a restful and relaxing vacation or getaway. The main house features 14 distinctively decorated guest rooms with private baths. Every morning guests will be greeted with Dawn's delicious Continental breakfast featuring delightful "made from scratch" pastries, served buffet-style in the dining room. Dawn's breakfasts receive high commendation from the guide book, *Best Places to Stay in New England.*

Hosts: Jon and Dawn Cunningham
Rooms: 18 (PB) $75-105
Continental Breakfast
Credit Cards: A, B
Notes: 2, 7, 9, 10, 11, 12, 14

Sally Webster Inn

34 Mount Pleasant Street, 01966
(978) 546-9251

Gracious Colonial Inn (circa 1832) steeped in local history sits just two blocks from the gal-

Sally Webster Inn

leries, shops, and restaurants of Rockport village and is surrounded by ocean beaches. Whether guests come to Rockport to whale watch, sail, golf, shop, or antique, coming home to the inn will be the best part of the day. Rockport is a wonderful place to settle in and explore New England—Boston, Salem, Newburyport, Essex, Gloucester, Marblehead, all within 35 miles.

Hosts: Rick and Carolyn Steere
Rooms: 8 (PB) $70-94
Continental Breakfast
Credit Cards: A, B
Notes: 2, 5, 7, 9, 11, 12

Seacrest Manor

99 Marmion Way, 01966
(978) 546-2211
www.rockportusa.com/seacrestmanor/

Decidedly small, intentionally quiet. Gracious hospitality in luxurious surroundings with

Seacrest Manor

7 No smoking; 8 Children welcome; 9 Social drinking allowed; 10 Tennis nearby; 11 Swimming nearby; 12 Golf nearby; 13 Skiing nearby; 14 May be booked through a travel agent; 15 Handicapped accessible.

magnificent views overlooking woods and sea. Spacious grounds, lovely gardens, and ample parking. Famous full breakfast and afternoon tea included. Fresh flowers, cable TV, free daily paper, mints, and turndown. Mobil-rated three stars. Across from the nine-acre John Kieran Nature Preserve. An hour north of Boston by car or train. No pets. No smoking. Not recommended for children. Closed December through March.

Hosts: Leighton Saville and Dwight MacCormack
Rooms: 8 (6 PB; 2 SB) $102-148
Full Breakfast
Credit Cards: None
Notes: 2, 7, 9, 11, 12

The Tuck Inn Bed & Breakfast

17 High Street, 01966
(978) 546-7260; (800) 789-7260
www.rockportusa.com/tuckinn/

A cozy 1790 Colonial home on a quiet secondary street, one block from the village center. The inn features the charm of yesterday with antiques, quilts, wide-pine floors, and living room with fireplace, coupled with modern conveniences such as private baths, cable TVs, air conditioning, and a pool. Guests have remarked on the lavish home-baked buffet breakfast and are treated to good old-fashioned New England hospitality. Train and golfing are three blocks away. Nonsmoking.

The Tuck Inn

Hosts: Liz and Scott Wood
Rooms: 11 (PB) $59-99
Continental Breakfast
Credit Cards: A, B
Notes: 2, 5, 7, 8, 9, 10, 11, 12, 14

SALEM

Amelia Payson House

16 Winter Street, 01970
(978) 744-8304; e-mail: bbamelia@aol.com
www.salemweb.com/biz/ameliapayson/

A five-minute stroll from the elegantly restored 1845 Greek Revival finds the Peabody & Essex Museum, the Salem Witch Museum, Salem Maritime National Historic Site, the House of Seven Gables, shops, waterfront dining, and the Amtrak train to Boston. The seaside towns of Rockport and Gloucester are a short drive up the coast. Comfort amenities include private baths, TV, and air conditioning. Color brochure available. Children over 12 welcome. Nonsmoking host home.

Hosts: Ada and Donald Roberts
Rooms: 4 (PB) $75-125
Continental Breakfast
Credit Cards: A, B, C
Notes: 7, 9, 10, 11, 12

Bed & Breakfast Reservations North Shore, Greater Boston, Cape Cod

P.O. Box 600035, Newtonville, 02460
(617) 964-1606; (800) 832-2632
FAX (617) 332-8572; e-mail: info@bbreserve.com
www.bbreserve.com

5. Inn on the Green. In the heart of Salem, this historic Greek Revival-style inn was built in 1846. It has been elegantly restored. Each of seven guest rooms has period furnishings, queen-size bed, private bath, cable TV, and air conditioning. Sunny breakfast room where complimentary Continental breakfast is served. Relax in the beautiful formal living room with marble decorative fireplace. Walk to historic

sites, shopping, great restaurants, and commuter rail train to Boston. Cat in residence. No smoking. $102-115.

161. Salem Common. Classic Greek Revival, built in 1850 in historic district, overlooking Common. Steps away from visitor sites, and a short walk to waterfront area shops and restaurants. The Commuter Rail train to Boston is easy walking distance. Guest rooms have private baths, cable TV, VCR, air conditioning, telephones, coffee makers, and refrigerators. The Honeymoon Suite features a four-poster bed, fireplace, beamed ceilings, and private Jacuzzi bath. Each day at the inn begins with the aroma of freshly brewed coffee and a complimentary elegant Continental breakfast. Free on-site parking. No smoking. Open year-round. Premium rates charged during Foliage season and Salem Haunted Happenings. $95-165.

Coach House Inn

284 Lafayette Street, 01970
(978) 744-4092; (800) 688-8689
FAX (978) 745-8031; e-mail: coachhse@star.net
www.salemweb.com/biz/coachhouse

Victorian mansion, built by a sea captain in 1879, retains the charm and elegance of an earlier era. Colorful, bright rooms are decorated with antique furnishings. In historic district two blocks from the ocean.

Host: Patricia Kessler
Rooms: 11 (9 PB; 2 SB) $78-135
Continental Breakfast
Credit Cards: A, B, C, D
Notes: 5, 7, 8, 9, 10, 11, 12

The Inn at Seven Winter Street

7 Winter Street, 01970
(508) 745-9520; (800) 932-5547

Come, be a guest at the Inn at Seven Winter Street! This magnificently restored French Victorian inn is an award winner. Each room finely

The Inn at Seven Winter Street

appointed with period antiques and furnishings. All rooms have something beautifully unique: marble fireplace, canopied bed, Jacuzzi, or sun deck. In a historic area, within a one-minute walk of the waterfront, historic sites, dining, and museums. Off-street parking available. No smoking.

Hosts: Sally Flint, Jill and D. L. Coté
Rooms: 10 (PB) $85-185
Continental Breakfast
Credit Cards: A, B, C
Notes: 2, 5, 7, 9

The Salem Inn

7 Summer Street, 01970
(978) 741-0680; (800) 446-2995
www.SalemInnMA.com

Three elegantly restored homes in the heart of Salem's historic district. Thirty-nine comfortably appointed rooms with private baths. Direct-dial telephones, cable TVs, and air conditioning. Hearty Continental breakfast. Some rooms with canopied beds, whirlpool baths and/or working fireplaces. Within walking distance of the museums and other attractions.

Hosts: Richard and Diane Pabich
Rooms: 39 (PB) $109-290
Continental Breakfast
Credit Cards: A, B, C, D, E, F
Notes: 4, 5, 6, 8, 10, 11, 12, 14

7 No smoking; 8 Children welcome; 9 Social drinking allowed; 10 Tennis nearby; 11 Swimming nearby; 12 Golf nearby; 13 Skiing nearby; 14 May be booked through a travel agent; 15 Handicapped accessible.

Stephen Daniels House

1 Daniels Street, 01970
(508) 744-5709

Built by a sea captain in 1667 and enlarged in 1756, the house is beautifully restored and furnished with antiques. Wood-burning fireplaces in the bedrooms with charming canopied beds. Continental breakfast is served before two huge fireplaces. Walk to 11 points of interest in Salem.

Host: Catherine Gill
Rooms: 5 (3 PB; 2 SB) $75-125
Continental Breakfast
Credit Cards: C
Notes: 2, 5, 6, 8, 9, 10, 11, 12, 14

Suzannah Flint House

98 Essex Street, 01970
(978) 744-5281; (800) 893-9973
www.salemweb.com/biz/suzannahflint

Built in 1808, the Suzannah Flint House is a fine example of Federal period architecture. Each spacious room features antique furnishings, oriental rugs over original hardwood floors, decorative fireplaces, private baths, cable color TV/VCR, and air conditioning. The inn is in Salem's historic district, adjacent to Salem Common, and one block to the waterfront wharves, mu-seums, historic sites, shops, and fine dining. Also walk to train station.

Host: Scott Eklind
Rooms: 3 (PB) $60-110
Continental Breakfast
Credit Cards: A, B, C, D
Notes: 2, 5, 7, 9, 10, 11, 12

SANDWICH (CAPE COD) _____

Bed & Breakfast Cape Cod

P.O. Box 1312, Orleans, 02653
(508) 255-3824; (800) 541-6226
FAX (508) 240-0599
e-mail: info@BedandBreakfastCapeCod.com
www.BedandBreakfastCapeCod.com

SAN 05. Cape Cod at its best. A Colonial home one mile from spectacular Sandy Neck Beach. Large four-poster bedroom with attached bath and sliders that go out to guests' own private deck. High ceilings, TV, sitting area as well. Great area for relaxing. $115.

Belfry Inne and Bistro

8 Jarves Street, P.O. Box 2211, 02563
(508) 888-8550; (800) 844-4542
FAX (508) 888-3922; e-mail: info@belfryinn.com
www.belfryinn.com

Belfry Inne exemplifies an era renowned for gentility and grace. Authentic "painted lady" in the heart of Sandwich, Cape Cod historic district. All rooms with private bath, some with whirlpools, fireplaces, soaking tubs, and private balconies. Pamperings include down comforters and individual selected antiques— room service, telephones, some TVs. Hospitality at its finest. Bistro offers beverages, desserts as well as dinner—neo-French cuisine. Relax on the porch with a glass of wine or iced tea.

Host: Christopher Wilson
Rooms: 9 (PB) $85-165
Full Breakfast
Credit Cards: A, B, C
Notes: 2, 4, 5, 7, 8, 10, 11, 12, 14

Capt. Ezra Nye House

152 Main Street, 02563
(508) 888-6142; (800) 388-2278

Comfort and warmth amid antique-filled rooms, some with fireplaces and canopies, make any stay a treat in this 1829 Federal home. Museums, lake, and restaurants within a block. Featured in *Glamour* and *Innsider* magazines and chosen Best Bed and Breakfast, Upper Cape, by *Cape Cod Life* magazine in 1993, 1994, 1996, and 1998. "Thank you for opening your hearts and your home to us....You have made our first trip to Cape Cod a memorable one!" Children over 10 welcome.

NOTES: Credit cards accepted: A MasterCard; B Visa; C American Express; D Discover; E Diner's Club; F Other; 2 Personal checks accepted; 3 Lunch available; 4 Dinner available; 5 Open all year; 6 Pets welcome;

Capt. Ezra Nye House

Hosts: Elaine and Harry Dickson
Rooms: 5 (PB) $85-110
Suite: 1 (PB)
Full Breakfast
Credit Cards: A, B, C, D, F
Notes: 2, 5, 7, 9, 10, 11, 12, 14

The Cranberry House

The Cranberry House

50 Main Street, (Route 130), 02563
(508) 888-1281

The Cranberry House is a friendly place to stay on Cape Cod. A full breakfast is served in the dining room or on the deck. Relax in the den overlooking the beautifully landscaped yard, or relax in the gazebo. Hosts offer cable TV and complimentary soft drinks. Sandwich, the cape's oldest town, has many shops, restaurants, museums, gardens, and beaches. The Cape Cod canal has walking and biking

trails. No smoking in house. Children over 10 welcome.

Hosts: John and Sara Connolly
Rooms: 4 (PB) $65-85
Full Breakfast
Credit Cards: A, B, F
Notes: 5, 7, 9, 10, 11, 12

Dillingham House

71 Main Street, 02563
(508) 833-0065

Built circa 1650, the Dillingham House is one of the oldest in the country. It offers its guests an interesting historical experience while providing a quiet and comfortable natural environment off the beaten path. Sandwich has many historical attractions, as well as quiet beaches for relaxation and a scenic waterfront nearby.

Host: Kathy Kenney and Sheryl Siebert
Rooms: 4 (2 PB; 2 SB) $85-95
Continental Breakfast
Credit Cards: None
Notes: 2, 6, 7, 8, 9, 10, 11, 12

The Dunbar House

1 Water Street, 02563
(508) 833-2485; FAX (508) 833-4713
e-mail: dunbar@capecod.net
www.dunbarteashop.com

An old Colonial home, circa 1740, in the heart of historic Sandwich village offers three en

The Dunbar House

7 No smoking; 8 Children welcome; 9 Social drinking allowed; 10 Tennis nearby; 11 Swimming nearby; 12 Golf nearby; 13 Skiing nearby; 14 May be booked through a travel agent; 15 Handicapped accessible.

suite guest rooms, a full breakfast, and an English tearoom in the adjacent carriage house. The Dunbar House overlooks Shawme Pond and is within walking distance of five museums and the beach.

Hosts: Nancy Iribarren and David Bell
Rooms: 3 (PB) $80-100
Full Breakfast
Credit Cards: A, B, D
Notes: 3, 4, 5, 7, 8, 9, 10, 11, 12, 14

Inn at Sandwich Center

118 Tupper Road, 02563
(508) 888-6958; (800) 249-6949
FAX (508) 833-0574; e-mail: innsan@aol.com
www.bfbooks.com/innsan.html

Elegant 1829 inn listed in the National Register of Historic Places in historic Sandwich village. Antique and art lovingly create warm ambiance. Five bedrooms, fireplaces, four-poster beds, private bathrooms. Breakfast served in keeping room with circa 1750 fireplace. Homemade Continental plus breakfast. Special amenities. Nonsmoking. French, Italian, and some Spanish spoken. Children over 12 welcome.

Hosts: Eliane and Alan Thomas
Rooms: 5 (PB) $75-120
Continental Breakfast
Credit Cards: A, B, C, D
Notes: 2, 7, 9, 10, 11, 12, 14

Isaiah Jones Homestead

165 Main Street, 02563
(508) 888-9115; (800) 526-1625

Elegant 1849 Victorian Italianate bed and breakfast fully restored with Victorian antique furniture, oriental rugs, accessories, and tapestries throughout. Five guest rooms, with queen-size beds. All private baths, two with oversize whirlpool tubs. Three rooms with fireplaces. Full breakfast and complimentary beverages. On Main Street of historic Sandwich village, the oldest town on Cape Cod, and a 15-minute walk to the beach.

Hosts: Jan and Doug Klapper
Rooms: 5 (PB) $75-155
Full Breakfast
Credit Cards: A, B, C, D
Notes: 2, 5, 7, 9, 10, 11, 12, 14

The Summer House

The Summer House

158 Main Street, 02563
(508) 888-4991; (800) 241-3609
e-mail: sumhouse@capecod.net
www.capecod.net/summerhouse

Elegant circa 1835 Greek Revival bed and breakfast featured in *Country Living* magazine, in the heart of historic Sandwich village, Cape Cod's oldest town (settled 1637). Antiques, hand-stitched quilts, working fireplaces, flowers, large sunny rooms, and English-style gardens. Close to dining, museums, shops, pond, and gristmill; boardwalk to beach. Bountiful breakfast, elegantly served. Afternoon tea in the garden included. Working fireplaces in all guest rooms, plus one in the parlor, and one in the breakfast room. Children over six welcome. Seasonal rates.

Hosts: Erik Suby and Phyllis Burg
Rooms: 5 (PB) $65-105
Full Breakfast
Credit Cards: A, B, C, D
Notes: 2, 5, 7, 9, 10, 11, 12, 14

NOTES: Credit cards accepted: A MasterCard; B Visa; C American Express; D Discover; E Diner's Club; F Other; 2 Personal checks accepted; 3 Lunch available; 4 Dinner available; 5 Open all year; 6 Pets welcome;

SCITUATE

The Allen House

18 Allen Place, 02066
(781) 545-8221
e-mail: allenhousebnb@worldnet.att.net
www.allenhousebnb.com

Sleep comfortably and quietly in a gracious, gabled Victorian merchant's home overlooking an unspoiled New England fishing town and harbor, only an hour's drive south of Boston. Then wake to classical music and gourmet cuisine. The hosts are English, professional caterers, and cat lovers. On every sunny, warm day expect a full breakfast—and sometimes afternoon tea—on the porch overlooking the harbor.

Hosts: Christine and Iain Gilmour
Rooms: 6 (PB) $69-199
Full Breakfast
Credit Cards: A, B, C, D
Notes: 2, 5, 7, 9, 11, 12, 14, 15

The Allen House

Bed & Breakfast Cape Cod

P.O. Box 1312, Orleans, 02653
(508) 255-3824; (800) 541-6226
FAX (508) 240-0599
e-mail: info@BedandBreakfastCapeCod.com
www.BedandBreakfastCapeCod.com

SCI 02. This wonderful Boston South Shore village has beautiful ocean views from miles of pristine beach and harbors. The 10-year-old three-level home has spectacular views of the ocean, marshes, and beaches. The air-conditioned suite has a king-size bed, living room, bath, sliders to a private patio, and views of the water. A great spot for weekly stays or less for

parties of up to four persons. Enjoy a breakfast in an antique-filled dining room served formally. Fifteen dollars for extra person in suite. $80-125.

Bed & Breakfast Reservations North Shore, Greater Boston, Cape Cod

P.O. Box 600035, Newtonville, 02460
(617) 964-1606; (800) 832-2632
FAX (617) 332-8572; e-mail: info@bbreserve.com
www.bbreserve.com

108. Seashell Bed and Breakfast. Halfway between Cape Cod and Boston, this bed and breakfast offers panoramic ocean views from guests' suite and private patio. On "third cliff," just one mile from scenic Scituate Harbor, where guests will enjoy quaint shops and a variety of interesting restaurants. Guest quarters include own private suite, private bath, dining/living room, full kitchen, TV, air conditioning, telephone. Full breakfast is served in the upstairs dining room for shorter stays. For longer stays, the host will stock guests' cupboards and refrigerator with breakfast foods. Extra bedroom upstairs with private bath available only in conjunction with suite. Smoking is not permitted. Infants and children over 12 are welcome. $85-125.

SHEFFIELD

Covered Bridge

69 Maple Avenue, Norfolk, CT 06058
(860) 542-5944; FAX (860) 542-5690
e-mail: tremblay@esslink.com
www.obs-us.com/chesler/coveredbridge

1SHMA. This charming log home, commanding a sweeping view of the Berkshires, is the perfect spot for an idyllic, pastoral retreat. A horse grazes nearby, and it's a short walk across the fields to the swimming pond. A full breakfast is served in the kitchen or on the porch. The host, an actress, has traveled extensively and is also well informed about area activities. There are two double guest rooms that share a bath. $85-95.

Ivanhoe Country House

Ivanhoe Country House

254 South Undermountain Road (Route 41), 01257
(413) 229-2143

In the Berkshire Hills on 20 wooded acres. Swimming pool, hiking trails including the Appalachian. All rooms with private baths, some with fireplace and kitchen. Near Tanglewood, antique shops, shopping outlets, ski areas, golf, and tennis. Excellent restaurants nearby. Continental breakfast served outside each bedroom. Brochure available.

Hosts: Carole and Dick Maghery
Rooms: 9 (PB) $75-125
Continental Breakfast
Credit Cards: None
Notes: 2, 5, 6, 8, 9, 10, 12, 13

Nutmeg Bed & Breakfast Agency

P.O. Box 271117, West Hartford, 06127-1117
(860) 236-6698; (800) 727-7592
FAX (860) 232-7680

314. A New England barn built in 1790. Rustic reservation, very woodsie with a brook running through the five acres. Wonderful location for hiking—walking distance to Appalachian Trail. Fifteen rooms in the lodge—many are suites, all with private baths. Three bungalows, each can sleep family of five. Central air in lodge, units in bungalows. Fifteen minutes to

Lime Rock; 40 minutes to Tanglewood. Continental breakfast. Children welcome. No smoking. No resident pets. Pets accepted in bungalows (extra charge).

Ramblewood Inn

Box 729, 01257
(413) 229-3363; (800) 854-1862
www.bbonline.com/ma/ramblewood

This stylish country house, furnished for comfort and romance, is in a beautiful natural setting of mountains, pine forest, and serene private lake for swimming and canoeing. Private baths, fireplaces, central air, lovely gardens, and gourmet breakfasts. Convenient to all Berkshire attractions: Tanglewood, drama/dance festivals, antiques, Lime Rock racing, skiing, and hiking. Minimum stay requirements for weekends and holidays. Suite available.

Hosts: June and Martin Ederer
Rooms: 6 (PB) $80-125
Full Breakfast
Credit Cards: A, B
Notes: 2, 5, 7, 8, 9, 10, 11, 12, 13, 14

Ramblewood Inn

SOUTH DENNIS

Country Pineapple Inn

370 Main Street, P.O. Box 719, 02660
(508) 394-7474; e-mail: irret8848@aol.com

Enjoy the elegant simplicity of a restored 1839 sea captain's home in the historic village of

Country Pineapple Inn

South Dennis, Cape Cod. Hosts strive to make their guests feel as family. Hosts serve a full country breakfast, along with house specialties that are available throughout the day. The inn is in the "Sea Captains' Village," close to the beautiful Bass River, three golf courses, boating, and swimming, and the famous Cape Cod Bike Rail Trail. Enjoy one acre of grounds and solitude. Children over 10 welcome.

Rooms: 4 (3 PB; 1 SB) $65-95
Full Breakfast
Credit Cards: None
Notes: 2, 5, 7, 9, 10, 11, 12, 15

SOUTH EGREMONT

The Egremont Inn

Old Sheffield Road, P.O. Box 418, 01258
(413) 528-2111; FAX (413) 528-3284

In the National Register of Historic Places, this 1780 stagecoach stop has 20 rooms, suites, and connecting rooms, all with private baths and air conditioning. Three fireplaced first-floor sitting rooms, lovely wraparound porch, tavern, and dining room with outstanding cuisine. Pool and tennis courts on premises. The inn is a short drive to downhill and cross-country skiing, hiking, cycling, water attractions, a wealth of live theater, concerts, and dance festivals, and world-renowned antique shops.

Hosts: Karen and Steven Waller
Rooms: 20 (PB) $90-185
Full and Continental Breakfast
Credit Cards: A, B, C, D
Notes: 2, 4, 5, 8, 10, 11, 12, 13, 14

Weathervane Inn

Route 23, P.O. Box 388, 01258
(800) 528-9580; FAX (413) 528-1713

The Weathervane Inn began life as a 1785 farmhouse and still has the original fireplace with its beehive oven, rarely seen today but a necessity in bygone days for both cooking and heating. Today, the Weathervane sits on 10 beautifully landscaped acres of gardens and trees, and features 11 period-appointed bedrooms, all with private bath, plenty of common rooms for guests to sit and relax by a fire or read a book, a bountiful country breakfast each morning, and an afternoon tea with fresh-baked goodies. Located in the historic town of South Egremont in the Berkshires, the Weathervane is central to Tanglewood, summer theater, hiking trails, natural attractions, skiing, and antiquing.

Hosts: Maxine and Jeffrey Lane
Rooms: 11 (PB) $135-245
Full Breakfast
Credit Cards: A, B, C
Notes: 2, 5, 7, 8, 9, 10, 11, 12, 13, 15

Weathervane Inn

SOUTHAMPTON

Diantha's Garden Bed & Breakfast

20 Wolcott Road, 01073
(413) 529-0093; (888) 332-7797
FAX (413) 529-0456

Early 1800s farmhouse on more than four acres. Guest areas include a comfortable large living room, a sitting room with TV and refrigerator, and a lovely screened porch. Two air-conditioned bedrooms—larger furnished with a queen-size bed and day bed, the smaller with a double bed. Spacious shared bath. Many heirlooms throughout. Located in the foothills of the Pioneer Valley, this charming home is easily accessible to Springfield, Westfield, Northampton, Amherst, and South Hadley. Homemade breakfasts featuring both traditional and unique favorites as well as host's special muffins. Children over 10 welcome.

Hosts: Linda and Jim Cooper
Rooms: 2 (SB) $65-75
Full Breakfast
Credit Cards: A, B, D
Notes: 2, 5, 7, 12, 14

SOUTH ORLEANS
Hillbourne House

Route 28, #654, 02662
(508) 255-0780; FAX (508) 240-1850

This charming bed and breakfast was built in 1798 and during the Civil War was part of the Underground Railroad. A circular hiding place is still in evidence beneath the trap door in the common room. Enjoy a magnificent view of Pleasant Bay and the great dunes of Outer Beach on the Atlantic. Convenient to all cape activities. Private beach and dock. Continental plus breakfast served.

Hosts: Jack and Barbara Hayes
Rooms: 8 (PB) $50-105
Continental Breakfast
Credit Cards: None
Notes: 2, 5, 7, 9, 10, 11, 12

STERLING
Sterling Orchards Bed & Breakfast

60 Kendall Hill Road, P.O. Box 455, 01564-0455
(978) 422-6595; FAX (978) 422-3200
e-mail: jvassociat@aol.com

Built in 1740, this Colonial home features many original details such as the 12-foot center chimney, Indian shutters, and wide-pine floors. A full country breakfast is served in solarium overlooking lawn and gardens. No smoking. Many shops in area. Closed January to March. Exit 6 from I-90.

Hosts: Bob and Sue Smiley
Rooms: 2 (PB) $65-85
Full Breakfast
Credit Cards: None
Notes: 2, 7, 8, 9, 11, 12, 13, 14

STOCKBRIDGE
Arbor Rose Bed & Breakfast

8 Yale Hill, 01262-0114
(413) 298-4744; www.arborrose.com

Charming 1810 mill and farmhouse with flowing pond, gardens, antiques, tranquility, home baking, and smiles. Close to Stockbridge center, museums, restaurants, and Berkshire Theater. Private baths, four-poster beds, fireplaces, gallery shop, ski packages. No smoking. Families welcome.

Hosts: Christina Alsop and Family
Rooms: 6 (PB) $85-165
Full Breakfast
Credit Cards: A, B, C
Notes: 2, 5, 7, 8, 9, 10, 11, 12, 13, 14

Arbor Rose

Historic Merrell Inn

1565 Pleasant Street, South Lee, 01260
(413) 243-1794; (800) 243-1794
FAX (413) 243-2669
e-mail: info@merrell-inn.com
www.merrell-inn.com

NOTES: Credit cards accepted: A MasterCard; B Visa; C American Express; D Discover; E Diner's Club; F Other; 2 Personal checks accepted; 3 Lunch available; 4 Dinner available; 5 Open all year; 6 Pets welcome;

Historic Merrell Inn

This 200-year-old brick stagecoach inn in a small New England village along the banks of the Housatonic River is listed in the National Register of Historic Places. Rooms with fireplaces, canopied beds, and antique furnishings. Full breakfast is served in the original tavern room. One mile to Norman Rockwell's beloved Stockbridge.

Hosts: Charles and Faith Reynolds
Rooms: 9 (PB) $75-165
Full Breakfast
Credit Cards: A, B
Notes: 2, 5, 7, 9, 11, 13, 14

The Inn at Stockbridge

Route 7 North, P.O. Box 618, 01262
(413) 298-3337; FAX (413) 298-3406

Consummate hospitality and outstanding breakfasts distinguish a visit at this turn-of-the-

The Inn at Stockbridge

century Georgian Colonial estate on 12 secluded acres in the heart of the Berkshires. Close to the Norman Rockwell Museum, Tanglewood, Hancock Shaker Village, summer theaters, and four-season recreation. The inn has a gracious, English country feeling, with two well-appointed living rooms, a formal dining room, and a baby grand piano.

Hosts: Alice and Len Schiller
Rooms: 12 (PB) $100-270
Full Breakfast
Credit Cards: A, B, C, D
Notes: 2, 5, 7, 9, 10, 11, 12, 13, 14, 15

The Roeder House

The Roeder House Bed & Breakfast

Route 183, Box 525, 01262
(413) 298-4015; www.roederhouse.com

On four acres in Stockbridge near the Rockwell and Chesterwood museums. Full breakfast served on porch in summer with views of pool and grounds. Queen-size four-poster beds, private baths, air conditioning, period antiques, and Audubon print collection. Cancellation and no smoking policies. Winter ski package.

Hosts: Diane and Vernon Reuss
Rooms: 7 (PB) $95-245
Full Breakfast
Credit Cards: A, B, C, D, F
Notes: 2, 5, 7, 10, 12, 13, 14

7 No smoking; 8 Children welcome; 9 Social drinking allowed; 10 Tennis nearby; 11 Swimming nearby; 12 Golf nearby; 13 Skiing nearby; 14 May be booked through a travel agent; 15 Handicapped accessible.

Seasons on Main

Seasons on Main Bed & Breakfast

47 Main Street, P.O. Box 634, 01262
(413) 298-5419

Lovingly restored and refurbished 1860 Greek Revival home in the heart of the village of Stockbridge, "Norman Rockwell's Main Street," with beautiful gardens and large front porch. The bed and breakfast has four guest rooms, private baths, paddle fans, air conditioning, and fine heirloom antique furnishings. Fireplace and TV in front parlors. An easy walk to shops, fine restaurants, Berkshire theater, and recreation in a four-season area. Dog in residence. Afternoon refreshments and seasonal package arrangements. Inquire about cancellation policy. Minimum two- to-three-night stay on Tanglewood weekends and holidays. Not suitable for children.

Hosts: Greg and Pat O'Neill
Rooms: 4 (PB) $125-235
Full Breakfast
Credit Cards: A, B, C, D
Notes: 2, 5, 7, 9, 10, 11, 12, 13

STURBRIDGE

Bed & Breakfast Reservations North Shore, Greater Boston, Cape Cod

P.O. Box 600035, Newtonville, 02460
(617) 964-1606; (800) 832-2632

FAX (617) 332-8572; e-mail: info@bbreserve.com
www.bbreserve.com

24. The Village Bed and Breakfast. Less than one hour from Boston and the Berkshires, tour Old Sturbridge Village, where life in an 1830s rural New England town is re-created. This accommodation is very convenient to the town of Brimfield, where one of the largest and most famous flea markets in Massachusetts is held. At day's end enjoy the comforts of this cozy gambrel-roofed Colonial-style bed and breakfast with three beautiful guest rooms (shared/private baths). There is also a separate entrance suite, perfect for extended stays, with half-bath, refrigerator, microwave, desk. Guests may use the cozy sitting room with TV or relax on outside screened porch/deck. Full breakfast and afternoon tea included. Children over 12 welcome. No smoking. $95-100.

Sturbridge Country Inn

530 Main Street, P.O. Box 60, 01566
(508) 347-5503; FAX (508) 347-5319

Circa 1840. Shaded by an old silver maple, this classic Greek Revival house boasts a two-story columned entrance. The attached carriage house now serves as the lobby and displays the original post-and-beam construction and exposed rafters. All guest rooms have individual fireplaces and whirlpool tubs. They are gracefully appointed in reproduction colonial furnishings, including queen-size four-poster bed. A patio and gazebo are favorite summertime retreats.

Host: Patricia Affenito
Rooms: 9 (PB) $59-169
Continental Breakfast
Credit Cards: A, B, C, D
Notes: 5, 9, 10, 11, 12, 13, 14

SUDBURY

Sudbury Bed & Breakfast

3 Drum Lane, 01776
(978) 443-2860

NOTES: Credit cards accepted: A MasterCard; B Visa; C American Express; D Discover; E Diner's Club; F Other; 2 Personal checks accepted; 3 Lunch available; 4 Dinner available; 5 Open all year; 6 Pets welcome;

A large Garrison Colonial home with traditional furnishings on a quiet tree-studded acre.
A Continental breakfast is served with homemade muffins and rolls. Close to Boston, Lexington, and Concord. An abundance of outdoor
recreation and historical sights nearby. Friendly
hospitality for the New England visitor.

Hosts: Don and Nancy Somers
Rooms: 2 (S1.5B) $55-65
Continental Breakfast
Credit Cards: None
Notes: 2, 5, 7, 8, 10, 11, 12, 13

TRURO

Bed & Breakfast Cape Cod

P.O. Box 1312, Orleans, 02653
(508) 255-3824; (800) 541-6226
fax (508) 240-0599
e-mail: info@BedandBreakfastCapeCod.com
www.BedandBreakfastCapeCod.com

TRU 01. A gracious old Victorian inn restored
with Old World charm and elegance. There are
five spacious guest rooms. Three rooms have
private baths and the other two share a bath.
One room has an efficiency kitchenette. Soak
away your cares in the hot tub or spend a lazy
afternoon on the grand front porch. Near the
National Seashore beaches and minutes from
Provincetown. There are two cottages and a
carriage house available. The cottages are pet
friendly. Children are welcome in the cottages
and carriage house. Special weekly rates available. Seasonal rates. $59-139.

Parker House

P.O. Box 1111, 02666
(508) 349-3358

The Parker House is an 1820 classic full-Cape
nestled into the side of Truro Center between
the Cobb Memorial Library and the Blacksmith Shop restaurant. Clean ocean and bay
beaches two miles to east or west. Many art
galleries and restaurants in Provincetown and
Wellfleet are 10 minutes away by car. Golf,

Parker House

tennis, sailing, and whale watches nearby. The
Cape Cod National Seashore and Audubon
Sanctuary offer many trails and guided walks.
The Parker House offers haven to a limited
number of guests who can rest and read or
enjoy the many activities nearby.

Host: Stephen Williams
Rooms: 2 (SB) $55
Continental Breakfast
Credit Cards: None
Notes: 2, 5, 10, 11, 12

TYRINGHAM

The Golden Goose

123 Main Road, Box 336, 01264
(413) 243-3008

Small, friendly, 1800 country home nestled in
Tyringham Valley in the Berkshires. Victorian
antiques. Within one-half hour are Tanglewood, Stockbridge, Jacob's Pillow, Hancock
Shaker Village, the Norman Rockwell

The Golden Goose

Museum, Berkshire Theatre Festival, skiing, golf, and tennis. One mile off the Appalachian Trail. Near Butternut, Otis, Jiminy Peak, and Catamount ski slopes. Air-conditioned guest rooms. Children welcome. Coffee, tea, and cereals provided in rooms. Three-night minimum weekend stays summer and fall. Shorter stays accepted depend on mid-week bookings.

Hosts: Lilja and Joe Rizzo
Studio Apartment: $90-125
Barn Loft: $130-160
Credit Cards: A, B, C, D
Notes: 2, 5, 7, 8, 9, 10, 11, 12, 13, 14

Greenwood House

VINEYARD HAVEN (MARTHA'S VINEYARD) __

Captain Dexter House of Vineyard Haven

92 Main Street, Box 2457, 02568
(508) 693-6564; FAX (508) 693-8448

A perfect country inn! Built in 1840, the house has been meticulously restored and exquisitely furnished to reflect the charm of that period. Be surrounded by flowers from the garden and pampered by innkeepers who believe in old-fashioned hospitality. The inn's eight romantic guest rooms are distinctively decorated. Several rooms have working fireplaces (as does the parlor) and four-poster canopied beds. Stroll to town and harbor. Continental plus breakfast.

Host: Birdie
Rooms: 8 (PB) $95-275
Continental Breakfast
Credit Cards: A, B, C
Notes: 2, 5, 7, 8, 9, 10, 11, 12, 14

Greenwood House Bed & Breakfast

40 Greenwood Avenue, Box 2734, 02568-2734
(508) 693-6150; FAX (508) 696-8113
e-mail: innkeeper@greenwoodhouse.com

This Martha's Vineyard Island inn is uniquely nestled in a quiet residential neighborhood two blocks from historic district and Main Street. The spacious 1906 home has rooms with pri-

vate baths, color cable TV, telephones, and more. Awake each morning to a delicious breakfast before heading out to explore the island. The unique and captivating charm of Martha's Vineyard can be fully captured and experienced with a stay at Greenwood House.

Hosts: Kathy Stinson and Larry Gomez
Rooms: 5 (PB) $109-269
Full Breakfast
Credit Cards: A, B, C, E, F
Notes: 5, 7, 9, 10, 11, 12, 14

The Hanover House

28 Edgartown Road; P.O. Box 2107, 02568
(508) 693-1066; (800) 339-1066
FAX (508) 696-6009

Within walking distance of the Vineyard Haven harbor and the ferries from the main-

The Hanover House

NOTES: Credit cards accepted: A MasterCard; B Visa; C American Express; D Discover; E Diner's Club; F Other; 2 Personal checks accepted; 3 Lunch available; 4 Dinner available; 5 Open all year; 6 Pets welcome;

land, the Hanover House offers the charm of a cozy country house with the convenience of a village inn. The impeccably maintained guest rooms and suites all feature private baths, color TV, queen-size or two double beds, and air conditioning. A homemade Continental plus breakfast is served on the sun porch. The Hanover House is a AAA three-diamond, Mobil three-star, nonsmoking property.

Hosts: Kay and Ron Nelson
Rooms: 15 (PB) $118-275
Continental Breakfast
Credit Cards: A, B, C, D
Notes: 7, 9, 10, 11, 12, 14

High Haven House

85 Summer Street, P.O. Box 289, 02568
(508) 693-9204; (800) 232-9204
FAX (508) 693-7807

A charming bed and breakfast on Martha's Vineyard. A perfect vacation spot with something for everyone. The beautiful beaches bring visitors from all over the world. High Haven House offers a variety of meticulously maintained accommodations that will suit everyone's budget and needs. Pool. Hot tub. Homemade Vineyard breakfast. In-room telephones. Call for details and off-season rates. "Best ambiance in Vineyard Haven."—*Boston's Best Guide.*

Hosts: Joe and Kathleen Schreck
Rooms: 12 (7 PB; 5 SB) $79-199
Continental Breakfast
Credit Cards: A, B, D
Notes: 2, 5, 8, 9, 10, 11, 12, 14

The Look Inn

13 Look Street, 02568
(508) 693-6893

A charming, early 1800s farmhouse, reasonable rates, walking distance to shops, restaurants, beaches, and ferries. Complimentary Continental breakfast. Hot tub, massage, yoga available on site. Walking and photography tours. The innkeepers knowledge on Martha's

Vineyard Island will make your visit a joy! Children over 12 welcome.

Hosts: Freddy Rundlet and Catherine Keller
Rooms: 3 (3 SB) $90-125
Continental Breakfast
Credit Cards: A, B, F
Notes: 2, 5, 7, 9, 10, 11, 12

Lambert's Cove Country Inn

Lambert's Cove Country Inn

Rural Route 1, Box 422, 02568
(508) 693-2298

Once a lovely country estate, Lambert's Cove Country Inn in West Tisbury offers guest rooms in three charming buildings: the original 1790 residence, a converted 18th-century barn, and a carriage house. The setting is seven and one-half acres of lawn, meadows, gardens, and woodlands, with towering trees, an orchard, and vine-covered stone walls. Each room has its own charm. The dining room, which is open to the public, features some of the finest meals on the island.

Hosts: Katherine and Louis Costabel
Rooms: 15 (PB) $85-195
Full Breakfast
Credit Cards: A, B, C
Notes: 2, 4, 5, 7, 8, 10, 11, 12

Lothrop Merry House

Owen Park, Box 1939, 02568
(508) 693-1646

The Lothrop Merry House, built in the 1790s, overlooks Vineyard Haven Harbor and has a flower-bordered terrace, a private beach, and

7 No smoking; 8 Children welcome; 9 Social drinking allowed; 10 Tennis nearby; 11 Swimming nearby; 12 Golf nearby; 13 Skiing nearby; 14 May be booked through a travel agent; 15 Handicapped accessible.

Lothrop Merry House

an expansive lawn. Most rooms have ocean views and a fireplace. All are furnished with antiques and fresh flowers. Complimentary canoe and Sunfish for guests' use. Close to ferry and shops. Personal checks accepted for deposit only.

Hosts: John and Mary Clarke
Rooms: 7 (4 PB; 3 SB) $68-215
Continental Breakfast
Credit Cards: A, B
Notes: 2, 5, 7, 8, 9, 10, 11, 12

WARE (STURBRIDGE)

Antique 1880 Inn Bed & Breakfast

14 Pleasant Street, 01082
(413) 967-7847

Relax in yesterday's charm. This 12-room Colonial is complete with six fireplaces, rustic beams, and hardwood floors. Breakfast may be served on the porch or in the dining room. Enjoy afternoon tea before the cozy fireplace. Midpoint between Boston and the Berkshires. Enjoy a country drive to Sturbridge Village and historic Deerfield. A short drive to five area colleges: Amherst, Mass-Hampshire, Mount Holyoke, and Smith.

Host: Margaret Skutnik
Rooms: 3 (1 PB; 2 SB) $55-75
Full Breakfast
Credit Cards: None
Notes: 2, 5, 7, 8, 9, 10, 11, 12, 14

WAREHAM

Little Harbor Bed & Breakfast

20 Stockton Shortcut, 02571
(508) 295-6329

The Little Harbor Bed and Breakfast is a large rambling Cape Cod-style home built in the late 1600s, which is surrounded on all four sides by the Little Harbor Golf Course. This is an 18-hole par three golf course. The bed and breakfast has a pool with hot tub, a private putting green, privacy, and is less than one-half mile away from the Little Harbor Beach. Most rooms have one or two double beds, two rooms have a queen-size bed each.

Hosts: Dennis or Ken
Rooms: 5 (1 PB; 4 SB) $77-90
Continental Breakfast
Credit Cards: A, B
Notes: 2, 5, 8, 9, 11, 12

Mulberry Bed & Breakfast

257 High Street, 02571-1407
(508) 295-0684; FAX (508) 291-2909

Mulberry Bed and Breakfast sits on a half-acre lot shaded by the majestic mulberry tree in the historic section of Wareham. This Cape Cod-style bed and breakfast home, built in 1847 by a blacksmith, offers three cozy guest rooms with two shared baths. Furnishings and decor are in keeping with the home's vintage. Enjoy a hearty New England breakfast. Within an hour's drive are historic Plymouth, Boston, and Newport, the whaling-fishing city of New Bedford, and scenic Cape Cod. Wareham boasts 54 miles of coastline. Thus saltwater activities of every description are available. Two cats in residence. Cross-country skiing nearby. Inquire about handicapped accessibility. Two-night minimum stay preferred on weekends July and August. Ask about a clambake to go.

Host: Frances A. Murphy
Rooms: 3 (3 S2B) $50-75
Full Breakfast
Credit Cards: A, B, C, D
Notes: 2, 5, 7, 8, 9, 10 ,11, 12, 13, 14, 15

NOTES: Credit cards accepted: A MasterCard; B Visa; C American Express; D Discover; E Diner's Club; F Other; 2 Personal checks accepted; 3 Lunch available; 4 Dinner available; 5 Open all year; 6 Pets welcome;

WELLESLEY

Bed & Breakfast Associates Bay Colony, Ltd.

P.O. Box 57166, Babson Park, Boston, 02457-0166
(781) 449-5302; (888) 429-7591
FAX (781) 449-5958; e-mail: info@bnbboston.com
www.bnbboston.com

M503. Light in the Window. A pleasant suburban Colonial-style home on a quiet road close to Wellesley College and Babson College. Walk to commuter train to Boston. This mature host couple offers two guest rooms on the second floor of their home. One is a comfortable room with wicker decor, cable TV, and king-size bed. The other is a smaller, cozy room with double bed, cable TV, and reading chair. Full bath in hall; can be private. $75-95.

WELLFLEET

Bed & Breakfast Cape Cod

P.O. Box 1312, Orleans, 02653
(508) 255-3824; (800) 541-6226
FAX (508) 240-0599
e-mail: info@BedandBreakfastCapeCod.com
www.BedandBreakfastCapeCod.com

WEL 01. Only 150 yards from a beach on the back side of the Wellfleet Harbor, guests may walk to Wellfleet Center from Uncle Tim's bridge near this perfect upside down 3/4 Cape house. The first floor is completely private with a queen-size bedroom and large full bath. There is a trundle bedroom available for families or people traveling together. In addition, a lovely private studio with queen-size bed, private bath, patio, and kitchenette is on the ground level. The refrigerator is stocked for breakfast, which is served on the spacious deck. Forty dollars for extra person. All children are welcome. The bed and breakfast is pet friendly. $90-140.

The Inn at Duck Creeke

The Inn at Duck Creeke

P.O. Box 364, 02667
(508) 349-9333; FAX (508) 349-0234
www.capecod.net/duckinn

On a rustic five acres with views of pond and tidal marsh, this cozy country inn has 25 attractive guest rooms within three lodging buildings, an exceptional restaurant, and the town's oldest tavern. Within the historic district, just a short walk to galleries and shops, it is also close to the harbor, ponds, and beaches. The friendly and energetic staff work to make guests' stay a pleasant and memorable one. "We welcome your visit."

Hosts: Bob Morrill and Judy Pihl
Rooms: 25 (17 PB; 8 SB) $65-95
Continental Breakfast
Credit Cards: A, B, C
Notes: 2, 4, 8, 9, 10, 11, 12

WEST HARWICH (CAPE COD)

Bed & Breakfast Reservations North Shore, Greater Boston, Cape Cod

P.O. Box 600035, Newtonville, 02460
(617) 964-1606; (800) 832-2632
FAX (617) 332-8572; e-mail: info@bbreserve.com
www.bbreserve.com

109. The Inn at West Harwich. This fully restored 200-year-old inn is five minutes from

7 No smoking; 8 Children welcome; 9 Social drinking allowed; 10 Tennis nearby; 11 Swimming nearby; 12 Golf nearby; 13 Skiing nearby; 14 May be booked through a travel agent; 15 Handicapped accessible.

the Nantucket ferry. Six sparkling guest rooms, all with private bath, TV, air conditioning, and refrigerator. Two of the rooms are large deluxe suites with Jacuzzis and fireplaces. One suite is handicapped accessible. Cozy sitting room with fireplace. A wonderful Continental plus breakfast is delivered to room. Great central location for all Cape Cod attractions. Families with children welcome. No smoking. $85-140.

WEST HARWICH

Cape Cod Claddagh Inn

77 Main Street, Route 28, 02671-0667
(508) 432-9628 (info); (508) 430-2440 (pub)
(800) 356-9628 (reservations)
FAX (508) 432-6039
www.capecodcladdaghinn.com

Irish hospitality in a Victorian ambiance would remind guests of an intimate Irish manor with authentic pub and fine dining poolside or fireside. All rooms en suite. Duplex cottage set in the pines for extended stays. Call for colored brochure.

Hosts: Eileen and Jack Connell
Rooms: 8 (PB) $75-125
Full Breakfast
Credit Cards: A, B, C
Notes: 2, 3, 4, 5, 6, 8, 9, 10, 11, 12, 14, 15

Cape Cod Claddagh

Cape Winds by the Sea

28 Shore Road, 02671-0623
(508) 432-1418; e-mail: capewind@banet.net
www.telecottage.com/capewind

Nestled in a quiet residential neighborhood, Cape Winds by the Sea offers peaceful rooms with beautiful views of Nantucket Sound. A short walk offers a choice of three beaches. The front porch, complete with colonial rockers, is a great place to watch the water or read a favorite book. Bike trails, golf courses, and many artisan shops are just a few minutes away by car. "We look forward to having you stay with us."

Hosts: Ed and Judi Shank
Rooms: 6 (PB) $90-110
Continental Breakfast
Credit Cards: None
Notes: 2, 5, 7, 10, 11, 12

WESTON

Webb-Bigelow House

863 Boston Post Road, 02193
(617) 899-2444

Built in 1827, this elegantly furnished Federal house on three acres is 20 minutes from Boston and ideal for visiting colleges, corporations, historic areas, or family. Whether visiting, attending business meetings, or sightseeing, the restful atmosphere in an exclusive suburb provides a place to relax with amenities of a pool and deck. Three bedrooms and adjoining baths include terry-cloth robes, hair dryers, and air conditioning. No children under 10. Excellent restaurants nearby. Open since 1983. Closed January through March.

Hosts: Jane and Bob Webb
Rooms: 4 (3 PB; 1 SB) $95-120
Full Breakfast
Credit Cards: None
Notes: 2, 7, 9, 10, 11

WEST STOCKBRIDGE

Elaine's Bed & Breakfast Selections

4987 Kingston Road, Elbridge, 13060
(315) 689-2082 (11 A.M.-7 P.M.)

Traditional country inn with first-floor public restaurant, tavern, and patio dining. This 200-

NOTES: Credit cards accepted: A MasterCard; B Visa; C American Express; D Discover; E Diner's Club; F Other; 2 Personal checks accepted; 3 Lunch available; 4 Dinner available; 5 Open all year; 6 Pets welcome;

year-old inn was originally a stagecoach stop. Guest rooms on the second floor have antique brass, iron beds, and private baths. Quick drive to Stockbridge, Lenox, and Lee. Seasonal rates.

Shaker Mill Inn

2 Oak Street, Box 521, 01266
(413) 232-8596; FAX (413) 232-4644
e-mail: shakerres@aol.com
www.shakermillinn.com

This may just be the best buy in the Berkshires. Enormous, modern deluxe rooms with king- or queen-sized beds, all with patios or balconies, come complete with small kitchens. The suites have two full bedrooms, two full baths, large, fully stocked kitchen, living room, two TVs, and just about anything else guests might want. There are 10 rooms in a converted Shaker house.

Host: Jonathan Rick
Rooms: 10 (PB) $95-250
Continental Breakfast
Credit Cards: A, B, C
Notes: 2, 5, 6, 7, 9, 10, 11, 12, 13, 14

The Williamsville Inn

Route 41, 01266
(413) 274-6118; FAX (413) 274-3539

The Williamsville Inn offers gracious lodging and candlelight dining in a historic 1797 Berkshire farmhouse, a peaceful country setting at the foot of Tom Ball Mountain. The restaurant, which serves elegant country cuisine nightly, except Tuesdays, is recommended by the *New York Times* and *Bon Appétit*. Old World charm and modern amenities, cordial atmosphere, and the opportunity to enjoy the gentle pleasures of quiet country life bring guests from all over the world. Antiquing, shopping, and hiking are nearby. Minutes from Tanglewood and the Norman Rockwell Museum.

Hosts: Gail and Kathleen Ryan
Rooms: 16 (PB) $120-185
Full Breakfast
Credit Cards: A, B, C
Notes: 2, 4, 5, 7, 8, 9, 10, 11, 12, 13, 14

WEST TISBURY

The House at New Lane

44 New Lane, P.O. Box 156, 02578
(508) 696-7331; e-mail: housenl@vineyard.net

A simple and elegant West Tisbury bed and breakfast comfortably on seven acres of woods and gardens. Access to all-season country walks, beaches, nature trails, bike paths. Fireplaces in breakfast and sitting rooms.

Rooms: 4 (4 S2B) $65-85
Full Breakfast
Credit Cards: None
Notes: 2, 5, 7, 8, 9, 10, 11, 12

WESTWOOD

Bed & Breakfast Associates Bay Colony, Ltd.

P.O. Box 57166, Babson Park, Boston, 02457-0166
(781) 449-5302; (888) 429-7591
FAX (781) 449-5958; e-mail: info@bnbboston.com
www.bnbboston.com

IW725. Copper Beech Bed and Breakfast. Built in 1720, this historic home is filled with antiques and has a private setting with in-ground pool, gardens, and patio. The carriage house sleeps six with two bedrooms, one and one-half baths, kitchen, living/dining room. Three guest rooms in the main house with shared bath, but private bath arrangements can be made. Family rates available. $70-175

WEST YARMOUTH

The Manor House Bed & Breakfast

57 Maine Avenue, 02673
(508) 771-3433; (800) 9MANOR9

The Manor House is a lovely 1920s six-bedroom Dutch Colonial bed and breakfast overlooking Lewis Bay. Each room has a private bath and all are decorated differently and

---

7 No smoking; 8 Children welcome; 9 Social drinking allowed; 10 Tennis nearby; 11 Swimming nearby; 12 Golf nearby; 13 Skiing nearby; 14 May be booked through a travel agent; 15 Handicapped accessible.

The Manor House

named after special little touches of Cape Cod, such as Cranberry Bog and Whale Watch. Easy access to virtually everything the cape has to offer. Enjoy a bountiful breakfast, afternoon tea, and friendly hospitality at the Manor House.

Hosts: Rick and Liz Latshaw
Rooms: 6 (PB) $78-128
Full Breakfast
Credit Cards: A, B, C
Notes: 2, 5, 7, 9, 10, 11, 12

WEYMOUTH

Host Homes of Boston

P.O. Box 117, Waban Branch, Boston, 02468-0001
(617) 244-1308; (800) 600-1308
FAX (617) 244-5156

Willowreeds. Bright and spacious 1990 Williamsburg Colonial with 18th-century furnishings, country atmosphere. Large deck overlooking huge swimming pool and adjacent wooded conservation land. Second-floor guest room with double canopied bed. Pine room with queen-size bed. Two hall baths. Resident toy poodle. First-floor guest parlor. Breakfast in sunny gourmet kitchen or on deck. Three miles to Red Line. Near fine restaurants. No smoking. Air conditioning. TV and swimming pool. $75-87.

WILLIAMSTOWN

Field Farm Guest House

554 Sloan Road, 01267
(413) 458-3135

At the foot of the Taconic Range, Field Farm offers charming accommodations in a country setting. Four miles of trails wind through 296 acres of forest, fields, and wetlands, home to a variety of wildlife. The 1948 American-Modern style house has large dining and living rooms with fireplace, games, and books. Verandas overlook the swimming pool and tennis court. Picture windows frame formal gardens, sculptures, and stunning views of Mount Greylock—Massachusetts's highest mountain.

Hosts: Jean and Sean Cowhig (innkeepers);
Owners: The Trustees of Reservations
Rooms: 5 (PB) $125
Full Breakfast
Credit Cards: A, B, D
Notes: 2, 5, 7, 9, 10, 11, 12, 13

Steep Acres Farm Bed & Breakfast

520 White Oaks Road, 01267
(413) 458-3774

Two miles from Williams College and the Williamstown Theatre Festival. A country home on a high knoll with spectacular views of the Berkshire Hills and Vermont's Green Mountains. Trout and swimming pond are tempting on this farm's 52 acres adjacent to the Appalachian and Long Trails. Short distance to Tanglewood and Jacob's Pillow.

Hosts: Mary and Marvin Gangemi
Rooms: 4 (SB) $50-85
Full Breakfast
Credit Cards: None
Notes: 2, 5, 7, 8, 9, 10, 11, 12, 13, 14

NOTES: Credit cards accepted: A MasterCard; B Visa; C American Express; D Discover; E Diner's Club; F Other; 2 Personal checks accepted; 3 Lunch available; 4 Dinner available; 5 Open all year; 6 Pets welcome;

WINDSOR

Windfields Farm

154 Windsor Bush Road, Cummington, 01026
(413) 684-3786

Secluded 100-acre homestead on a dirt road surrounded by gardens, birds, fields, and forests, with swimming pond and hiking and ski trails. Guests have private entrance, book-lined living room, fireplace, piano, and dining room. Family antiques, paintings, and flowers. Organic produce, eggs, maple syrup, raspberries, and wild blueberries enrich the hearty breakfasts. Near Tanglewood, Williams and Smith Colleges, and the new Norman Rockwell Museum. Closed March and April. Children over 12 are welcome.

Hosts: Carolyn and Arnold Westwood
Rooms: 2 (SB) $70-80
Full Breakfast
Credit Cards: None
Notes: 2, 7, 9, 10, 11, 13

YARMOUTH

Bed & Breakfast Cape Cod

P.O. Box 1312, Orleans, 02653
(508) 255-3824; (800) 541-6226
FAX (508) 240-0599
e-mail: info@BedandBreakfastCapeCod.com
www.BedandBreakfastCapeCod.com

YAR 02. Built in 1712, this homestead has been made into a charming home and bed and breakfast accommodation. It is on high ground with distant views of Bass River. Breakfast is served on the patio or in the main house. Room one has a private bath and entrance and a studio-style kitchenette. Room two has an additional sitting room with sofa bed and private bath and entrance. The carriage house has barn-board walls, open beams, wood-burning stove,

kitchen, private bath, and a loft with extra beds. Weekly rates available. Seasonal rates. $65-85.

YARMOUTH PORT (CAPE COD)

Bed & Breakfast Cape Cod

P.O. Box 1312, Orleans, 02653
(508) 255-3824; (800) 541-6226
FAX (508) 240-0599
e-mail: info@BedandBreakfastCapeCod.com
www.BedandBreakfastCapeCod.com

YRP 06. Built in 1850 and in the National Register of Historic Places, this lovely old home sits on a quiet street off of the Olde King's Highway. There is a fresh-water pond with beach at the end of the street. This house can be rented for two to six people. There is a king-size bedroom with sitting area and private bath. There are two other rooms with a queen-size bed and a twin bed that can be rented to one party. Very gracious hospitality in a quiet, antique setting.

YRP 07. Built in 1825 as a luxurious sea captain's home, this beautiful location offers the visitor the warmth and charm of Cape Cod in a by-gone era. There are nine beautifully and traditionally appointed rooms, all with private baths, air conditioning, and cable TV. There are five rooms in the main house, each with its own uniqueness. There are four extraordinary rooms in the newly renovated carriage house that offers fireplaces, one room is handicapped accessible, and one room has a whirlpool bath tub. Explore historic and picturesque Route 6A from this special inn. Children welcome.

Colonial House Inn & Restaurant

Route 6A (277 Main Street), 02675
(508) 362-4348; (800) 999-3416
FAX (508) 362-8034
e-mail: colhseinn@capecod.net
www.capecod.net/colonialhouseinn

A year-round, full service country inn with a restaurant and lounge, in the center of the cape

7 No smoking; 8 Children welcome; 9 Social drinking allowed; 10 Tennis nearby; 11 Swimming nearby; 12 Golf nearby; 13 Skiing nearby; 14 May be booked through a travel agent; 15 Handicapped accessible.

Colonial House Inn

on historic Route 6A. A historic landmark with 21 rooms, all with private baths, TVs, telephones, data ports, air conditioning, canopied beds, antiques. Heated indoor pool and Jacuzzi, sun deck, beautiful garden sitting area, waterfall and fountain. Available for receptions up to 150 people. Within walking distance are nature trails, golf, tennis, fresh- and saltwater beaches and antique shops.

Host: Malcolm J. Perna
Rooms: 21 (PB) $70-95
Continental Breakfast
Credit Cards: A, B, C, D
Notes: 2, 3, 4, 5, 6, 8, 9, 10, 11, 12, 13, 14, 15

Liberty Hill Inn on Cape Cod

77 Main Street, 02675
(508) 362-3976; (800) 821-3977
e-mail: libertyh@capecod.net
www.capecod.net/libertyhillinn

Casual elegance in a historic seaside village on the old Kings Highway. Romantic fireplaces, canopied beds, whirlpool, gourmet breakfast. Stroll to village shops and first-class restaurants. Meander country lanes to Cape Cod Bay. Take a run on the beach. A perfect central location provides easy access to all of Cape Cod's attractions. Mobil-rated three stars. Special honeymoon package. Handicapped accessible. Cable TV, air conditioning. "An elegant country inn…in an attractive setting of trees and flower-edged lawns. Romantic"–Fodor's.

Hosts: Jack and Beth Flanagan
Rooms: 9 (PB) $90-190
Full Breakfast
Credit Cards: A, B, C
Notes: 2, 5, 8, 9, 10, 11, 12, 14, 15

Olde Captain's Inn

101 Main Street, 02675-1709
(508) 362-4496; (888) 407-7161
e-mail: general@oldecaptainsinn.com
www.oldecaptainsinn.com

Charming 1812 sea captain's home in the historic district. Fine lodgings and superb Continental breakfast. Cable TV. The inn has a truly friendly, elegant atmosphere. Walk to shops and restaurants. No smoking in the inn. Continental plus breakfast is served. Stay two nights and the third night is free. Suites are available starting at $476 per week.

Hosts: Betsy O'Connor and Sven Tilly
Rooms: 5 (3 PB; 2 SB) $50-100
Continental Breakfast
Credit Cards: None
Notes: 2, 5, 7, 8, 9, 10, 11, 12, 14

One Centre Street Inn

Route 6A and Old Kings Highway, 02675
(508) 362-8910; (888) 407-1653
FAX (508) 362-0195

Step back in time in this 1824 parsonage on the historic north side of Cape Cod. Its understated elegance affords guests both comfort and style in six individually dec- orated guest rooms. Most rooms are hand-stenciled and most have private baths. Fresh coffee awakens guests, along with homemade muffins and scones, seasonal fruits, and a special entrée—perhaps French toast with strawberry Grand Marnier sauce or cranberry-toasted pecan pancakes. Beaches, antiques, galleries, restaurants one mile away. Children over eight welcome.

Host: Karen Iannello
Rooms: 6 (4 PB; 2 SB) $95-145
Full Breakfast
Credit Cards: A, B, D
Notes: 2, 5, 7, 9, 10, 11, 12

NOTES: Credit cards accepted: A MasterCard; B Visa; C American Express; D Discover; E Diner's Club; F Other; 2 Personal checks accepted; 3 Lunch available; 4 Dinner available; 5 Open all year; 6 Pets welcome;

The Village Inn

The Village Inn

92 Main Street, Route 6A, P.O. Box 1, 02675
(508) 362-3182

This charming sea captain's home built in 1795 has been an inn since 1946. Noted for cordial hospitality and comfortable rooms with private baths. Public rooms, screened porch, and shaded lawn. The inn is within easy walking distance of Cape Cod Bay, excellent restaurants, and antique shops. No smoking.

Hosts: Mac and Esther Hickey
Rooms: 10 (8 PB; 2 SB) $40-95
Full Breakfast
Credit Cards: A, B
Notes: 2, 5, 6, 7, 8, 9, 10, 11, 12, 14

Wedgewood Inn

83 Main Street, 02675
(508) 362-5157

In the historic area of Cape Cod, the inn is in the National Register of Historic Places and has been featured in *Colonial Homes*. Near beaches, art galleries, antique shops, golf, boating, and fine restaurants. Fireplaces and private screened porches. Luxury suites in newly restored barn.

Hosts: Milt and Gerrie Graham
Rooms: 9 (PB) $125-185
Full Breakfast
Credit Cards: A, B, C, E
Notes: 2, 5, 12, 14

Wedgewood Inn

7 No smoking; 8 Children welcome; 9 Social drinking allowed; 10 Tennis nearby; 11 Swimming nearby; 12 Golf nearby; 13 Skiing nearby; 14 May be booked through a travel agent; 15 Handicapped accessible.

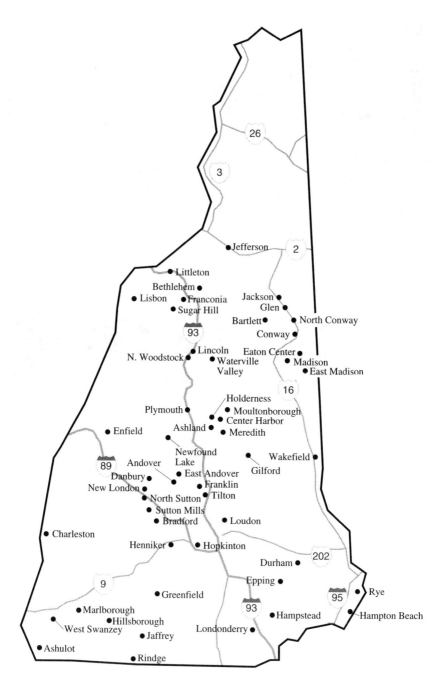

Jefferson

Littleton
Bethlehem
Lisbon   Franconia   Jackson
         Sugar Hill   Glen
                  Bartlett   North Conway
                       Conway

N. Woodstock   Lincoln   Eaton Center
              Waterville   Madison
              Valley   East Madison

                  Holderness
Plymouth   Moultonborough
                  Center Harbor
         Ashland   Meredith

Enfield

                  Newfound
                  Lake   Wakefield
Andover   Gilford
Danbury   East Andover
New London   Franklin
         North Sutton   Tilton
         Sutton Mills
         Bradford   Loudon

Charleston
         Henniker   Hopkinton
                            Durham
                       Epping
                  Greenfield

Marlborough
    Hillsborough
West Swanzey   Londonderry   Hampstead   Rye
         Jaffrey   Hampton Beach
Ashulot
         Rindge

New Hampshire

New Hampshire

Highland Lake Inn

ANDOVER

Highland Lake Inn

32 Maple Street, P.O. Box 164, East Andover, 03231
(603) 735-6426; FAX (603) 735-5355
www.highlandlakeinn.com

Enjoy the perfect New England getaway—
"New Hampshire at its most magical." Built in
1767 and expanded in 1805, this classic building overlooks Highland Lake, Kearsarge,
Tucker, and Ragged Mountains. Beautifully
decorated, the inn has been renovated to
include private baths, en suite in the guest
rooms. A sumptuous and different breakfast is
served each morning. Cross-country and alpine
trails, hiking, fishing, swimming, championship golf courses, country fairs, antiquing,
outlet shopping all nearby. AAA three-diamond-rated. Barn gift/craft shop.

Hosts: The Peter Petras Family
Rooms: 10 (PB) $85-125
Full Breakfast
Credit Cards: A, B, C, D
Notes: 5, 7, 10, 12, 13

ASHLAND

Elaine's Bed & Breakfast Selections

4987 Kingston Road, Elbridge, NY 13060
(315) 689-2082 (call between 10:30 A.M.–7:00 P.M.)

Perfect romantic getaway in Victorian style.
Extremely popular—booked months in advance.
Imagine rich dark woodwork, carved lace-
canopied beds, in-room fireplaces, and Jacuzzis.
If guests love the grandeur of old, then they will
love this Victorian bed and breakfast. In the heart
of the White Mountains, just minutes away from
Squaw Lake, as well as world-class alpine skiing
and cross-country trails, swimming, fishing, hiking, biking, tennis, golf, and antiquing. $85-155.

Glynn House Victorian Inn

43 Highland Street, P.O. Box 719, 03217
(603) 968-3775; (800) 637-9599
FAX (603) 968-3129; e-mail: glynnhse@lr.net
www.bbonline. com/nh/glynnhouse/

Step back in time to Victorian yesteryear. A
romantic escape in the heart of the White

Glynn House Victorian Inn

NOTES: Credit cards accepted: A MasterCard; B Visa; C American Express; D Discover; E Diner's Club;
F Other; 2 Personal checks accepted; 3 Lunch available; 4 Dinner available; 5 Open all year; 6 Pets welcome;
7 No smoking; 8 Children welcome; 9 Social drinking allowed; 10 Tennis nearby; 11 Swimming nearby;
12 Golf nearby; 13 Skiing nearby; 14 May be booked through a travel agent; 15 Handicapped accessible.

Mountains and *On Golden Pond* lakes region of New Hampshire. Come enjoy the local colors of each season. Nine gracious bedrooms with private baths. Whirlpool tub and fireplace amenities. Gourmet breakfast is served. Waterville Valley and Tenney Mountain nearby. Just two hours from Boston; one hour from Manchester airport; I-94, exit 24. No smoking in bedrooms.

Hosts: Karol and Betsy Paterman
Rooms: 9 (PB) $85-155
Full Breakfast
Credit Cards: A, B
Notes: 2, 5, 8, 9, 10, 11, 12, 13, 14

ASHUELOT

Elaine's Bed & Breakfast Selections

4987 Kingston Road, Elbridge, NY 13060
(315) 689-2082 (call between 10:30 A.M.–7:00 P.M.)

Owner-designed and built, this dream pavilion guest house is on top of a mountain with a view of three states. Marble floors throughout except in the master bedroom where there is wall-to-wall carpet. Complete kitchen, spacious marble bath with large whirlpool tub and separate shower. Thick terry-cloth robes for guests' comfort. A full gourmet breakfast is delivered from the owner's house in the morning. Nice location for parties, conferences, and weddings with a chapel on premises. Helicopter shuttle access from Keene airport. Very secluded private location. Rated A plus by the ABBA. Two-night minimum on weekends and three-night minimum for holiday weekends. $250.

BARTLETT

The Notchland Inn

Hart's Location, Route 302, 03812
(603) 374-6131; (800) 866-6131
FAX (603) 374-6168; e-mail: notchland@aol.com
www.notchland.com

The Notchland Inn

A traditional country inn where hospitality has not been forgotten. There are 12 guest rooms, all with working fireplaces and private baths; several with Jacuzzi tubs. Delicious gourmet dining, spectacular mountain views, hiking, cross-country skiing, and swimming are some of the many recreations offered at this secluded mountain estate. MAP available.

Hosts: Les Schoof and Ed Butler
Rooms: 12 (PB) $168-270
Full Breakfast
Credit Cards: A, B, C, D
Notes: 2, 4, 5, 7, 9, 10, 11, 12, 13, 14

BETHLEHEM

Adair Country Inn

80 Guider Lane, 03574
(603) 444-2600; (888) 444-2600
FAX (603) 444-4823; e-mail: adair@connriver.net
www.adairinn.com

Adair Country Inn is a Georgian Colonial Revival mansion, sited on a knoll surrounded by 200 acres. Its extensive landscaping and gardens were designed originally by the Olmsted Brothers. Most rooms have wonderful views of either the Presidential or Dalton mountain ranges. Colorful and flavorful food is emphasized from hearty breakfasts to fine

---

evening dining (in season). Hiking, skiing, golf, and shopping nearby. Adair is a recipient of the prestigious AAA four-diamond award.

Hosts: Judy and Bill Whitman
Rooms: 10 (PB) $145-300
Full Breakfast
Credit Cards: A, B, C
Notes: 2, 4, 5, 7, 9, 10, 11, 12, 13, 14

The Mulburn Inn at Bethlehem

2370 Main Street, 03574
(603) 869-3389; www.mulburninn.com

Step back in time and visit this picturesque English Tudor-style mansion which served as the Woolworth family summer estate. Built by the famous architect Sylvanius D. Morgan, the intricate details of this home are breathtaking. Relax in the cozy yet romantic atmosphere where legends such as Cary Grant and Barbara Hutton spent their honeymoon. Spacious rooms include private baths. The inn boasts three fireplaces and two wraparound porches. Nestled in the White Mountains; golf, skiing, hiking, and a variety of other activities are just minutes away.

Hosts: Alecia Loveless and Christina Ferraro
Rooms: 7 (PB) $70.20-108.00
Full Breakfast
Credit Cards: A, B, C
Notes: 2, 5, 7, 8, 9, 10, 11, 12, 13, 14

The Mulburn Inn

Northern Star Inn

157 Maple Street, 03574
(877) 869-4395; FAX (603) 869-4351

Northern Star Inn

A quaint country inn nestled in the heart of New Hampshire's White Mountains. The host provides a peaceful country setting in a four-season resort region. Minutes to two-course PGA golf, fishing, tennis, and all major attractions. The inn graciously features 14 guest rooms with private bath and TV. Also wake to a delicious home-cooked breakfast. AAA-approved. "Come and let us be your hosts."

Host: Deborah Ford
Rooms: 14 (PB) $55-85
Credit Cards: A, B, D
Notes: 2, 4, 5, 8, 9, 10, 11, 12, 13

Wayside Inn

Wayside Inn

Route 302 at Pierce Bridge, P.O. Box 480, 03574-0480
(603) 869-3364; (800) 448-9557
FAX (603) 869-5765; www.thewaysideinn.com

A traditional New England country inn in the White Mountains. Quiet location by the Ammonoosuc River. Spacious, newly renovated rooms with a European flair. Rooms in the River House are suitable for families with children and offer cable TV, small refrigerators, and balconies overlooking the river. All rooms are air conditioned. Sandy beach by the river. Tennis and fishing on premises. Excel-

7 No smoking; 8 Children welcome; 9 Social drinking allowed; 10 Tennis nearby; 11 Swimming nearby; 12 Golf nearby; 13 Skiing nearby; 14 May be booked through a travel agent; 15 Handicapped accessible.

lent meals in the dining room. Swiss specialties. B&B, MAP, Golf packages. AAA- and
Mobil-rated.

Hosts: Victor and Kathe Hofmann
Rooms: 26 (PB) $75-135
Full Breakfast
Credit Cards: A, B, C, D
Notes: 4, 5, 8, 9, 10, 11, 12, 13, 14, 15

BRADFORD

Candlelite Inn

Candlelite Inn Bed & Breakfast

5 Greenhouse Lane, 03221
(603) 938-5571; (888) 812-5571
FAX (603) 938-2564
e-mail: candlelite@conknet.com

Built in 1897, this historic country Victorian
inn is nestled on three acres of peaceful, rural
countryside in the Lake Sunapee Region. The
Candlelite Inn has all the grace and charm for
that perfect getaway. The three-course breakfast—down to dessert—is served in the Sun
Room overlooking the pond. Walk the back-
roads of Bradford as the leaves change or
cross-country ski and snowshoe the hills
while exploring the beautiful scenery here in
town. "Come and experience the relaxed
atmosphere and the quiet elegance of this all
seasons inn."

Hosts: Les and Marilyn Gordon
Rooms: 6 (PB) $70-95
Full Breakfast
Credit Cards: A, B, C, D
Notes: 2, 5, 7, 9, 10, 11, 12, 13

Mountain Lake Inn

Route 114, Box 443, 03221
(603) 938-2136; (800) 662-6005
e-mail: rfoor@conknet.com
www.mountainlakeinn.amtg.com

Circa 1760 white Colonial house on 168 acres
overlooking Lake Massasecum and mountain
peaks. A sandy beach on the lake for swimming, fishing, boating, and ice skating. Trails
on the property for hiking or snowshoeing and
snowmobiling. Located minutes from Ski
Resorts, golf courses, antiques, and Lake
Sunapee. Enjoy the wall coverings of Currier
and Ives prints while relaxing by the fireplace.
Breakfast is in the dining room with a different
hot dish offered each morning while enjoying
the vintage wood-burning stove. Close to Concord and New London. Lunch and dinner available upon request. Inquire about
accommodations for pets. Smoking permitted
on porch only.

Hosts: Bob and Tracy Foor (new innkeepers)
Rooms: 9 (PB) $80-85
Full Breakfast
Credit Cards: A, B, C, D
Notes: 2, 5, 8, 11, 12, 13, 14

Rosewood Country Inn

67 Pleasant View Road, 03221
(603) 938-5253 (phone/FAX–call first)
(800) 938-5273; e-mail: rosewood@conknet.com

Elegant and romantic country inn on a quiet
country road, but just minutes away from the

Rosewood Country Inn

NOTES: Credit cards accepted: A MasterCard; B Visa; C American Express; D Discover; E Diner's Club;
F Other; 2 Personal checks accepted; 3 Lunch available; 4 Dinner available; 5 Open all year; 6 Pets welcome;

lakes and mountains. Cross-country skiing from the front door. Twelve tastefully decorated suites, all with private baths. Drift off to sleep in a canopied or four-poster bed. Mozart and Vivaldi set the mood for the three-course candlelight and crystal breakfast served before a crackling fire in the dining room, or on one of the lovely sunlit porches. The perfect romantic getaway.

Hosts: Lesley and Dick Marquis
Rooms: 12 (PB) $85-175
Full Breakfast
Credit Cards: A, B, C
Notes: 2, 5, 7, 9, 11, 12, 13

Thistle & Shamrock

Thistle & Shamrock Inn & Restaurant

11 West Main Street, 03221
(603) 938-5553; (888) 938-5553
FAX (603) 938-5554
e-mail: stay@thistleand shamrock.com
www.thistleandshamrock.com

Turn-of-the-century country hotel, furnished with pieces that reflect the era. Guest rooms with private baths. Guests will enjoy a homemade breakfast in the dining room downstairs. A grand parlor with fireplace is always ready for guests to enjoy. The restaurant offers casual gourmet dining with full liquor service in an elegant setting.

Hosts: Jim and Lynn Horigan
Rooms: 11 (PB) $75-91
Full Breakfast
Credit Cards: A, B, C, D
Notes: 2, 4, 5, 7, 8, 9, 10, 11, 12, 13, 14, 15

CENTER HARBOR

Red Hill Inn

Rural Free Delivery 1, Box 99M, 03226
(603) 279-7001; (800) 5-RED HILL
FAX (603) 279-7003

Restored country estate on 60 acres overlooking Squam Lake and White Mountains. Twenty-six rooms, each with private bath, many with fireplace and Jacuzzi. Outdoor hot tub and swimming pool. Air conditioned. Country gourmet restaurant serving all meals; entertainment in the Runabout Lounge. Cross-country skiing and rentals on property. Two hours north of Boston.

Hosts: Rick Miller and Don Leavitt
Rooms: 26 (PB) $105-175
Full Breakfast
Credit Cards: A, B, C, D
Notes: 2, 3, 4, 5, 8, 11, 12, 13, 14

CHARLESTOWN

MapleHedge Bed & Breakfast Inn

355 Main Street, P.O. Box 638, 03603
(800) 9-MAPLE-9; FAX (603) 826-5237
e-mail: debrine@fmis.net
www.maplehedge.com

An elegant home in the national historic register equipped with all modern amenities, MapleHedge is in historic rural New Hampshire on a site with 200-year-old maples and

MapleHedge

7 No smoking; 8 Children welcome; 9 Social drinking allowed; 10 Tennis nearby; 11 Swimming nearby; 12 Golf nearby; 13 Skiing nearby; 14 May be booked through a travel agent; 15 Handicapped accessible.

beautiful gardens. MapleHedge is remembered for its three-course breakfast, wine and cheese social hour, and friendly, caring hosts. All rooms and their private baths are individually decorated with antiques. Hosts pamper guests with exquisitely ironed sheets, fluffy towels, and a turndown service. Inn is on the Connecticut River, the western boundary between New Hampshire and Vermont, and is highly rated by both Mobil and ABBA. Children over 12 welcome.

Hosts: Joan and Dick DeBrine
Rooms: 5 (PB) $90-105
Full Breakfast
Credit Cards: A, B
Notes: 2, 7, 9, 10, 11, 12, 13, 14

CONWAY

Darby Field Inn

Bald Hill Road, P.O. Box D 03818
(603) 447-2181; (800) 426-4147
www.darbyfield.com

A charming, out-of-the-way country inn that offers excellent dining, a cozy atmosphere, award-winning gardens, and spectacular mountain views. An outdoor pool, cross-country ski trails, outdoor hot tub, and a staff that is both friendly and courteous. Reservations recommended. Rate includes breakfast. Midweek and off-season packages. Minimum stay on weekends is two nights and on holidays is two to three nights. Inquire about accommodations for children.

Darby Field Inn

Hosts: Marc and Maria Donaldson
Rooms: 15 (PB) $90-190
Full Breakfast
Credit Cards: A, B
Notes: 2, 4, 9, 10, 11, 12, 13, 14

DANBURY

The Inn at Danbury

Route 104, 03230
(603) 768-3318; www.innatdanbury.com

In rural New Hampshire, the Inn at Danbury is ideally positioned for those seeking quiet and relaxation. The comfortable, friendly surroundings offer guests the opportunity to unwind from the daily grind. The inn features a full country breakfast, an indoor heated swimming pool, and a restaurant. The restaurant offers a delightful menu prepared by innkeeper Edna Greene and her son Jon with family recipes handed down three generations. Guests can take advantage of the many seasonal outdoor activities available in New Hampshire. A dorm with eight beds is also available.

Hosts: Tom, Edna, and Jonathan Greene
Rooms: 14 (PB) $79-99
Full Breakfast
Credit Cards: A, B, C
Notes: 2, 4, 5, 7, 8, 9, 11, 12, 13, 14

DURHAM

Bed & Breakfast Reservations North Shore, Greater Boston, Cape Cod

P.O. Box 600035, Newtonville, MA 02460
(617) 964-1606; (800) 832-2632
FAX (617) 332-8572; e-mail: info@bbreserve.com
www.bbreserve.com

135. The Inn at Oyster River. Listed in the National Register of Historic Places, the inn is one of the oldest buildings in New Hampshire, dating back to 1649. The inn offers luxurious accommodations. Guest rooms have four-poster canopied beds and private baths.

NOTES: Credit cards accepted: A MasterCard; B Visa; C American Express; D Discover; E Diner's Club; F Other; 2 Personal checks accepted; 3 Lunch available; 4 Dinner available; 5 Open all year; 6 Pets welcome;

Selected rooms offer working fireplaces. Jacuzzis and oversize tubs. In-room amenities include telephones, TVs, and data ports. Full gourmet breakfast. Very close to the University of New Hampshire in Durham. A short drive to the seacoast town of Portsmouth and the Kittery, Maine, outlets. No smoking. Open year-round. Children 12 and older are welcome. $159-199.

Three Chimneys Inn

Three Chimneys Inn

17 Newmarket Road, 03824
(603) 868-7800; (888) 399-9777 (outside NH)
FAX (603) 868-2964
e-mail: chimney3@nh.ultranet.com

This 1649 three-and-one-half-acre estate overlooks, the Oyster River and Old Mill Falls on New Hampshire's seacoast A stone's throw from the University of New Hampshire, the inn provides an elegant alternative for New England fine dining, accommodation, and conference or private gathering space. The inn boasts 23 luxurious guest rooms with full private bath or Jacuzzi, color TV, business-size desk, and telephone with data port. A lavish complimentary breakfast is served in Coppers and guests may choose between upscale American cuisine in the inn's three-hearth dining rooms or casual fare and conversation in the ffrost Sawyer Tavern.

Hosts: Ron and Jane Peterson
Rooms: 23 (PB) $149-189
Full Breakfast
Credit Cards: A, B, C, D
Notes: 3, 4, 5, 7, 9, 10, 11, 12, 14, 15

EAST ANDOVER

Bed & Breakfast Reservations North Shore, Greater Boston, Cape Cod

P.O. Box 600035, Newtonville, MA 02460
(617) 964-1606; (800) 832-2632
FAX (617) 332-8572; e-mail: info@bbreserve.com
www.bbreserve.com

66. The Lakeside Inn. This charming Colonial farmhouse inn, originally built in 1767 and enlarged in the 1800s, is nestled in a rural landscape, surrounded by fields, barns, stone walls, shady sugar maples, and century-old farmhouses. The inn has been completely and lovingly restored by its present owners to add modern amenities and additional space for guests' comfort and relaxation. The 10 spacious and beautifully appointed guest rooms include private baths, luxurious bedding, and fine linens. Several rooms have working fireplaces. Full country breakfast included. Children over eight are welcome. No smoking. $125-150.

EAST MADISON

Purity Spring Resort

HC 63, Box 40, Route 153, 03849
(603) 367-8896 (business)
(800) 373-3754 (reservations)
FAX (603) 367-8664

For nearly 100 years the Hoyt family has been welcoming families to Purity Spring Resort, 1,000 private acres accented by pris-

Purity Spring Resort

7 No smoking; 8 Children welcome; 9 Social drinking allowed; 10 Tennis nearby; 11 Swimming nearby; 12 Golf nearby; 13 Skiing nearby; 14 May be booked through a travel agent; 15 Handicapped accessible.

tine 150-acre Purity Lake and King Pine Ski area. It's the ideal destination resort for families in all seasons. Summer guests enjoy swimming in the lake, boating, canoeing, and water skiing. Winter families welcome the ease and affordability of King Pine Ski area. Enjoy the open hospitality of a traditional all-inclusive resort that offers the most value for the money.

Hosts: The Hoyt Family
Rooms: 48 (44 PB; 4 SB) $54-216
Full Breakfast
Credit Cards: A, B, C, D
Notes: 2, 3, 4, 5, 8, 9, 10, 11, 12, 13, 14, 15

EATON CENTER

The Inn at Crystal Lake

Route 153, P.O. Box 12, 03832
(603) 447-2120; (800) 343-7336
FAX (603) 447-3599

Unwind in a restored 1884 country Victorian inn, in a quiet scenic corner of the Mount Washington Valley. Eleven guest rooms are furnished with antiques and have private baths. Relax in the living room with fireplace and large-screen TV or retreat to the antique parlor or library, or in the new billiards room. Swim, fish, sail, canoe, ski, skate, or outlet shop. Smoking is permitted in designated areas only. Children over 10 are welcome.

Hosts: Richard and Janice Octeau
Rooms: 11 (PB) $70-140
Full Breakfast
Credit Cards: A, B, C, D, E
Notes: 2, 5, 9, 10, 11, 12, 13

ENFIELD

Boulder Cottage on Crystal Lake

Rural Route 1, Box 257, 03748
(603) 632-7355

A turn-of-the-century Victorian cottage owned by the hosts' family for 75 years. The inn, in the Dartmouth-Sunapee region, faces beautiful Crystal Lake where swimming, boating, and fishing are accessible. A full country breakfast is served in the Great Room or sun porch. Afternoon refreshments are offered. Many enjoy an extended stay with kitchen privileges. Open May through November.

Hosts: Barbara and Harry Reed
Rooms: 4 (2 PB; 2 SB) $40-65
Full Breakfast
Credit Cards: None
Notes: 2, 7, 8, 9, 11, 12

Mary Keane House

Mary Keane House

Lower Shaker Village, Box 5, 03748
(603) 632-4241; (888) 239-2153
www.tneorg.com/marykeane/

Unusual late-Victorian-style bed and breakfast overlooking Mascoma Lake, with five spacious and light-filled one- and two-room suites combines for guests' pleasure elegance and whimsy, antiques and comfort, sunrise balconies and sunset porches. Complete with glider swing, warm fires, and great breakfasts. Summer wine or winter hot cider on porch or by the fire. Lawns and gardens for strolling, private beach for swimming and canoeing. Shaker Museum nearby. Just 20 minutes to Hanover.

Hosts: David and Sharon Carr
Rooms: 5 (PB) $85-135
Full Breakfast
Credit Cards: A, B, C
Notes: 2, 5, 6, 7, 8, 9, 11, 12, 13, 14

NOTES: Credit cards accepted: A MasterCard; B Visa; C American Express; D Discover; E Diner's Club; F Other; 2 Personal checks accepted; 3 Lunch available; 4 Dinner available; 5 Open all year; 6 Pets welcome;

Shaker Farm Bed & Breakfast

Route 4-A, Mascoma Lake, 03748
(603) 632-7664; (603) 632-9290; (800) 613-7664

Historic Shaker residence, circa 1794, features gunstock corners, original pegboards, and Shaker cupboards. Extra-large rooms with period wallpaper, tastefully furnished, king-size beds, fully carpeted, TV, air conditioning, lake and mountain views, hiking trails, winter sports, and lake sports. Fifteen minutes to Dartmouth College. Hearty country breakfast. Warm hospitality, lovely rooms, and great food.

Hosts: Hal and Charlotte Toms
Rooms: 6 (3 PB; 3 SB) $60-125
Full Breakfast
Credit Cards: A, B
Notes: 2, 10, 11, 12, 13

Shaker Hill Bed & Breakfast

Rural Route 4, Box 100, 259 Shaker Hill Road, 03748
(603) 632-4519; (877) 516-1370
e-mail: shakerhillb&b@valley.net

Shaker Hill Bed and Breakfast…an updated 1790s Colonial home set on 24 acres in northern New England. Original wide-board floors set off the charm of each unique bedroom. Each is designed for comfort with down comforters and pillows, comfortable chairs, and plenty of light for reading. The house is wrapped in a large covered porch, perfect for relaxing after a busy day. Home-baked afternoon refreshments are served. The living room

Shaker Hill

is stocked with books, games, TV, and VCR. A full breakfast is served in the paneled dining room—in front of a crackling fire during the chilly winter months. Readily accessiblr to many attractions and events in both New Hampshire and Vermont, the Shaker Hill Bed and Breakfast is designed to make guests' stay a special one.

Hosts: Allen and Nancy Smith
Rooms: 4 (PB) $75-95
Full Breakfast
Credit Cards: A, B
Notes: 2, 5, 7, 9, 11, 12, 13

The Shaker Inn

447 Route 4A, 03748
(888) 707-4257; FAX (603) 632-7922
e-mail: info@theshakerinn.com

A comfortable 1841 granite Shaker dwelling overlooking Lake Mascoma. Museum on the premises. Guests stay in the original sleeping chamber outfitted with historic Shaker built-ins and furnished in an authentic Shaker style and dine in the original Shaker dining room on Shaker inspired cuisine. Listed in the national historic register. Featured in *House Beautiful*, *Condé Nast Traveler* magazines.

Rooms: 24 (PB) $105-155
Full Breakfast
Credit Cards: A, B, C, D, E, F
Notes: 2, 3, 4, 5, 7, 8, 11, 12, 13, 14

FRANCONIA

Bungay Jar Bed & Breakfast

P.O. Box 15, Easton Valley Road, 03580
(603) 823-7775; (800) 421-0701
FAX (603) 444-0100; www.bungayjar.com

Secluded woodlands with spectacular mountain views, brook, and gardens make this home built from an 18th-century barn memorable. King or queen suites, private balconies, skylights, six-foot soaking tub, sauna, canopied

7 No smoking; 8 Children welcome; 9 Social drinking allowed; 10 Tennis nearby; 11 Swimming nearby; 12 Golf nearby; 13 Skiing nearby; 14 May be booked through a travel agent; 15 Handicapped accessible.

Bungay Jar

bed. Two-story common area with fireplace for reading, music, and talk. Mountain-gaze in the morning sun while breakfasting outside in summer. Small in scale; intimate. Owners are a landscape architect, a patent attorney, and their young son. New suite with fireplace and two-person Jacuzzi. Display garden and garden shop/classes. Children and pets welcome in cottage only.

Owners/Innkeepers: Kate Kerivan and Lee Strimbeck
Rooms: 7 (PB) $100-225
Cottage 1 (PB)
Full Breakfast
Credit Cards: A, B, C, D
Notes: 2, 5, 7, 9, 10, 11, 12, 13

Franconia Inn

Easton Road, 03580
(603) 823-5542; (800) 473-5299
FAX (603) 823-8078

A charming inn on 107 acres in the Easton Valley, affording breathtaking views of the White Mountains. The inn's 34 rooms are decorated simply, yet beautifully. Elegant American cui-

sine highlights the inn's quiet country sophistication. On-premises recreational activities include four clay tennis courts, outdoor heated pool and Jacuzzi, mountain bikes, horseback riding, glider rides on airfield, sleigh rides, lighted ice skating, cross-country ski center with 65K groomed trails. Children are welcome. On Route 116. Closed April 1 through May 15.

Hosts: The Morris Family
Rooms: 34 (30 PB; 4 SB) $91-156
Full Breakfast
Credit Cards: A, B, C
Notes: 4, 8, 9, 10, 11, 12, 13, 14, 15

The Hilltop Inn

Main Street, Sugar Hill, 03585
(603) 823-5695; (800) 770-5695
FAX (603) 823-5518
e-mail: amcah@hilltopinn.com

A charming Victorian country inn, circa 1895. Antique furnishings throughout make each of the guest rooms unique and the common rooms cozy and inviting. All guest rooms include English cotton sheets and handmade quilts. Pets are welcome if they can get along with the resident dogs. AAA-rated three diamonds. Now available is a two-bedroom cottage with full kitchen, bath, and fireplaced living room. Featured in *Outside, Yankee, Country Victorian, Country Almanac*, and numerous travel guides. Boxed lunches available for hikers.

Hosts: Meri and Mike Hern
Rooms: 6 (PB) $90-195
Cottage: $195-225
Full Breakfast
Credit Cards: A, B, D
Notes: 2, 5, 6, 9, 10, 11, 12, 13

The Inn at Forest Hills

P.O. Box 783, Route 142, 03580
(603) 823 9550; (800) 280-9550 (reservations)
e-mail: amerbb@innfhills.com
www.innatforesthills.com

This charming, historic 18-room, more than 100-year-old Tudor manor house beguiles

Franconia Inn

guests to enjoy the majestic scenery and year-round attractions of the White Mountains of New Hampshire. Enjoy gracious hospitality in seven comfortable guest rooms, all with private baths. Relax in country casualness in the sun-filled solarium or by the fireplaces in the living room and alpine room. Savor a gourmet New England breakfast by the fireplace in a fine old country inn!

Hosts: Joanne and Gordon Haym
Rooms: 7 (PB) $90-160
Full Breakfast
Credit Cards: A, B
Notes: 2, 5, 7, 9, 10, 11, 12, 13

FRANKLIN

The Atwood Inn

Route 3A, 03235
(603) 934-3666; e-mail: atwoodinn@cyberportal.net
www.atwoodinn.com

Nestled in the heart of the lakes region, the inn is convenient for all tourist attractions, restaurants, seasonal sports, and activities. This 1830 brick Federal home was restored in 1984 preserving the original features, among them Indian shutters, Count Rumford fireplaces, and old turnkey locks. Hosts offer old-fashioned hospitality, scrumptious breakfasts, and comfortable accommodations. Let this be "your home away from home."

Hosts: Fred and Sandi Hoffmeister
Rooms: 7 (PB) $70-90

The Atwood Inn

Full Breakfast
Credit Cards: A, B, C, D
Notes: 2, 5, 7, 8, 9, 10, 11, 12, 13, 14

GILFORD

Gunstock Inn & Fitness Center

580 Cherry Valley Road, 03246
(603) 293-2021; (800) 654-0180
www.gunstockinn.com

Nestled in a traditional New England setting with a spectacular view of New Hampshire's Lake Winnipesaukee and surrounding mountains. this country inn has 25 guest rooms furnished with lovely antiques. Tavern-family dining, pool table. The health club features a 75-foot pool, saunas, steam rooms, and fully equipped exercise room. Within minutes of golf courses, boating, hiking, skiing, tennis,

Gunstock Inn

7 No smoking; 8 Children welcome; 9 Social drinking allowed; 10 Tennis nearby; 11 Swimming nearby; 12 Golf nearby; 13 Skiing nearby; 14 May be booked through a travel agent; 15 Handicapped accessible.

horseback riding, and area attractions. Pantry breakfast is included in the rates.

Rooms: 25 (PB) $60-175
Credit Cards: A, B, C, D
Notes: 2, 4, 5, 8, 9, 10, 11, 12, 13, 15

GLEN

Covered Bridge House

Route 302, P.O. Box 989, 03838
(603) 383-9109; (800) 232-9109
e-mail: cbhouse@landmarknet.net
www.coveredbridgehouse.com

Feel at home at this cozy bed and breakfast in the Mount Washington Valley next to an 1850s covered bridge. In warm weather, cool off in the Saco River at the private beach or explore all the valley has to offer—hiking, biking, golf, shops, restaurants, attractions, and more. In winter, five major downhill ski areas and six cross-country ski networks are nearby. Relax in the outdoor hot tub that is open year-round. AAA three-diamond-rated.

Hosts: Dan and Nancy Wanek
Rooms: 6 (4 PB; 2 SB) $49-89
Full Breakfast
Credit Cards: A, B, C, D
Notes: 2, 5, 7, 8, 9, 11, 12, 13, 14

GREENFIELD

Greenfield Bed & Breakfast Inn

Junction Routes 136 and 31, Box 400, 03047
(603) 547-6327
e-mail: innkeeper@thegreenfieldinn.com
www.greenfieldinn.com

A romantic Victorian mansion on three acres of lawn in Greenfield, a mountain valley village between Keene and Manchester just 90 minutes from Boston. Enjoy the relaxing mountain view from the spacious veranda. A full hot breakfast is served with crystal, china, and Mozart. Very close to skiing, swimming, hiking, tennis, golf, biking, and bargain antique shopping (no sales tax). A favorite of Mr. and Mrs. Bob Hope and

honeymooners of all ages. Senior citizen discount. Two ski lodge-style suites and sleep-six year-round cottage also available. Smoking permitted in designated areas only.

Hosts: Vic and Barbara Mangini
Rooms: 12 (8 PB; 4 SB) $49-119
Cottage: 2 $159
Full Breakfast
Credit Cards: A, B, C
Notes: 2, 5, 8, 9, 10, 11, 12, 13, 14, 15

HAMPSTEAD

Stillmeadow Bed & Breakfast at Hampstead

545 Main Street, P.O. Box 565, 03841
(603) 329-8381; e-mail: stillmeadowb@yahoo.com

Southern New Hampshire's premier bed and breakfast, Stillmeadow is an 1850 Greek Renaissance Italianate Colonial house accessible to both the mountains and the seacoast. Four rooms with private bath and refrigerator are available, including one family suite with crib, changing table, and "secret stairs" that lead to a children's playroom and playyard. Attractions nearby include the Robert Frost Farm, America's Stonehenge, Kingston State Park, and Rockingham Race Track. Between Manchester and Boston. Antique hardwood floors and a cookie jar that is always full.

Hosts: Lori and Randy Offord
Rooms: 4 (PB) $65-90
Continental Breakfast
Credit Cards: A, B, C, D
Notes: 2, 5, 7, 8, 9, 10, 11, 12, 13

Stillmeadow

NOTES: Credit cards accepted: A MasterCard; B Visa; C American Express; D Discover; E Diner's Club; F Other; 2 Personal checks accepted; 3 Lunch available; 4 Dinner available; 5 Open all year; 6 Pets welcome;

HAMPTON BEACH

Oceanside Inn

365 Ocean Boulevard, 03842
(603) 926-3542

The Oceanside overlooks the Atlantic Ocean
and its beautiful sandy beaches. Each of the 10
rooms is tastefully and individually decorated,
many with period antiques and all with private
modern baths. A complimentary Continental
breakfast is served each day and features
homemade bread and pastries. This gracious
inn is in a less congested part of Hampton
Beach within easy walking distance of restaurants, shops, and other attractions. Closed mid-
October through mid-May.

Hosts: Skip and Debbie Windemiller
Rooms: 10 (PB) $100-150
Continental Breakfast
Credit Cards: A, B, C, D
Notes: 7, 9, 10, 11, 12

HENNIKER

Colby Hill Inn

3 The Oaks, P.O. B 779, 03242
(603) 428-3281; (800) 531-0330
FAX (603) 428-9218
e-mail: info@colbyhillinn.com
www.colbyhillinn.com

Congenial inn-dog, Delilah, awaits
with a handshake, and the
cookie jar beckons at
this rambling 1789 inn,
a complex of farm-
house, carriage house,
and barns on five village acres. Sixteen
antique-filled guest rooms, some with working
fireplace, all with private bath and telephone
with data port and a private line. And the food
is memorable—from the bountiful breakfasts
to the acclaimed candlelit dinners served every
night in the gardenside dining room.

Hosts: Ellie and John Day; Laurel Day Mack
Rooms: 16 (PB) $85-175
Full Breakfast

Credit Cards: A, B, C, D, E
Notes: 2, 4, 5, 7, 9, 10, 11, 12, 13, 14

Meeting House Inn

Meeting House Inn

35 Flanders Road, 03242
(603) 428-3228
e-mail: meetinghouse@conknet.com
www.conknet.com/meetinghouse/

The Meeting House Inn is family owned and
operated. It is a renovated country farmstead
(established 1982). A relaxed and cozy atmosphere where special attention is paid to individual comfort. A nonsmoking inn. The restaurant
serves a delicious selection of individually prepared entrées. Rooms are filled with family
furnishings and antiques, and all have private
baths. A hot full breakfast is brought to the
room in a country basket. Air conditioned.
AAA-approved. Private hot tub and sauna are
available. Inquire about accommodations for
children.

Rooms: 6 (PB) $65-105
Full Breakfast
Credit Cards: A, B, C, D
Notes: 4, 5, 7, 9, 10, 11, 12, 13

HILLSBOROUGH

The Inn at Maplewood Farm

447 Center Road, P.O. Box 1478, 03244
(603) 464-4242; (800) 644-6695
www.conknet.com/maplewoodfarm/

Award-winning country lodgings in the heart
of New Hampshire. Guest rooms are tastefully

7 No smoking; 8 Children welcome; 9 Social drinking allowed; 10 Tennis nearby; 11 Swimming nearby;
12 Golf nearby; 13 Skiing nearby; 14 May be booked through a travel agent; 15 Handicapped accessible.

appointed with American and European antiques, an inviting bed, and unique amenities. The inn is a great starting point for a retreat of hiking, swimming, or golfing. In the heart of antique country and on 14 acres of foliage trees. The Inn at Maplewood Farm has its own vintage radio station. Homemade breakfast every day. The inn was named one of America's 25 favorite bed and breakfasts. An all-suites bed and breakfast. AAA-rated and a *Yankee* Editor's Pick.

Hosts: Laura and Jayme Simoes
Rooms: 4 (PB) $75-125
Full Breakfast
Credit Cards: A, B, C, D, E
Notes: 2, 7, 8, 9, 10, 11, 12, 14

HOLDERNESS

The Inn on Golden Pond

Route 3, P.O. Box 680, 03245
(603) 968-7269

An 1879 Colonial home on 50 wooded acres. Bright and cheerful setting, breakfast, and game rooms. Close to major ski areas. Nearby is Squam Lake, the setting for the film *On Golden Pond*. Minimum stay on holidays. Children over 12 welcome.

Hosts: Bill and Bonnie Webb
Rooms: 9 (PB) $115-140
Full Breakfast
Credit Cards: A, B, C, D
Notes: 2, 5, 7, 9, 10, 11, 12, 13, 14

The Inn on Golden Pond

HOPKINTON

The Country Porch Bed & Breakfast

281 Moran Road, 03229
(603) 746-6391

On 15 peaceful acres of lawn, pasture, and forest, this bed and breakfast is a reproduction of an 18th-century Colonial. Sit on the wrap-around porch and gaze out over the meadow, bask in the sun, and then cool off in the pool. The comfortably appointed rooms have a Colonial, Amish, or Shaker theme and have king- or twin-size beds. Summer and winter activities are plentiful, and fine country dining is a short drive away. "Come and sit a spell." No smoking permitted indoors.

Hosts: Tom and Wendy Solomon
Rooms: 3 (PB) $70-80
Full Breakfast
Credit Cards: A, B
Notes: 2, 5, 7, 9, 10, 11, 12, 13, 14

Elaine's Bed & Breakfast Selections

4987 Kingston Road, Elbridge, NY 13060
(315) 689-2082 (call between 10:30 A.M.–7:00 P.M.)

This delightful nonsmoking bed and breakfast has beautifully reproduced Early American wide-pine floors, beamed ceilings, and fireplaces. The guest rooms have new private baths. Full breakfast served. Can accommodate business conferences and special get-togethers. Outdoor pool. No pets. Inquire about accommodations for children. Two-night minimum on race weekends and graduation weekends. Murder mystery evening for groups of six available January through April. $70-80.

JACKSON

Dana Place Inn

Box L, Pinkham Notch, 03846
(603) 383-6822; (800) 537-9276
e-mail: dpi@ncia.net; www.danaplace.com

Century-old inn at the base of Mount Washington on 300 acres along the Ellis River. Dana Place features cozy rooms, fine dining, indoor heated pool, river swimming, Jacuzzi, tennis, hiking, walking trails, fishing, and cross-country skiing on the premises. Golf, outlet shopping, downhill skiing, and White Mountain attractions all are nearby. Inquire about the seasonal escape packages available.

Hosts: Harris and Mary Lou Levine
Rooms: 33 (29 PB; 4 SB) $95-155
Full Breakfast
Credit Cards: A, B, C, D, E
Notes: 2, 3, 4, 5, 6, 7, 8, 9, 10, 11, 12, 13, 14

Ellis River House

Route 16, P.O. Box 656, 03846
(603) 383-9339; (800) 233-8309
FAX (603) 383-4142
e-mail: innkeeper@erhinn.com; www.erhinn.com

Offering romance and rejuvenation, this enchanting small hotel is just a short stroll from the village. The comfortable guest rooms are decorated with Laura Ashley prints, some with fireplaces and two-person Jacuzzis, cable TV, telephones, scenic balconies, and period antiques and all with individually controlled

Ellis River House

heat and air conditioning. Two-room suites, riverfront cottage, hot tub, sauna, heated pool, sitting and game rooms, and sun deck overlooking the pristine Ellis River. Enjoy a full country breakfast with homemade breads or a romantic candlelight dinner. Afterwards relax with libations and billiards in the pub. Seasonal rates available. Children 16 years and older welcome.

Hosts: Barry and Barbara Lubao
Rooms: 18 (15 PB; 3 SB) $89-289
Full Breakfast
Credit Cards: A, B, C, D, E
Notes: 2, 4, 5, 7, 9, 10, 11, 12, 13, 14, 15

Inn at Jackson

Inn at Jackson

P.O. Box 807, 03846
(603) 383-4321; (800) 289-8600
fax (603) 383-4085; e-mail: innjack@ncia.net
www.innatjackson.com

Designed by architect Stanford White and built in 1902, the Inn served as summer residence for the Baldwin family of New York (of piano fame) and turned into an inn in 1922. The Inn offers a grand foyer, 14 spacious guest rooms, hardwood floors, fireplaces, TVs, air conditioning, and outdoor hot tub Jacuzzi. A Continental plus breakfast with home-baked goodies is served in the fireplaced dining room or on the sun porch overlooking the mountains. AAA-rated three diamonds.

Hosts: Bob Bowman and Lori Tradewell
Rooms: 14 (PB) $65-159
Full Breakfast
Credit Cards: A, B, C, D, E
Notes: 2, 5, 7, 8, 9, 10, 11, 12, 13, 14

7 No smoking; 8 Children welcome; 9 Social drinking allowed; 10 Tennis nearby; 11 Swimming nearby; 12 Golf nearby; 13 Skiing nearby; 14 May be booked through a travel agent; 15 Handicapped accessible.

The Village House

The Village House

P.O. Box 359, 03846
(603) 383-6666

Just over the covered bridge in the village of Jackson is the Village House. The Village House has enjoyed more than 100 years of hospitality. The circa 1860 inn offers its visitors all the amenities of a large resort, with the charm and personality of a small bed and breakfast. The outdoor pool, Jacuzzi, tennis court, and wraparound porch are perfect for summer nights. In the winter, after a day of alpine or Nordic skiing, enjoy the fire or sit under the stars in the Jacuzzi. In any season, guests are welcome. Full breakfast served in the fall and winter; Continental breakfast served in the summer.

Host: Robin Crocker
Rooms: 13 (PB) $65-140
Full and Continental Breakfast
Credit Cards: A, B, D
Notes: 2, 5, 6, 7, 8, 9, 10, 11, 12, 13, 14

JAFFREY

Woodbound Inn & Lake Front Cabins

62 Woodbound Road, 03461
(603) 532-8341; (800) 688-7770
FAX (603) 532-8341 ext. 213
e-mail: woodbound@aol.com

Come enjoy a country inn resort. There is plenty to do on 165 acres, including free golf on a nine-hole course, tennis, private beach, hiking and cross-country ski trails, arcade, gift shop, restaurant, lounge, meeting/banquet facilities for 5 to 200 people, and more. Accommodations include 19 rooms in a 100-year-old bed and breakfast, 14 modern rooms, and 11 lakefront cabins with fireplaces. A perfect place in any season for an escape weekend, wedding, business meeting, or vacation. Pets welcome in cabins only.

Rooms: 44 (39 PB; 5 SB) $60-135
Full Breakfast
Credit Cards: A, B, C
Notes: 2, 5, 8, 9, 10, 11,1 2, 13, 14

JEFFERSON

Applebrook Bed & Breakfast

Route 115A, 03583-0178
(603) 586-7713; (800) 545-6504

Taste the midsummer raspberries while enjoying spectacular mountain views from this old Victorian farmhouse. Bike, hike, fish, ski, go antiquing, or just relax in the sitting room by the goldfish pool. Near Santa's Village and Six Gun City. Family suite available in addition to private guest rooms. The newest room, Nellie's Nook, boasts a king-size bed, private balcony overlooking the mountains, and tucked in the corner is a two-person spa. Brochure available. Try the hot tub under the stars!

Hosts: Sandra J. Conley and Martin M. Kelly
Rooms: 12 (7 PB; 5 SB) $55-905
Dorm Rooms: $25 per person
Full Breakfast
Credit Cards: A, B
Notes: 2, 6, 7, 8, 9, 10, 11, 12, 13, 14

Applebrook

NOTES: Credit cards accepted: A MasterCard; B Visa; C American Express; D Discover; E Diner's Club; F Other; 2 Personal checks accepted; 3 Lunch available; 4 Dinner available; 5 Open all year; 6 Pets welcome;

The Jefferson Inn

The Jefferson Inn

Route 2, RR 1, Box 68A, 03583
(603) 586-7998; (800) 729-7908

A comfortably gracious 1896 Victorian nestled in the northern White Mountains near Mount Washington. Eleven unique accommodations with spectacular views, private baths, and sumptuous breakfasts. Guests are encouraged to bring their boots, binoculars, and bicycle. Three of New Hampshire's 50 best rides start here. Golf, hiking trails, swimming, ice-skating, antiques, and crafts within walking distance. Close to several restaurants, cross-country and downhill skiing, snowmobile trails, summer theater, and children's attractions. The perfect getaway for all ages. AAA-rated three diamonds.

Hosts: Marla Mason and Don Garretson
Rooms: 11 (PB) $80-175
Full Breakfast
Credit Cards: A, B, C, D
Notes: 2, 5, 8, 9, 11, 12, 13, 14, 15

LINCOLN

Red Sleigh Inn

Pollard Road, P.O. Box 562, 03251
(603) 745-8517

Family-run inn with mountain views. Just off the scenic Kancamagus Highway. One mile to Loon Mountains. Waterville, Cannon, and Bretton Woods nearby. Many summer attractions and superb fall foliage. Shopping, dining, and theater are minutes away. Hiking, swimming, golf, and train rides are available. Children over 12 are welcome.

Hosts: Bill and Loretta Deppe
Rooms: 6 (2 PB; 4 SB) $65-85
Full Breakfast
Credit Cards: A, B
Notes: 2, 5, 7, 9, 10, 11, 12, 13, 14

LISBON

Ammonoosuc Inn

641 Bishop Road, 03585
(603) 838-6118; (888) 546-6118
FAX (603) 838-5591

This 19th-century farmhouse is by a nine-hole golf course on the banks of the Ammonoosuc River. Its wraparound front porch overlooks the course and the river, and provides a quiet and peaceful setting. The inn is 15 minutes from Franconia Notch, and is convenient to all the White Mountains have to offer. An ample Continental breakfast is served, and MAP and golf packages are available.

Hosts: Jeni and Jim Lewis
Rooms: 9 (PB) $60-120
Continental Breakfast
Credit Cards: A, B
Notes: 4, 5, 10, 12, 13

Ammonoosuc Inn

7 No smoking; 8 Children welcome; 9 Social drinking allowed; 10 Tennis nearby; 11 Swimming nearby; 12 Golf nearby; 13 Skiing nearby; 14 May be booked through a travel agent; 15 Handicapped accessible.

LITTLETON

The Beal House Inn

2 West Main Street, 03561
(603) 444-2661; (888) 616-BEAL
e-mail:Beal.House.inn@connriver.net
www.bealhouseinn.com

Come enjoy the good things in
life at this 1833 Main Street inn.
Delight in the antiques,
down comforters, and
fireplaces. Escape to the
romantic suite. Soak in the
antique claw-foot tubs. Two
common rooms with fire-
places. Read a book, chat,
or watch TV and movies in
the parlor. Watch the town
of Littleton go by from the wicker-filled
enclosed front porch. Eight rooms with private
baths, whimsical beds, and some with TV/VCR
and air conditioning. Sip a favorite beverage on
the outdoor deck while viewing the mountains
and star-filled skies. The jazzy bistro restaurant
features a contemporary mix of classic cuisine,
wood-grilled items, fine wines and spirits. Walk
to town for shopping, movies, and dining after a
day of exploring the White Mountains. Inquire
about accommodations for pets.

Hosts: Pat and Michael McGuin
Rooms: 10 (PB) $85-150
Full Breakfast
Credit Cards: A, B, C, D
Notes: 2, 3, 4, 5, 7, 8, 9, 10, 11, 12, 13, 14

LONDONDERRY

Bed & Breakfast Reservations North Shore, Greater Boston, Cape Cod

P.O. Box 600035, Newtonville, MA 02460
(617) 964-1606; (800) 832-2632
FAX (617) 332-8572; e-mail: info@bbreserve.com
www.bbreserve.com

134. Orchard Hill Bed and Breakfast. This quiet
country farmhouse overlooks acres of "U-Pick"
apple orchards. The hosts have made extensive
renovations to the farmhouse, which was originally built in 1850. The cozy accommodations
offer two comfortable guest rooms, sharing a
bath when both rooms are occupied. The spacious common room offers guests a wonderful
place to relax before or after a long day of travel
or sightseeing. Full country breakfast. Local
attractions include horse-drawn farm tours,
Stoneyfield Yogurt Factory tours, Canobie Lake
Amusement Park, horseback riding, golf, and
even hot-air balloon rides. No smoking. $75-85.

LOUDON

Elaine's Bed & Breakfast Selections

4987 Kingston Road, Elbridge, NY 13060
(315) 689-2082 (call between 10:30 A.M.–7:00 P.M.)

This Georgian Colonial was built in 1790 and
offers elegant accommodations in this house
and also in the attached carriage house. All
seven guest rooms have private baths, reading
lights, and ceiling fans. The family room has
games, TV, an extensive book collection, and a
wood stove. Complimentary beverages and
snacks are served here. A full hearty country
breakfast is served. Hiking, mountain biking,
cross-country skiing and snowmobiling, all
accessible from the farm's doorway. Nearby is
alpine skiing, canoeing, golfing, horseback riding, fishing, antiquing, and tax-free shopping.
Well-traveled host is fluent in French and Spanish. Two suites have fireplaces and one has a
sitting area and large modern bath. $115-125.

MADISON

Elaine's Bed & Breakfast Selections

4987 Kingston Road, Elbridge, NY 13060
(315) 689-2082 (call between 10:30 A.M.–7:00 P.M.)

This large rambling farmhouse is on 216 acres.
The four guest rooms on the second floor are

spacious and have private baths, and a family suite on the third floor has two bedrooms, private bath, a sleeper-sofa, TV, and a table with chairs. Relax on the large open wraparound porch with a mountain view. There are two guest living rooms, one with a woodstove and the other with a keyboard. Full homemade country breakfast. Moderate rates.

MARLBOROUGH

Peep-Willow Farm

51 Bixby Street, 03455
(603) 876-3807

Peep-Willow Farm is a 20-acre working Thorough-bred horse farm that also caters to humans, with a view all the way to the Connecticut River valley. Guests are welcome to help with chores or watch the young horses frolic in the fields, but there is no riding. Flexibility and serenity are the key ingredients to enjoying the stay. Pets and children welcome by prior arrangement. Cross-country skiing.

Host: Noel Aderer
Rooms: 3 (SB) $35-55
Full Breakfast
Credit Cards: None
Notes: 2, 5, 7, 9, 10, 11, 12, 13

MEREDITH

Elaine's Bed & Breakfast Selections

4987 Kingston Road, Elbridge, NY 13060
(315) 689-2082 (call between 10:30 A.M.–7:00 P.M.)

1. This 200-plus-year-old bed and breakfast has eight guest rooms with private baths. There are multiple fireplaces, an outdoor swimming pool, a game room with pool table, and a guest kitchen. AAA-rated three diamonds. No smoking. Full breakfast served between 8:00-9:30 A.M. Children over six welcome. $79-99.

2. This Victorian "Painted Lady" has spacious rooms with fireplaces, whirlpools, and two first-floor handicapped accessible rooms. No smoking. All guest rooms have TVs and telephones. Full breakfast. Open year-round. Seasonal rates. $79-149.

The Inns at Mill Falls

312 Daniel Webster Highway #28, 03253
(603) 279-7006; (800) 622-MILL
FAX (603) 279-6797
e-mail: info@millfalls-baypoint.com

The Inns at Mill Falls offer the best of the Lakes Region. A 40-foot waterfall is between the 54-room inn at Mill Falls and the marketplace which has 18 shops and restaurants. Bay Point offers 24 luxury lake view rooms and the popular Boathouse Grille. The new Chase House offers 23-lakeview rooms and suites, plus a state-of-the-art 200-seat conference center. The Inns have rooms and rates for all.

Rooms: 101 (PB) $89-249
Credit Cards: A, B, C, D
Notes: 2, 3, 4, 5, 8, 9, 10, 11, 12, 13, 14, 15

MOULTONBOROUGH

Olde Orchard Inn

Route 1, Box 256, 03254
(603) 476-5004; (800) 598-5845

This bed and breakfast features nine guest rooms, with private baths, in a beautifully restored farmhouse. The inn is on 13 acres with a mountain brook and pond. Hosts offer guests a large country breakfast with home-baked goods and all the fixings. Only one mile from beautiful Lake Winnipesaukee and only minutes away from many other lakes, regional

Olde Orchard Inn

7 No smoking; 8 Children welcome; 9 Social drinking allowed; 10 Tennis nearby; 11 Swimming nearby; 12 Golf nearby; 13 Skiing nearby; 14 May be booked through a travel agent; 15 Handicapped accessible.

attractions, and activities. Within one hour's drive, guests will find five major ski areas, or guests may decide to take a cross-country ski tour from the inn's front door. The foliage is stunning in Autumn, but anytime is a delightful time to stay here.

Hosts: The Senner Family
Rooms: 9 (PB) $75-140
Full Breakfast
Credit Cards: A, B, D
Notes: 2, 5, 7, 8, 9, 10, 11, 12, 13, 14

NEWFOUND LAKE

The Inn on Newfound Lake

Route 3A, Bridgewater, 03222
(603) 744-9111; (800) 745-7990
FAX (603) 744-3894
e-mail: inonlk@cyberportal.net
www.newfoundlake.com

Beautiful Victorian inn that has been welcoming guests since 1840. Resting on the shore of one of the most pristine lakes in the country. Hiking, biking, skiing. Truly a four-season destination spot. Dine in the renowned restaurant, or just watch the beautiful sunsets from the 120-foot veranda. Return to a bygone era. One of New Hampshire's hidden secrets. Near Wellington State Park, the White Mountains, and tax-free outlet shopping.

Hosts: Larry Delangis and Phelps Boyce
Rooms: 31 (24 PB; 7 SB) $105-135
Continental Breakfast
Credit Cards: A, B, C, D
Notes: 2, 4, 5, 7, 9, 10, 11, 12, 13, 14

The Inn on Newfound Lake

NEW LONDON

The Inn at Pleasant Lake

125 Pleasant Street, P.O. Box 1030, 03257
(603) 526-6271; (800) 626-4907
FAX (603) 526-4111
e-mail: bmackenz@kear.tds.net
www.innatpleasantlake.com

Descending 500 feet from Main Street, visitors will find the inn on the shore of Pleasant Lake with Mount Kearsarge as its backdrop. All rooms have beautiful views, private baths, and are furnished with antiques. Dining room serves a prix fixe five-course one-sitting dinner—reservations required. Five acres of woods, pastures, and gardens surround the inn. Hiking trails nearby. The lake provides swimming and fishing in summer; skiing and skating are equally popular in winter. Children are welcome.

Hosts: Linda and Brian Mackenzie
Rooms: 11 (PB) $95-155
Full Breakfast
Credit Cards: A, B, D
Notes: 2, 5, 7, 8, 9, 10, 11, 12, 13, 14

The Inn at Pleasant Lake

NORTH CONWAY

The Buttonwood Inn

Mount Surprise Road, P.O. Box 1817, 03860
(603) 356-2625; (800) 258-2625 U.S. and Canada
FAX (603) 356-3140
e-mail: button_w@moose.ncia.net
www.buttonwoodinn.com

Nationally recognized for superior innkeeping. Visit this 1820s farmhouse on 17 secluded

NOTES: Credit cards accepted: A MasterCard; B Visa; C American Express; D Discover; E Diner's Club; F Other; 2 Personal checks accepted; 3 Lunch available; 4 Dinner available; 5 Open all year; 6 Pets welcome;

The Buttonwood Inn

acres, two miles from the village of North Conway. Guests enjoy a peaceful, rural setting, with the convenience of being close to everything. Decorated with Shaker furniture, stenciling, and antiques. Breakfasts are second to none. Three-time award-winning perennial gardens surround the inn. Hike or cross-country ski from the back door. Individually prepared daily itineraries. A memorable blend of hospitality, laughter, and kindness.

Hosts: Claudia and Peter Needham
Rooms: 10 (PB) $95-250
Full Breakfast
Credit Cards: A, B, C, D
Notes: 2, 5, 7, 8, 9, 10, 11, 12, 13, 14

Cabernet Inn

Box 489, 03860
(603) 356-4704; (800) 866-4704
e-mail: info@cabernetinn.com; www.cabentinn.com

Nestled in a grove of towering pines, this 1842 Victorian cottage was refurbished and enhanced into an elegant nonsmoking inn. Deluxe rooms have either Jacuzzis or gas fireplaces, queen-size beds, and air conditioning. Two guest living rooms with fireplaces open to shaded outdoor patios and provide relaxing ambiance. Period lighting and furnishings are found throughout the inn. When guests step into the large gourmet kitchen, the secrets behind the delicious, bountiful breakfasts are revealed.

Hosts: Chris and Bob Wyner
Rooms: 10 (PB) $75-175
Full Breakfast
Credit Cards: A, B, C, D
Notes: 2, 5, 7, 10, 11, 12, 13, 15

The Farm by the River Bed & Breakfast

2555 West Side Road, 03860
(603) 356-2694 (phone/FAX); (888) 414-8353
e-mail: info@farmbytheriver.com
www.farmbytheriver.com

Unwind in this charming, historic 1785 inn within a spectacular mountain setting, on 65 acres with river frontage. Each room is uniquely decorated, some have two-person Jacuzzis and fireplaces—family suites available also. Enjoy a fireside or patio breakfast with views to the mountains, gardens, and horses. On site: horseback and sleigh rides, snowshoeing, fly-fishing, and swimming with private beach. AAA-rated three diamonds.

Hosts: Rick and Charlene Davis
Rooms: 10 (8 PB; 2 SB) $65-170
Full Breakfast
Credit Cards: A, B
Notes: 5, 7, 8, 9, 10, 11, 12, 13, 14

The Forest: A Country Inn

P.O. Box 37, Intervale, 03845
(603) 356-9772; (800) 448-3534
FAX (603) 356-5652

Step into an era of old-fashioned charm and hospitality at the beautifully maintained 1890

The Forest: A Country Inn

7 No smoking; 8 Children welcome; 9 Social drinking allowed; 10 Tennis nearby; 11 Swimming nearby; 12 Golf nearby; 13 Skiing nearby; 14 May be booked through a travel agent; 15 Handicapped accessible.

Victorian inn set on 25 quiet, wooded acres just minutes from North Conway. Eleven lovely rooms are furnished with antiques and some rooms have fireplaces. A romantic stone cottage with a fireplace and a cottage with a whirlpool tub are romantic hideaways. The guests-only dining room serves a country breakfast each morning. Enjoy the large screened veranda, outdoor pool, and 65K of cross-country ski trails at the back door. Seasonal variations. Packages available.

Rooms: 11 (PB) $79-169
Full Breakfast
Credit Cards: A, B, C, D
Notes: 2, 5, 7, 8, 9, 10, 11, 12, 13, 14

Nereledge Inn

River Road (off Main Street, Route 16)
P.O. Box 547, 03860
(603) 356-2831

This small 1787 traditional bed and breakfast with views of Cathedral Ledge offers charm, hospitality, and relaxation. Daydream in a rocking chair on the front porch, relax by the fire, or enjoy a game of darts or backgammon. A friendly, informal atmosphere awaits guests. The country breakfast includes warm apple crumble with ice cream. Close to hiking, biking, rock and ice climbing, and skiing. Walk to the village for dining, theater, and shopping or to the river for swimming, fishing, and canoeing.

Hosts: Valerie and Dave
Rooms: 11 (6 PB; 5 SB) $60-130
Full Breakfast
Credit Cards: A, B, C, D
Notes: 2, 5, 7, 8, 9, 10, 11, 12, 13, 14

Old Red Inn & Cottages

P.O. Box 467, 03860
(603) 356 2642; (800) 338-1356
FAX (603) 356-6626; e-mail: oldredin@nxi.com
www.oldredinn.com

One hundred ninety years of caring for travelers to the White Mountains. Guests experience the warmth and hospitality that this grand

home shares with each guest. Stroll into town for dining, summer theater, golf, shopping. Watch a nightly baseball game on the common in summer or ice skate in the park in winter. Fireplaced cottages also available for relaxing with that someone special, or bring the whole family and use one of the two-bedroom cottages. Every guest starts the day off with a full breakfast served fireside in winter or on the front porch in the summer. Spotless and comfortable accommodations make this the number one choice for visitors from anywhere in the world as well as right here in the USA.

Hosts: Terry and Dick Potochniak
Rooms: 17 (15 PB; 2 SB) $59-165
Full Breakfast
Credit Cards: A, B, C, D
Notes: 5, 7, 8, 10, 11, 12, 13, 14

Scottish Lion Inn & Restaurant

P.O. Box 1527, 03860-1527
(888) 356-4945; FAX (603) 356-4802
e-mail: info@scottishlioninn.com

At the Scottish Lion, guests will find a genuine country inn atmosphere with eight lovely rooms, all with private baths and air conditioning. Splendid cuisine consisting of American, Scottish, and international fare with an award-winning wine list to complement each dish. The Black Watch Pub features a very large selection of single malts and also Scotch whiskies, ales, brandies and liqueurs.

Hosts: Michael and Janet Procopio
Rooms: 8 (PB) $65-130
Full Breakfast
Credit Cards: A, B, D, E
Notes: 3, 4, 5, 8, 9, 10, 11, 12, 13, 14

The 1785 Inn & Restaurant

3582 White Mountain Highway
P.O. Box 1785, 03860-1785
(603) 356-9025; (800) 421-1785 (reservations)
FAX (603) 356-6081; e-mail: the1785inn@aol.com

The 1785 Inn has a famous view of Mount Washington popularized by the White Moun-

---

NOTES: Credit cards accepted: A MasterCard; B Visa; C American Express; D Discover; E Diner's Club; F Other; 2 Personal checks accepted; 3 Lunch available; 4 Dinner available; 5 Open all year; 6 Pets welcome;

tain School of Art in the 1800s. The inn was completely refurbished by the current owners and offers romantic accommodations where guests can relax and savor the view while being pampered with fine dining and friendly service. On six pristine acres with swimming pool, skiing, nature trails, 210-year-old fireplaces, hiking, biking, fishing. Free color brochure.

Hosts: Becky and Charlie Mallar
Rooms: 17 (12 PB; 5 SB) $69-239
Full Breakfast
Credit Cards: A, B, C, D, E, F
Notes: 2, 4, 5, 7, 8, 9, 10, 11, 12, 13, 14

Wyatt House Country Inn

Main Street, Route 16, P.O. Box 777, 03860
(603) 356-7977; (800) 527-7978
FAX (603) 356-2183; e-mail: wyatthouse@webtv.net
www.wyatthouse.com

Experience the charm of an elegant country Victorian inn with panoramic mountain and river views. New suite with two-person Jacuzzi bath and mountain views. Gourmet multi-entrée breakfast is served with candlelight. Early morning coffee and muffins and Victorian tea time are served in the handsome study. Village location, and minutes to downhill and cross-country skiing. Stroll from the back yard to the Saco River for swimming or fishing. Tax-free outlet shopping. Air conditioning, color cable TV, optional breakfast in bed. AAA-rated. Smoking limited to Victorian wraparound porch and grounds. Children over seven welcome.

Hosts: Bill and Arlene Strickland
Rooms: 7 (5 PB; 2 SB) $65-95
Full Breakfast
Credit Cards: A, B, C, D
Notes: 3, 5, 7, 9, 10, 11, 12, 13, 14

NORTH CONWAY (INTERVALE)

Elaine's Bed & Breakfast Selections

4987 Kingston Road, Elbridge, NY 13060
(315) 689-2082 (call between 10:30 A.M.–7:00 P.M.)

This is a unique country lodge with resort amenities. Central to all activities in Mount Washington Valley, on the Intervale Resort Loop—just north of North Conway. All rooms have TV, refrigerators, and air conditioning. Two swimming pools, an outdoor Jacuzzi, tennis, fishing, and hiking on premises. Cross-country ski on groomed trails. Just five minutes away is excellent alpine skiing at either Cranmore or Attitash/Bear Peak. Open year-round. Continental breakfast. $55-220.

NORTH SUTTON

Follansbee Inn on Kezar Lake

P.O. Box 92, 03260
(603) 927-4221; (800) 626-4221
e-mail: follansbeeinn@conknet.com
www.follansbeeinn.com

An authentic 1840 New England inn with white clapboard and green trim. On peaceful Kezar

Follansbee Inn

7 No smoking; 8 Children welcome; 9 Social drinking allowed; 10 Tennis nearby; 11 Swimming nearby; 12 Golf nearby; 13 Skiing nearby; 14 May be booked through a travel agent; 15 Handicapped accessible.

Lake, with an old-fashioned porch, comfortable sitting rooms with fireplaces, and charming antique furnishings. Nestled in a small country village but convenient to all area activities (New London, 4 miles; Hanover/Dartmouth, 20 miles; Lake Sunapee, 8 miles). One and one-half hours from Boston and less than four hours from Montreal and Cape Cod. Private pier with rowboat, canoe, paddleboat, and windsurfer for guests. Beautiful walk around the lake during all seasons. Beer and wine license. Healthy nonsmoking inn. Closed parts of November and April. Children over eight welcome.

Hosts: Dick and Sandy Reilein
Rooms: 23 (11 PB; 12 SB) $90-120
Full Breakfast
Credit Cards: A, B
Notes: 2, 7, 9, 10, 11, 12, 13

NORTH WOODSTOCK

Wilderness Inn Bed & Breakfast

Routes 3 and 112, RFD Box 69, 03262
(603) 745-3890; (800) 200-WILD
www.musar.com/wildernessinn

Built in 1912, the Wilderness Inn is decorated with antiques and turn-of-the- century photographs. Guest rooms have views of Lost River or the mountains. Avid skiers, canoers, and hikers themselves, the owners are delighted to help guests explore the area. Breakfasts include fresh fruit and juice, home-baked muffins, a choice of apple or cranberry-walnut pancakes, crêpes with sour cream, applesauce, and chopped nuts, or vegetable omelets. Cottage with fireplace.

Hosts: Michael and Rosanna Yarnell
Rooms: 8 (6 PB; 2 SB) $45-120
Full Breakfast
Credit Cards: A, B, C
Notes: 2, 5, 7, 8, 9, 10, 11, 12, 13, 14

PLYMOUTH

Colonel Spencer Inn

Rural Route 1, Box 206, 03264
(603) 536-3438; (603) 536-1944

The inn is a tastefully restored 1764 Colonial home featuring hewn post-and-beam construction, Indian shutters, gunstock corners, wainscoting, paneling, and wide-pine floors. Seven antique-appointed bedrooms with private baths welcome guests with New England warmth and hospitality. A full country breakfast is served in a fireplaced dining room within view of the White Mountains and the Pemigewasset River. Convenient to lake and mountain attractions, at exit 27, off I-93, one-half mile south on Route 3.

Hosts: Carolyn and Alan Hill
Rooms: 7 (PB) $45-65
Full Breakfast
Credit Cards: None
Notes: 2, 5, 7, 8, 9, 10, 11, 12, 13, 14

RINDGE

Cathedral House

63 Cathedral Entrance, 03461
(603) 899-6790

The Cathedral House is on the grounds of the internationally renowned Cathedral of the

Cathedral House

NOTES: Credit cards accepted: A MasterCard; B Visa; C American Express; D Discover; E Diner's Club; F Other; 2 Personal checks accepted; 3 Lunch available; 4 Dinner available; 5 Open all year; 6 Pets welcome;

Pines. Here guests and their families can enjoy the comforts of a tasteful 1850s farmhouse surrounded by meadows and mountain ranges. Marked trails lead to a grassy pond for fishing and canoeing or to the cathedral gardens and chapels where outdoor weddings, christenings, and services are conducted. Bring the family and step back to a time when traveling meant being welcomed into a stranger's house only to find a home away from home.

Hosts: Donald and Shirley Mahoney
Rooms: 5 (1 PB; 4 SB) $50-125
Full Breakfast
Credit Cards: A, B
Notes: 2, 5, 7, 8, 11, 12, 13

RYE

Rock Ledge Manor Bed & Breakfast

1413 Ocean Boulevard, Route 1A, 03870
(603) 431-1413

Gracious traditional seaside manor home (1840-80) with wraparound porch. All rooms have paddle fans, an ocean view, and queen-size beds. Six minutes to historic Portsmouth; 20 minutes to University of New Hampshire; 15 minutes to Hampton; 10 minutes to southern Maine's seacoast attractions. Open year-round. Children over 15 welcome.

Hosts: Stan and Sandi Smith
Rooms: 4 (2 PB; 2 SB) $90-145
Full Breakfast
Credit Cards: None
Notes: 2, 5, 7, 9, 10, 11, 12, 13

SUGAR HILL

The Homestead Inn

Route 117, P.O. Box 619, 03585
(603) 823-5564; (800) 823-5564
FAX (603) 823-9599; e-mail: homested@together.net
www.thehomestead1820.com

Spanning seven generations, this is one of the oldest family inns in America. Its atmosphere

is relaxing and comfortable, while the local unspoiled beauty and breathtaking mountain views compel many a return visit. Nearby is the renowned Franconia State Park and "Old Man of the Mountains." Other attractions include the Flume Gorge, the Aeriel Tramway, four train rides, seven golf courses, six museums, the Mount Washington area, several children theme parks, 1,200 miles of hiking trails, bike path, covered bridges, and waterfalls. Full country breakfast. Three major ski areas nearby. Cross-country skiing on property.

Host: Paul Hayward
Rooms: 19 (9 PB; 10 SB) $60-108
Full Breakfast
Credit Cards: A, B, C, D
Notes: 2, 5, 6, 7, 8, 9, 10, 11, 12, 13, 14

SUTTON MILLS

The Village House at Sutton Mills

14 Grist Mill Road, 03221
(603) 927-4765; e-mail: jm_paige@conknet.com
www.xcity.com/sutton/villahse.htm

The Village House is an 1857 country Victorian house on four private acres overlooking a quaint New England village in a four-season resort area. The rooms are comfortably appointed, each with its own unique charm. Jack operates a blacksmith shop in the barn, and Marilyn creates canvas floorcloths, popular in the 18th and 19th centuries in New England. Full country breakfast included.

The Village House

Hosts: Marilyn and Jack Paige
Rooms: 3 (PB) 80
Full Breakfast
Credit Cards: A, B
Notes: 2, 5, 7, 8, 9, 11, 12, 13

TILTON

Black Swan Inn

354 West Main Street, 03276
(603) 286-4524; FAX (603) 286-8260

An elegant Victorian built in 1880 awaits guests—exceptional mahogany, walnut, and oak woodwork abounds. In the Lakes region 18 miles north of Concord. Two fireplaces for guests to enjoy as well as two screened porches and lovely gardens in the summer. Shaker village, Tilton Academy, outlet mall shopping are but a few attractions. Nice restaurants in the area. AAA-rated three diamonds, Mobil Travel Guide, 1st Traveler choice on internet, Inns & Outs. Exit 20 off I-93. Children 10 and older welcome. Two suites in the Carriage House are handicapped accessible, but not the main inn.

Host: Janet Foster
Rooms: 9 (5 PB; 4 SB) $75-100
Full Breakfast
Credit Cards: A, B, C, D, E
Notes: 2, 5, 9, 10, 11, 12, 13, 14

Tilton Manor

40 Chestnut Street, 03276
(603) 286-3457 (phone/FAX)
e-mail: tiltonmanor@worldpath.net
www.tiltonmanor.com

This 16-room turn-of-the-century Victorian bed and breakfast welcomes guests. Specializing in the utmost comforts, the inn is nestled in a tranquil three and one-half acre setting. The bedrooms, furnished with antiques and handmade afghans, will warm guests' spirits. Books, games, and TV are there only for guests' pleasure in the spacious sitting room. Come join us, and relax by the fireside in the living room. Awake to the aroma of home cooking and freshly baked muffins. Start the day with the heartiest country breakfast in New Hampshire.

Hosts: Diane and Chip
Rooms: 4 (2 PB; 2 SB) $75-80
Full Breakfast
Credit Cards: A, B, C, D
Notes: 2, 4, 5, 6, 7, 8, 10, 11, 12, 13

WAKEFIELD

Elaine's Bed & Breakfast Selections

4987 Kingston Road, Elbridge, NY 13060
(315) 689-2082 (call between 10:30 A.M.–7:00 P.M.)

History buffs are enchanted with this 200-year-old inn. The seven guest rooms are individually decorated and have private baths and ceiling fans. The living room has a three-sided fireplace, TV, sofa, and comfortable chairs and shares the fireplace with the dining room that has a large picture window overlooking the patio, garden, and yard where guests can watch the birds. Guests may play a piano is set between the living room and dining room. There are more than six acres of walking trails. The innkeeper also holds quilting weekends, mystery weekends, and small weddings and/or receptions. Full breakfast. Moderate rates.

The Wakefield Inn

2723 Wakefield Road, 03872
(603) 522-8272; (800) 245-0841

Within the national historic district of Wakefield Corner, the inn and its surrounding homes are all 19th-century white wooden structures surrounded by gracious fence-encircled yards and historic landmarks, such as a hay scale, granite horse trough, and town pound. Built in 1804, the inn features a free-standing spiral staircase, a three-sided fireplace, Indian shutters, and a wraparound porch. Comfortable, immaculate guest rooms are large with attractive furnishings featuring Lou's handmade quilts.

NOTES: Credit cards accepted: A MasterCard; B Visa; C American Express; D Discover; E Diner's Club; F Other; 2 Personal checks accepted; 3 Lunch available; 4 Dinner available; 5 Open all year; 6 Pets welcome;

Hosts: Harry and Lou Sisson
Rooms: 7 (PB) $70-80
Full Breakfast
Credit Cards: A, B
Notes: 2, 5, 12

WATERVILLE VALLEY

Silver Fox Inn

10 Snowsbrook Road, P.O. Box 358, 03215
(888) 236-3699; e-mail: wvlodge@together.net

Located in a beautiful resort in the heart of the White Mountain National Forest. The Silver Fox offers comfortable air-conditioned rooms. Lounge in the living room and partake of the wine and cheese social every afternoon. Enjoy an expansive Continental breakfast while gazing at spectacular mountain views in the dining room. Ski all winter and play all summer, there are activities for everyone to enjoy. Walk to restaurants and shops in the resort's Town Square.

Hosts: Tor and Susan Brunvand
Rooms: 32 (PB) $49-119
Continental Breakfast
Credit Cards: A, B, C, D, E
Notes: 2, 5, 7, 8, 9, 10, 11, 12, 13, 14, 15

WEST SWANZEY

The Loafer Inn at the 1792 Whitcomb House Bed & Breakfast

27 Main Street, 03446
(603) 357-6624; FAX (603) 357-6621
e-mail: loaferinn@monad.net

Five covered bridges and lovely English gardens cast a relaxing spell. Classic 22-room mansion. Loaf, swim, fish, bike, jog, golf, tennis, canoe, go antiquing, or "shop till you drop" in nearby Keene. Antique furnishings; "At your leisure" country breakfast buffet.

Hosts: Richard and Cheryl Munson
Rooms: 6 (2 PB; 4 SB) $65-75
Full Breakfast
Credit Cards: A, B, C
Notes: 2, 5, 7, 9, 10, 11, 12

7 No smoking; 8 Children welcome; 9 Social drinking allowed; 10 Tennis nearby; 11 Swimming nearby; 12 Golf nearby; 13 Skiing nearby; 14 May be booked through a travel agent; 15 Handicapped accessible.

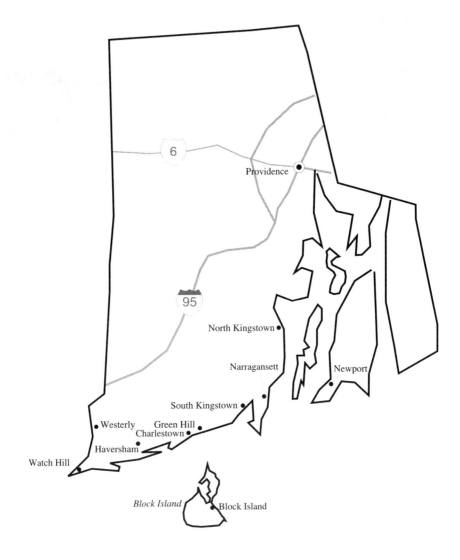

6

95

Providence •

North Kingstown •

Narragansett

Newport

•

South Kingstown •

• Westerly   Green Hill •
Charlestown •

Haversham

Watch Hill   •

Block Island

Block Island
•

Rhode Island

Rhode Island

The Barrington Inn

BLOCK ISLAND

The Barrington Inn

Corner of Beach and Ocean Avenues, P.O. Box 397, 02807
(401) 466-5510; FAX (401) 466-5880
e-mail: barrington@ids.net

Known for its warmth and hospitality, the Barrington Inn is an 1886 farmhouse on a knoll overlooking the New Harbor area of Block Island. There are six individually decorated guest rooms with private baths, and two housekeeping apartments. A light breakfast is served each morning by the innkeepers. Amenities include two guest sitting rooms, guest refrigerator, ceiling fans, comfortable beds, front porch, back deck, and afternoon beverages. No smoking. Continental plus breakfast served. Children over 12 welcome.

Hosts: Joan and Howard Ballard
Rooms: 6 (PB) $70-168
Continental Breakfast
Credit Cards: A, B, D
Notes: 2, 7, 9, 10, 11

Old Town Inn

P.O. Box 351, 02807
(401) 466-5958

The Old Town Inn is at the junction of Old Town Road and Center Road, about one mile from the ferry landing. Ten guest rooms, four in the old section featuring antique furniture and six in the new east wing featuring queen-size beds, full baths, refrigerators. Continental breakfasts are served in the 19th-century dining rooms. On about four acres of landscaped area.

Hosts: Ralph, Monica, and David Gunter
Rooms: 10 (8 PB; 2 SB) $85-125
Continental Breakfast
Credit Cards: A, B
Notes: 2, 7

The 1661 Inn & Hotel Manisses

Spring Street, 02807
(401) 466-2421; FAX (401) 466-3162
e-mail: biresorts@aol.com

Enjoy the New England decor of the 1661 Inn and the Victorian charm of the Hotel Manisses. Each room is individually decorated and many rooms feature whirlpool tubs, decks, ocean views, or fireplaces. Marvel at the spectacular views of the Atlantic Ocean from the covered porch while enjoying a complimentary full buffet breakfast. Enjoy fine dining in the casual elegance of the Manisses Dining Room as featured in *Gourmet* magazine. There are also a unique farm and garden with many exotic animals including llamas, emus, zebu, and more.

The 1661 Inn

NOTES: Credit cards accepted: A MasterCard; B Visa; C American Express; D Discover; E Diner's Club; F Other; 2 Personal checks accepted; 3 Lunch available; 4 Dinner available; 5 Open all year; 6 Pets welcome; 7 No smoking; 8 Children welcome; 9 Social drinking allowed; 10 Tennis nearby; 11 Swimming nearby; 12 Golf nearby; 13 Skiing nearby; 14 May be booked through a travel agent; 15 Handicapped accessible.

All rates include breakfast, the wine and nibble hour, and a tour of the island. Rooms open year-round. Children welcome.

Hosts: Joan and Justin Abrams; Rita and Steve
    Draper
Rooms: 55 (51 PB: 4 SB) $50-335
Full Breakfast
Credit Cards: A, B
Notes: 2, 3, 4, 5, 7, 8, 9, 10, 11, 14

The White House

The White House

02807-0447
(401) 466-2653

Large island manor house. Part 18th century. Two bedrooms sharing two baths and opening onto balconies overlooking the ocean. French Provincial antique furnishings. Notable collection of presidential autographs and documents. Full breakfast. All kinds of in-house services and amenities. Open year-round.

Host: Mrs. Joseph V. Connolly
Rooms: 2 (SB) $55-120
Full Breakfast
Credit Cards: A, B
Notes: 2, 5, 9, 10, 11

CHARLESTOWN

Bed & Breakfast Referrals of South Coast Rhode Island— (800) 853-7479

P.O. Box 562, 02813-0562

Bed and Breakfast Referrals of South Coast Rhode Island offers free information year-round on availabilities at 24 bed and breakfasts. They are an excellent resource for finding those last-minute "must getaways." Bed and breakfasts are in quiet rural settings, historic villages, and waterfront communities. All are an easy drive to beautiful sandy beaches, Newport, Providence, University of Rhode Island and Brown University, Mystic Seaport, Watch Hill, Foxwoods and Mohegan Sun casinos, and the new Mashantucket Pequot Museum. Excellent restaurants, entertainments, all sports, bird watching and more.

One Willow by the Sea

1 Willow Road, 02813-4162
(401) 364-0802; e-mail: josyrealty@ids.net

A warm, inviting "kick your shoes off and relax" stay on the beautiful Atlantic South Coast. Enjoy peaceful nights and delicious breakfasts on sun deck in summer. There's lots to do: miles of sandy beaches, sea and land sports, fine dining, entertainments and festivals. Visit historic New England villages and Narragansett Indian ceremonies. Easy drives to events in the capital city, Providence, Newport, Mystic, Foxwoods and Mohegan Sun casinos, and the new Mashantucket Pequot "state of the art" museum. French spoken.

Host: Denise Dillon Fuge
Rooms: 2 (SB) $70
Suite: 1 (PB-2 rooms) $80
Full Breakfast
Credit Cards: None
Notes: 2, 5, 7, 9, 10, 11, 12,

GREEN HILL

Green Shadows Bed & Breakfast

803 Green Hill Beach Road, Wakefield, 02879-6228
(401) 783-9752

This new home is in the beautiful Green Hill area of South Coast Rhode Island. Set on a wooded acre; the ocean and the beach are a 10-minute walk away. Light-filled bedrooms with king-size beds and private baths, quiet lounge with cable TV, VCR, and screened porch for breakfast and relaxing with views of Green Hill Pond. First-floor accommodations, full breakfast. Within easy drive of Mystic Seaport, Foxwoods Casino, wildlife preserves, flea markets, antique shops, summer theater, and Newport.

Hosts: Don and Mercedes Kratz
Rooms: 2 (PB) $95-105
Full Breakfast
Credit Cards: None
Notes: 2, 5, 7, 9, 11, 12, 15

HAVERSHAM

Covered Bridge

69 Maple Avenue, Norfolk, CT 06058
(860) 542-5944; FAX (860) 542-5690
e-mail: tremblay@esslink.com
www.obs-us.com/chesler/coveredbridge

1HR1. Early 1900s beach home the artist/architect owner has redone to create a spectacular home in a secluded setting overlooking a saltwater pond with a view of the ocean. There are two guest rooms in the main house, one with a balcony, which are decorated with antiques and paintings done by the owner. There in one cottage on the grounds. A Continental plus breakfast is served in the dining room or on the terrace overlooking the water. $95-150.

NARRAGANSETT

The Admiral Washburn Maynard House at Namcook

93 Old Boston Neck Road, 028228
(800) 877-6646; FAX (401) 788-9385
e-mail: namcook@aol.com

This luxurious New England estate with its in-ground swimming pool and stone walls is on three acres of beautifully landscaped property overlooking Beaver Tail Lighthouse and the Atlantic Ocean. Constructed in 1905 by the Admiral and his wife Bessie as their retirement home, this tastefully appointed shingle-style home offers two spacious bedrooms, each with private bath and fireplace. For guests with a need for additional space, a charming room is available. The house is replete with oriental rugs, antiques, heirlooms, art, and period books. Sea breezes are flirting in every nook and cranny. An elegant breakfast, afternoon and evening refreshments are included.

Hosts: Brigadier General (Ret.) Jack and Marguerite Apperson
Rooms: 2 (PB) $175
Credit Cards: None
Full Breakfast
Notes: 2, 5, 7, 11, 12, 13

The Canterbury

The Canterbury

4 Sumac Trail, 02882
(401) 783-0046

The Canterbury is a Cape Ann Colonial on a half-acre of private fenced-in lawn and gardens. There are two large bedroom suites on the second floor with a shared full bath. Rooms feature a choice of king-size or twin beds, each with its own sitting area, a color cable TV, and VCR.

Host: Eunice Keenan
Rooms: 2 (SB) $65-80
Credit Cards: None
Full Breakfast
Notes: 2, 5, 8, 9, 10, 11

Four Gables

12 South Pier Road, 02882
(401) 789-6948

Built by an architect in 1898, this charming Arts and Craft-style home has many interesting features. It is furnished with antiques and unique handcrafted items. Fishing equipment and advice available. Breakfast is served in the dining room overlooking the ocean, or guests may choose to enjoy the veranda with its spectacular views. Within walking distance of the beach, restaurants, and shops, and within a short drive to many attractions.

Hosts: Terry and Barbara Higgins
Rooms: 2 (SB) $60-90
Full Breakfast
Credit Cards: A, B, C
Notes: 2, 5, 7, 9, 10, 11, 12, 14

1900 House

59 Kingston Road, 02882
(401) 789-7971

Restored Victorian, circa 1900, with antique furniture, quiet street, lavender front door, and pretty gardens. Each room is unique, but all include country antiques, wooden bed frames, canopied beds, thick oriental rugs, and small special touches, such as the original owners' marriage certificate. Beach is a five-minute walk. Guests have use of a porch, which has cool sea breezes. Full gourmet breakfast served.

Hosts: Bill and Sandra Panzeri
Rooms: 3 (1 PB; 2 SB) $55-95
Full Breakfast
Credit Cards: None
Notes: 2, 5, 7, 10, 9, 11, 12, 14

Pleasant Cottage

104 Robinson Street, 02882
(401) 783-6895

This charming cottage is on a half-acre of woods and gardens. A quiet, serene atmosphere awaits guests just blocks from lovely Narragansett Beach. Enclosed outdoor shower. Relax on large screened porch. Bedrooms with shared bath, or private bath and private entrance. Full breakfast served, including a treat for coffee lovers. Reservations and advance deposit required.

Hosts: Fred and Terry Sepp
Rooms: 2 (1 PB; 1 SB) $65-80
Full Breakfast
Credit Cards: None
Notes: 2, 5, 7, 9, 10, 11, 12

The Richards

144 Gibson Avenue, 02882
(401) 789-7746

These gracious and elegant accommodations are in an 1884 historic manse. Relax by the crackling fire in the library or in the guest rooms which have fireplaces. Enjoy a leisurely and delicious full breakfast, complete with homemade muffins, strudels, and blintzes. The hostess's special touches will spoil anyone—down comforters, canopied beds, and flowers fresh from the gardens. There are minimum-stay requirements for weekends and holidays. Special suite rates are available for couples who are traveling together.

Hosts: Steven and Nancy Richards
Rooms: 2 (1 PB; 1 SB) $90-100
Suite: 2 (PB) $125-180
Full Breakfast
Credit Cards: None
Notes: 2, 5, 7, 9, 10, 11, 12

Seafield Cottage

110 Boon Street, 02882
(401) 783-2432

A charming, 17-room Victorian home filled with lace, charm, and ambiance. Guest bedrooms have period furnishings including swooner couches, canopied beds, down pillows and comforters. Guests also have semi-private bathrooms. Full breakfast is served on antique china in the breakfast room. Guests enjoy freshly ground imported coffee, juices, fruit compote along with either breakfast calzones, French toast, Belgian waffles, or specialty pancakes. One block from the beach, the cottage is a short distance from Newport, the International Tennis Hall of Fame, and Block Island. Also available is a one-bedroom apartment on Pru-

---

NOTES: Credit cards accepted: A MasterCard; B Visa; C American Express; D Discover; E Diner's Club; F Other; 2 Personal checks accepted; 3 Lunch available; 4 Dinner available; 5 Open all year; 6 Pets welcome;

dence Island, a 20-minute ferry ride from historic Bristol. Smoking permitted on porch only.

Hosts: Carl, Anne and Pam Cottle
Rooms: 2(1 PB; 1 SB) $75
Full Breakfast
Credit Cards: None
Notes: 2, 11, 12

NEWPORT

Admiral Benbow Inn

93 Pelham Street, 02840
(800) 343-2863
e-mail: 5star@admiralinns.com
www.admiralinns.com

Walking distance to all Newport has to offer. This 15-room Victorian has something for everyone. A welcoming inn with many returning guests. The Admiral Benbow Inn was built in 1855 as an inn, to welcome seafarers and travelers, by Sea Captain Augustus Littlefield. The tradition continues to offer Old-World hospitality and grace. Individually decorated rooms with whirlpool tubs. Breakfast served each morning in the summer kitchen.

Host: Pam Royality
Rooms: 15(PB) $65-185
Continental Breakfast
Credit Cards: A, B, C, D
Notes: 7, 9, 10, 11, 12, 14

Bannister's Wharf Guest Rooms

Bannister's Wharf, 02840
(401) 846-4500; FAX (401) 849-8750
e-mail: janb@bannisterswharf.com
www.bannisterswharf.com

Rooms and suites with harborside decks. At the center of the best shopping, dining, and waterfront activities in Newport. Guests may watch the lobster and deep sea trawlers unload their catch as well as the arrival and departure of visiting yachtmen. Just off America's Cup Avenue guests will view all of Newport's magnificent harbor and enjoy its cool evening breezes. Rooms have private baths, air conditioning, TVs, telephones, refrigerators. Free parking.

Host: Jan Buchner
Rooms: 8 (PB) $75-245
Credit Cards: A, B, C, D
Notes: 2, 3, 4, 5, 8, 9, 10, 11, 12

Beech Tree Inn

34 Rhode Island Avenue, 02840
(401) 847-9794; (800) 748-6565
FAX (401) 847-6824; www.beechtreeinn.com

The Beech Tree Inn is a bed and breakfast offering the largest breakfast with the greatest variety of entrées in Newport. The inn was completely renovated in 1994, and all guest rooms are large with new bathrooms. Some rooms have fireplaces and Jacuzzis. Some have outside decks. A casual and relaxed atmosphere with charming Colonial decor. No smoking in guest rooms. AAA three-diamond-rated.

Hosts: Ed and Kathy Wudyka
Rooms: 8 (PB)
Full Breakfast
Credit Cards: A, B, C, D
Notes: 5, 8, 9, 10, 11, 12, 14

Bellevue House Bed & Breakfast

14 Catherine Street, 02840
(401) 847-1828; (800) 820-1828
FAX: (401) 847-4946
e-mail: JM@BellevueHouse.com
www.bellevuehouse.com

Built in 1774, Bellevue House was converted into the first summer hotel in Newport in 1828. On top of historic hill, off the famous Bellevue Avenue and three blocks from the harbor, the house retains a combination of ideal location, colonial history, economical rates, and a friendly host and hostess. All guest rooms have air conditioning and are nonsmoking. Children over 12 welcome.

Hosts: Joan and Vic Farmer
Rooms: 8 (6 PB; 2 SB) $85-150
Continental Breakfast
Credit Cards: None
Notes: 2, 7, 9, 10, 11, 12, 14

7 No smoking; 8 Children welcome; 9 Social drinking allowed; 10 Tennis nearby; 11 Swimming nearby; 12 Golf nearby; 13 Skiing nearby; 14 May be booked through a travel agent; 15 Handicapped accessible.

Black Duck Inn

29 Pelham Street, 02840
(401) 841-5548; (800) 206-5212
FAX (401) 846-4873
e-mail: mary@blackduckinn.com
www.blackduckinn.com

A charming inn in the waterfront area footsteps away from harborfront shops, restaurants, and sailing. A short stroll to the Cliff Walk and Newport mansions. For that romantic getaway, stay in one of the Jacuzzi and fireplace rooms where guests can relax in comfort. The inn has central air and each room has TV, telephone, and off-street parking. No smoking.

Host: Mary A. Rolando
Rooms: 8 (6 PB; 2 SB) $95-190
Continental Breakfast
Credit Cards: A, B, C
Notes: 5, 7, 8, 10, 11, 14

Brinley Victorian Inn

23 Brinley Street, 02840
(401) 849-7645; (800) 999-8523
FAX (401) 845-9634

Romantic year-round, the inn becomes a Victorian Christmas dream come true. Comfortable antiques and fresh flowers fill every room. Friendly, unpretentious service and attention to detail will make this inn a traveler's haven in Newport. Park and walk everywhere. AAA-approved. Minimum stay on weekends is two nights and on holidays is three nights. A suite with Jacuzzi and fireplace is available. Children over 12 welcome.

Hosts: John and Jennifer Sweetman
Rooms: 15 (PB) $79-199
Continental Breakfast
Credit Cards: A, B, C
Notes: 2, 5, 7, 9, 10, 11, 12, 14

Castle Hill Inn & Resort

Ocean Drive, 02840
(401) 849-3800; (888) 466-1355
FAX (401) 84 9-3838
www.castlehillinn.com

Castle Hill Inn

On a 40-acre peninsula at the top of Newport's world-renowned Ocean Drive, Castle Hill offers guests the seclusion, beauty, and romance of a private oceanfront retreat. An elegant Victorian mansion with luxuriously appointed water-view rooms provides an escape from daily routines and cares. The exclusive Beach Houses offer rooms on a private sandy beach. Enjoy regional cooking with an international flair. Lunch, dinner, and Sunday Jazz Brunch, including outdoor dining. Open year-round. Gourmet-served breakfast is included in the rates.

Host: Paul O'Reilly
Rooms: 35 (PB) $145-450
Credit Cards: A, B, C, D
Notes: 3, 4, 5, 7, 8, 9, 10, 11, 12, 15

Cliff View Guest House

4 Cliff Terrace, 02840
(401) 846-0885

A two-story 1870 Victorian on a quiet dead-end street leading to the beautiful Cliff Walk, a three-mile path bordering the ocean. Five-minute walk to beach; 15-minute walk to downtown harbor area. Ten-room house with four guest bedrooms; two share a bath and have view of ocean; two have private baths, but no ocean view. Three rooms have air conditioning. The hostess's French-speaking grandson is on the premises during school summer vacation.

Host: Pauline Shea
Rooms: 4 (2 PB; 2 SB) $75-85
Continental Breakfast
Credit Cards: A, B
Notes: 2, 7, 11, 12

NOTES: Credit cards accepted: A MasterCard; B Visa; C American Express; D Discover; E Diner's Club; F Other; 2 Personal checks accepted; 3 Lunch available; 4 Dinner available; 5 Open all year; 6 Pets welcome;

1855 Marshall Slocum Guest House

1855 Marshall Slocum Guest House

29 Kay Street, 02840
(800) 372-5120; FAX (401) 846-3787
e-mail: marshallslocuminn@edgenet.net
www.marshallslocuminn.com

This home has been meticulously restored to reflect the charm and beauty of its Victorian heritage. Breakfast is often served on the deck overlooking the expansive back yard. Refreshments served daily at 5:00 P.M. Guests staying three nights midweek enjoy a complimentary New England clambake. A 5-minute walk to downtown and a 10-minute walk to the beaches; plenty of off-street parking for guests.

Hosts: Joan and Julie Wilson
Rooms: 5 (PB) $90-155
Full Breakfast
Credit Cards: A, B, C
Notes: 2, 3, 4, 5, 7, 9, 10, 11, 12, 14

Gardenview

8 Binney Street, 02840
(401) 849-5799

Gardenview is a cozy, quaint, countrified private home bed and breakfast. It is a short distance from the mansions, beaches, and famous Ocean Drive. The yard is filled with flowers, a fish pond with a waterfall, and many birds to view and enjoy. Hosts offer two quiet rooms for their guests: a cozy room that faces the gar-

dens and a suite with a sitting area. Both rooms have private whirlpool baths, air conditioning, fireplaces, cable TVs, antiques, and handmade quilts. A separate common room is available and the dining room has a fireplace.

Hosts: Mary and Andrew Fitzgerald
Rooms: 2 (PB) $85-180
Full Breakfast
Credit Cards: None
Notes: 2, 5, 7, 9, 10, 11, 12

Halidon Hill Guest House

Halidon Avenue, 02840
(401) 847-8318

Halidon Hill is up the street from the Ida Lewis and the New York Yacht Clubs. Relax around the large in-ground pool and spacious deck. It is close to shopping, restaurants, mansions, and beaches. All rooms are beautifully decorated and furnished with air conditioning, small refrigerators, and TVs. Full breakfast served.

Hosts: Helen and Paul Burke
Rooms: 2 $55
Apartments: 2 $250
Full Breakfast
Credit Cards: C, D, E
Notes: 2, 5, 8, 9, 11, 12

Hydrangea House Inn: A Bed & Breakfast

16 Bellevue Avenue, 02840
(401)846-4435; (800) 945-4667
FAX: (401) 846-6602
e-mail: hydrangeahouse@home.com
www.hydrangeahouse.com

The Hydrangea House Inn is at the center of the seaside resort of Newport, between Boston and New York City. Built during the "gilded" period of Newport, the inn, carefully transformed with seven rooms, is sumptuously decorated with fine fabrics and antiques. Some rooms have Jacuzzis and fireplaces. Plush carpeting, thick cozy towels, crystal water glasses, long-stemmed goblets for your wine setups, and afternoon tea are some amenities that will

---

7 No smoking; 8 Children welcome; 9 Social drinking allowed; 10 Tennis nearby; 11 Swimming nearby; 12 Golf nearby; 13 Skiing nearby; 14 May be booked through a travel agent; 15 Handicapped accessible.

make your stay in Newport not just a stopover, but more…a real luxury!

Hosts: Grant Edmonson and Dennis Blair
Rooms: 7 (PB)$125-280
Full Breakfast
Credit Cards: A, B, C
Notes: 2, 5, 7, 9, 10, 11, 12, 14

The Inn at Shadow Lawn

120 Miantonomi Avenue, Middletown/Newport
   02842 (401) 847-0902; (800) 352-3750
FAX (401) 848-6529

The Inn at Shadow Lawn, one of Newport County's finest bed and breakfast inns, is on two acres of beautifully landscaped lawns and gardens. This 1850s Victorian mansion, with its crystal chandeliers and stained-glass windows, has eight large bedrooms, each with private bath, cable TV with VCR, refrigerator, telephone, and air conditioning. Four rooms also have attached kitchens, and six rooms have working fireplaces. Complimentary shuttle to Newport Harbor district. Enjoy a complimentary bottle of wine and join the hosts daily for a glass of sherry.

Hosts: Randy and Selma Fabricant
Rooms: 8 (PB) $85-185
Full Breakfast
Credit Cards: A, B, C, D, E, F
Notes: 5, 7, 8, 9, 10, 11, 12, 14

Jenkins Guest House

206 South Rhode Island Avenue, 02840
(401) 847-6801

The hosts built this Cape Cod when they were married. Since their eight children, who were raised in this house, are now grown and on their own, the hosts have been using the extra rooms for guests since 1978. Having lived in Newport all their lives, they have interesting stories to tell from a local viewpoint and can provide helpful information about restaurants and places to visit. On a quiet little street just a 3-minute walk from the beach or a 10-minute walk to the mansions or the harbor, with plenty

Jenkins Guest House

of parking on the grounds. Enjoy the homemade muffins for breakfast in a country-in-the-city atmosphere. Air conditioned. Smoking permitted on the deck only.

Hosts: David and Sally Jenkins
Rooms: 3 (1 PB; 2SB) $75
Continental Breakfast
Credit Cards: None
Notes: 2, 7, 8, 9, 10, 11, 12, 14

The Melville House

39 Clark Street, 02840
(401) 847-0640
e-mail: innkeeper@ids.net
www.melvillehouse.com

Step back into the past and stay at a Colonial inn, built circa 1750, "where the past is present." The Melville House is in the National Register of Historic Places and is in the heart of Newport's beautiful historic district. Walk around the corner to the Brick Market and the wharves. Enjoy a leisurely homemade breakfast in the morning, afternoon tea, and join the hosts for complimentary tea and sherry before dinner. Off-street parking.

The Melville House

NOTES: Credit cards accepted: A MasterCard; B Visa; C American Express; D Discover; E Diner's Club; F Other; 2 Personal checks accepted; 3 Lunch available; 4 Dinner available; 5 Open all year; 6 Pets welcome;

Hosts: Vince DeRico and Christine Leene
Rooms: 7 (5 PB; 2 SB) $85-165
Suite: $165
Full Breakfast
Credit Cards: A, B, C, D
Notes: 2, 3, 5, 7, 9, 10, 11, 12, 14

Mount Vernon Inn

26 Mount Vernon Street, 02840
(401) 846-6314; (888) MT VERNON
FAX (401) 846-0530;
e-mail: marcia@mountvernoninn.com
www.mountvernoninn.com

A charming 1850 Victorian bed and breakfast
with lovely spacious rooms furnished with
king-, queen-size, or twin beds, antiques and
wicker. A six-minute walk to the harbor, town,
restaurants, and more. Ideal for families, small
weddings, and groups. On a lovely, quiet
street. Off-street parking, air conditioning, and
full breakfast.

Hosts: Marcia and Kevin Smith
Rooms: 5 (3 PB; 2 SB) $90-155
Full Breakfast
Credit Cards: A, B, C, D
Notes: 2, 5, 7, 8, 9, 10, 11, 12, 14

The Old Beach Inn

19 Old Beach Road, 02840
(401) 849-3479; (888) 303-5033
FAX (401) 847-1236
e-mail: info@oldbeachinn.com
www.oldbeachinn.com

Elegant Victorian bed and breakfast in one of
Newport's most prestigious areas. Built in
1879, this inn was once the home of an affluent
physician and commodore and is now listed in
the Rhode Island historic register. The fabled
mansions, Cliff Walk, beaches, and historic
harborfront are only a short walk away. Each of
the romantic guest rooms has a private bath,
and several have fireplaces. Continental plus
breakfast served Monday through Saturday. A
full entrée is served as well on Sundays. Seasonal rates. Children over 12 welcome.

Hosts: Luke and Cynthia Murray
Rooms: 7 (PB) $95-185
Continental Breakfast
Credit Cards: A, B, C, D
Notes: 2, 5, 7, 9, 10, 11, 12

Pilgrim House Inn

Pilgrim House Inn

123 Spring Street, 02840
(401) 846-0040(800) 525-8373
FAX (401) 848-0357
www.pilgrimhouseinn.com

The Pilgrim House Inn is on Newport's historic
hill and offers 11 spacious rooms with private
baths. Each room is furnished in Victorian
decor and is immaculate. Breakfast is served
each morning and parking is conveniently
behind the inn. In warmer weather guests enjoy
a spectacular harbor view from the deck while
eating breakfast and watching sailboats glide
through Newport Harbor. During cooler
months sherry and shortbread are served fireside. The inn is one block from Thames
Street—a short stroll to Newport's restaurants
and unique shops. Come and enjoy fresh flowers and the charm of a bygone era. Children
over 12 welcome.

Host: Donna Messerlian
Rooms: 11 (9 PB; 2 SB) $50-155
Continental Breakfast
Credit Cards: A, B
Notes: 2, 7, 9, 10, 11, 12, 14

7 No smoking; 8 Children welcome; 9 Social drinking allowed; 10 Tennis nearby; 11 Swimming nearby;
12 Golf nearby; 13 Skiing nearby; 14 May be booked through a travel agent; 15 Handicapped accessible.

The Queen Anne Inn

16 Clarke Street, 02840
(401) 846-5676; (888) 407-1616
FAX (401) 841-8509
e-mail: queenanne@cwix.com
www.queenanneinnnewport.com

The Queen Anne Inn, a charming, beautifully preserved 19th-century inn on quiet, historic Clarke Street, is the quintessence of Newport. Rich in history and tradition, Newport combines small-town quaintness, superb restaurants and beautiful beaches, making it a perfect weekend and vacation destination. An island of old-fashioned serenity amidst the excitement of downtown. The Queen Anne will help make guests' visit everything they want it to be. Also available is a two-room suite with sitting room. Rooms are air conditioned, and parking is plentiful. Children eight and older are welcome.

Hosts: Flavia and Paul Gardiner
Rooms: 8 (6 PB; 2 SB) $85-160
Continental Breakfast
Credit Cards: A, B, C
Notes: 2, 5, 7, 9, 10, 11, 12, 14

Rhode Island House

77 Rhode Island Avenue, 02840
(401) 848-7787; FAX (401) 849-3104

Spacious, elegant, grand 1881 Victorian residence featuring unsurpassed sun-filled rooms, personalized decor, and relaxed ambiance. Each bedroom has a private bath, fine linens, queen-size bed, and air conditioning. Fireplaces, Jacuzzis, and private deck available. Easy walk to restaurants, shopping, beach, and tourism sites. A full gourmet breakfast is prepared by a renowned chef to the Newport summer colony.

Host: Michael Dupre
Rooms: 5 (PB) $145-250
Full Breakfast
Credit Cards: A, B, C
Notes: 2, 7, 9, 10, 11, 12

Spring Street Inn

Spring Street Inn

Corner of Howard Street, 353 Spring Street, 02840
(401) 847-4767; e-mail: sprngstinn@aol.com
www.springstreetinn.com

Circa 1858 Empire Victorian, centrally in downtown Newport on a residential street. Open February through December. Cozy, quaint, and romantic. The inn's amenities include a gourmet full breakfast with choice of hot entrées, afternoon refreshments in the guest living room/library, on-site parking, air conditioning, fresh flowers throughout inn, and concierge services. No smoking. AAA- and ABBA-approved. Five guest rooms with private baths, one harbor-view suite, one two-bedroom suite are offered.

Hosts: Patricia Golder and Jack Lang
Rooms: 5 (PB) $69-269
Suites: 2
Full Breakfast
Credit Cards: A, B
Notes: 2, 7, 9, 10, 11, 12, 14

NOTES: Credit cards accepted: A MasterCard; B Visa; C American Express; D Discover; E Diner's Club; F Other; 2 Personal checks accepted; 3 Lunch available; 4 Dinner available; 5 Open all year; 6 Pets welcome;

Stella Maris Inn

91 Washington Street, 02840
(401) 849-2862

Elegant, romantic 1861 Victorian mansion completely restored in 1990. Some rooms with water views and fireplaces, all tastefully furnished with antiques. Large wraparound front porch with water view. Spacious gardens. Hearty Continental breakfast featuring homemade muffins and breads. Walking distance to town. Parking on premises. Elevator.

Hosts: Dorothy and Ed Madden
Rooms: 8 (PB) $85-195
Continental Breakfast
Credit Cards: None
Notes: 2, 5, 7, 9, 10, 11, 12, 14

The Victorian Ladies Inn

63 Memorial Boulevard, 02840
(401) 849-9960

The inn is circa 1850s. Established and totally refurbished in 1985. The inn is appointed with period pieces. The rooms have down quilts, lots of wonderful fabrics; all rooms are light, airy, and fresh. There are lovely courtyards, with a profusion of flowers and plants. The inn is just three blocks from the public beaches, shops, and restaurants. The inn has been featured in many popular publications, such as *Bride's*, *Glamour*, *Country Inns*, etc.

Hosts: Don and Hélène O'Neill
Rooms: 11 (PB) $95-185
Full Breakfast
Credit Cards: A, B
Notes: 2, 7, 9, 10, 11, 12

Villa Liberté

22 Liberty Street, 02840-3221
(401) 846-7444; (800) 392-3717
www.villaliberte.com

Neatly tucked away off historic Bellevue Avenue, the Villa Liberté offers the charm and romance of the City by the Sea. From warm cherrywood furnishings to lush imported bedding, the villa offers uniquely appointed queen-size rooms, elegant master suites, and comfortable apartment suites; each with private bath, air conditioning, telephone, TV, and parking. Dramatic black and white tile baths feature pedestal sinks and arched alcoves. Enjoy buffet Continental breakfast in the tea room or on the terrace sun deck. Walk to the mansions, Newport's beautiful beaches, Brick Marketplace, and the wharf area.

Host: Leigh Anne Mosco
Rooms: 15 (PB) $99-235
Continental Breakfast
Credit Cards: A, B, C
Notes: 7, 8, 10, 11, 12

The Willows of Newport, Romantic Inn & Garden

8 Willow Street, Historic Point, 02840-1927
(401) 846-5486
www.newportri.com/users/willows

In the historic section of Newport, the Willows pampers guests with secret gardens, handcrafted canopied beds, fresh flowers, mints on pillows, champagne glasses and silver ice bucket, and the lights on dim. Breakfast in bed on bone china and silver service. Three blocks from downtown/ waterfront. Parking and air conditioning. A Continental plus breakfast served. Open year-round. Three-star rating from Mobil. Award of Excellence by American Bed & Breakfast Association. Awarded "Best

The Willows of Newport

7 No smoking; 8 Children welcome; 9 Social drinking allowed; 10 Tennis nearby; 11 Swimming nearby; 12 Golf nearby; 13 Skiing nearby; 14 May be booked through a travel agent; 15 Handicapped accessible.

Garden," "Best Place to Kiss," in *Country Inns*, 1998 and was the main feature in *Wedding Day*, 1998.

Host: Patricia Murphy
Rooms: 5 (PB) $128-325
Continental Breakfast
Credit Cards: None
Notes: 2, 5, 7, 9, 10, 11, 12, 14

NEWPORT/MIDDLETOWN

Polly's Place

349 Valley Road, Route 214, 02842
(401) 847-2160
www.bbonline.com/ri/pollysplace/

A quiet retreat one mile from Newport's harbor, historic homes, and sandy beaches. Polly is a long-time Newport resident willing to give helpful advice to travelers interested in the area. Rooms are large, clean, and very attractive. Breakfast is served in the dining room with a lovely view of wildlife and birds of the area. The hostess also offers a one-bedroom apartment that is available by the week and completely equipped. This bed and breakfast has been inspected and approved for cleanliness and quality. Children over 12 welcome.

Host: Polly Canning
Rooms: 4 (2 PB; 2 SB) $80-125
Apartment: 1
Full Breakfast
Credit Cards: None
Notes: 2, 5, 7, 9, 10, 11, 12, 14

NORTH KINGSTOWN

The Fifty Seven Bed & Breakfast

57 Thomas Street, 02852
(401) 294-7201

Enjoy a friendly stay at Fifty Seven—a comfortable contemporary Cape cottage, three minutes from Wickford's historic district, harbor, and shopping. Guest bedroom with private

bath has access to a large outdoor pool and landscaped garden. Air conditioning and TV/VCR in room. Near South County beaches, sailing, golf, and bird watching. Home-cooked breakfasts are a special feature.

Host: Audrey Ebrahim
Rooms: 1 (PB) $65-75
Full Breakfast
Credit Cards: None
Notes: 2, 5, 7, 11, 12, 13

PROVIDENCE

Old Court Bed & Breakfast

144 Benefit Street, 02903
(401) 751-2002

In the heart of Providence's historic Benefit Street area, guests will find the Old Court, where tradition is combined with contemporary standards of luxury. The Old Court was built in 1863 and reflects early Victorian styles. In rooms that overlook downtown Providence and Brown Universities, visitors feel as if they have entered a more gracious era. Children 12 and older welcome. Smoking is not permitted in the house.

Host: David Dolbashian
Rooms: 11 (PB) $95-250
Full Breakfast
Credit Cards: A, B, C, D
Notes: 2, 5, 7, 14

State House Inn

43 Jewett Street, 02908
(401) 351-6111

In the center of a quiet and quaint neighborhood, the State House Inn is a 100-year-old building newly restored and renovated into a country bed and breakfast. Minutes from downtown Providence and the many local colleges and universities. Brings country living to the big city.

State House Inn

Hosts: Frank and Monica Hopton
Rooms: 10 (PB) $89-139
Full Breakfast
Credit Cards: A, B, C, D
Notes: 5, 7, 8, 9, 10, 12, 13, 14

PROVIDENCE AREA

Historic Jacob Hill Farm Bed & Breakfast/Inn

120 Jacob Street, Seekonk, MA 02771
(508) 336-9165; (888) 336-9165
FAX (508) 336-0951

Casual elegance. Built in 1722, with a long history of hosting some of America's most affluent families, including the Vanderbilts. Recently updated rooms are spacious with queen- and king-size beds and private bathrooms or suites. Some with a Jacuzzi. Each room individually appointed with antiques and traditional wall coverings, some with fireplaces and whirlpool tubs. In-ground pool, tennis, stable, and riding lessons available, or just relax in

Historic Jacob Hill Farm

the gazebo. Ten minutes from Providence, Rhode Island. One hour from Boston, Cape Cod, Newport, or Mystic, CT.

Hosts: Bill and Eleonora Rezek
Rooms: 6 (PB) $110-225
Full Breakfast
Credit Cards: A, B, C, D, E
Notes: 5, 7, 9, 10, 11, 12, 13,

SOUTH KINGSTOWN

The Kings' Rose

1747 Mooresfield Road, 02879
(401) 783-5222; (888) 230-ROSE

This mini-estate (1933) offers two acres of rose-filled gardens, tennis, sunny public rooms, easy access to a half-dozen ocean beaches. Just east of historic Kingston village and the University of Rhode Island, the inn is 30 minutes from Newport's mansions and Mystic (Connecticut) Seaport and Aquarium. Fine dining, antiquing, wildlife preserves, music, and theater nearby. On Rhode Island Route 138, three and one-half miles west of U.S. Route 1, two miles east of West Kingston (Amtrak) Railroad station. Inquire about accommodations for pets.

Hosts: Barbara and Perry Viles
Rooms: 5 (PB and SB) $90-140
Full Breakfast
Credit Cards: None
Notes: 2, 5, 6, 7, 8, 9, 10, 11, 12, 13, 14

Larchwood Inn

521 Main Street, Wakefield, 02879
(401) 783-5454; (800) 275-5450
FAX (401) 783-1800

The Larchwood Inn is a family-run country inn that has kept pace with the 20th century without sacrificing its rural beauty. Most rooms have private baths, and all guests are encouraged to use the services of the main inn, which includes three dining rooms (all of which serve three meals daily) and a cocktail lounge (with lunch and happy hour daily and live music on the weekends). Near beaches, boating, hiking,

7 No smoking; 8 Children welcome; 9 Social drinking allowed; 10 Tennis nearby; 11 Swimming nearby; 12 Golf nearby; 13 Skiing nearby; 14 May be booked through a travel agent; 15 Handicapped accessible.

Larchwood Inn

horseback and bike riding, and skiing. Breakfast not included in rates.

Hosts: Francis and Diann Browning
Rooms: 18 (12 PB; 6 SB) $50-130
Credit Cards: A, B, C, D, E
Notes: 2, 3, 4, 5, 6, 8, 9, 10, 11, 12, 13, 14

WATCH HILL

Watch Hill Inn & Restaurant

38 Bay Street, 02891
(800) 356-9314; FAX (401) 348-6301
www.watchhillinn.com

A romantic seaside inn overlooking the bay in historic Watch Hill village. Pleasant stroll to breathtaking beaches, quaint shops, famous carousel. Grille restaurant serves fresh seafood, steaks, pastas, grilled pizzas. Relax with a favorite beverage on the outside deck and enjoy the most spectacular sunsets in the area. Well-suited for a romantic getaway, the Watch Hill Inn also specializes in wedding receptions, rehearsal dinners, private parties, and corporate meeting and seminars for up to 200 guests. Lunch, dinner, and cocktails available seasonally.

Hosts: Mark Szaro, general manager
Rooms: 16 (PB) $95-195
Continental Breakfast
Credit Cards: A, B
Notes: 3, 4, 5, 8, 9, 10, 11, 12, 14

WESTERLY

Grandview Bed & Breakfast

212 Shore Road, 02891
(800) 447-6384

Turn-of-the-century hilltop home with splendid ocean view. Large, cheery sunporch for breakfast. Sit on wraparound stone porch. Walk to tennis or golf. Short drive to beaches, Watch Hill, Mystic Seaport/Aquarium, Newport mansions and Foxwoods Casino.

Host: Patricia Grande
Rooms: 9 (5 PB; 4 SB) $85-100
Continental Breakfast
Credit Cards: A, B, C
Notes: 2, 5, 7, 8, 9, 10, 11, 12. 14

Nutmeg Bed & Breakfast Agency

P.O. Box 1117, West Hartford, 06127-1117
(860) 236-6698; (800) 727-7592
FAX (860) 232-7680
e-mail: Nutmegbnb@home. com
www. BnB-link.com

504. Savor the splendid views from the wraparound stone porch of this turn-of-the-century bed and breakfast. There are 11 guest rooms, four with private baths. The home has a large family room equipped with a player piano, cable TV, games, and a variety of reading material. Pick-up available from local train station or airport. If guests love the beach, this home is a perfect base for enjoying the five Rhode Island beaches nearby. Only minutes from Mystic, Connecticut. Continental breakfast. Limited smoking. Children welcome. Pets in residence.

507. Five minutes from the beach, this renovated 1920 summer home is by a saltwater pond that looks out to the ocean. Originally a working farm, it provides the perfect quiet getaway. One guest room has two double beds, many windows, and a private bath with shower. The second guest room has a canopied double bed, private deck with a view of the water, and a private bath with a tub. For the family get-

NOTES: Credit cards accepted: A MasterCard; B Visa; C American Express; D Discover; E Diner's Club; F Other; 2 Personal checks accepted; 3 Lunch available; 4 Dinner available; 5 Open all year; 6 Pets welcome;

away, there are also two summer cottages available, one with three bedrooms and the other with six. Continental breakfast. No smoking. Children welcome. Pets in residence.

The Villa

190 Shore Road, 02891
(401) 596-1054; FAX (401) 596-6268
e-mail: villa@riconnect.com

A lovely Mediterranean-style bed and breakfast set on one and one-half acres near many attractions, beaches, and fine restaurants. Enjoy six comfortable suites, all with private baths, some with double Jacuzzis and fireplaces. Complimentary Continental plus breakfast. In-ground pool and hot tub in season. Visit nearby Mystic, Newport, Watch Hill, Foxwoods Casino, or just relax and enjoy the surroundings of the villa.

Hosts: Angela Craig and Peter Gagnon
Rooms: 6 (PB) $95-245
Continental Breakfast
Credit Cards: A, B, C, D
Notes: 2, 5, 7, 11, 12, 14

Woody Hill Bed & Breakfast

149 South Woody Hill Road, 02891
(401) 322-0452

The hostess, a high school English teacher, invites guests to share this reproduction Colonial home with antiques and gardens. Snuggle under quilts, relax on the porch swing, visit nearby Newport and Mystic, and swim in the pool or at beautiful ocean beaches. Westerly has it all!

Host: Dr. Ellen L. Madison
Rooms: 5 (4 PB or SB) $65-125
Full Breakfast
Credit Cards: None
Notes: 2, 5, 7, 8, 9, 10, 11, 12

Woody Hill

Alburg

North Hero

North Hero Island

2

89

Enosberg Falls

Montgomery Center

Derby Line

Morgan

91

Fairfax

Jeffersonville

Jericho

Essex

Burlington

Wolcott

Greensboro

Lyndonville

Stowe

Cabot

St. Johnsbury

Bolton Valley

Waterbury Center

Lower Waterford

Waterbury

2

Montpelier

Waitsfield

Northfield

Warren

Brookfield

Newbury

7

East Middlebury

Chelsea

Middlebury

89

Ripton

Hancock

Goshen

Rochester

Fairlee

Orwell

Brandon

Bethel

Royalton

Pittsfield

Killington

Fair Haven

4

Rutland

Woodstock

Shrewsbury

Hartland

Poultney

Windsor

Middletown Springs

Wallingford

91

Danby

Ludlow

Proctorsville

Weston

Springfield

Dorset

Andover

Manchester Village

7

Peru

Chester

Manchester Center

Londonderry

Manchester

South Londonderry

Bellows Falls

Sandgate

Arlington

Jamaica

Newfane

Putney

Mount Snow Valley

South Newfane

West Dover

East Dover

Bennington

Brattleboro

Wilmington

Jacksonville

Vermont

Vermont

Thomas Mott

ALBURG

Thomas Mott Bed & Breakfast

63 Blue Rock Road, 05440-9620
(802) 796-3736 (phone/FAX); (800) 348-0843
e-mail: tmott@together.net
www.go-native.com/Inns/0162.html
www.thomas-mott-bb.com

Hosted by Patrick J. Schallert, a prominent importer and distributor of fine wines, retired, this pre-Civil War shoreline property offers a full view of the Green Mountains or the Adirondacks from all rooms in this beautifully restored bed and breakfast. One hour from Burlington or Montréal Island. Enjoy four-season lake activities; cross-country skiing, lawn games, complimentary canoes, private 75-foot dock, swimming, fishing, or sunning; 12 Ben & Jerry's ice creams (complimentary); AAA three diamonds; ABBA three crowns. Children over six are welcome.

Host: Patrick J. Schallert Sr.
Rooms: 5 (PB) $75-95
Full Breakfast
Credit Cards: A, B, C, D, E, F
Notes: 2, 5, 7, 9, 10, 11, 12, 13, 14

ANDOVER

Inn at HighView

753 East Hill Road, 05143
(802) 875-2724; FAX (802) 875-4021
e-mail: hiview@aol.com; www.innathighview.com

Vermont the way guests always dreamed it would be, but the way they've never found it. Secluded and relaxed elegance; breathtaking views of countryside from overlook gazebo and screened porch. Classically restored 18th-century farmhouse comfortably furnished. Warm conversation by a blazing fire, hearty breakfasts, and gourmet dinners. All guest rooms have private baths. Cross-country skiing-hiking trails on 72 acres. Rock garden and swimming pool. Ten minutes from Okemo Mountain, Weston, and Chester. Conference facilities and planning services available.

Hosts: Greg Bohan and Sal Massaro
Rooms: 8 (PB) $95-155
Full Breakfast
Credit Cards: A, B
Notes: 2, 4, 5, 6, 7, 8, 9, 10, 11, 12, 13, 14

ARLINGTON

The Arlington Inn

Historic Route 7A, P.O. Box 369, 05250
(800) 443-9442
e-mail: arlingtoninn@compuserve.com
www.arlingtoninn.com

An elegant, romantic, 1848 Greek Revival mansion. Eighteen luxurious rooms, many with Jacuzzis and fireplaces, all with private

NOTES: Credit cards accepted: A MasterCard; B Visa; C American Express; D Discover; E Diner's Club; F Other; 2 Personal checks accepted; 3 Lunch available; 4 Dinner available; 5 Open all year; 6 Pets welcome; 7 No smoking; 8 Children welcome; 9 Social drinking allowed; 10 Tennis nearby; 11 Swimming nearby; 12 Golf nearby; 13 Skiing nearby; 14 May be booked through a travel agent; 15 Handicapped accessible.

Arlington Inn

baths, antiques, TVs, and some with telephones. Gourmet candlelight dinning. "Editor's Pick" in *Yankee* magazine's Travel Guide to New England.

Hosts: Deborah and Mark Gagnon
Rooms: 18 (PB) $70-205
Full Breakfast
Credit Cards: A, B, C, D, E
Notes: 3, 4, 5, 7, 8, 9, 10, 11, 12, 13, 14, 15

Arlington Manor House Bed & Breakfast

Buck Hill Road, RR2 #59, 05250-8648
(802) 375-6784;
e-mail: kitandal@arlingtonmanorhouse.com
www.arlingtonmanorhouse.com

The Arlington Manor House is a charming, unusual Dutch Colonial home which was built in 1905 as a summer estate. In 1987 Al and Kit McAllister purchased the home. In August 1991 it was converted into a bed and breakfast with the added feature of many beautiful antiques for sale. Nutmeg, a golden retriever, known for her friendly greeting as well as a sad face when guests leave. Bring a camcorder for a bed and breakfast's "funniest home movies." Terrace char-grill (BYO). Tea social at 4 P.M.—ice (BYOB). Bikers' workshop. Bench stand. Beautiful views of lawns and four mountain peaks. River tubes. Garage parking for two available. Rates include a full breakfast and brunch. Children 10 and older welcome. Tennis court. Three rooms with fireplaces and two with climate control.

Hosts: Kit and Al McAllister
Rooms: 5 (3 PB; 2 SB) $65-130
Full Breakfast
Credit Cards: A, B, C
Notes: 2, 3, 5, 7, 10, 11, 12, 13, 14

Arlington's West Mountain Inn

River Road, P.O. Box 481, 05250
(802) 375-6516

Nestled on a mountainside, the century-old, seven-gabled West Mountain Inn invites guests to discover its many treasures. Distinctively decorated guest rooms, comfortable common areas, 150 acres of woodlands, wildflowers, meadows, a bird sanctuary, and llamas provide space to relax and rejuvenate the body and spirit. Miles of wilderness skiing or hiking trails and the Battenkill River provide seasonal outdoor activities. A hearty breakfast, complete with apple pie, and a savory country dinner in front of an open hearth round-out a comfortable stay.

Hosts: The Carlson Family
Rooms: 18 (PB) $121-225
Full Breakfast
Credit Cards: A, B, C, D
Notes: 2, 3, 4, 5, 7, 8, 9, 10, 11, 12, 13, 14, 15

Country Willows

332 East Arlington Road, 05250
(802) 375-0019; (800) 796-2585
FAX (802) 375-8302; e-mail: cw@sover.net
www.bbonline.com/vt/countrywillows/index.html

Country Willows, a gracious 1860s Victorian with a wraparound porch, is a village historic landmark on spacious parklike lawns in the heart of this village's picturesque historic district. The town of Arlington is hugged by the Green Mountains and meanders along the pristine waters of the famed Battenkill River. Choose from one of the individually appointed, antique-filled spacious rooms. Victorian and country decor. All rooms have queen-size beds,

---

NOTES: Credit cards accepted: A MasterCard; B Visa; C American Express; D Discover; E Diner's Club; F Other; 2 Personal checks accepted; 3 Lunch available; 4 Dinner available; 5 Open all year; 6 Pets welcome;

Country Willows

private baths, and handmade quilts. Some with fireplaces and claw-foot tubs.

Hosts: Craig and Kathleen Yanez
Rooms: 3 (PB) $65-145
Full Breakfast
Credit Cards: None
Notes: 2, 5, 7, 8, 10, 11, 12, 13, 14

Hill Farm Inn

Rural Route 2, Box 2015, 05250
(802) 375-2269; (800) 882-2545
www.hillfarminn.com

Take a step back in time and experience the quiet, comfortable nature of this historic inn on 50 acres of farmland, with a mile of frontage on the Battenkill River. Guests will enjoy magnificent mountain views in every direction. Full country breakfast cooked to order. Complimentary jar of homemade maple butter. Make

Hill Farm Inn

Hill Farm Inn a place in the country to be surrounded with caring comfort. Four seasonal cabins (May through October) with baths also available. Families welcome. Conservation land and walking areas.

Hosts: Craig and Kathleen Yanez
Rooms: 15 (13 PB; 2 SB) $70-150
Full Breakfast
Credit Cards: A, B, D
Notes: 2, 5, 8, 10, 11, 12, 13

Shenandoah Farm

Shenandoah Farm
Bed & Breakfast

Route 313 West, 05250
(802) 375-6372

Guests can enjoy quiet country lodging amid the glorious beauty of Vermont. This lovely 1820 Colonial is comfortably furnished with beautiful antiques and colonial furniture. It maintains the "at home" atmosphere that was its hallmark during the time it was a roadhouse in 1930. The Battenkill River offers fishing, canoeing, and tubing. Ski areas, golf, tennis, swimming, the Norman Rockwell Museum, Mount Equinox, and delightful craft shops are only minutes away in Arlington and Manchester.

Hosts: Woody and Donna Masterson
Rooms: 5 (1 PB; 4 SB) $70-80
Full Breakfast
Credit Cards: A, B
Notes: 2, 5, 7, 8, 9, 10, 11, 12, 13

7 No smoking; 8 Children welcome; 9 Social drinking allowed; 10 Tennis nearby; 11 Swimming nearby; 12 Golf nearby; 13 Skiing nearby; 14 May be booked through a travel agent; 15 Handicapped accessible.

BELLOWS FALLS

River Mist Bed & Breakfast

7 Burt Street, 05101
(802) 463-9023; FAX (802) 463-1571
e-mail: rmistbnb@vermontel.net
www.river-mist.com

Nestled in the historic village of Bellows Falls, in southeastern Vermont's beautiful Connecticut River Valley. The lovely circa 1880 Queen Anne Victorian is guests' home away from home as they explore all southern Vermont has to offer. There's plenty to do: take an excursion on the scenic Green Mountain Flyer Railroad, hike, antique, or take a walking tour of the village and admire street after street of beautifully restored Victorian homes. Whatever the reason—sightseeing, family reunion, or business—guests are invited to share in the breathtaking beauty of Vermont and the year-round hospitality of River Mist.

Hosts: John and Linda Maresea
Rooms: 4 (3 PB; 1 SB) $69-89
Full Breakfast
Credit Cards: A, B, C, D
Notes: 2, 5, 7, 8, 9, 10, 11, 12, 13

BENNINGTON

American Country Collection

1353 Union Street, Schenectady, NY 12308
(518) 370-4948; (800) 810-4948
FAX (518) 393-1634 (call first)
e-mail: carolbnbres@mon.com
www.bandpreservations.com

041. This carefully landscaped Victorian has a stream on the back property and a large front porch for rocking. There's a wood-burning stove on the brick hearth in the first-floor common room. Braided rugs cover wide-plank pine floors. Five guest rooms, all with private baths, and one cottage with king-size bed and private bath with Jacuzzi. Full gourmet breakfast includes pancakes, French toast, eggs, Belgian waffles, blintzes, or quiche. Smoking outdoors only. Children over 11 welcome. Ten percent gratuity. $85-145.

The Four Chimneys

21 West Road, 05201
(802) 447-3500; FAX (802) 447-3692
www.fourchimneys.com

This Georgian Revival mansion, on an 11-acre parklike setting, combines elegance with comfort and relaxation. The full service restaurant is considered one of the finest in the state. All rooms have been renovated and provide all the modern amenities, yet retain the Old World charm that makes this inn so unique. The inn provides a respite from the hectic pace of everyday life. Rated three diamonds by AAA and three stars by Mobil. Continental plus breakfast served. Come explore the well-kept secret of historic Old Bennington.

Hosts: Christine and Harold Cullison
Rooms: 11 (PB) $125-185
Continental Breakfast
Credit Cards: A, B, C, D, E
Notes: 2, 3, 4, 5, 7, 9, 10, 11, 12, 13, 14, 15

Molly Stark Inn

1067 East Main Street, 05201
(802) 442-9631; (800) 356-3076
FAX (802) 442-5224
e-mail: mollyinn@vermontel.com
www.mollystarkinn.com

A true country inn with an intimate atmosphere, this 1890 Victorian home is on the main road through a historic town in southwestern Vermont and welcomes visitors year-round. Decorated and tastefully furnished with

Molly Stark

NOTES: Credit cards accepted: A MasterCard; B Visa; C American Express; D Discover; E Diner's Club; F Other; 2 Personal checks accepted; 3 Lunch available; 4 Dinner available; 5 Open all year; 6 Pets welcome;

antiques, country collectibles, braided rugs on gleaming hardwood floors, and patchwork quilts on the beds. Private guest cottage with brass bed, Jacuzzi, and woodstove. Guests are invited to use the wraparound front porch with rocking chairs, and the den and parlor with wood-burning stoves are most inviting on those cool Vermont nights. Clean, affordable. Champagne dinner packages available.

Hosts: Cammi and Reed Fendler
Rooms: 7 (PB) $70-95
Cottage: $145
Full Breakfast
Credit Cards: A, B, C, D
Notes: 2, 4, 5, 7, 8, 9, 12, 13, 14

BETHEL

Greenhurst Inn

Rural Route 2, Box 60, River Street, 05032-9404
(802) 234-9474; (800) 521-2553

Queen Anne Victorian mansion listed in the National Register of Historic Places. In central Vermont near I-89, halfway between Boston and Montréal. Mints on the pillows and a library of 3,000 volumes. The inn was featured in the *New York Times* on March 3, 1991. Inquire about accommodations for pets.

Host: Lyle Wolf
Rooms: 13 (7 PB; 6 SB) $50-100
Continental Breakfast
Credit Cards: A, B
Notes: 2, 5, 6, 8, 9, 10, 11, 12, 13, 14

Greenhurst Inn

BOLTON VALLEY

Black Bear Inn

Black Bear Inn

HC 33, Box 717, 05477 (mailing)
Bolton Access Road (location)
(802) 434-2126; (800) 395-6335
FAX (802) 434-5161; e-mail: blkbear@wcvt.com
www.blkbearinn.com

A true Vermont country inn 2,000 feet above the valley floor with fantastic views of the Green Mountain range or fall foliage. Minutes from Burlington, one hour from Canada, antiquing, golfing, fishing, and 6,000 private acres for hiking, fishing, biking, and horseback riding. Twenty-four decorated rooms with antiques, handmade quilts, telephones, color TVs, fireplaces, hot tubs, and Vermont firestoves. Relax poolside or soak in the hot tubs. Enjoy gourmet dining in the evening and a hearty Vermont breakfast.

Hosts: The Richardson and Wallace Families
Rooms: 24 (PB) $69-109
Full and Continental Breakfast
Credit Cards: A, B
Notes: 4, 5, 7, 8, 9, 10, 11, 12, 13, 14, 15

BRANDON

The Brandon Inn

20 Park Street, 05733
(802) 247-5766; (800) 639-8485
FAX (802) 247-5768
www.brandoninn.com

7 No smoking; 8 Children welcome; 9 Social drinking allowed; 10 Tennis nearby; 11 Swimming nearby; 12 Golf nearby; 13 Skiing nearby; 14 May be booked through a travel agent; 15 Handicapped accessible.

Restored 1786 inn in the national historic register, on the village green. Individually decorated guest rooms have private baths. Beautifully appointed spacious public rooms. Secluded pool. Fine award-winning dining. Lunch and dinner. Terrace. Ask about family rates—children welcome. Weddings are a specialty.

Hosts: Sarah and Louis Pattis
Rooms: 37 (PB) $100-155
Full Breakfast
Credit Cards: A, B, C, D
Notes: 2, 3, 4, 5, 8, 10, 11, 12, 13, 14, 15

Churchill House Inn

3128 Forest Dale Road, Route 73 East, 05733
(802) 247-3078; (877) 248-7444
FAX (802) 247-0113
e-mail: innkeeper@churchillhouseinn.com

A century-old inn at the edge of the Green Mountain National Forest is a center for outdoor activities with extensive hiking, biking, and cross-country skiing from its doorstep. Outdoor pool. The inn's welcoming atmosphere, award-winning cuisine, and comfortable, antique-appointed accommodations complement an active day. All nine rooms have private baths, some with Jacuzzis. The sky-lit porch and two sitting rooms provide a casual setting. A candle-lit, four-course dinner served around an antique oak table completes the house-party atmosphere. Picnic lunches available. MAP rates available.

Hosts: Linda and Richard Daybell
Rooms: 9 (PB) $95-190
Full Breakfast and Dinner
Credit Cards: A, B, C
Notes: 2, 4, 7, 8, 9, 10, 11, 12, 13, 14

BRATTLEBORO

40 Putney Road Bed & Breakfast

40 Putney Road, 05301
(802) 254-6268; (800) 941-2413
FAX (802) 258-2673; e-mail: frtyptny@sover.net

40 Putney Road

One of Brattleboro's finest architectural landmarks, this antique-filled estate is nestled along the West River yet is within walking distance to downtown. The grounds feature classically landscaped gardens, mature trees, and fountains. Four individually decorated guest rooms, two with gas fireplaces, offer queen-size beds, telephone with modem, TV/VCR, Caswell-Massey toiletries, refrigerators, iron and ironing board, hair dryers, bathrobes, and fresh flowers. Other amenities include a full breakfast, turndown service, self-serve selection of beverages and fresh fruit, port wine, a video library, and air conditioning. Featured in *Vermont* magazine.

Hosts: Dan and Gwen Pasco
Rooms: 4 (PB) $105-175
Full Breakfast
Credit Cards: A, B, C, D
Notes: 2, 5, 7, 9, 10, 11, 12, 13, 14

The Tudor Bed & Breakfast

300 Western Avenue, 05301
(802) 257-4983; FAX (802) 258-2632

Enjoy luxurious casual comfort and personalized service. The Tudor is an elegantly furnished brick mansion with striking formal gardens. All rooms have queen-size beds, private bathrooms and telephone lines, cable TVs, air conditioning, and fireplaces. A Yamaha grand piano awaits guests in the lovingly appointed living room for their playing pleasure and relaxation. Savor a gourmet breakfast, customized private dining, and culinary classes. Convenient to four seasons' recreation, tourist destinations, fine restaurants, and shopping. "Welcome to your home!" Corporate welcome.

Host: Deborah Morgan
Rooms: 3 (PB) $120-150
Continental to Full Breakfast
Credit Cards: A, B, C
Notes: 2, 5, 7, 9, 10, 11, 12, 13

BROOKFIELD

Green Trails Inn

By the Floating Bridge, 05036
(802) 276-3412; (800) 243-3412

Comfortably elegant 13-room historic inn—relax and be pampered! Suites with Jacuzzis or fireplaces, lake-view rooms. Thirty-five-kilometer cross-county skiing from the front door. Ice skating, snowshoeing, sledding, and horse-drawn sleigh rides available in winter. Fishing, swimming, canoeing, hiking, and biking can be enjoyed summer and fall. An antique clock collection is displayed throughout the inn; clocks repaired and sold on premises. Bed and breakfast year-round. Wonderful dining just across the road. Children older than 10 welcome.

Hosts: Sue and Mark Erwin
Rooms: 13 (8 PB; 6 SB) $79-130
Credit Cards: A, B, D
Notes: 2, 5, 7, 9, 10, 11, 12, 13, 14

Green Trails Inn

BURLINGTON

Burlington Redstone Bed & Breakfast

497 South Willard Street, Route 7, 05401
(802) 862-0508

Burlington Redstone

In the national historic register. This lovingly restored home offers warm hospitality and gracious accommodations with art and antiques from around the world. Begin the day with coffee in the solarium overlooking Lake Champlain and the Adirondacks, followed by a country breakfast in the formal dining room. Guests are invited to wander about the patio and porches or stroll the flower-filled gardens. Walk to Church Street Marketplace, shopping, restaurants, theater, and the university. Discount tickets to Shelburne Museum and local restaurants.

Host: Helen Sellstedt
Room: 3 (SB) $75-115
Full Breakfast
Credit Cards: None
Notes: 2, 5, 7, 9, 10, 11, 12, 13

Hartwell House Bed & Breakfast

170 Ferguson Avenue, 05401
(888) 658-9242
http://members.aol.com/hartwellbb

Hartwell House offers a warm homelike atmosphere in a quiet Burlington neighborhood. Easy access to downtown shopping and activities or short walks to nearby lake, beach, bike path, and shopping centers. Convenient location provides guests varied options—restaurants, theaters, museums, boat rides, colleges, churches, hiking, skiing, swimming. Continental breakfast, fireplaced living room,

7 No smoking; 8 Children welcome; 9 Social drinking allowed; 10 Tennis nearby; 11 Swimming nearby; 12 Golf nearby; 13 Skiing nearby; 14 May be booked through a travel agent; 15 Handicapped accessible.

large deck, and pool provide families, couples, singles comforts of home. Hartwell House welcomes everyone!

Host: Linda Hartwell
Rooms: 2-3 (SB) $45-65
Continental Breakfast
Credit Cards: None
Notes: 2, 5, 7, 8, 9, 10, 11, 12, 13

CABOT

Creamery Inn Bed & Breakfast

P.O. Box 187, 05647
(802) 563-2819

This spacious and comfortable home, circa 1835, is picturesquely set only a mile from Cabot Creamery, with new lambs each spring. Guests may walk the country roads, enjoy ponds and waterfalls, drive to Burke Mountain or Stowe for skiing, or just relax. Sitting room, original stenciling. Enjoy the full, homemade breakfasts, featuring fruit, baked dish, and sweet breads. Special rates for stays of more than two nights. Candlelight dinners by advance reservation.

Host: Dan Lloyd
Rooms: 3 (PB) $55-75
Full Breakfast
Credit Cards: None
Notes: 2, 4, 5, 7, 8, 9, 11, 13, 15

Creamery Inn

CHELSEA

Shire Inn

Shire Inn

Main Street, 05038
(802) 685-3031; e-mail: J&K@shireinn.com
www.shireinn.com

Vermont before factory outlets and ski resorts? Come to Chelsea! In an 1832 brick mansion, bright, antique-furnished guest rooms with canopied beds, wood-burning fireplaces, 10-foot ceilings, and tall windows await guests. On 23 acres with gardens, a river, farm bridge, and hiking trails. Candlelight gourmet dinners. A romantic respite in a historic, unspoiled village. Ideal central location for exploring the best of Vermont. Come see!

Hosts: Jay and Karen Keller
Rooms: 6 (PB) $95-205
Cottage: 1
Full Breakfast
Credit Cards: A, B, D
Notes: 2, 4, 5, 7, 9, 10, 11, 12, 13, 14

CHESTER

Henry Farm Inn

2206 Green Mountain Turnpike, P.O. Box 646, 05143
(802) 875-2674; (800) 723-8213
FAX (802) 875-1510; e-mail: hfinn@vermontel.net
www.henryfarm@vermontel.net

A converted 1700s stagecoach stop on a quiet country road, the Henry Farm Inn offers an ideal Vermont getaway. This quintessential

NOTES: Credit cards accepted: A MasterCard; B Visa; C American Express; D Discover; E Diner's Club; F Other; 2 Personal checks accepted; 3 Lunch available; 4 Dinner available; 5 Open all year; 6 Pets welcome;

Henry Farm Inn

rural New England bed and breakfast has large sunny guest rooms, private baths, sumptuous country breakfasts. Set on 50 acres of rolling meadows and woodland with on-site pond and trout stream, trails to hike, bike or cross-country ski. Close to three major ski areas and one very charming Vermont village.

Host: Lee and Stuart Gaw
Rooms: 7 (PB) $75-125
Full Breakfast
Credit Cards: A, B
Notes: 2, 5, 7, 8, 9, 10, 11, 12, 13, 14

The Hugging Bear Inn & Shoppe

244 Main Street, 05143
(802) 875-2412; (800) 325-0519
e-mail: Inn@huggingBear.com
www.huggingbear.com

Bed, breakfast, and bears. Charming Victorian home on the village green. The shop has more than 9,000 teddy bears, and guests may "adopt" a bear for the night as long as he is

The Hugging Bear Inn

back to work in the shop by 9:00 A.M. Puppet show often performed at breakfast; breakfast music provided by an 1890 music box. Two lovable cats in residence. A magical place to visit! Two-night minimum stay required for holidays and high season weekends.

Hosts: The Thomases
Rooms: 6 (PB) $85-125
Full Breakfast
Credit Cards: A, B, C, D
Notes: 2, 5, 7, 8, 9, 10, 11, 12, 13

Night with a Native Bed & Breakfast

P.O. Box 327, 05143-0327
(802) 875-2616

Feel at home at this bed and breakfast. Enjoy the warm ambiance of hand-stenciled rooms, family-made rugs, antiques and collectibles, and wood stoves. TV in living room. The host, a sixth-generation Vermonter, offers true Vermont hospitality. Complimentary refreshments. Delicious breakfast served in dining room which was originally a one-room schoolhouse. Walking distance to restaurants and shops.

Host: Doris Hastings
Rooms: 2 (PB) $60-95
Full Breakfast
Credit Cards: None
Notes: 2, 5, 7, 9, 10, 11, 12, 13

"Second Wind" Bed & Breakfast

289 Grafton Street, P.O. Box 348, 05143
(802) 875-3438

Quiet, Victorian farmhouse-comfortably applied. Two suites with queen-size beds, private sitting rooms, cable TV, and air conditioning; one common living room. A sumptuous breakfast and warm hospitality. A short walk to Chester's main street green, and lovely restaurants. Southern exposure, wraparound deck bedecked with flowers and plants. Three inn dogs, "We're not fancy, but a great place to hang your hat. Welcome!" Children 12 and older welcome.

7 No smoking; 8 Children welcome; 9 Social drinking allowed; 10 Tennis nearby; 11 Swimming nearby; 12 Golf nearby; 13 Skiing nearby; 14 May be booked through a travel agent; 15 Handicapped accessible.

Hosts: Stephen and Sieglinde "Siggy" Wrobel
Rooms: 3 (2 PB; 1 SB) $70
Full Breakfast
Notes: 2, 5, 7, 9, 10, 11, 12, 13

The Stone Hearth Inn

698 Vermont Route 11 West, 05143
(802) 875-2525; FAX (802) 875-4688
e-mail: shinn@vermontel.com

This 1810 country inn is in southern Vermont.
Close to skiing, snowmobiling, snowboarding,
golf, tennis, and fishing. Ten guest rooms, English-style pub, and recreation room with hot tub.
Great getaway for families, couples, and groups.

Hosts: Don and Janet Strohmeyer
Rooms: 10 (PB) $45-150
Full Breakfast
Credit Cards: A, B, C, D
Notes: 2, 4, 5, 7, 8, 9, 10, 11, 12, 13, 14

DANBY

Silas Griffith Inn

178 Main Street, 05739
(802) 293-5567; (800) 545-1509
www.silasgriffith.com

Built in 1891 by Vermont's first millionaire, a
lovingly restored gracious Victorian mansion
and carriage house. Relax in a quiet 19th-century
village and walk to antique and gift shops. Full
hearty breakfast and elegant dining in the carriage house. "Come, enjoy our beautiful views."

Hosts: Paul and Lois Dansereau
Rooms: 17 (14 PB; 3 SB) $72-94
Full Breakfast
Credit Cards: A, B
Notes: 2, 4, 7, 8, 9, 10, 11, 12, 13, 14

DERBY LINE

The Birchwood Bed & Breakfast

502 Main Street, P.O. Box 550, 05830
(802) 873-9104; FAX (802) 873-9121
e-mail: birchwd@together.net
www.together.net/~birchwd

The Birchwood

A 1920 lovingly restored home in a charming
village in the Northeast Kingdom at the Canadian border. Three individually decorated,
antique-filled bedrooms include private bathrooms. A full breakfast is served each morning
in the sunlit dining room. The region offers
miles of unspoiled scenery. Enjoy the beauty of
the area as well as the comfort and spaciousness of this home. A warm welcome awaits
guests at the Birchwood Bed and Breakfast.

Hosts: Betty and Dick Fletcher
Rooms: 3 (PB) $75
Full Breakfast
Credit Cards: None
Notes: 2, 5, 7, 9, 10, 11, 12, 13

Derby Village Inn

440 Main Street, P.O. Box 1085, 05830
(802) 873-3604; FAX (802) 873-3047
e-mail: dvibandb@together.net
http://homepages.together.net/~dvibandb

Neoclassical elegance in a circa 1902 home on
the Canadian border. Five lovely bedrooms,
each with its own individual personality and
private bath. Enjoy beautiful sunsets, golfing,
downhill and cross-country skiing, hiking,
water sports, cycling, snowmobiling, fishing,
sleigh rides, antiquing, and most of all—peace
and tranquility. Within walking distance of the
world's only international library and opera
house. Delicious home cooking.

Hosts: Catherine McCormick and Sheila Steplar
Rooms: 5 (PB) $75-100
Credit Cards: A, B, C, D
Notes: 2, 5, 7, 8, 9, 10, 11, 12, 13

DORSET

Marble West Inn

Dorset West Road, 05251
(802) 867-4155; (800)453-7629;
FAX (802) 867-5731; e-mail: Marwest@saver.net
www.marblewestinn.com

Circa 1840 Greek Revival mansion nestled between two mountains just outside a quintessential village setting which captures the essence of Vermont. The grounds are beautifully manicured and include two small ponds which are fed by a rolling mountain brook behind the inn. Inside, guests are greeted by a stenciled hallway, polished dark pine floors and antiques. Retreat to the library or music rooms to relax in front of the fireplaces. The Dorset area offers, biking, hiking, fishing, canoeing, swimming, tennis, cross country, and down-hill skiing, and the Dorset Playhouse. Manchester Center, only minutes away, offers designer outlet and specialty stores, as well as many fabulous restaurants.

Hosts: Bonnie and Paul Quinn
Rooms: 8 (PB) $90-175
Full Breakfast
Credit Cards: A, B, C
Notes: 2, 5, 7, 9, 10, 11, 12, 13

EAST DOVER

Cooper Hill Inn

Cooper Hill Road, Box 146, 05341
(802) 348-6333; (800) 783-3229
e-mail: cooperhill@juno.com
www.CooperHillInn.com

Informal and cozy hilltop inn with "one of the most spectacular mountain panoramas in all New England." Quiet country road location. Hearty home-cooked meals. Five double rooms, three two-bedroom family suites, and two large family rooms, all with private baths. Close to area activities. Direct access from inn to mountain biking, hiking, snowmobiling, and cross-country skiing. Just 12 minutes to downhill skiing. Closed for one week in April and November.

Hosts: Pat and Marilyn Hunt
Rooms: 10 (PB) $72-120
Full Breakfast
Credit Cards: A, B, D
Notes: 2, 4, 5, 7, 8, 9, 10, 11, 12, 13, 14

EAST MIDDLEBURY

Waybury Inn

Route 125, 05753
(802) 388-4015; (800) 348-1810

Built in 1810, the Waybury Inn has 14 individually appointed guest rooms, all with private baths. Known to many as the inn featured on *The Bob Newhart Show*, the inn offers dinner daily and Sunday brunch. The Pub opens at 4:00 P.M. No smoking.

Hosts: Marty and Marcia Schuppert
Rooms: 14 (PB) $85-120
Credit Cards: A, B, D, E
Notes: 2, 4, 5, 7, 8, 10, 11, 12, 13, 14

ENOSBURG FALLS

Berkson Farms

Route 108 North
1205 West Berkshire Road, 05450-5205
(802) 933-2522

Berkson Farms is a full working dairy farm sitting on a picture-postcard 600 acres up near the Canadian border. The inn offers homey and comfortable lodging in a century-old restored farmhouse where guests can relax and enjoy all the simple, wonderful joys of nature, people,

7 No smoking; 8 Children welcome; 9 Social drinking allowed; 10 Tennis nearby; 11 Swimming nearby; 12 Golf nearby; 13 Skiing nearby; 14 May be booked through a travel agent; 15 Handicapped accessible.

Berkson Farms

and of life itself. The hosts serve home-cooked country-style meals and warm, friendly Vermont hospitality.

Hosts: Dick and Joanne Keesler
Rooms: 4 (1 PB; 3 SB) $55-65
Full Breakfast
Credit Cards: None
Notes: 2, 3, 4, 5, 6, 7, 8, 10, 11, 12, 13

FAIRFAX

American Country Collection

1353 Union Street, Schenectady, NY 12308
(518) 370-4948; (800) 810-4948
FAX (518) 393-1634 (call first)
e-mail: carolbnbres@mon.com
www.bandbreservations.com

149. Imagine being in a completely renovated New England carriage house in the year 1790, and begin the journey through this inn with original exposed beams and wood-burning stove. Four rooms are available for guests. Two rooms on the second floor share a bath, and two rooms on the first floor share another bath and a whirlpool tub. Snacks, wine, beer, and soft drinks available, and a fax machine, Macintosh computer, copier, and antique and gift shop are on premises. In the spring, enjoy watching maple syrup being made. Full breakfast. $48-78.

FAIR HAVEN

Maplewood Inn

Route 22A South, 05743
(802) 265-8039; (800) 253-7729 (reservations only)
e-mail: maplewd@sover.net
www.sover.net/~maplewd

Romantic 1843 Greek Revival listed in the National Register of Historic Places offering exquisitely appointed guest rooms and suites with private baths, antiques, working fireplaces, in-room color cable TVs, radios, telephones, and air conditioning. Common rooms include gathering room/library, breakfast room with hot beverage bar, and parlor with games and complimentary cordial bar. Near lakes, skiing, restaurants, and many other attractions. Area's only three-star Mobil-, three-diamond AAA-rated inn. Hearty Continental plus breakfast. Innkeeper/Realtor.

Hosts: Cindy and Doug Baird
Rooms: 5 (PB) $80-140
Continental Breakfast
Credit Cards: A, B, C, D
Notes: 2, 5, 9, 10, 11, 12, 13, 14

Maplewood Inn

FAIRLEE

American Country Collection

1353 Union Street, Schenectady, NY 12308
(518) 370-4948; (800) 810-4948
FAX (518) 393-1637 (call first)
e-mail: carolbnbres@msn.com
www.bandbreservations.com

178. This is a large country home surrounded by 125 acres of open fields and of woods and wonderful views. It has a living room with fireplace, cozy sitting room with wood stove, and a screened veranda. A second-floor sitting room has TV/VCR. Bedrooms have individually controlled heating and are comfortably furnished with carpets or area rugs, reading lamps, sitting areas, and down pillows and comforters. Children are welcome; 14 and under stay free in the same room as parents; half-price for children under 18 staying in separate room. No resident pets. Smoking permitted outside. Continental breakfast served. $90-135.

Silver Maple Lodge

Elaine's Bed & Breakfast Selections

4987 Kingston Road, Elbridge, NY 13060
(315) 689-2082 (call between 10:30 A.M.–7:00 P.M.)

There are eight guest rooms in the main house, which is more than 200 years old, and three duplex cottages plus a single cottage for a total of 15 rooms. Six rooms in the main house have private baths and two share one. All cottages have private baths, three have fireplaces, and two have kitchenettes. Main house is non-smoking. All outdoor activities nearby as well as Quechee Gorge, Maple Grove Maple Museum, Ben & Jerry's Ice Cream Factory, the Cabot Farmer's Cooperative Creamery, Calvin Coolidge homestead, and many other historic sites. Continental breakfast is served in the dining room. Extra person in room six dollars. $54-79.

Silver Maple Lodge and Cottages

Route 5, 05045
(802) 333-4326; (800) 666-1946
e-mail: scott@Silvermaplelodge.com;
www.Silvermaplelodge.com

Historic bed and breakfast country inn. Cozy rooms with antiques or knotty pine cottages, some with fireplaces. Enjoy the beach, boating, fishing, and swimming at Lake Morey, one mile away. Golf, tennis, skiing, and hot-air balloon rides are nearby. Dartmouth College is 17 miles away. Walk to restaurants. Two-night minimum stay required for holidays.

Hosts: Scott and Sharon Wright
Rooms: 16 (14 PB; 2 SB) $59-89
Continental Breakfast
Credit Cards: A, B, C, D
Notes: 2, 6, 8, 9, 10, 11, 12, 13, 14, 15

GOSHEN

Judith's Garden Bed & Breakfast

423 The Goshen-Ripton Road, 05733
(802) 247-4707; e-mail: gardenbb@together.net

A peaceful mountain oasis! Abundant perennial gardens, brimming with flowers. Spacious guest rooms and antique-filled living room. Praise-winning breakfasts served in the large country kitchen, featuring delicious home baking. Walking and hiking on quiet country roads and numerous mountain trails in the Moosalamoo Recreation Area of the Green Mountain

Judith's Garden

7 No smoking; 8 Children welcome; 9 Social drinking allowed; 10 Tennis nearby; 11 Swimming nearby; 12 Golf nearby; 13 Skiing nearby; 14 May be booked through a travel agent; 15 Handicapped accessible.

National Forest. Cross-country skiing and snowshoeing from the front door on Blueberry Hill's renowned 40-mile trail system. Near Brandon and Middlebury.

Hosts: Judith Irven and Dick Conrad
Rooms: 3 (PB) $75-95
Full Breakfast
Credit Cards: None
Notes: 2, 4, 5, 7, 9, 11, 12, 13, 14

GREENSBORO

Highland Lodge

Rural Route 1, Box 1290, Craftsbury Road, 05841
(802) 533-2647; FAX (802) 533-7494
e-mail: hlodge@connriver.net
www.pbpub.com/vermont/hiland.htm

Highland Lodge is a family-owned country inn and resort in a turn-of-the-century summer community on Caspian Lake. The lodge has a clay tennis court, lawn games, and a private beach for swimming and boating. Dirt roads for biking and hiking lead through farm country and a nature preserve. Cross-country skiing accessible on the grounds. Golf is nearby in the village. Children love the play program. The delicious food is complimented by all. Admire the breathtaking vistas at fall foliage time and from the lodge's own cross-country ski trails. Dinner and breakfast are both included in the rates per person per night.

Highland Lodge

Hosts: David and Wilhelmina Smith
Rooms: 11 (PB) $95-125 MAP
Cottages: 11
Full breakfast
Credit Cards: A, B, D
Notes: 2, 3, 4, 5, 8, 9, 10, 11, 12, 13, 14, 15

HANCOCK

Sweet Onion Inn

P.O. Box 66, Route 100, 05748
(802) 767-3734; FAX (802) 767-9227
e-mail: SweetO@madriver.com
www.madriver.com/lodging/SweetO

Peaceful country inn in mid-Vermont on scenic Route 100. Serving vegetarian breakfasts "prepared from scratch with the finest ingredients." Dinners with reservations. Freshly decorated rooms, wide plank floors and stenciled walls. Warm hospitality near walking, hiking, and biking trails in the Green Mountains. In November through April guests' third night is free.

Hosts: Ron and Kathy Heatley
Rooms: 8 (4 PB; 4 SB) $65-90
Full Breakfast
Credit Cards: A, B, C, D, E
Notes: 2, 4, 5, 7, 8, 9, 11, 12, 13, 14

HARTLAND

American Country Collection

1353 Union Street, Schenectady, NY 12308
(518) 370-4948; (800) 810-4948
FAX (518) 393-1634 (call first)
e-mail: carolbnbres@mon.com
www.bandbreservations.com

163. Contemporary home in a rural farm setting with a spectacular view. Guests have the privacy of the entire first floor, including private entrance, if desired. Soft country decor with handmade quilts. Continental breakfast. Two rooms, one with twin beds and one with a double bed; each has a private bath. Common room with fireplace and TV. Resident cat. Children welcome. No smoking. $65-75.

NOTES: Credit cards accepted: A MasterCard; B Visa; C American Express; D Discover; E Diner's Club; F Other; 2 Personal checks accepted; 3 Lunch available; 4 Dinner available; 5 Open all year; 6 Pets welcome;

JACKSONVILLE

American Country Collection

1353 Union Street, Schenectady, NY 12308
(518) 370-4948; (800) 810-4948
FAX (518) 393-1634 (call first)
e-mail: carolbnbres@mon.com
www.bandbreservations.com

165. Colonial-style country home built in 1840. Queen Anne Colonial furnishings and country accessories. Dining room with fireplace, living room, and sitting room with TV. Four guest rooms with private and shared baths. In-ground swimming pool. Twenty minutes from Mount Snow. Full breakfast. Children welcome. Smoking outside. $60-80.

JAMAICA

Three Mountain Inn

P.O. Box 180 A, 05343
(802) 874-4140

Small, romantic 1780s authentic country inn. Fine food and comfortable rooms. Many original details can be found, including three wood-burning fireplaces on the main floor, and several guest rooms also boast original fireplaces. In a historic village, just four blocks to hiking in the state park and cross-country skiing. Swimming pool on premises. Ten minutes to Stratton. The innkeepers plan special day trips with detailed local maps of the area. Special midweek rates. Honeymoon suites available. Small weddings, reunions, meetings. Bed and breakfast and modified American plan available.

Three Mountain Inn

Hosts: Charles and Elaine Murray
Rooms: 16 (14 PB; 2 SB) $75-180
Full Breakfast
Credit Cards: A, B, C, D
Notes: 2, 4, 7, 8, 9, 10, 11, 12, 13, 14

JEFFERSONVILLE

Jefferson House Bed and Breakfast

Main Street, P.O. Box 288, 05464
(802) 644-2030; (800) 253-9630
e-mail: jeffhouse@pwshift.com
www.pbpub.com/smugglers/jeffhouse.htm

Enjoy the picturesque beauty of this turn-of-the-century Victorian home in historic Jeffersonville. It features a large wraparound porch; a warm, friendly atmosphere; attractive, comfortable rooms; and a hearty, home-cooked breakfast. In spring and summer bike the country roads, hike the Long Trail or Mount Mansfield. Autumn's foliage is a sight to behold. In the winter, nearby Smugglers' Notch offers great skiing while other activities are only minutes away.

Hosts: Dick and Joan Walker
Rooms: 3 (PB) $60-75
Full Breakfast
Credit Cards: A, B, D
Notes: 2, 5, 7, 8, 9, 12, 13

Mannsview Inn

916 Route 108 South, 05464
(802) 644-8321; (888) 937-6266
FAX (802) 644-2006
e-mail:r.s.v.p.@mannsview.com
www.mannsview.com

Set on a plateau on 10 acres on Route 108, Vermont's most scenic highway. Fifteen minutes from Stowe. The inn is superbly decorated with antiques from the 10,000- square-foot antique center next door. Queen-size high poster beds, billiard room, library, sunroom, parlor, whirlpool bath, and outdoor spa. Sumptuous full country breakfast in the sunroom with window views of Smugglers' Notch and

Mount Mansfield. The inn is also Smugglers' Notch Canoe Touring. Canoe vacation packages from $189. Children over 10 welcome. Kennel facilities for visiting pets.

Hosts: Kelley and Bette Mann
Rooms: 6 (2 PB; 4 SB) $50-85
Full Breakfast
Credit Cards: A, B, C, D
Notes: 2, 5, 7, 9, 10, 11, 12, 13

Smugglers' Notch Inn

Smugglers' Notch Inn

Church Street, 05464
(802) 644-2412; (800) 845-3101
e-mail: info@smugglers-notch-inn.com/
www.smugglers-notch-inn.com

Escape to a warm, friendly, 200-year-old Vermont country inn in an authentic rural village. Eleven guest rooms with private baths, one with a Jacuzzi, and one with gas fireplace. Lounge, fireplace, great restaurant, outdoor hot tub, pool. See why generations of artists return here again and again. Wide variety of activities, from casual to vigorous. Great road or mountain biking, fly-fishing, ice or rock climbing, canoeing, skiing, golfing, hiking, antiquing. Covered bridges.

Hosts: Cynthia Barber and Jon Day
Rooms: 11 (PB) $60-125
Full Breakfast
Credit Cards: A, B, C
Notes: 2, 4, 5, 7, 8, 9, 10, 11, 12, 13

JERICHO

Homeplace

P.O. Box 96, 05465
(802) 899-4694

A quiet spot in a 100-acre wood. The spacious house is filled with European and American antiques. The living room has a large fireplace and looks out on Mount Mansfield. The house is surrounded by perennial gardens, and there are many wooded trails on the property. Friendly house and barn animals complete the picture.

Host: Mariot Huessy
Rooms: 3 (1 PB; 2 SB) $55-65
Full Breakfast
Credit Cards: None
Notes: 2, 5, 7, 8, 9, 10, 11, 12, 13, 14

Sinclair Inn Bed & Breakfast

389 Vermont Route 15, 05465
(802) 899-2234; (800) 433-4658

A showcase of builder Edmund Sinclair's craftsmanship, fully restored in 1993, this 1890 Victorian "painted lady" has been described as "a study in architectural styles, incorporating features such as turrets, colored glass, and an intricately carved fretwork across the living room and stairway." Halfway between Burlington and Smugglers' Notch. Enjoy the nearby hiking, boating, sailing, biking, festivals, and shows. Discount ski lift tickets available. One room has a fireplace and another room is handicapped accessible. Children over 12 welcome. Social drinking permitted in rooms. Specializing in garden weddings.

Hosts: Jeanne and Andy Buchanan
Rooms: 6 (PB) $80-115
Full Breakfast
Credit Cards: A, B, D
Notes: 2, 7, 9, 10, 11, 12, 13, 14, 15

NOTES: Credit cards accepted: A MasterCard; B Visa; C American Express; D Discover; E Diner's Club; F Other; 2 Personal checks accepted; 3 Lunch available; 4 Dinner available; 5 Open all year; 6 Pets welcome;

KILLINGTON

Elaine's Bed and Breakfast Selections

4987 Kingston Road, Elbridge, NY 13060
(315) 689-2082 (call between 10:30 A.M.-7:00 P.M.)

This lodge, open year-round, has 6 suites, 11 nonsmoking rooms, and 35 smoking rooms. All the rooms have modern private baths and TVs. There is a pool, hot tub, sauna, exercise room, adjoining lounge for games or cards. Full breakfast. Inquire about accommodations for pets. Children welcome and baby-sitters can be arranged. Killington Mountain is near great hiking and biking trails, fishing streams, rafting rivers, native craft shops, antiquing. Several golf courses are nearby. There is also a restaurant on the premises. $109-269.

Mountain Meadows Lodge

285 Thundering Brook Road, 05751
(802) 775-1010; (800) 370-4567
e-mail: havefun@mtmeadowslodge.com
www.mtmeadowslodge.com

A year-round lakeside resort on the Appalachian Trail. Outdoor, indoor, and lake activities abundantly available. On-site cross-country ski center. Fireside dining with country fare and vegetarian menu. Complete breakfasts feature granola, fresh fruit, and griddle cakes. All-day snacks, cheese, wine available. Boxed lunches. On-site, state-licensed children's farm and adventure program.

Hosts: Mark and Michelle Werle
Rooms: 19 (PB) $105-250
Full Breakfast
Credit Cards: A, B, C
Notes: 2, 3, 4, 5, 7, 8, 10, 11, 12, 13, 14, 15

The Peak Chalet

South View Path, P.O. Box 511, 05751
(802) 422-4278; e-mail: home@thepeakchalet.com
www.thepeakchalet.com

The Peak Chalet

The Peak Chalet is a four-room bed and breakfast within the beautiful Green Mountains of Vermont. The exterior is authentically European alpine. The interior is furnished with a fine country inn flavor and reflects high quality with attention to detail. The bed and breakfast offers panoramic mountain views with a cozy stone fireplace to unwind by. All rooms have queen-size beds and private baths. Within the Killington Ski Resort, this is a truly relaxing experience. Children over 12 welcome. Mobil and AAA three-diamond-rated.

Hosts: Diane and Greg Becker
Rooms: 4 (PB) $50-110
Continental Breakfast
Credit Cards: A, B, C, E
Notes: 2, 5, 7, 9, 10, 11, 12, 13, 14

Red Clover Inn

7 Woodward Road, Mendon, 05701
(802) 775-2290; (800) 752-0571
e-mail: redclovr@vermontel.com
www.redcloverinn.com

Down a winding country road, nestled on 13 acres, this 1840s lovingly restored farmhouse estate offers guests warmth, pampering, and an award-winning wine list to complement the exquisite cuisine. From enticing rooms with

---

7 No smoking; 8 Children welcome; 9 Social drinking allowed; 10 Tennis nearby; 11 Swimming nearby; 12 Golf nearby; 13 Skiing nearby; 14 May be booked through a travel agent; 15 Handicapped accessible.

private baths, antiques, some with double whirlpools and gas fireplaces, to sumptuous breakfasts and candlelight dining, the atmosphere is relaxed and peaceful. Hiking and biking. Knoll-top pool. Inquire about pet accommodations. AAA three-diamond-rated. Mobil three-star-rated. Selected as a romantic hideaway by the *Discerning* Traveler.

Hosts: Sue and Harris Zuckerman
Rooms: 14 (PB) $110-325
Full Breakfast
Credit Cards: A, B, D
Notes: 2, 4, 7, 9, 10, 11, 12, 13, 14

The Vermont Inn

The Vermont Inn

Route 4, 05751
(802) 775-0708; (800) 541-7795
FAX (802) 773-2440; e-mail: vtinn@aol.com

Built as a farmhouse in 1840, the Vermont Inn has been known for many years for its fine dining and lodging. The original wood beams are exposed in the living room, the lounge has a wood stove, and there is an old-fashioned game room. The rooms are individually decorated and some have a fireplace. Outdoor pool and tennis. Indoor hot tub and sauna. Screened porch and extensive gardens.

Hosts: Megan and Greg Smith
Rooms: 18 (PB) $50-185
Full Breakfast
Credit Cards: A, B, C, E
Notes: 2, 4, 5, 7, 8, 9, 10, 11, 12, 13, 14, 15

LONDONDERRY

The Blue Gentian Lodge

Magic Mountain Road, Rural Route 1, Box 29, 05148
(802) 824-5908; (800) 456-2405
FAX (802) 824-3531

In scenic south central Vermont, the lodge has 13 comfortable rooms and an outstanding view of Magic Mountain. All rooms have private baths, most have cable TVs, one is completely handicapped accessible. Lovely lounge with fireplace; dining area can accommodate 40 guests. Outdoor pool and hot tub on premises. Centrally between many must-see attractions, such as outlet shopping, museums, summer theaters, hiking, and skiing.

Hosts: The Alberti Family
Rooms: 13 (PB) $50-80
Full Breakfast
Credit Cards: A, B
Notes: 2, 5, 7, 8, 10, 11, 12, 13, 15

Swiss Inn

Route 11, Rural Route 1, Box 140, 05148
(802) 824-3442; (800) 847-9477

The Swiss Inn is in the heart of the Green Mountains with spectacular views of the surrounding area. These cozy, comfortable rooms all feature cable TVs, telephones, and private baths. Full Vermont breakfast is served daily. Two fireside sitting rooms and library are available. Restaurant on premises features Swiss specialties. Both downhill and cross-country skiing nearby in the winter. Shopping, antiques, golf, summer theater, and fall foliage at its best.

Hosts: Joe and Pat Donahue
Rooms: 18 (PB) $54-99
Full Breakfast
Credit Cards: A, B
Notes: 2, 4, 5, 8, 9, 10, 11, 12, 13

NOTES: Credit cards accepted: A MasterCard; B Visa; C American Express; D Discover; E Diner's Club; F Other; 2 Personal checks accepted; 3 Lunch available; 4 Dinner available; 5 Open all year; 6 Pets welcome;

LOWER WATERFORD

Rabbit Hill Inn

Lower Waterford Road, 05848
(800) 76-BUNNY; FAX (802) 748-8342
e-mail: Info@RabbitHillInn.com
www.RabbitHillInn.com

It is here that guests will find that romantic departure from their hectic world. This 200-year-old classic country inn is set on 15 acres above the Connecticut River. Enjoy pampering service, adventurous gourmet dining, and truly heartfelt hospitality unlike anything ever experienced. Enchanting candlelit guest rooms and suites—some with fireplaces, whirlpool tubs for two, and private porches. Repeatedly chosen one of American's Ten Best Inns. Rated four-diamonds by AAA and four-stars by Mobil.

Hosts: Brian and Leslie Mulcahy
Rooms: 21 (PB)
Full Breakfast
Credit Cards: A, B, C
Notes: 2, 4, 5, 7, 9, 10, 11, 12, 13, 14, 15

Rabbit Hill Inn

LUDLOW

The Combes Family Inn

953 East Lake Road, 05149
(802) 228-8799; (800) 822-8799
e-mail: billcfi@aol.com
www.combesfamilyinn.com

Bring the family to the Combes Family Inn in Vermont. The inn, a century-old farmhouse on a country back road, offers a quiet respite from the hustle and bustle of today's hectic lifestyle. Relax and socialize (BYOB) in the Vermont barn-board keeping room, furnished with turn-of-the-century oak. Sample Bill's country breakfasts and Ruth's delicious home cooking. Lush Green Mountains invite a relaxing, casual vacation. Eleven cozy, country-inspired guest rooms—all with private baths. Minimum-stay requirements for fall and winter weekends and for holidays. Closed April 15 through May 15.

Hosts: Ruth and Bill Combes
Rooms: 11 (PB) $55-124
Full Breakfast
Credit Cards: A, B, C, D
Notes: 2, 4, 6, 8, 9, 10, 11, 12, 13, 14

The Governor's Inn

86 Main Street, 05149
(802) 228-8830; (800) GOVERNOR
FAX (802) 228-2961

The Governor's Inn is a stylish, romantic Victorian country house in Ludlow, Vermont, just a mile from Okemo Mountain, in an area surrounded by crystal clear lakes. Some guest rooms have fireplaces. All are furnished with antiques and have private baths. Rates include afternoon tea and full breakfast for two, served at private tables beautifully set with silver, crystal, and heirloom china. Dinner available Wednesdays through Sundays. Golfing, fishing, skiing, and antiquing are all nearby.

Hosts: Jim and Cathy Kubec
Rooms: 9 (PB) $95-185
Suite: $265
Full Breakfast
Credit Cards: A, B
Notes: 2, 4, 5, 7, 9, 12, 13, 14

LYNDONVILLE

The Wildflower Inn

Darlington Hill Road, 05851
(802) 626-8310; (800) 627-8310

7 No smoking; 8 Children welcome; 9 Social drinking allowed; 10 Tennis nearby; 11 Swimming nearby; 12 Golf nearby; 13 Skiing nearby; 14 May be booked through a travel agent; 15 Handicapped accessible.

FAX (802) 626-3069; e-mail: wldflwrinn@aol.com
www.wildflowerinn.com

The Wildflower Inn sits on 500 acres in Vermont's pristine Northeast Kingdom. This is the region of Vermont where even Vermonters escape to. Whether it's a hike above the cliffs of Mount Pisgah, a swim in the glacial carved Willoughby Lake, an inquisitive visit to the Fairbanks Museum, a sweet tour of the Maple Grove Farms, an invigorating ski down Burke Mountain, or just relaxing by the inn's pool, your stay will be renewing.

Hosts: Jim and Mary O'Reilly
Rooms: 21 (PB) $85-250
Full Breakfast
Credit Cards: A, B
Notes: 2, 3, 4, 5, 7, 8, 10, 11, 12, 13, 14, 15

MANCHESTER

1811 House

Box 39, 05254
(802) 362-1811; (800) 432-1811
FAX (802) 362-2443

This classic Vermont inn offers guests the warmth and comfort of their own home. Built in the 1770s, the house has operated as an inn since 1811 except for one brief period when it was the residence of Abraham Lincoln's granddaughter. All guest rooms have private baths; some have fireplaces, oriental rugs, fine paintings, and canopied beds. More than seven acres of lawn contain flower gardens and a pond and offer an exceptional view of the Green Mountains. Walk to golf and tennis, near skiing, fishing, canoeing, and all sports. Young people over 16 welcome.

1811 House

Hosts: Marnie and Bruce Duff
Rooms: 14 (PB) $120-220
Full Breakfast
Credit Cards: A, B, C, D
Notes: 2, 5, 7, 9, 10, 11, 12, 13, 14

The Inn at Manchester

Historic Route 7A, Box 41, 05254-0041
(802) 362-1793; (800) 273-1793
FAX (802) 362-3218; www.innatmanchester.com

Beautifully restored turn-of-the-century classic Queen-Anne, listed on the National Register of Historic Places. The inn sits on 4 acres of birches, lawns, flower gardens, and towering pines and spruces. Elegantly antique-furnished rooms and suites all with  private baths and air conditioning. Most suites with separate sitting rooms, fireplaces, and canopied beds. Luscious full breakfast and afternoon tea. Secluded pool and wonderful views of the mountains provide a spectacular setting for the inn.

Hosts: Stan and Harriet Rosenberg
Rooms: 18 (PB) $100-145
Suites: 4
Full Breakfast
Credit Cards: A, B, C, D, E
Notes: 2, 5, 7, 9, 10, 11, 12, 13, 14

Manchester Highlands Inn

Box 1754 AD, Highland Avenue, 05255
(802) 362-4565; (800) 743-4565
FAX (802) 362-4028
e-mail: relax@highlandsinn.com
www.highlandsinn.com

Discover Manchester's first "painted lady," a graceful Queen Anne Victorian inn on a hilltop overlooking town. Front porch with rocking chairs, large outdoor pool, game room, and pub with stone fireplace. Rooms individually decorated with feather beds, down comforters, and lace curtains; many with canopied beds.

NOTES: Credit cards accepted: A MasterCard; B Visa; C American Express; D Discover; E Diner's Club; F Other; 2 Personal checks accepted; 3 Lunch available; 4 Dinner available; 5 Open all year; 6 Pets welcome;

Manchester Highlands Inn

Gourmet country breakfasts and afternoon snacks are served. Air conditioned.

Hosts: Robert and Patricia Eichorn
Rooms: 15 (PB) $105-145
Full Breakfast
Credit Cards: A, B, C
Notes: 2, 5, 7, 8, 9, 10, 11, 12, 13, 14

MANCHESTER CENTER

The Inn at Ormsby Hill

Historic Route 7A,1824 Main Street, 05255
(802) 362-1163; (800) 670-2841
FAX (802) 362-5176
e-mail: ormsby@vermontel.com
www.ormsbyhill.com

This splendid restored manor house is on two and one-half acres overlooking the Green Mountains. Listed in Vermont register of historic places, the inn offers 10 luxurious bed chambers, all with private baths, fireplaces and two-person whirlpools. The inn is known for its exceptional dining in the conservatory. Manchester is a four-season resort community with a full assortment of sports and cultural activities.

Hosts: Ted and Chris Sprague
Rooms: 10 (PB) $165-325
Full Breakfast
Credit Cards: A, B, D
Notes: 2, 4, 5, 7, 9, 10, 11, 12, 13, 14, 15

River Meadow Farm

P.O. Box 822, 05255
(802) 362-1602

Secluded farm at the end of a country lane with beautiful views of the surrounding countryside. The remodeled farmhouse was built just prior to 1800. Four guest bedrooms sharing two and one-half baths, large country kitchen with a fireplace and adjoining screened-in, glassed-in porch, pleasant dining room, living room with baby grand piano, and den with TV. Ninety acres to hike or cross-country ski, bordered by the famous Battenkill River. Swimming is available 15 miles away.

Host: Patricia J. Dupree
Rooms: 5 (SB) $60
Full Breakfast
Credit Cards: None
Notes: 2, 5, 7, 8, 9, 10, 11, 12, 13

MANCHESTER VILLAGE

The Reluctant Panther Inn & Restaurant

17-39 West Road, 05254-0678
(802) 362-2568; (800) 822-2331
FAX (802) 362-2586; e-mail: panther@sover.net

Handsome collection of exquisitely decorated deluxe accommodations and romantic suites. Many with Jacuzzi for two, and a fireplace in bathroom, another in bedroom. Classic European and modern American cuisine served around impressive fieldstone fireplace or in Greenhouse. Acclaimed by *New York Times, Country Inns,* and *Gourmet.* "Country hospitality for the sophisticated traveler." MAP rates available.

Hosts: Maye and Robert H. Bachofen
Rooms: 21 (PB) $198-650
Full Breakfast
Credit Cards: A, B, C, D, E
Notes: 2, 4, 5, 7, 9, 10, 11, 12, 13, 14

---

7 No smoking; 8 Children welcome; 9 Social drinking allowed; 10 Tennis nearby; 11 Swimming nearby; 12 Golf nearby; 13 Skiing nearby; 14 May be booked through a travel agent; 15 Handicapped accessible.

MIDDLEBURY

The Annex

Route 125, 05740
(802) 388-3233

This 1830 Greek Revival home was originally
built as an annex to the Bob Newhart "Stratford
Inn." The annex features six rooms decorated
in a blend of country, antiques, and homemade
quilts. The nearby national forest provides hiking, skiing, and biking trails. Visit the UVM
Morgan Horse Farm and the Shelburne
Museum while in the area. Please inquire about
accommodations for children.

Host: T. D. Hutchins
Rooms: 6 (4 PB; 2 SB) $50-80
Continental Breakfast
Credit Cards: None
Notes: 2, 5, 7, 9, 10, 11, 12, 13

The Annex

The Middlebury Inn

Courthouse Square, P.O. Box 631, 05753
(802) 388-4961; (800) 842-4666

Traditional 1827 New England inn within
scenic college town enhanced by a legion of
historical, cultural, and entertaining attractions.
Walking distance to museums, boutique shops,
magnificent waterfall. Elegantly restored
rooms in the main house, Porter Mansion and
contemporary motel. All rooms provide cable
color TVs, direct-dial telephones, private bathrooms with amenities, telephones, and hair

The Middlebury Inn

dryers. Fine dining, afternoon tea, Sunday
brunch, special packages. Gift shop. AAA
three-diamond-rated. Member of Historic
Hotels of America. Inquire about accommodations for pets. Smoking permitted in designated
areas only.

Hosts: Frank and Jane Emanuel
Rooms: 75 (PB) $80-260
Continental Breakfast
Credit Cards: A, B, C, D, E
Notes: 2, 3, 4, 5, 6, 7, 8, 9, 10, 11, 12, 13, 14, 15

MIDDLETOWN SPRINGS

American Country Collection

1353 Union Street, Schenectady, NY 12308
(518) 370-4948; (800) 810-4948
FAX (518) 393-1634 (call first)
e-mail: carolbnbres@mon.com
www.bandbreservations.com

147. There is a treat waiting for guests as they
step back 100 years in time to an age of elegance in this rural New England village. Listed
in the National Register of Historic Places, this
historic home is filled with antiques and a large
music box collection. Near Lake St. Catherine
for boating and picnicking. Fishermen will
love the trout that can be caught in a stream
bordering the property. Six guest rooms are
available, all with private baths and a full
breakfast. Dinner available nightly. $78-85.

NOTES: Credit cards accepted: A MasterCard; B Visa; C American Express; D Discover; E Diner's Club;
F Other; 2 Personal checks accepted; 3 Lunch available; 4 Dinner available; 5 Open all year; 6 Pets welcome;

MONTGOMERY CENTER

The Inn on Trout River

P.O. Box 76, The Main Street, 05471
(802) 326-4391; (800) 338-7049
FAX (802) 326-3194; e-mail: info@troutinn.com
www.troutinn.com

Surrounded by magnificent mountain ranges in a quaint Currier and Ives-style village, this 100-year-old country Victorian inn features private baths, queen-size beds, down comforters, feather pillows, flannel sheets, cozy fireplaces, antiques, gourmet restaurant, a pub, and game room. Close to summer and winter sports, covered bridges, and shopping. A full menu at breakfast is always included. AAA three-diamond historic country inn and AAA three-diamond restaurant.

Hosts: Michael and Lee Forman
Rooms: 10 (PB) $86-112
Full Breakfast
Credit Cards: A, B, C, D
Notes: 4, 5, 7, 8, 9, 10, 11, 12, 13, 14

The Inn on Trout River

Phineas Swann Bed & Breakfast

The Main Street, P.O. Box 43, 05471
(802) 326-4306

Phineas Swann is a classic intimate Vermont country bed and breakfast. Written about recently in *Country Living* magazine, the *Boston Phoenix*, and *Out* magazine. The main house is a 100-year-old gingerbread Victorian with hardwood floors, two fireplaces, and

canopied and carved-wood beds. The Carriage House suites have upscale accommodations with in-room Jacuzzis, fireplaces, and queen-size beds. The inn is at the base of Jay Peak Ski resort and one mile from world-class cross-country skiing; rentals available.

Hosts: Michael Bindler and Glen Bartolomeo
Rooms: 4 (2 PB; 2 SB) $69-89
Suites: 2 (PB) $125-145
Full Breakfast
Credit Cards: A, B, D
Notes: 2, 5, 7, 8, 9, 10, 11, 12, 13, 14

MONTPELIER

Betsy's Bed & Breakfast

74 East State Street, 05602
(802) 229-0466; FAX (802) 229-5412
e-mail: betsybb@together.net
www.central-vt.com/business/betsybb

Betsy's Bed and Breakfast is a warm and inviting Queen Anne home in the nation's smallest capital. The rooms are furnished with period antiques. Guests are invited to linger over a cup of coffee in the sun-filled dining room, chat with the owners by a crackling fire in the formal parlor, lift weights or cycle in the exercise room, rock on the front porch, or hide away in their room and enjoy the peace and quiet.

Hosts: Jon and Betsy Anderson
Rooms: 12 (PB) $55-125
Full Breakfast
Credit Cards: A, B, C, D
Notes: 2, 5, 7, 8, 9, 11, 12, 13, 14

MORGAN

Hunts Hideaway

236 Coche Brook Crossing
West Charleston, 05872
(802) 895-4432; (802) 334-8322

7 No smoking; 8 Children welcome; 9 Social drinking allowed; 10 Tennis nearby; 11 Swimming nearby; 12 Golf nearby; 13 Skiing nearby; 14 May be booked through a travel agent; 15 Handicapped accessible.

Contemporary split-level on 100 acres: brook, pond, and a 44-foot in-ground pool. In Morgan, six miles from I-91, near the Canadian border. Guests may use kitchen and laundry facilities. Lake Seymour is two miles away; 18-hole golf courses at Newport and Orleans; bicycling, jogging, skiing at Jay Peak and Burke Mountain, antiquing, bird watching, and fishing.

Host: Pat Hunt
Rooms: 3 (SB) $40
Full Breakfast
Credit Cards: None
Notes: 2, 5, 6, 8, 9, 11, 12, 13

MOUNT SNOW VALLEY

Snow Goose Inn

Route 100, P.O. Box 366, West Dover, 05356
(802) 464-3984; (888) 604-7964
FAX (802) 464-5322; e-mail: gooseinn@aol.com
www.snowgooseinn.com

Three acres of Vermont wooded countryside create a cozy, secluded setting. Each room is appointed with period antique furniture, private bath, cable TV, and plush featherbeds. Many of the rooms also have wood-burning fireplaces, two-person Jacuzzis, and private decks. In the evening, complimentary wine and hors d'oeuvres are served in front of a fireplace or on one of the many porches overlooking the perennial gardens. Close to skiing, hiking, and boating.

Hosts: Eric and Karen Falberg
Rooms: 12 (PB) $95-300
Full Breakfast
Credit Cards: A, B, C, E
Notes: 2, 5, 6, 7, 8, 9, 10, 11, 12, 13, 15

NEWBURY

Peach Brook Inn Bed & Breakfast

Doe Hill, 05051
(802) 866-3389

A 1780s manse on a country lane just off Route 5 overlooking the Connecticut River and Valley

viewing fields, farms, village, and majestic mountains. Plenty of farm animals and places to walk. Breakfast on the veranda to enjoy the view. French toast or pancakes with Vermont maple syrup. Children over 10 welcome. Cross-country skiing nearby.

Hosts: Joyce and Raoul Emery
Rooms: 3 (1 PB; 2 SB) $50-70
Full Breakfast
Credit Cards: None
Notes: 2, 5, 7, 9, 10, 11, 12, 13

NEWFANE

West River Lodge & Stables

117 Hill Road, 05345
(802) 365-7745; www.westriverlodge.com

Established in 1930, the West River Lodge, a charming country farmhouse, has been noted for its warm informal comforts and hearty breakfasts. Surrounded by wooded hills and rivers, guests can explore countryside by horseback, hiking, cycling, fishing, swimming, or canoeing. Simply relax with a book on our lovely front porch or wander through the abundant antique shops, enjoy the seasonal festivals, brilliant foliage, and all winter festivities, including horse-drawn sleigh rides and nearby skiing. Newly renovated stables are available for full boarding facilities and overnight horse lodging year round. Riding ring and trails. Lodge is open for small dinner parties, receptions, and family reunions. Children seven and older welcome.

Hosts: Ellen and Jim
Rooms: 8 (2 PB; 6 SB) $85-95
Full Breakfast
Credit Cards: A, B
Notes: 2, 5, 7, 10, 11, 12, 13

NOTES: Credit cards accepted: A MasterCard; B Visa; C American Express; D Discover; E Diner's Club; F Other; 2 Personal checks accepted; 3 Lunch available; 4 Dinner available; 5 Open all year; 6 Pets welcome;

NORTHFIELD

Northfield Inn

228 Highland Avenue, 05663
(802) 485-8558

Turn-of-the-century mansion, restored to its original Victorian elegance with magnificent panoramic views of the Green Mountains and the Northfield Valley. Graceful porches, gardens, gentle breezes, golden sunsets, romantic ambiance. Rated three-diamond by AAA, three-star by Mobil, and three-crown by ABBA. Dinner available for groups only.

Host: Aglaia Stalb
Rooms: 8 (PB) $85-130
Full Breakfast
Credit Cards: A, B
Notes: 2, 5, 7, 9, 10, 11, 12, 13, 14

Northfield Inn

NORTH HERO

The North Hero House

P.O. Box 155, Route 2, 05474
(802) 372-4732; 372-4735; (888) 525-3644
FAX (802) 372-3218; e-mail: Nhhlake@aol.com
www.northherohouse.com

Whether guests are drawn to the Lake Champlain islands of Northern Vermont by the wide-open vistas or the calming sound of water lapping at the shore's edge, the North Hero House will warmly welcome them into the heart of the nation's "Sixth Great Lake." The main inn, built in 1891, first provided a retreat for guests arriving by steamship. Guests are enchanted with the beautifully restored buildings, antiques, and collectibles, yet equally pleased to find all the modern conveniences

they expect while traveling. The area's quiet rural charm, waterside farms, orchards, and sandy beaches are complemented by festivals, craft fairs, historical day trips, and plenty of outdoor activities to keep guests busy exploring the string of islands.

Host: Walter Blasberg (owner)
Rooms: 26 (PB) $89-249
Full Breakfast
Credit Cards: A, B, C
Notes: 2, 4, 5, 7, 8, 9, 10, 11, 12, 13, 14, 15

NORTH HERO ISLAND

Charlie's Northland Lodge

3829 US Route 2, 05474-9713
(802) 372-8822

Early 1800s guest house in a quiet village setting on North Hero Island in Lake Champlain. Two guest rooms furnished with country antiques share a modern bath, private entrance, and living room. A place to fish, sail, canoe, kayak, bike, or just plain relax. In winter, guests may ice fish and cross-country ski. Guest cottages available upon request.

Hosts: Dorice and Charlie Clark
Rooms: 2 (SB) $60-65
Continental Breakfast
Credit Cards: A, B
Notes: 2, 5, 9, 10, 11, 12, 13, 14

ORWELL

Historic Brookside Farms— A Four Season Country Inn

Route 22A, 05760
(802) 948-2727; FAX (802) 948-2800

This 1789-1843 historic register Greek Revival mansion is on 300 acres. All rooms are furnished in period antiques. Enjoy a full country breakfast, afternoon tea, and romantic candlelit gourmet dinner. Cross-country ski on miles of trails through 78 acres of magnificent forest. Hiking, lawn games, boating, and fishing on a 20-acre lake. There is a lovely antique

7 No smoking; 8 Children welcome; 9 Social drinking allowed; 10 Tennis nearby; 11 Swimming nearby; 12 Golf nearby; 13 Skiing nearby; 14 May be booked through a travel agent; 15 Handicapped accessible.

shop on the premises. Family-owned and - operated. Smoking permitted in designated areas only. Suite and all common rooms are handicapped accessible.

Rooms: 7 (4 PB; 3 SB) $85-165
Full Breakfast
Credit Cards: None
Notes: 2, 3, 4, 5, 8, 9, 10, 11, 12, 13, 14, 15

PERU

Johnny Seesaw's

P.O. Box 68, Route 11, 05152
(802) 824-5533 (phone/FAX)
e-mail: gary@jseesaw.com

Elegantly rustic log lodge offering private guest rooms, family suites, and two-bedroom cabins with living room and fireplace. Magnificent country cuisine and wine list. On Bromley Mountain, 400 yards from lifts, and minutes to Stratton Mountain and cross-country skiing. Red clay tennis court and Olympic-size pool on premises. Pets selectively permitted.

Hosts: Gary and Nancy Okun
Rooms: 21 (PB) $76-190
Full Breakfast
Credit Cards: A, B, D
Notes: 2, 4, 6, 8, 9, 10, 11, 12, 13, 14

PITTSFIELD

Swiss Farm Inn

Route 100, P.O. Box 510, 05762
(802) 746-8341; (800) 245-5126
www.swissfarminn.com

A family tradition for 50 years now. Roger and Joyce Stevens make guests feel right at home from the minute of arrival. Breakfast and dinner are prepared and served by the hosts and promise to be a true homemade country delight. Twelve miles from Killington ski resort. Biking, hiking, snowmobiling, horseback riding, golf, tennis, and great swimming. Children are always welcome. Having lived in the Caribbean for some time, the Stevens family creates a warm blend of Caribbean and country life.

Hosts: Roger and Joyce Stevens
Rooms: 17 (14 PB; 3 SB) $50-60
Full Breakfast
Credit Cards: A, B
Notes: 2, 4, 5, 8, 9, 10, 11, 12, 13, 14

POULTNEY

Elaine's Bed & Breakfast Selections

4987 Kingston Road, Elbridge NY, 13060
(315) 689-2082 (call between 10:30 A.M.–7:00 P.M.)

This homey Victorian bed and breakfast is very close to Poultney which is the home of Green Mountain College. The guest rooms are sizable with two having private baths and two sharing a bath. Guests will enjoy the fireplace lounge and the piano parlor. Outdoor hot tub. Picnic lunches can be prepared at a fee with advance notice. Bikes and boats may be rented nearby. No smoking. Allergy-free home. Ten dollars for each additional person. Hostess will cater dessert for special occasions or hold barbeque cookout if requested. $70-80.

Tower Hall Bed & Breakfast

399 Bentley Avenue, 05764-1176
(800) 894-4004; e-mail: towerhal@sover.net
www.sover.net/~towerhal

An 1890s Queen Anne Victorian with three-story tower, wraparound porch, and westerly views of mountains and meadows. Adjacent to Green Mountain College in the village. Only five miles to lakes with sailboat and motorboat availability. Thirty miles to skiing or shopping. Hiking, biking, snowmobiling, and cross-country skiing from the house. Tennis across the street. Piano parlour, fireplace lounge, and TV room in common areas. Bountiful breakfast in sunny dining room. Children and well-behaved dogs welcome. First-floor room available for people with disabilities. Extended capacity for larger groups of 20-24 people.

NOTES: Credit cards accepted: A MasterCard; B Visa; C American Express; D Discover; E Diner's Club; F Other; 2 Personal checks accepted; 3 Lunch available; 4 Dinner available; 5 Open all year; 6 Pets welcome;

Host: Pat Perrine
Rooms: 4 (2 PB; 2 SB) $65-85
Continental Breakfast
Credit Cards: D
Notes: 2, 5, 7, 8, 10, 11, 12, 13, 14

PROCTORSVILLE

Golden Stage Inn

399 Depot Street, 05153
(802) 226-7744; (800) 253-8226
TTY (802) 226-7136; FAX (802) 226-7882
e-mail:gldstgin@ludl.tds.net

History galore: 1700s stagecoach stop; Underground Railroad safe house; Otis Skinner family residence. Full breakfasts and five-course gourmet dinners (optional) often feature inn's own harvest. Homemade breads a specialty. Large, sunny rooms reflect traditions of warm hospitality. Abundant fishing in nearby lakes and rivers. "You catch and clean 'em, we cook 'em (or freeze 'em) for you." Swimming pool. Bicycles available for leisurely exploring. Modified American plan available.

Hosts: Micki and Paul
Rooms: 8 (PB) $99-218
Suite: 1
Full Breakfast
Credit Cards: A, B, D
Notes: 2, 4, 5, 7, 8, 9, 11, 12, 13, 14, 15

Whitney Brook Bed & Breakfast

2423 Twenty Mile Stream Road, 05153
(802) 226-7460; whitney_brook@yahoo.com

An 1870 Vermont farmhouse, Whitney Brook Bed and Breakfast sits on a private and quiet 10 acres with stone walls, streams, meadows, and woods. The house has been renovated to provide a comfortable home atmosphere, while maintaining the old farmhouse charm. A large living room with fireplace and an upstairs sitting area with a selection of games are available for guests. Nearby are antique and specialty shops such as the well-known Vermont Country Store. For the sports-minded, our area provides

downhill (Okemo) and cross-country skiing within 10 minutes and great hiking, biking, golfing, fishing, and horseback riding. The picnic table and adirondack chairs are always ready for a pleasant afternoon of reading.

Hosts: Jim and Ellen Parrish
Rooms: 4 (2 PB; 2 SB) $55-95
Full Breakfast
Credit Cards A, B, C, D
Notes: 2, 5, 7, 9, 10, 11, 12, 13

PUTNEY

Hickory Ridge House Bed & Breakfast

Rural Delivery 3, Box 1410, 05346
(802) 387-5709; (800) 380-9218
FAX (802) 387-4328

Gracious 1808 Federal manor on eight beautiful acres in country setting. Large guest rooms with fireplaces, high ceilings, private baths, air conditioning, TV/VCRs, telephones, and robes. Full breakfast served. Great restaurants and shopping nearby. Hiking, biking, swimming, and cross-country skiing nearby. Theater and art galleries abound.

Hosts: Linda and Jack Bisbee
Rooms: 8 (PB) $105-145
Full Breakfast
Credit Cards: A, B, C
Notes: 2, 5, 7, 9, 10, 11, 12, 13, 14, 15

Hickory Ridge House

7 No smoking; 8 Children welcome; 9 Social drinking allowed; 10 Tennis nearby; 11 Swimming nearby; 12 Golf nearby; 13 Skiing nearby; 14 May be booked through a travel agent; 15 Handicapped accessible.

The Putney Inn

The Putney Inn

P.O. Box 181, 05346
(800) 653-5517; FAX (802) 387-5211
e-mail: putneyin@sover.net
www.Putneyinn.com

In the heart of southern Vermont. Nationally acclaimed cuisine. Concerts, theater, meandering strolls, and artisan studios. Voted area's best in lodging and dining. Small inn charm with the luxury of privacy. Incredible food; gracious friendliness. Chef Ann Cooper offers locally farmed New England fare, from wholesomely simple to extravagantly delightful. So bring bikes, canoes, hiking boots. Come to play or to just enjoy exquisite food and quietude.

Host: Randi Ziter
Rooms: 25 (PB) $68-148
Full Breakfast
Credit Cards: A, B, C, D
Notes: 2, 3, 4, 5, 6, 8, 9, 10, 11, 12, 13, 14, 15

RIPTON

The Chipman Inn

Route 125, 05766
(802) 388-2390; (800) 890-2390
e-mail: smudge@together.net

A traditional Vermont inn built in 1828 in the Green Mountain National Forest. Fine food, wine, and spirits for guests. Eight rooms, all with private baths. Fully licensed bar and large fireplace. Closed November 15 to December 26 and April 1 to May 15. Children over 12 welcome.

Hosts: Joyce Henderson and Bill Pierce
Rooms: 8 (PB) $85-115

Full Breakfast
Credit Cards: A, B, C, D
Notes: 2, 4, 9, 11, 12, 13

ROCHESTER

The New Homestead

Route 100, 05767-0025
(802) 767-4751

Just a small village on a blue highway in a narrow winding valley of the Green Mountains. Delightfully seedy gardens surround the house. Hens cluck contentedly in the barn, providing the basis for memorable breakfasts. "We keep our price low to attract people like us." Sandy also practices law. David dabbles in domestic art/architecture. Ike and Tina are resident cats.

Hosts: Sandra Haas and David Marmor
Rooms: 5 (3 PB; 2 SB) $40
Full Breakfast
Credit Cards: None
Notes: 2, 5, 7, 8, 9, 10, 11, 12, 13

The New Homestead

NOTES: Credit cards accepted: A MasterCard; B Visa; C American Express; D Discover; E Diner's Club; F Other; 2 Personal checks accepted; 3 Lunch available; 4 Dinner available; 5 Open all year; 6 Pets welcome;

ROYALTON

Fox Stand Inn

Route 14, 05068
(802) 763-8437

Built in 1818 as a stagecoach stop on the banks of the White River. The dining room and tavern are open to the public and offer international creations. The inn's second floor has five comfortably furnished guest rooms. In the center of one of Vermont's acclaimed recreational regions. Swimming, canoeing, tubing, bicycling, hiking, and fishing are readily at hand. Antique shops, auctions, flea markets, and horse shows are found throughout the countryside.

Hosts: Jean and Gary Curley
Rooms: 5 (SB) $50-75
Full Breakfast
Credit Cards: A, B
Notes: 2, 4, 5, 7, 9, 10, 11, 12, 13

Fox Stand Inn

RUTLAND

Elaine's Bed & Breakfast Selections

4987 Kingston Road, Elbridge, NY 13060
(315) 689-2082 (call between 10:30 A.M.–7:00 P.M.)

A truly unique stay! Full breakfast in formal dining room consists of many different entrées. A first-floor suite has a canopied bed, a living room, and a large private bath with a whirlpool. Upstairs are two more guest rooms that share a bath. Another apartment is in a separate building. There is a billiard table and a Ping-Pong table in the basement, and a clay tennis court in the back yard. Open year-round. No smoking. Twelve dollars each additional person in a room. $90-100.

The Inn at Rutland

The Inn at Rutland

70 North Main Street, Route 7, 05701
(802) 773-0575; (800) 808-0575

The Inn at Rutland is an 1890s Victorian mansion restored to its original condition. Guest rooms have been tastefully decorated to re-create the past while maintaining modern comforts. All rooms have private bathrooms, telephones, and cable TVs, with some rooms having air conditioning and VCRs. A large breakfast is served. The common rooms offer a comfortable atmosphere for conversation, reading by the fireplace, or just relaxing. Carriage house for ski or bike storage, with some mountain bikes available for guests. AAA-, Mobil-, ABBA-rated.

Hosts: Bob and Tanya Liberman
Rooms: 12 (PB) $65-195
Full Breakfast
Credit Cards: A, B, C, D, E
Notes: 5, 7, 8, 9, 10, 11, 12, 13, 14

7 No smoking; 8 Children welcome; 9 Social drinking allowed; 10 Tennis nearby; 11 Swimming nearby; 12 Golf nearby; 13 Skiing nearby; 14 May be booked through a travel agent; 15 Handicapped accessible.

ST. JOHNSBURY

Bed & Breakfast Reservations North Shore, Greater Boston, and Cape Cod

P.O. Box 600035, Newtonville, MA 02460
(617) 964-1606; (800) 832-2632
FAX (617) 332-8572; e-mail: info@bbreserve.com
www.bbreserve.com

156. The Nichols House. Restored 1846 Federal-style farmhouse sits in a secluded setting in Victorian-era town, known as the "Capital" of Vermont's Northeast Kingdom. On the first floor, there is a suite with private bath and sitting area. The second floor has rooms with shared bath and large den with TV and VCR. Just 10 minutes away from Peacham, the most photographed town in the United States, 45 minutes from Franconia Notch and White Mountains, 20 minutes away is Burke Mountain Ski Resort for both downhill and cross-country. Forty miles away, is the Canadian border. Within walking distance is downtown St. Johnsbury with its world-renown athenaeum/art gallery, museums, planetarium, shopping and fine dining. Full breakfast and afternoon tea. No smoking. Closed in April. Children welcome. $70-85.

SHREWSBURY

The Buckmaster Inn

Rural Route 1, Box 118, Lincoln Hill Road, 05738
(802) 492-3720; e-mail: buckinn@sover.net

A beautiful country inn circa 1801 is listed in the National Register of Historic Homes. Shrewsbury is a picturesque, quiet community, wonderful for hiking, biking, cross-country skiing, or simply relaxing. Four guest rooms with shared baths. The decor is New England country flare and comfortable for resting after a long day in the fresh air. Fireside breakfast dining or breakfast served on a very large screened-in porch during the warmer months. A friendly and hospitable inn and guests are made to feel as though they are at a home away from home. Centrally positioned on the backside of Killington Mountain between Rutland and Ludlow, Vermont. Accessible by major roads and highways. Children over eight welcome.

Hosts: Elizabeth and Richard Davis
Rooms: 4 (2 PB; 2 SB) $89
Full Breakfast
Credit Cards: none (MC and Visa coming soon)
Notes: 2, 5, 7, 8, 9, 10, 11, 12, 13, 14

SOUTH LONDONDERRY

The Londonderry Inn

P.O. Box 301-70, 05155-0301
(802) 824-5226; FAX (802) 824-3146
e-mail: londinn@sover.net
www.londonderryinn.com

An 1826 homestead that has been welcoming guests for 50 years overlooks the West River and the quiet village of South Londonderry in the Green Mountains of southern Vermont. Special family accommodations. Living room with huge fireplace; billiard and Ping-Pong rooms. Dinner available on weekends and holidays.

Hosts: Jean and Jim Cavanagh
Rooms: 25 (20 PB; 5 SB) $41-116
Full Breakfast
Credit Cards: None
Notes: 2, 5, 8, 10, 11, 12, 13, 14

The Londonderry Inn

SOUTH NEWFANE

The Inn at South Newfane

The Inn at South Newfane

369 Dover Road, 05351-7901
(802) 348-7191; e-mail: cullinn@sover.net
www.innatsouthnewfane.com

A charming turn-of-the-century country inn provides elegant relaxation, international cuisine, and warm hospitality. The incredible beauty and serenity of the more than 100 private acres surrounding the inn are ideal for any occasion. Three fireplaces. Guest rooms are delightfully distinctive—each with a private bath. Lunch (seasonal) and dinner served. Fully licensed bar. Antique and specialty shops. Many winter sports and other activities nearby. Children over 10 welcome.

Hosts: Neville and Dawn Cullen
Rooms: 6 (PB) $95-130
Full Breakfast
Credit Cards: A, B, C, D
Notes: 4, 5, 7, 11, 12, 13, 14

Rock River Bed & Breakfast

408 Dover Road, 05351
(802) 348-6301; e-mail: chrsptrk@sover.net
www.sover.net/~chrsptrk

A quiet retreat from the busy-ness of life. Set in the peaceful green hills of southeastern Vermont, the old home, circa 1795, has unique rooms, the collected antiques and art of three generations, and a family atmosphere. These combine to provide a warm and restful setting where guests can relax and rejuvenate, and then venture forth to experience the rich opportunities of the area.

Rooms: 3 (2 PB; 1 SB) $65-95
Full Breakfast
Notes: 2, 5, 7, 11, 12, 13

SPRINGFIELD

Hartness House

30 Orchard Street, 05156
(802) 885-2115; (800) 732-4789
www.hartnesshouse.com

This beautiful 1903 inn is listed in the National Register of Historic Places. Once the home of Gov. James Hartness, this inn invites guests to step back in time to a setting of gracious living, with carved beams, majestic fireplaces, and a grand staircase leading up to 11 beautifully decorated rooms. Guests may also choose from 29 modern rooms in the annex. Enjoy swimming, gracious poolside dining, and unique features: a 1910 tracking telescope and a small underground museum reached via a 240-foot tunnel. Lunch available Monday through Friday. Dinner available Monday through Saturday. Smoking permitted in designated areas only. Dining room is handicapped accessible.

Hosts: The Blair Family
Rooms: 40 (PB) $80-130
Full Breakfast
Credit Cards: A, B, C, D, E
Notes: 2, 3, 4, 5, 8, 9, 10, 12, 13, 14, 15

Hartness House

---

7 No smoking; 8 Children welcome; 9 Social drinking allowed; 10 Tennis nearby; 11 Swimming nearby; 12 Golf nearby; 13 Skiing nearby; 14 May be booked through a travel agent; 15 Handicapped accessible.

STOWE

Andersen Lodge— an Austrian Inn

3430 Mountain Road, 05672
(802) 253-7336; (800) 336-7336

A small Tyrolean inn ideal for the gourmet who appreciates European delights. Open grounds with swimming pool and tennis courts. Exercise room with Jacuzzi and sauna, recreation path. Open seasonally. Some rooms are nonsmoking.

Hosts: Dietmar and Gertrude Heiss
Rooms: 18 (PB) $68-120
Full Breakfast
Credit Cards: A, B, C, D
Notes: 2, 4, 5, 6, 8, 9, 10, 11, 12, 13, 14, 15

Brass Lantern Inn

717 Maple Street, 05672
(802) 253-2229; (800) 729-2980
FAX (802) 753-7425; e-mail: brasslntrn@aol.com
www.brasslanterninn.com

A traditional Vermont bed and breakfast inn in the heart of Stowe. Award-winning restoration of an 1810 farmhouse and carriage barn overlooking Mount Mansfield, Vermont's most prominent mountain. The inn features period antiques, air conditioning, handmade quilts, and planked floors. Some rooms have whirlpools and/or fireplaces and most have views. Award-winning breakfast. An intimate spot for house guests only. AAA three-diamond inn. Special packages include honeymoon, adventure, skiing, golf, air travel, sleigh and surrey rides, and more.

Host: Andy Aldrich
Rooms: 9 (PB) $80-225
Full Breakfast
Credit Cards: A, B, C
Notes: 2, 5, 7, 9, 10, 11, 12, 13, 14

Fitch Hill Inn

258 Fitch Hill Road, Hyde Park, 05655
(802) 888-3834; (800) 639-2903
FAX (802) 888-7789; e-mail: fitchinn@aol.com
www.stoweinfo.com/sea/fitchhill

Friendly affordable elegance on a hilltop overlooking Vermont's highest mountains in the beautiful Lamoille River Valley. Ten miles north of Stowe, the historic Fitch Hill Inn, circa 1797, offers four guest rooms and two suites. There are three common living room areas and more than 300 video movies for guests to enjoy. Three porches offer spectacular views; rest and relax in the beautiful gardens. A full gourmet breakfast is served, and candlelit four-course dinners are available by reservation for six or more. Packages available. Seasonal rates. Minimum stays for holidays and most weekends. Some rooms have fireplaces, hot tub, and Jacuzzis.

Hosts: Richard A. Pugliese and Stanley E. Corklin
Rooms: 4 (PB) $85-135
Suites: 2 (PB) $145-189
Full Breakfast
Credit Cards: A, B, C, D
Notes: 2, 3, 4, 5, 7, 9, 10, 11, 12, 13, 14

Honeywood Inn

4583 Mountain Road, 05672
(802) 253-4846; (800) 659-6289

Welcome to this cozy inn. Eight large double rooms each unique all with private bath and two suites with fireplace and Jacuzzi. Large guest living room with fireplace and separate TV. Room with satellite TV. Outdoor Jacuzzi, babbling brook, walking trails, small waterfall, and two outdoor pools (in the summer only). Cross-country ski from front door. Close to hiking, biking, downhill skiing, Full gourmet breakfast and afternoon refreshments. Midweek special stay, five-pay-four, Sunday arrival only. Not valid during peak periods and some restrictions could apply.

Hosts: Christel and Jim Horman
Rooms: 8 (PB) $79-119
Suites: 2 $129-199
Full Breakfast
Credit Cards: A, B, C, D
Notes: 4, 5, 7, 9, 10, 11, 12, 13, 14

Nichols Lodge

P.O. Box 1028, 05672
(802) 253-7683

Rustic farmhouse inn with assortment of rooms—dormitory. Rooms with baths in hall, connecting and private. Some with air conditioning. Fireplaced lounge and recreation room. Continental breakfast available during winter months. Walks through campground and uphill. Bike path one and one-half miles away, accessible from lodge. Brochure available. Swimming pool on premises.

Host: Kathryn K. Nichols
Rooms: 12 (2 PB; 8 SB) $16-62
Credit Cards: A, B, C
Notes: 2, 5, 6, 8, 10, 11, 12, 13, 14

Stowe Inn at Little River

123 Mountain Road, 05672
(802) 253-4836; (800) 227-1108
FAX (802) 253-7308; e-mail: info@stoweinn.com
www.stoweinn.com

Stowe Inn at Little River

A beautifully restored, 1825 Stowe village inn, just a moment's walk from Main Street. The skiing and summer sports for which Stowe is so famous are on the Mountain Road, right outside the door. Antique sitting rooms, a superb bar, window-walled restaurant, and riverside patio together with hot tub and and heated pool. Fifty-one bedrooms include traditional country and modern deluxe with bathroom, cable TV, and air conditioning.

Host: Miranda Batiste
Rooms: 57 (PB) $65-240
Continental Breakfast
Credit Cards: A, B, C
Notes: 2, 3, 4, 5, 7, 8, 9, 10, 11, 12, 13, 14, 15

WalkAbout Creek Lodge

199 Edson Hill Road, 05672
(802) 253-7354; (800) 426-6697
FAX (802) 253-8429; e-mail: walkcreek@aol.com
www.walkaboutcreeklodge.com

Experience the authenticity of a classic mountain lodge and retreat to this secluded haven. WalkAbout Creek Lodge is nestled on five wooded acres beside a flowing mountainside creek and is a true historic gem, one of the oldest of its kind. Solidly built of hewn logs and fieldstone, this is the perfect place to relax with friends and family. Guests can look forward to the fieldstone fireplaces, expansive living areas, individually furnished rooms, outdoor hot tub, swimming pool, rustic Billabong Pub, hearty breakfasts, and on-site access to unlimited trails, for the hiker, biker, and cross-country skier alike. Let this season be yours to discover WalkAbout Creek Lodge, for it is a winter wonderland, a fall spectacular, and a summer haven, with all the attractions and activities of Stowe close at hand.

Hosts: Joni and Crew
Rooms: 17 (PB) $90-150
Full Breakfast
Credit Cards: A, B, C
Notes: 5, 6, 8, 13,

7 No smoking; 8 Children welcome; 9 Social drinking allowed; 10 Tennis nearby; 11 Swimming nearby; 12 Golf nearby; 13 Skiing nearby; 14 May be booked through a travel agent; 15 Handicapped accessible.

WAITSFIELD

Elaine's Bed & Breakfast Selections

4987 Kingston Road, Elbridge, NY 13060
(315) 689-2082 (call between 10:30 A.M.–7:00 P.M.)

This elegant yet comfortable rural house was originally built in 1824 and added onto over the years. There are eight guest rooms, all with modern, private baths. Full breakfasts. Large outdoor hot tub. Mad River is just across the road for fishing and swimming. Sugar Bush ski area is just a few minutes drive. Dinners available by prior arrangement for a few or a larger group. The two dining rooms can seat 22 people. Nonsmoking. Children over 10 welcome. No guest pets. Two resident dogs and a cat. The inn also hosts special holiday celebrations on Christmas, New Years, and Thanksgiving.

Hyde Away Inn

Route 17, Rural Route 1, Box 65, 05673
(802) 496-2322; (800) 777-HYDE
e-mail: hydeaway@madriver.com

A comfortable, casual, circa 1820 inn less than five minutes from Sugarbush and Mad River Glen ski areas, hiking and biking trails, and historic Waitsfield Village. Twelve rooms, common area with TV, children's toy area. Unpretentious and friendly atmosphere. Hearty breakfast each morning. Public restaurant with outstanding, affordable American cuisine. Rustic tavern with pub fare and summer deck dining. Some rooms where pets may be allowed. Smoking permitted in designated areas only.

Hosts: Bruce and Margaret
Rooms: 12 (4 PB; 8 SB) $49-89
Full Breakfast
Credit Cards: A, B, C
Notes: 4, 5, 8, 9, 10, 11, 12, 13, 14

Inn at Mad River Barn

Box 88, Route 17, 05673
(802) 496-3310
e-mail: MadRiverBarn@MadRiver.com
www.MadRiverBarn.com

The Inn at Mad River Barn preserves the rich, warm atmosphere of a 1940s traditional ski lodge in a mountain setting. The barn houses a large game room, a lounge with a fireplace and full bar, a restaurant, and many comfortable, deep chairs. The pine-paneled guest rooms are usually large and nicely furnished. The beds have quilts made by the hostess. The Annex is a small farmhouse dating from 1820. It has been remodeled to provide deluxe rooms, each with a sauna, TV, and kitchenette. Up the road is Mad River Glen, a favorite spot for cross-country and downhill skiers. Other year-round activities include local theatre, horseback riding, and gliding. Fifty years in business.

Host: Betsy Pratt
Rooms: 15 (PB) seasonal
Full Breakfast
Credit Cards: A, B, C, D
Notes: 2, 4, 5, 8, 10, 11, 12, 13, 14

Lareau Farm Country Inn

Box 563, Route 100, 05673
(802) 496-4949

In an open meadow near the Mad River, this 1832 Greek Revival farmhouse is only minutes from skiing, shopping, dining, soaring, and golf. Sleigh rides, cross-country skiing, and swimming on the premises. When guests come, they feel at home and relaxed. Hospitality is the inn's specialty. "One of the top 50 inns in America"—*Inn Times.*

Hosts: Susan Easley
Rooms: 13 (11 PB; 2 SB) $60-125
Full Breakfast
Credit Cards: A, B
Notes: 2, 5, 7, 8, 10, 11, 12, 13, 14

The Mad River Inn
Bed & Breakfast

Tremblay Road, P.O. Box 75, 05673
(802) 496-7900; (800) TEA-TART

A romantic 1860s country Victorian inn nestled alongside the Mad River with picturesque mountain views. Ten unique guest rooms with feather beds and private baths. Gourmet breakfast and afternoon tea included daily. Porches, gardens, gazebo, Jacuzzi, and swimming hole. Fireplace, library, BYOB lounge. Catered weddings. Midweek specials. Families and groups welcome. Walk to new recreation path.

Hosts: Luc and Rita Maranda
Rooms: 9 (PB) $59-125
Full Breakfast
Credit Cards: A, B, C
Notes: 2, 5, 7, 8, 9, 10, 11, 12, 13, 14

Millbrook Inn

Route 17, 533 McCullough Highway, 05673
(802) 496-2405; (800) 477-2809
FAX (802) 496-9735; e-mail: millbrkinn@aol.com
www.millbrookinn.com

Relax in the friendly, unhurried atmosphere of this cozy 1850s inn. Seven guest rooms are decorated with hand stenciling, antique bedsteads, and handmade quilts. Breakfast and dinner included in the daily rate. Dine in the romantic small restaurant that features hand-rolled pasta, fresh fish, veal, shrimp, and homemade desserts from a varied menu. Bed and breakfast rates are available during the summer only, Modified American Plan during winter and fall. Two-day minimum stay required for weekends, three-nights for holidays. Closed from April 1 to June 15 and October 20 to mid-December. Also available is the newly renovated, two-bedroom, two-bathroom Octagon House. Inquire about accommodations for pets. Children over six are welcome.

Hosts: Joan and Thom Gorman
Rooms: 7 (PB) $78-140
Credit Cards: A, B, C
Notes: 2, 4, 7, 9, 10, 11, 12, 13

Mountain View Inn

Mountain View Inn

1912 McCullough Highway, Fayston, 05673
(802) 496-2426

This small country inn (circa 1826) has seven guest rooms, each with private bath, accommodating two people. The rooms are decorated with stenciling, quilts, braided rugs, and antique furniture. Meals are served family-style around an antique harvest table. Good fellowship is enjoyed around the wood-burning fireplace in the living room. Two-night minimum stay required on weekends.

Hosts: Fred and Susan Spencer
Rooms: 7 (PB) $100-120
Full Breakfast
Credit Cards: None
Notes: 2, 5, 7, 8, 9, 10, 11, 12, 13, 14

The Waitsfield Inn

Route 100, Box 969, 05673
(802) 496-3979; (800) 758-3801
FAX (802) 496-3970
e-mail: waitsfieldinn@madriver.com
www.waitsfieldinn.com

This gracious 1820s restored Colonial inn is in the heart of the beautiful Mad River Valley. The inn, just minutes from Sugarbush, is convenient to spectacular skiing and wonderful hiking, shopping, antiquing, and much more. Relax in one of the 14 rooms, all of which are beautifully appointed with antiques, quilts, and private baths. Enjoy a delicious full breakfast

7 No smoking; 8 Children welcome; 9 Social drinking allowed; 10 Tennis nearby; 11 Swimming nearby; 12 Golf nearby; 13 Skiing nearby; 14 May be booked through a travel agent; 15 Handicapped accessible.

and let the "innspired" hosts make every stay a memorable one.

Hosts: Pat and Jim Masson
Rooms: 14 (PB) $89-150
Full Breakfast
Credit Cards: A, B, C, D
Notes: 2, 5, 7, 8, 9, 10, 11, 12, 13, 14

WALLINGFORD

American Country Collection

1353 Union Street, Schenectady, NY 12308
(518) 370-4948; (800) 810-4948
FAX (518) 393-1634 (call first)
e-mail: carolbnbres@mon.com
www.bandbreservations.com

241. The Victorian warmth and Italian architectural motifs carry through to the individually decorated rooms. Antique furnishings and special touches make this bed and breakfast a true country pleasure. North of Manchester, near Killington and Pico and a short drive to the Appalachian Trail, this bed and breakfast is in the heart of Vermont. Claw-foot tubs, canopied beds, wicker on the porch complete the scene. Seven rooms with private baths. Children over 12 welcome. $100-160.

I. B. Munson House Bed & Breakfast Inn

7 South Main Street, P.O. Box 427, 05773
(802) 446-2860; FAX (802) 446-3336

Elegant 1856 Italianate Victorian inn, in the national historic register. Exquisitely restored to former glory. Seven guest rooms with private baths, some with claw-foot tubs and wood-burning fireplaces. Full breakfast by fireside or on deck overlooking garden (seasonal). Beautiful large common rooms with stunning chandeliers. In a quaint historic village. Dining nearby. Boyhood home of Paul P. Harris, founder of Rotary International. Children 12 and older welcome.

Hosts: Karen and Phillip Pimental
Rooms: 7 (PB) $65-150
Full Breakfast
Credit Cards: A, B, C, D
Notes: 2, 7, 9, 10, 11, 12, 13, 14

WARREN

Sugartree Inn

Rural Route 1, Box 38
Sugarbush Access Road, 05674
(802) 583-3211; (800) 666-8907
FAX (802) 583-3203
e-mail: sugartree@madriver.com

An intimate mountainside inn at Sugarbush. Nine guest rooms furnished with antiques, brass or canopied beds, and one fireplaced suite. In summer, flowers abound. Relax in the gingerbread gazebo. Golf, tennis, hiking, and swimming holes nearby. Winter brings cross-country and downhill skiing just a quarter-mile away. Warm up with hot cider by the parlor fireplace. Hearty country breakfasts. Picnic lunches available. Dinner is available for groups.

Hosts: Frank and Kathy Partsch
Rooms: 9 (PB) 80-135
Full Breakfast
Credit Cards: A, B, C, D
Notes: 2, 5, 7, 9, 10, 11, 12, 13, 14

Sugartree Inn

West Hill House

West Hill House Bed & Breakfast

1496 West Hill Road, 05674
(802) 496-7162; (800) 898-1427
FAX (802) 496-6443
e-mail: westhill@madriver.com
www.westhillhouse.com

Up a quiet country lane, nine acres with gardens, pond, views, this 1850s farmhouse is just one mile from Sugarbush Ski Resort, adjacent to championship golf course and cross-country ski trails. Extraordinary hiking, cycling, canoeing, fishing. Near fine restaurants, quaint villages, covered bridges. Enjoy comfortable porches, fireplaces, library, great room, sunroom. Guest rooms—six with fireplace and/or Jacuzzi—offer premium linens, down comforters, good reading lights. Dinner available by reservation with six-guest minimum. Children over 12 welcome.

Hosts: Dotty Kyle and Eric Brattstrom
Rooms: 7 (PB) $100-155
Full Breakfast
Credit Cards: A, B, C, D
Notes: 2, 5, 7, 9, 10, 11, 12, 13, 14

WATERBURY

American Country Collection

1353 Union Street, Schenectady, NY 12308
(518) 370-4948; (800) 810-4948
FAX (518) 393-1634 (call first)
e-mail: carolbnbres@mon.com
www.bandbreservations.com

039. This 1790 Cape Cod was once a stagecoach stop and is now a haven for modern-day travelers seeking country comfort and hospitality. The six guest rooms are filled with country antiques. One room has a working fireplace. All have private baths. The inn has a library, living room, dining room, large porch, and country kitchen, where a full breakfast is served at the long trestle table next to the brick hearth. Smoking in common areas only. Children over six are welcome. Three-night minimum stay over holiday weekends. $85-140.

Grünberg Haus

Grünberg Haus Bed & Breakfast & Cabins

Rural Route 2, Box 1595 AD, Route 100 S, 05676
(802) 244-7726; (800) 800-7760
e-mail: grunhaus@aol.com
www.waterbury.org/grunberg

Romantic Austrian chalet on a quiet mountainside, hand-built of native timber and fieldstone. Gorgeous guest rooms, secluded cabins, and spectacular carriage house suite. Warm-weather Jacuzzi, cold-weather sauna, cross-country ski and walking trails, year-round fireplace, and BYOB pub. Savor memorable breakfast feasts. In Ben & Jerry's hometown, between Stowe and Sugarbush ski resorts. "Home of hospitable innkeepers, chickens, and teddy bears." Central to Stowe, Burlington, Montpelier, covered bridges, and waterfalls.

Hosts: Christopher Sellers and Mark Frohman
Rooms: 13 (7 PB; 6 SB) $59-145
Full Breakfast
Credit Cards: A, B, D
Notes: 2, 5, 7, 8, 9, 10, 11, 12, 13, 14

7 No smoking; 8 Children welcome; 9 Social drinking allowed; 10 Tennis nearby; 11 Swimming nearby; 12 Golf nearby; 13 Skiing nearby; 14 May be booked through a travel agent; 15 Handicapped accessible.

Inn at Blush Hill

Blush Hill Road, Box 1266, 05676
(802) 244-7529; (800) 736-7522
www.blushhill.com

Waterbury's oldest inn, a circa 1790 restored Cape on five acres with beautiful mountain views. The inn has four fireplaces, a large sitting room, fireplaced guest room, canopied bed, down comforters, and lots of antiques. One room has a Jacuzzi. Across from a golf course, and all summer sports are nearby. Enjoy skiing at Stowe, Sugarbush, and Bolton Valley. Back-to-back to Ben & Jerry's Ice Cream Factory. Packages available. AAA- and Mobil-rated. Children over six welcome.

Hosts: Gary and Pam Gosselin
Rooms: 5 (PB) $59-130
Full Breakfast
Credit Cards: A, B, C, D
Notes: 2, 5, 7, 9, 10, 11, 12, 13, 14

Old Stagecoach Inn

18 North Main Street, 05676
(802) 244-5056; (800) 262-2206

Experience the charm of a bygone era in the heart of Vermont's premier recreational area. Beautiful rooms, antiques throughout, listed in the National Register of Historic Places. Complimentary full breakfast. Minutes to world-class skiing, hiking, biking, water sports, and unmatched sightseeing. Just one-half mile south of I-89 on scenic Route 100 in the village of Waterbury. AAA-approved.

Hosts: Jack and John Barwick
Rooms: 11 (8 PB; 3 SB) $45-150
Full Breakfast
Credit Cards: A, B, C, D
Notes: 2, 4, 5, 6, 7, 8, 9, 10, 11, 12, 13, 14

WATERBURY CENTER

The Black Locust Inn

Route 100, Box 715, 05677
(802) 244-7490; (800) 366-5592 (reservations only)
FAX (802) 244-8473; www.blacklocustinn.com

The Black Locust Inn

Amid glorious black locust trees, the elegantly restored 1832 farmhouse is an unspoiled retreat from the world. Spend tranquil days and nights savoring relaxed conversation or sit back and reflect on life's delights. All rooms have guest-controlled heat and air conditioning and ceiling fans. The hosts take great pride in making each room an enchanting place to be. Scrumptious country breakfasts and evening wine and appetizers. Activities year-round in nearby Stowe and Waterbury. Easy access to Montpelier, Burlington, and the Northeast Kingdom. Exit 10 from I-89, five miles on route 100. Rated three diamonds by AAA and two stars by Mobil.

Hosts: Len, Nancy, and Valerie Vignola
Rooms: 6 (PB) $100-150
Full Breakfast
Credit Cards: A, B, C, D
Notes: 2, 5, 7, 8, 10, 11, 12, 13, 15

Elaine's Bed & Breakfast Selections

4987 Kingston Road, Elbridge, NY 13060
(315) 689-2082 (call between 10:30 A.M.–7:00 P.M.)

Newly renovated and restored large gambrel-roofed home. The guest annex has a separate entrance and plenty of storage area for skis and other sports equipment. The Gathering Room is fully equipped with sofas, chairs, tables, TV and VCR, microwave, and other amenities. The main house is open during busy fall foliage season and offers three guest rooms

NOTES: Credit cards accepted: A MasterCard; B Visa; C American Express; D Discover; E Diner's Club; F Other; 2 Personal checks accepted; 3 Lunch available; 4 Dinner available; 5 Open all year; 6 Pets welcome;

with private and shared baths. There are also eight guest rooms, some with private and some with shared baths. Afternoon tea is offered most days from 4:00 to 5:00 P.M. Nonsmoking. Visa and Mastercard. Children welcome. Port-a-crib, rollaway available for $10. Seasonal and mid-week rates, special group rates, and rates for extended stays are available.

Deerhill Inn

WEST DOVER

Austin Hill Inn

Route 100, P.O. Box 859, 05356
(800) 332-RELAX; FAX (802) 464-1229
e-mail: austinhi@sover.net
www.austinhillinn.com

Nestled in the woods, yet near everything. Twelve lovely guest rooms with country appointments, fireplaces, private baths, and most with wraparound balconies. Turndown service with burning votive candles. Full gourmet breakfasts each morning and afternoon wine and cheese served fireside. Close to summer and winter activities. Perfect location for weddings, honeymoons, reunions, and small business meetings. Two miles to Mount Snow. Swimming pool.

Hosts: Debbie and John Bailey
Rooms: 12 (PB) $105-155
Full Breakfast
Credit Cards: A, B, D
Notes: 2, 4, 5, 7, 8, 9, 10, 11, 12, 13, 14

Deerhill Inn and Restaurant

P.O. Box 136, Valleyview Road, 05356-0136
(802) 464-3100; (800) 99-DEER-9
e-mail: deehill@sover.net; www.deerhill.com

A friendly English-style country house with mountain views, candlelight dining, superb cuisine, spacious sitting rooms, fine antiques, art gallery, a licensed lounge, private baths, some rooms with fireplaces, lovely grounds, swimming pool. In Mount Snow area. Alpine and Nordic skiing, mountain biking, two championship golf courses, golf school, airport, walking, fishing, boating, antiquing, shopping, craft fairs, Marlboro Music Festival, and just plain relaxing. Weddings a specialty. Children over eight welcome.

Hosts: Michael and Linda Anelli
Rooms: 15 (PB) $95-220
Full Breakfast
Credit Cards: A, B, C
Notes: 2, 4, 5, 9, 10, 11, 12, 13

The Doveberry Inn & Restaurant

Route 100, P.O. Box 1736, 05356
(802) 464-5652; (800) 722-3204
FAX (802) 464-6229; e-mail: duveberry@aol.com
www.DoveberryInn.com

This quaint country inn rests in the Green Mountains of southern Vermont, featuring eight unique guest rooms, with private baths and TVs. The surrounding area offers fishing, hiking, some of the best biking, downhill, cross-country skiing, snowmobiling, and the famed Marlboro Music Festival. Ease into comfort with great breakfasts from an acclaimed restaurant, moderately priced for everyone to enjoy. Children over eight welcome. "Top 25 American Bed and Breakfast with Super Chefs." Dubbed "Homey" by *Condé Nast's Traveler*, April 99. "Memories of the Doveberry linger. These are the kind of dishes that encourage writers to excess!" *VT Magazine*, June 1999.

7 No smoking; 8 Children welcome; 9 Social drinking allowed; 10 Tennis nearby; 11 Swimming nearby; 12 Golf nearby; 13 Skiing nearby; 14 May be booked through a travel agent; 15 Handicapped accessible.

Hosts: Christine and Michael Fayette
Rooms: 8 (PB) $80-150
Credit Cards: A, B, C, F
Notes: 2, 4, 5, 7, 8, 10, 11, 12, 13, 14, 15

The Gray Ghost Inn

Route 100, P.O. Box 938, 05356
(802) 464-2474; (800) 745-3215

The guest book is filled with comments saying "super," "lovely," "warm and comfy," "better than home!" Of course it is; hosts cook breakfast, make the bed, even bake cookies for guests. Very clean rooms, nicely decorated, all with private baths. Guests are welcomed by caring, gracious host and hostess who live at the inn. They are happy to assist guests with information regarding dining, entertainment, sports, or whatever their needs are. A rural area with beautiful villages. Personal checks accepted for reservations only. Sixteen rooms are nonsmoking rooms and five rooms are handicapped accessible.

Hosts: John and Kaye Collingwood
Rooms: 25 (PB) $30-50
Full Breakfast
Credit Cards: A, B, C, D
Notes: 5, 8, 9, 10, 11, 12, 13, 14

West Dover Inn

Route 100, P.O. Box 1208, 05356
(802) 464-5207; FAX (802) 464-2173
e-mail: wdvrinn@sover.net
www.westdoverinn.com

Continuously operating for more than 150 years, this beautifully restored historic inn features individually appointed guest rooms, all with private baths, as well as luxurious fireplace suites with whirlpool tubs. Memorable dining at Gregory's Restaurant, featuring innovative country gourmet fare, relaxed ambiance, and an extensive wine list as well as a pub-like cocktail lounge. Within minutes of golf, skiing, mountain biking, tennis, and swimming. Recommended by *Fodor's, Frammer's,* and Mobil.

West Dover Inn

Closed late April through mid-May and early November. Children over eight welcome.

Hosts: Greg Gramas and Monique Phelan
Rooms: 12 (PB) $90-200
Full Breakfast
Credit Cards: A, B, C, D
Notes: 2, 4, 9, 10, 11, 12, 13, 14

WESTON

The Inn at Weston

Route 100, P.O. Box 179, 05161
(802) 824-6789; fax (802) 824-3073
e-mail: inweston@sover.net; www.innweston.com

Just imagine…a historically registered inn, handsome guest rooms and suites, hearty breakfasts, candlelight dining, cozy pub, six

The Inn at Weston

NOTES: Credit cards accepted: A MasterCard; B Visa; C American Express; D Discover; E Diner's Club; F Other; 2 Personal checks accepted; 3 Lunch available; 4 Dinner available; 5 Open all year; 6 Pets welcome;

acres of grounds and gardens all within easy walking distance of Village Green. Ideal setting for a romantic getaway, wedding, or corporate retreat. The public is cordially invited for dinner, served from 5:30 P.M. Dinner reservations are suggested.

Hosts: Lauren and Steve Bryant
Rooms: 13 (PB) $95-250
Full Breakfast
Credit Cards: A, B, C
Notes: 4, 5, 7, 9, 12, 13, 14

WILMINGTON

The Hermitage Inn

Coldbrook Road, P.O. Box 457, 05363
(802) 464-3511; FAX (802) 464-2688
e-mail: hermitag@sover.net
www.hermitageinn.com

Fifteen individually decorated guest rooms each with working fireplace, private bath, telephone, and cable TV. Fourteen guest rooms at nearby Brookbound. Award-winning restaurant serving Continental cuisine, and featuring home-raised gamebirds and venison. *Wine Spectator's* Grand Award winner yearly since 1984. More than 2,000 labels and 35,000 bottles in stock to complement every meal. Sporting clays course and hunting preserve on-site. A 55K ski touring center with equipment rentals and lessons. Wine and Gift shop offers homemade maple syrup, jams, and jellies. MAP rates available.

Host: James McGovern
Rooms: 15 (15 PB) $225-250
Credit Cards: A, B, C, E
Notes: 2, 3, 4, 5, 8, 9, 10, 11, 12, 13, 14

The Hermitage Inn

Nutmeg Inn

Nutmeg Inn

153 Route 9W (Molly Stark Trail), P.O. Box 818, Mount Snow Valley, 05363
(802) 464-7400; (800) 277-5402
www.nutmeginn.com

Just as guests always imagined a Vermont country inn to be. Cozy and romantic, warm and charming circa 1777 Vermont farmhouse appointed with period antiques. All rooms and suites with private baths, central air conditioning, and telephones; many with wood-burning fireplaces and TVs. All have king- or queen-size beds (four-poster, brass, and wrought iron). Luxurious suites with whirlpools, living rooms, wood-burning fireplaces, TVs, and VCRs. Common area with fireplace. Full gourmet "Country Breakfast."

Hosts: Dave and Pat Cerchio
Rooms: 14 (PB) $89-299
Full Breakfast
Credit Cards: A, B, C, D
Notes: 2, 5, 7, 9, 10, 11, 12, 13, 14

The Red Shutter Inn

Route 9 West, Box 636, 05363
(802) 464-3768; (800) 845-7548

This 1894 nine-room Colonial inn with fireplace suites sits on a hillside within walking distance of the town of Wilmington. Tucked behind the inn is the renovated carriage house with four rooms, one a two-room fireplace suite with a two-person whirlpool bath. A renowned restaurant with candlelight dining (alfresco dining on an awning-covered porch in the summertime). Championship golf (golf packages), skiing at Mount Snow and Haystack, cross-country skiing, hiking, boating, and antiquing are minutes away. Experience the congenial atmosphere of country inn life. Closed April. No smoking in inn.

Hosts: Renée and Tad Lyon
Rooms: 9 (PB) $105-210
Full Breakfast
Credit Cards: A, B, C, D
Notes: 2, 4, 7, 9, 10, 11, 12, 13, 14

Trail's End

Shearer Hill Farm Bed & Breakfast

Shearer Hill Road, P.O. Box 1453, 05363
(802) 464-3253; (800) 437-3104
e-mail: ppuseySHF@sover.net
www.sover.net/~puseyshf/

Wake to the aroma of freshly brewed coffee, homemade muffins, and breads. Enjoy the quiet setting of this small working farm with White-Faced Hereford Cows, on a pristine country road. The inn, just five miles from the center of Wilmington, has large rooms with private baths. The hosts serve a delicious Vermont breakfast. Near Mount Snow and Haystack ski areas, groomed cross-country skiing trails on property, connected to VAST trails, snowmobile rentals and sleigh rides nearby. Marlboro Music Festival just five miles away. Outstanding golf courses, swimming, hiking, boating, horseback riding, mountain biking, and many fine restaurants nearby.

Hosts: Bill and Patti Pusey
Rooms: 6 (PB) $70-90
Full Breakfast
Credit Cards: A, B, C, D
Notes: 2, 5, 7, 8, 9, 10, 11, 12, 13, 14, 15

Trail's End—A Country Inn

5 Trail's End Lane, 05363
(802) 464-2727; (800) 859-2585
e-mail: trailsnd@together.net
www.trailsendvt.com

A unique country inn tucked away on 10 acres with flower gardens, a clay tennis court, heated outdoor pool, and a large pond. Described as "irresistibly romantic" by the author of *Best Places to Kiss in New England.* Picture-perfect rooms, including fireplace rooms and fireplace suites with canopy beds and whirlpool tubs. Full breakfast menu and afternoon tea. Warm hospitality and attention to detail are the hosts' specialties. Ski and golf packages available as well as dining discounts.

Hosts: Debby and Kevin Stephens
Rooms: 15 (PB) $105-165
Suites: $155-195
Full Breakfast
Credit Cards: A, B, C, D
Notes: 2, 5, 7, 9, 10, 11, 12, 13, 14

The White House of Wilmington

Route 9, P.O. Box 757, 05363
(802) 464-2135; (800) 541-2135
FAX (802) 464-5222; e-mail: whitehse@sover.net
www.whitehouseinn.com

Set on the crest of a high rolling hill overlooking the Deerfield Valley, the White House of

NOTES: Credit cards accepted: A MasterCard; B Visa; C American Express; D Discover; E Diner's Club; F Other; 2 Personal checks accepted; 3 Lunch available; 4 Dinner available; 5 Open all year; 6 Pets welcome;

Wilmington is southern Vermont's premier landmark. Built in 1915 as a private summer home, the Victorian mansion now offers romantic accommodations amidst casual surroundings. It's easy to see why the inn was voted "one of the 10 most romantic inns" by both the *New York Times* and *Boston Herald.* Twenty-three guest rooms, 13 fireplaces, indoor and outdoor pools, whirlpool and sauna. Ski touring center.

Host: Robert Grinold
Rooms: 23 (PB) $108-195
Full Breakfast
Credit Cards: A, B, C, D, E
Notes: 2, 4, 5, 8, 9, 10, 12, 13, 14, 15

WINDSOR

Juniper Hill Inn

153 Penbroke Road, 05089
(802) 674-5273; (800) 359-2541
www.juniperhillinn.com

This elegant but informal inn allows guests to pamper themselves. Antique-furnished guest rooms, many with working fireplaces. Marvelous views. Sumptuous candlelit dinners and hearty breakfasts. Cool off in the pool, canoe, bike, hike, or visit antique and craft shops, covered bridges, and museums. Twenty minutes from Woodstock and Quechee, and Hanover, New Hampshire. A perfectly romantic inn. Mobil- and AAA-rated. Closed April.

Hosts: Rob and Susanne Pearl
Rooms: 16 (PB) $95-170

Juniper Hill Inn

Full Breakfast
Credit Cards: A, B, D
Notes: 2, 4, 7, 10, 11, 12, 13, 14

WOLCOTT

American Country Collection

1353 Union Street, Schenectady, NY 12308
(518) 370-4948; (800) 810-4948
FAX (518) 393-1634 (call first)
e-mail: carolbnbres@mon.com
www.bandbreservations.com

130. Twelve miles north of Stowe, this Greek Revival-style three-bedroom inn is bordered by the LaMoille River and has authentically appointed rooms and spacious bedchambers. The four guest rooms with private baths are decorated according to themes. One room has a gas-fired wood stove. Full breakfast. Smoking outdoors only. Children 12 and older welcome. $70-90.

WOODSTOCK

Applebutter Inn Bed & Breakfast

Happy Valley Road, 05091
(802) 457-4158 (phone/FAX); (800) 486-1734
e-mail:aplbtrn@aol.com

Delighfuly warm and friendly ambiance. Once a Jersey farm. Tucked away on quiet and relaxing hamlet three miles from center of Woodstock and Quechee Villages. 1850 home is appointed with traditional antiques, warm colors, and three sitting rooms with fireplaces. Breakfasts consist of a bountiful buffet of natural foods. Fine linens and down comforters on comfortable beds assure a fabulous sleep. Family is friendly, lovely gardens, and complete seasonal activities nearby. Innkeepers take genuine hospitality seriously. Inquire about accommodations for pets.

Hosts: Beverlee and Andrew Cook
Rooms: 6 (PB) $85-145
Full Breakfast
Credit Cards: A, B
Notes: 2, 5, 6, 7, 8, 9, 10, 11, 12, 13, 14

7 No smoking; 8 Children welcome; 9 Social drinking allowed; 10 Tennis nearby; 11 Swimming nearby; 12 Golf nearby; 13 Skiing nearby; 14 May be booked through a travel agent; 15 Handicapped accessible.

Bailey's Mills Bed & Breakfast

1347 Bailey's Mills Road, 05062
(802) 484-7809 (phone/FAX); (800) 639-3437
www.bbonline.com/vt/baileysmills

Romantic accommodations await beyond porch swings and rockers. Spacious Federal home. Rich architectural details. Savor candlelit breakfast buffet amidst heirloom antiques while gleaning colorful details of local history. Explore this secluded farming valley on unpaved roads and paths to pastures, woodlands, and the Hapgood Cemetery. Picnic at hilltop or pond. Sip afternoon tea over board games in the library, verdant solarium or among hummingbirds on the porch. Bailey's Brook serenades the emerging stars. Woodstock only 10 miles away. Deluxe Continental Breakfast

Hosts: Barbara Thaeder and Donald Whitaker
Rooms: 3 (PB) $75-135
Continental Breakfast
Credit Cards: A, B
Notes: 2, 5, 7, 9, 10, 11, 12, 13, 14

Canterbury House

43 Pleasant Street, 05091
(802) 457-3077

A 119-year-old village townhouse just east of the village green. This bed and breakfast, furnished with authentic Victorian antiques, has eight rooms with private baths. Living room with TV and VCR. Within walking distance of shops, the historic district, and restaurants. A full gourmet breakfast is served in the dining room. Guest rooms have air conditioning. Described as elegant but comfortable. Children over 17 welcome.

Hosts: The Frosts
Rooms: 8 (PB) $85-155
Full Breakfast
Credit Cards: A, B, C
Notes: 2, 5, 7, 9, 10, 11, 12, 13, 14

The Charleston House

The Charleston House

21 Pleasant Street, 05091
(802) 457-3843; (888) 475-3800
e-mail: nohl@together.net
www.charlestonhouse.com

A Greek Revival brick and clapboard townhouse, listed in the National Register of Historic Places, it is a part of the sophistication that is Woodstock. Resplendent with art and furnishings befitting the 1835 birthdate of this home, the guest rooms have private baths, and some include fireplaces, Jacuzzis, and TVs. Sumptuous candlelit breakfasts. Air conditioning. Nonsmoking.

Hosts: Dieter and Willa Nohl
Rooms: 9 (PB) $110-195
Full Breakfast
Credit Cards: A, B, C
Notes: 2, 7, 9, 10, 11, 12, 13, 14

Canterbury House

Four Pillars at Taftsville, circa 1836

Happy Valley Road, P.O. Box 132, Taftsville, 05073
(802) 457-2797; (800) 957-2797
e-mail: fpillars@vermontel.com
www.fourpillarsBB.com

Historic Greek Revival, circa 1836, restored home. Four huge hemlock trees were used to erect the "four pillars" on the front portico. Enjoy the splendor of Vermont all year, with everything from golfing to skiing. Each guest room is charming and unique with private baths. Delightful down comforters, lace curtains, wide-pine-board floors and lush towels are just a sampling of the amenities. Breakfasts may be candlelit with coffee, tea, juice, homemade sconces, muffins pancakes, eggs, french toast, or quiche. Enjoy country walks and wonderful bike paths. An authentic Russian stove graces the kitchen.

Innkeepers: Gail Childs
Rooms: 5 (PB) $75-140
Credit Cards: A, B
Notes: 2, 5, 7, 9, 10, 11, 12, 13

The Jackson House Inn

37 Old Route 4 West, 05091
(802) 457-2065; (800) 448-1890
FAX (802) 457-9290; www.jacksonhouse.com

"Vermont's hottest gourmet getaway"—*Country Inns* magazine. Fine dining and luxurious accommodations in an 1890 Victorian mansion in the National Register of Historic Places. Fif-

The Jackson House Inn

teen guest rooms, including six suites, are furnished with fine period antiques in various gracious styles. Memorable gourmet breakfast and evening wine/champagne bar included. Five beautifully landscaped acres of formal gardens with stream and pond. Spa with steam room.

Host: Juan Florin
Rooms: 15 (PB) $170-260
Full Breakfast
Credit Cards: A, B, C
Notes: 2, 4, 5, 7, 9, 10, 11, 12, 13, 14, 15

Kedron Valley Inn

Kedron Valley Inn

Route 106, South Woodstock, 05071
(800) 836-1193; FAX (802) 457-4469
e-mail: kedroninn@aol.com
www.innformation.com/vt/kedron

Historic country inn, nestled seven minutes south of picturesque Woodstock. Private baths, Jacuzzis, in-room fireplaces, queen-size canopied beds, heirloom quilts, private decks. Award of Excellence wine list with cuisine that is tied for top honors in all Vermont. Swimming lake with two white-sand beaches. Surrounded by skiing, antiques, historic estates, and shopping. Featured in *Country Living*, *Country Home*, and *Yankee*. Voted Inn of the Year by *Inn-Goers*. Midweek discounts for non-peak season.

Hosts: Max and Merrily Comins
Rooms: 26 (PB) $120-230
Full Breakfast
Credit Cards: A, B, C, D
Notes: 2, 4, 9, 10, 11, 12, 13, 14

7 No smoking; 8 Children welcome; 9 Social drinking allowed; 10 Tennis nearby; 11 Swimming nearby; 12 Golf nearby; 13 Skiing nearby; 14 May be booked through a travel agent; 15 Handicapped accessible.

The Lincoln Inn
at the Covered Bridge

Rural Route 2, Box 40, Route 4, 05091
(802) 457-3312; FAX (802) 457-5808
e-mail: lincon2@aol.com
www.pbpub.com/woodstock/lincoln.htm

A full service country inn set in a lovingly restored farmhouse. Six cozy guest rooms await, each with private bath, each unique in style and character. Just three miles west of the village, the inn sits on six acres of beautiful riverfront grounds. Dinner, available in the country-elegant dining room, is prepared by Swiss chef/owner for guests' delight. Nonsmoking.

Hosts: Kurt and Lori Hildbrand
Rooms: 6 (PB) $125
Full Breakfast
Credit Cards: A, B, D
Notes: 2, 4, 5, 7, 10, 11, 12, 13

The Woodstocker
Bed & Breakfast

Route 4, 61 River Street, 05091
(802) 457-3896; FAX (802) 457-3897
e-mail: woodstocker@valley.net
www.scenesofvermont.com/woodstocker/index.html

Nestled at the foot of Mount Tom, this charming 1830s Cape offers nine large, tastefully appointed air-conditioned rooms with private baths. Queen-size beds, full kitchens, and private sitting areas are among the many amenities available. Each morning begins with a sumptuous buffet breakfast, and complimentary refreshments are served in the afternoon.

Within the picturesque village of Woodstock, a short stroll over a covered bridge brings guests to fine dining and shopping.

Hosts: Tom and Nancy Blackford
Rooms: 9 (PB) $85-155
Full Breakfast
Credit Cards: A, B
Notes: 2, 5, 7, 8, 9, 10, 11, 12, 13, 14

Woodstock House
Bed & Breakfast

Route 106, P.O. Box 361, 05091
(802) 457-1758

Renovated old farmhouse with exposed hand-hewn beams and lovely mellow old floors. Three miles south of Woodstock on Route 106. Open May through December.

Host: Mary Fraser
Rooms: 5 (3 PB; 2 SB) $70-85
Full Breakfast
Credit Cards: B
Notes: 2, 4, 7, 9, 10, 11, 12, 13

Woodstock House

Canada

New Brunswick

New Brunswick

"Le Poirier"

CARAQUET

"Le Poirier" Bed & Breakfast

98 Boulevard St-Pierre Ouest, E1W 1B6
(506) 727-4359; FAX (506) 726-6084

Wonderful sunsets in a cozy seashore fishing town on the Acadian Peninsula. Minutes from the world-renowned Acadian Historical Village. Caraquet features the Acadian Festival August 6-16, one of the 100 best recommended festivals in North America, wind surfing, boating, deepsea fishing, kayak renting, horseback riding. "Le Poirier" homestead, built in 1927, has been restored to its original splendor and offers Acadian hospitality in a restful atmosphere.

Hosts: Roland and Martina Friolet
Rooms: 5 (2 PB; 3 SB) $45-65 Canadian
Continental Breakfast
Credit Cards: A
Notes: 2, 5, 7, 8, 9, 10, 11, 12

EDMUNDSTON

Auberge Le Fief Inn Bed & Breakfast

87 Rue de L'eglise/Church Street, E3V 1J6
(506) 735-0400; FAX (506) 735-0402

A Heritage Canada estate with themed rooms showing the history of the legendary Republic of Madawaska. All rooms have private (full) baths, air conditioning, telephones, TVs, and VCRs. Guests can borrow a book from hosts' private library or a movie from their collection of Academy Award winners. The licensed dining room offers fine regional cuisine in a romantic Victorian setting and can help create a wonderful memory.

Hosts: Sharon and Philip Bélanger
Rooms: 8 (PB) $69.95-124.95
Full Breakfast
Credit Cards: A, B
Notes: 4, 5, 7, 8, 9, 10, 11, 12, 13

EVANDALE AREA

Evandale Inn

Rural Route 3, Gagetown, E0G 1V0
(506) 468-1105; (888) 313-0022
FAX (506) 468-9442
e-mail: evandale@nb.aibn.com

Historic 110-year-old riverboat inn. Newly restored Victorian building. Antique furnishings. Positioned on the banks of large river with wetlands nearby. Home to many varieties of birds and waterfowl. Canoes and bicycles available to guests. Riverside walking trail. Magnificent pastoral scenery. All rooms feature breathtaking views of St. Johns River. Powerboat cruises also available. Rooms range from average to luxury suites with Roman-style baths.

Hosts: Trish and Chris Durnnian
Rooms: 8 (PB) $79-189
Continental Breakfast
Credit Cards: A, B
Notes: 3, 4, 7, 9, 11, 12, 14, 15

NOTES: Credit cards accepted: A MasterCard; B Visa; C American Express; D Discover; E Diner's Club; F Other; 2 Personal checks accepted; 3 Lunch available; 4 Dinner available; 5 Open all year; 6 Pets welcome; 7 No smoking; 8 Children welcome; 9 Social drinking allowed; 10 Tennis nearby; 11 Swimming nearby; 12 Golf nearby; 13 Skiing nearby; 14 May be booked through a travel agent; 15 Handicapped accessible.

GRAND FALLS

Cote Bed & Breakfast

575 Broadway Boulevard West, E3Z 2L2
(506) 473-1415; (877) 444-COTE (2683)
FAX (506) 473-1952
www.bbcanada.com/474.html

Five quiet, luxurious rooms with queen-size
beds and en suite bathrooms. Two have balconies. Falls and Gorge restaurants, shopping
within walking distance. Eighteen-hole golf
course 2km away. Homemade jams and pure
maple syrup enhance a full breakfast. Visit this
unique bilingual town.

Hosts: Norma and Noel Cote
Rooms: 5 (PB) $45-125
Full Breakfast
Credit Cards: A, B
Notes: 5, 7, 8, 10, 11, 12, 13

GRAND MANAN ISLAND

Compass Rose

North Head, E0G 2M0
(506) 662-8570; (514) 458-2607 (winter)
FAX (514) 458-3119

Two small turn-of-the-century houses overlooking the fisherman's wharf at North Head.
The bedrooms are made inviting with quilts
and pine furnishings. Breathtaking views of the
Bay of Fundy and the busy harbor make dining
in the Compass Rose always a special occasion. The menu features island-grown produce,
locally caught seafood, and baked goods fresh
from the ovens. Open May through October.

Hosts: Nora and Ed Parker
Rooms: 7 (PB) $89
Full Breakfast
Credit Cards: A, B
Notes: 3, 4, 7, 9, 10, 11, 12

McLaughlin's Wharf Inn

Seal Cove, E0G 3B0
(506) 662-8760; (506) 662-3672 (reservations)
FAX (506) 662-9998

Bed and breakfast with relaxed homey atmosphere in center of small fishing village and historic
property. Six cozy rooms with shared bathrooms,
TV lounge, dining room, deck overlooking tides
of Bay of Fundy. Dining room wheelchair accessible. Close to all island interests, local bird and
whale watching, and boat tours.

Host: Brenda McLaughlin
Rooms: 6 (SB) $69
Continental Breakfast
Credit Cards: A, B, C
Notes: 7, 8, 9, 10, 11, 12

RIVERSIDE

Cailswick Babbling Brook

Route 114, E02 2R0
(506) 882-2079; e-mail: cailsbb@nb.sympatico.ca
www.bbcanada.com/86.html

Babbling Brook is a century-old Victorian home
in the village of Riverside, Albert County, New
Brunswick, overlooking the Shepody Bay. The
home is surrounded by running books, trees,
flowers, and spacious land where one may relax
and enjoy the beauty of nature. Country-style
breakfasts served every morning in the spacious
kitchen. Come and explore the beauty of Albert
County and the hospitality of its people. The
Fundy National Park, bird sanctuary, Cape
Enrage, Hopewell Rocks, and a selection of
craft shops and galleries are all nearby.

Host: Eunice Cail
Rates: $45-50
Full Breakfast
Credit Cards: B
Notes: 2, 5, 7, 8, 9, 12, 13, 14

ST. ANDREWS

Eider Shores Guest House

100 Queen Street, P.O. Box 476, E0G 2X0
(506) 529-4795; FAX (506) 529-4644
e-mail: tshoal@nbnet.nb.ca

What better way to enjoy St. Andrew "By-the-
Sea" than one block from the water and central

NOTES: Credit cards accepted: A MasterCard; B Visa; C American Express; D Discover; E Diner's Club;
F Other; 2 Personal checks accepted; 3 Lunch available; 4 Dinner available; 5 Open all year; 6 Pets welcome;

to all attractions including fine dining, exclusive boutiques, fine gardens, and world-class golf? Guests can relax in the attractive well-appointed Fundy Room or Cottage Suite while making themselves at home with kitchenette facility and sunny sitting room off deck and yard. Eider Shores Guest House is perfect for overnight or extended visits, and package deals are available.

Hosts: Bill and Deborah Hogans
Rooms: 2 (PB) $70-90
Continental Breakfast
Credit Cards: B
Notes: 5, 7, 8, 9, 10, 11, 12

Kingsbrae Arms
Relais & Chateaux

219 King Street, E0G 2X0
(506) 529-1897 (reservations)
FAX (506) 529-1197; e-mail: kingbrae@nbnet.nb.ca
www.kingsbrae.com

Kingsbrae Arms is a sprawling manor house, first in Atlantic Canada to become Relais et Chateaux and distinctive Mobil four-star property. The estate serves guests as friends who have come to stay at a private country home. The cuisine changes daily and with the seasons. There is a heated pool in the private gardens. The house is filled with traditional art and antiques, yet is prepared for the 21st century with the latest communication devices and marble-appointed bathrooms in the guest quarters. MAP (breakfast and dinner) in season.

Hosts: Harry Chancey and David Oxford
Rooms: 9 (PB) $250-750 Canadian
Full Breakfast
Credit Cards: A, B
Notes: 2, 4, 5, 6, 7, 9, 10, 11, 12, 13, 14

ST. ANDREWS-BY-THE-SEA

Pansy Patch

59 Carleton Street, E0G 2X0
(506) 529-3834; (888) PANSY PATCH (726-7972)
FAX (506) 529-9042
e-mail: pansypatch@nb.aibn.com
www.pansypatch.com

Distinctively rated a four-star (Canada Select) and a three-diamond (AAA/CAA) destination for romance, relaxation, or business. "The most photographed home in New Brunswick"—*St. Croix Courier*. Featured in *New York Times*, *Canadian Homes*, *Bride's*. Designated a Canadian Heritage property. Renowned for its Canadian warmth and hospitality. Thoughtful, yet discreet, attention given to each guest's needs and tastes. Outstanding quality in furnishings, appointments, and amenities. Resort-class recreational facilities. Bike rentals. Full breakfasts, afternoon and evening fine dining, room service. Advance reservations suggested.

Host: Jeannie Foster
Rooms: 9 (PB) $135-200 Canadian
Full Breakfast
Credit Cards: A, B
Notes: 3, 4, 7, 8, 9, 10, 11, 12, 14

ST. JOHN

Five Chimneys Bed & Breakfast

238 Charlotte Street West, E2M 1Y3
(506) 635-1888; FAX (506) 672-2534
e-mail: 5chim@nb.aibn.com

A warm welcome awaits guests at this 1850s home. "As my mother says we are just "five moments away from everything"—some of the best restaurants in Canada, the Reversing Falls,

Five Chimneys

7 No smoking; 8 Children welcome; 9 Social drinking allowed; 10 Tennis nearby; 11 Swimming nearby; 12 Golf nearby; 13 Skiing nearby; 14 May be booked through a travel agent; 15 Handicapped accessible.

and Nature Parks. The Digby ferry terminal is closer than that. She also says, "recipes are not written in stone" so for those who have special needs I am used to experimenting with muffin and pancake recipes (low/no fat, wheat-free, corn-free, milk-free, etc.)."

Host: Linda Gates
Rooms: 3 (PB) $70-75
Full Breakfast
Credit Cards: A, B
Notes: 2, 5, 7, 8, 9, 10, 11, 12, 13

Linden Manor Bed & Breakfast

267 Charlotte Street West, E2M 1Y2
(506) 674-2754; e-mail: linden@fundy.net
http: //user.fundy.net/linden

A large Colonial home, circa 1830, with three spacious guest rooms all with private baths. One room is on the ground floor. Within walking distance of the ferry to Nova Scotia and just a five-minute drive to a nature park, downtown, or world-famous Reversing Falls. After a restful sleep in a king- or queen-size bed, enjoy breakfast in the dining room. Freshly baked muffins with fruit, coffee, or tea await guests, while French toast or eggs any style are being prepared. Special diets are accommodated. Four-star Canada Select.

Hosts: Linda and Gregg Molloy
Rooms: 3 (PB) $70-75 (Canadian) ($50-55 U.S.)
Full Breakfast
Credit Cards: A, B
Notes: 5, 7, 9, 11, 12

SHEDIAC

Auberge Belcourt Inn

310 Main Street, E0A 3G0
(506) 532-6098; FAX (506) 532-9398
e-mail: belcourt@nbnet.nb.ca
www.sn2000.nb.ca/comp/auberge-belcourt

Come and revisit a bygone era in an elegantly renovated Victorian-style house entirely furnished with period antiques. Seven uniquely furnished bedrooms are available (five with private baths). A full breakfast is served on antique china in an oval dining room. In the heart of Shediac within walking distance of shops and restaurants, and close to Parlee Beach, one of the finest beaches in New Brunswick. Dinner available September through April only.

Hosts: Pauline and Chris Pyke
Rooms: 7 (5 PB; 2 SB) $79-109 Canadian
Full Breakfast
Credit Cards: A, B, C, E
Notes: 5, 9, 11, 12

Auberge Belcourt Inn

NOTES: Credit cards accepted: A MasterCard; B Visa; C American Express; D Discover; E Diner's Club; F Other; 2 Personal checks accepted; 3 Lunch available; 4 Dinner available; 5 Open all year; 6 Pets welcome;

Nova Scotia

Goodwin's Chat & Chew Bed & Breakfast

Rural Route 2, B4H 3X9
(902) 661-0282

Guests will find this bed and breakfast on Route 366, just 20 miles from Amherst. Rural country side overlooking the beautiful Northumberland Strait. A five-minute walk to the beach, 45 minutes to the Conferdation Bridge to Prince Edward Island. Chat with the hosts in the living room. Lots of antiques and hand-made quilts grace the beds in the guest bedrooms. The 1927 Chevy Coupe is always on display. Full breakfast.

Hosts: Fraser and Arleen Goodwin
Rooms: 3 (3 S2B) $45-50
Full Breakfast
Credit Cards: None
Notes: 7, 8, 11, 12, 14

ANNAPOLIS ROYAL

The King George Inn

548 Upper St. George Street, B0S 1A0
(902) 532-5286; (888) 799-KING (5464)
e-mail: dms@ns.sympatico.ca
www3.ns.sympatico.ca/dms/king.htm

Grand Victorian sea captain's home, furnished completely in period antiques. In historic Annapolis Royal (Canada's oldest settlement). A short walk from all major attractions. Inn features large, bright rooms with tall ceilings, cove moldings, leaded glass, fireplaces, parquet floors, and legendary Nova Scotian hospitality. Family suites available. Some rooms

The King George Inn

with private deck, Jacuzzi, and TV. Free bicycles. Whale watching arranged.

Hosts: Michael and Donna Susnick; Faye McStravick
Rooms: 8 (6 PB; 2 SB) $59-159 Canadian
Full and Continental Breakfast
Credit Cards: A, B
Notes: 4, 6, 7, 8, 9, 10, 11, 12, 14

BADDECK

Castle Moffett

P.O. Box 678, B0E 1B0
(902) 756-9070; FAX (902) 756-3399
e-mail: castle@canadamail.com
www.castlemoffett.com

Castle Moffett spans a cascading brook on 185 mountainside acres overlooking the Bras d'Or Lake. Centrally positioned to the Cabot Trail, Bell Museum, Fortress Louisbourg, bird and

7 No smoking; 8 Children welcome; 9 Social drinking allowed; 10 Tennis nearby; 11 Swimming nearby; 12 Golf nearby; 13 Skiing nearby; 14 May be booked through a travel agent; 15 Handicapped accessible.

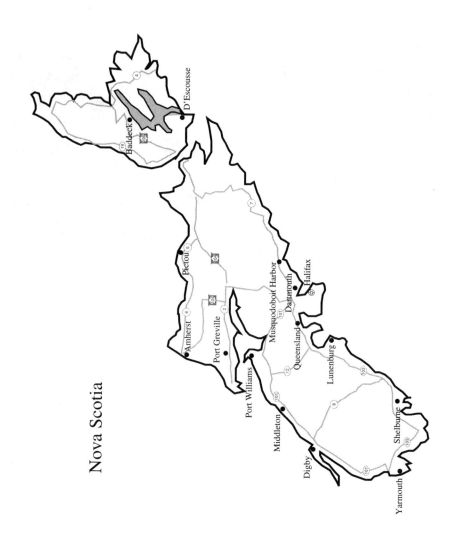

Nova Scotia

D'Escousse
Baddeck
Pictou
Amherst
Port Greville
Port Williams
Middleton
Digby
Yarmouth
Musquodoboit Harbor
Dartmouth
Halifax
Queensland
Lunenburg
Shelburne

whale cruises, and championship golfing. Each deluxe suite features a four-poster or canopied bed(s), large whirlpool bath, fireplace, antiques, and magnificent views. Enjoy the Great Hall with its grand piano and fireplace, a quiet walk, bird watching, and an alfresco champagne lobster supper in a five-star bed and breakfast. Two- to five-night honeymoon/adventure/golf packages available. Rates include a Continental buffet breakfast and are based on per couple per night. Guaranteed reservations on Visa and MasterCard. Dinner available with advance reservations. Fully licensed Dungeon Lounge.

Hosts: Mr. and Mrs. Desmond Moffett
Rooms: 8 (PB) $225-400
Continental Breakfast
Credit Cards: A, B
Notes: 4, 7, 9, 11, 12, 13, 14

BADDECK/CAPE BRENTON

The Broadwater Inn

Box 683, B0E 1B0
(902) 295-1101; (877) 818-FISH
e-mail: outdoorstore@ns.sympatico.com

Overlooking the Bras'dor Lakes and Beinn Bhreagh, the estate of Alexander Graham Bell, the Broadwater offers wooded and garden relaxation. Serving as guests' home-away-from-home during travel throughout the Cabot Trail, the hosts offer six suites, six log cottages, and adjoin a nationally renown golf course.

Hosts: John and Rosalie
Rooms: 6 (PB) $50-80 (U.S.)
Continental Breakfast
Credit Cards: A, B
Notes: 5, 7, 11, 12, 13, 15

CHESTER

Haddon Hall Inn

67 Haddon Hill Road, B0J 1J0
(902) 275-3577; FAX (902) 275-5159

Haddon Hall, one of Chester's renowned summer estates, was built in 1905 by Vernon Woolrich. On top of Haddon Hill, the residence offers a spectacular view of Mahone Bay and the town of Chester. This elegant country inn offers 10 beautiful guest rooms furnished in period furnishings, with private baths, TVs, and telephones. Guests are invited to swim in the outdoor pool or relax on the broad veranda. In the evening sit in front of a warm crackling fire in the Moose Room prior to dining in the elegant restaurant.

Host: Cynthia O'Connell
Rooms: 10 (PB) $150 and up
Continental Breakfast
Credit Cards: A, B
Notes: 4, 7, 9, 10, 11, 12, 14, 15

Mecklenburgh Inn

78 Queen Street, B0J 1J0
(902) 275-4638 (telephone/FAX)

A welcoming bed and breakfast in the heart of the celebrated seaside village of Chester. Full gourmet breakfasts are served at the large dining table before a crackling wood fire. Each room is unique in decor, but all enjoy downy duvets, designer sheets, fluffy towels, and comfy robes. The inn is the perfect home base from which to browse the shops, explore the area and islands, golf, sail, or just relax in the hammock on the covered balcony. In the evenings enjoy the theater, fine dining, or curl

Mecklenburgh Inn

NOTES: Credit cards accepted: A MasterCard; B Visa; C American Express; D Discover; E Diner's Club; F Other; 2 Personal checks accepted; 3 Lunch available; 4 Dinner available; 5 Open all year; 6 Pets welcome; 7 No smoking; 8 Children welcome; 9 Social drinking allowed; 10 Tennis nearby; 11 Swimming nearby; 12 Golf nearby; 13 Skiing nearby; 14 May be booked through a travel agent; 15 Handicapped accessible.

up with a book in front of the fire. Atmosphere is leisurely and casual.

Host: Sue Fraser
Rooms: 3 (SB) $55-75
Suite: 1 (PB) $115
Full Breakfast
Credit Cards: B, C
Notes: 3, 9, 10, 11, 12, 14

D'ESCOUSSE

D'Escousse Bed and Breakfast

Rural Route 1, Box 510, B0E 1K0
(902) 226-2936

Early 1800s home overlooking picturesque harbor. Two and one-half baths, four rooms, TV in lounge. Kitchen facilities available. Plenty of privacy (owner resides in separate dwelling). Breakfast 7:00 A.M. to 12:00 P.M. A half-minute walk to private beach. Rowboats available. In Canada's choice of seven best villages.

Hosts: Sara and Al McDonald
Rooms: 4 (SB) $52
Full Breakfast
Credit Cards: None
Notes: 7, 8, 11, 12

DIGBY

Thistle Down Country Inn

98 Montague Row, P.O. Box 508, B0V 1A0
(902) 245-4490; (800) 565-8081
FAX (902) 245-6717

Canada Select-rated three and one-half stars. Historic 1904 home on Digby Harbour with spectacular view of the fishing fleet and the Annapolis Basin. Delicious candlelight dinners for guests only in the Queen Alexandra dining room, at 6:30 P.M.; reservations appreciated. Public telephone in lobby gift shop. *On parle français.* Twelve gracious rooms, all with private bath. Six units directly on the water with refrigerators. Cable TV and VCR in lounge. Full breakfast served 7:30-9:00 A.M. Open May

1 through October 31. Inquire about accommodations for pets. Children over six welcome.

Hosts: Ed Reid and Lester Bartson
Rooms: 12 (PB) $65-110 Canadian
Full Breakfast
Credit Cards: A, B, C, E
Notes: 4, 7, 9, 11, 12

GRAND PRÉ

Inn the Vineyard

264 Old Post Road (Box 106), B0P 1M0
(902) 542-9554; (800) 565-0000
e-mail: 101610.2263@compuserve.com

One small twin and three lovely double rooms with private baths and working fireplaces, Nova Scotia antiques, and art. In the family since 1779. Comfortable parlour for relaxing. Telephone, fax, TV, and VCR available. Minutes from Grand Pré historic park and Wolfville Theatre and fine restaurants. The hosts take pride in their hospitality and excellent three-course breakfast. Exit 10 of Route 101, right on Grand Pré Road, right again on Old Post Road. Open June 1 through September 30.

Hosts: John Halbrook and Cally Jordan
Rooms: 4 (PB) $55-95
Full Breakfast
Credit Cards: A, B
Notes: 2, 6, 7, 9, 14

HALIFAX

Halliburton House Inn

5184 Morris Street, B3J 1B3
(902) 420-0658; FAX (902) 423-2324

Halliburton House Inn is a four-star registered Heritage property and is home to one of Halifax's finest restaurants. The inn's 28 comfortable guest rooms are tastefully furnished with period antiques. All have private baths, as well as the modern amenities expected by today's guests. Two suites have working fireplaces. The restaurant offers a relaxed, elegant setting

---

NOTES: Credit cards accepted: A MasterCard; B Visa; C American Express; D Discover; E Diner's Club; F Other; 2 Personal checks accepted; 3 Lunch available; 4 Dinner available; 5 Open all year; 6 Pets welcome;

Halliburton House

for dinners. The menu specializes in seafood and wild game. On-site parking.

Host: Robert B. Pretty
Rooms: 28 (PB) $110-160
Continental Breakfast
Credit Cards: A, B, C, E
Notes: 4, 5, 7, 8, 9, 12, 14

LUNENBURG

1826 Maplebird House Bed & Breakfast

36 Pelham Street, Box 278, B0J 2C0
(902) 634-3863(phone/FAX)
e-mail: barry.susie@ns.sympatico.ca
www3.ns.sympatico.ca/barry.susie

A restored Heritage home (circa 1826) with swimming pool and large garden overlooking Lunenburg Harbour and golf course. Within easy walking distance of the town centre and its restaurants, shops, architectural homes, renowned Fisheries Museum of the Atlantic, whale watching, and sailing. Rates quoted include all taxes and breakfast.

Hosts: Susie and Barry Scott
Rooms: 4 (3 PB; 1 SB) $69-92 Canadian
Full Breakfast
Credit Cards: A, B
Notes: 2, 5, 7, 8, 9, 10, 11, 12

Kaulbach House Historic Inn

75 Pelham Street, B0J 2C0
(902) 634-8818 (phone/FAX);
    (800) 568-8818 (reservations)

Award-winning restoration of registered Heritage inn (circa 1880). In the heart of the United Nations-designated World Heritage town and overlooking the waterfront, this inn offers elegant accommodation in a gracious Victorian atmosphere. Each of the seven beautifully appointed guest rooms has TV and private bath. A complimentary elaborate three-course breakfast includes specialities like Orange Soufflé with Strawberry Sauce, Apricot Glazed Pears, Peach 'n' Creme Crêpes, and Strawberry Crème Brulée. Off-street parking.

Hosts: Eva Wambsganz
Rooms: 7 (PB) $65-110
Full Breakfast
Credit Cards: A, B, C
Notes: 7, 9, 10, 11, 12, 14

Lion Inn

P.O. Box 487, B0J 2C0
(902) 634-8988; (888) 634-8988
FAX (902) 634-3386; e-mail: lioninn@tallships.ca
www.bbcanada.com/3050.html

The Lion Inn bed and breakfast is in the heart of Lunenburg's national historic district, it is a historical Georgian home built in 1835. Over the years the building has retained both its original residential and mid-19th-century character. Evening dining includes lamb, beef, and fresh seafood cooked to order. Featured in *Frommers* and *Where to Eat in Canada*. Visit the guest lounge featuring local art work.

Hosts: Lois and George Morin
Rooms: 3 (PB) $65-85
Full Breakfast
Credit Cards: A, B, C
Notes: 4, 5, 8, 9, 10, 11, 12

---

7 No smoking; 8 Children welcome; 9 Social drinking allowed; 10 Tennis nearby; 11 Swimming nearby; 12 Golf nearby; 13 Skiing nearby; 14 May be booked through a travel agent; 15 Handicapped accessible.

The Lunenburg Inn

26 Dufferin Street, P.O. Box 1407, B0J 2C0
(902) 634-3963; (800) 565-3963
FAX (902) 634-9419; e-mail: luninn@auracom.com
www.lunco.com/lunenburginn

The hosts take pride in providing their guests an at-home warmth during a stay at this beautifully restored, classic Victorian registered Heritage property (circa 1893). Breakfasts, featuring home-baking and preserves, are always a favorite with guests. On the edge of the UNESCO-designated World Heritage Site of Old Town Lunenburg. A short stroll brings guests to the waterfront and the living history that has made Lunenburg famous the world over. Off-street parking.

Hosts: Gail and Don Wallace
Rooms: 7 (PB) $70-145 Canadian
Full Breakfast
Credit Cards: A, B, C, E
Notes: 7, 8, 9, 10, 11, 12, 14

MIDDLETON

Fairfield Farm Inn

10 Main Street (Route 1 West), B0S 1P0
(902) 825-6989 (phone/FAX); (800) 237-9896
e-mail: griffith@glinx.com
www.valleyweb.com/fairfieldfarminn

Rated four stars, this 1886 Victorian farmhouse has been completely restored and furnished in period antiques to enhance its original charm. Guest rooms feature king- and queen-size beds, en suite private bathrooms, air conditioning, cable TV, clock radios, and hair dryers. The inn is on a 110-acre estate on the Annapolis River, with woodland, mountain, and meadow views. A historic church, museum, galleries, and shops are within walking distance, and a short drive will take guests to the Bay of Fundy, national parks, and historic sites.

Hosts: Richard and Shae Griffith
Rooms: 5 (PB) $60-75 Canadian
Full and Continental Breakfast
Credit Cards: A, B, C, D, E
Notes: 3, 4, 5, 7, 9, 10, 11, 12, 13, 14, 15

MUSQUODOBOIT HARBOUR

Wayward Goose Inn Bed & Breakfast

343 West Petpeswick Road, B0J 2L0
(902) 889-3654; (888) 790-1777
www.bbcanada.com/358.html

The Wayward Inn is a quiet inn where deer and loons visit regularly. Thirty minutes from Halifax-Dartmouth, the Wayward Goose blends the best of urban convenience with rural charm. The area offers the best of crafts, museums, and breathtaking scenery. Hike the trails, swim off the dock, sail in the daysailer, paddle a canoe, row a rowboat, relax in the private living room with fireplace, stereo, cable TV, and VCR. Rooms are tastefully appointed with private baths and other features. Honeymoon suite features a whirlpool bath for two. Packages are available. Open May through October 1. Canada Select three-star rating.

Hosts: Randy and Judy Skaling
Rooms: 3 (PB) $56-81
Full Breakfast
Credit Cards: A, B
Notes: 2, 7, 8, 9, 11, 12, 14

PICTOU

Willow House Inn

11 Willow Street, P.O. Box 1900, B0K 1H0
(902) 485-5740

The Willow House Inn, a registered historical property built in 1840, consists of eight rooms with private and semi-private baths. The Willow House Inn is in the historic town of Pictou overlooking the harbor. Join the hosts at the Willow House Inn with its shaded lawn, large airy rooms which are well appointed with

NOTES: Credit cards accepted: A MasterCard; B Visa; C American Express; D Discover; E Diner's Club; F Other; 2 Personal checks accepted; 3 Lunch available; 4 Dinner available; 5 Open all year; 6 Pets welcome;

antiques and decor that depicts a quieter, tranquil time.

Rooms: 8 (4 PB; 4 SB) $55-65 Canadian
Continental Breakfast
Credit Cards: A, B
Notes: 5, 7, 8, 9, 10, 11, 12

PORT GREVILLE

Homestead Bed 'N Breakfast

Brook Road, Box 5, B0M 1T0
(902) 348-2046

Newer split-entry home on a hill overlooking the Minas Basin/Bay of Fundy featuring two colonial decorated rooms, one with an adjoining bathroom. Relaxing country atmosphere with grand piano in upstairs living room, color TV/VCR in downstairs living room, artesian well water, and many walking trails, parks, scenic lookouts, blueberry fields, and ship building museum nearby. Full breakfast with homemade bread baked on premises. Cancellation 24-hours notice. Friendly house cat on premises.

Hosts: Helen and Ross Morris
Rooms: 2 (2 SB) $55
Full Breakfast
Credit Cards: None
Notes: 7

PORT WILLIAMS

Carwarden Bed & Breakfast

640 Church Street, Rural Route 1, B0P 1T0
(888) 763-3320; FAX (902) 678-0029
e-mail: carwarden@ns.sympatico.ca
www.bbcanada.com/1427.html

Serene and stately Queen Anne Revival-style registered Heritage property; spacious high-ceilinged rooms, antiques. Peaceful rural setting, broad lawns, beautiful shade trees. Sweeping view of the dykelands from the wide veranda. Fifteen minutes to mighty Bay of Fundy tides, agate, lobster, Cape Split hiking, Grand Pré National Historic site, Wolfville's Atlantic Theatre Festival. Kind and comfort-

able hospitality, a can't-eat-lunch breakfast. Open May 1 through October 31. Forty-eight hour cancellation policy.

Host: Mrs. Mary McMahon
Rooms: 3 (1.5 PB; 2 SB) $60-65 Canadian
Full Breakfast
Credit Cards: A, B
Notes: 7, 9, 11, 12

The Old Rectory Bed & Breakfast

1519 Highway 358, Rural Route 1, B0P 1T0
(902) 542-1815

Four miles from Wolfville. Recently renovated Victorian home with sunroom, gardens, and orchard. (U-Pick and cidermaking in season.) Evening tea served. Geology field trips can be arranged. Hike to Cape Split, visit historic Prescott House and Grand-Pré National Historic Site. Enjoy the many local art galleries and cultural events available in a university town.

Hosts: Ron and Carol Buckley
Rooms: 3 (1 PB; 2 SB) $60
Full Breakfast
Credit Cards: B
Notes: 7, 8, 11, 12, 14

QUEENSLAND

Surfside Inn

Rural Route 2 Hubbards, 9609 St. Margarets Bay Road, B0J 1T0
(902) 857-2417; (800) 373-2417
www.bbcanada.com/524.html

The inn overlooks Queensland Beach and is 30 minutes away from Halifax, Peggy's Cove, and Lunenburg. This sea captain's home, circa 1880, has been restored, keeping Victorian elegance, with all but modern amenities. Rooms feature color TVs, whirlpools, and special luxuries for guests' enjoyment. Guests will feel like royalty sleeping in one of the massive antique mahogany beds which come complete with Beautyrest mattress and cozy duvet. There is also an in-ground pool. Off-season

7 No smoking; 8 Children welcome; 9 Social drinking allowed; 10 Tennis nearby; 11 Swimming nearby; 12 Golf nearby; 13 Skiing nearby; 14 May be booked through a travel agent; 15 Handicapped accessible.

Surfside Inn

rates available. Canada Select three and one-half-star rating. AAA three-diamond rating. Continental plus breakfast served.

Hosts: Michelle and Bill Batcules
Rooms: 6 (PB) $65-135
Continental Breakfast
Credit cards: A, B, C, D
Notes: 5, 7, 9, 10, 11, 12, 13, 14

SHELBURNE

The Cooper's Inn & Restaurant

36 Dock Street, P. O. Box 959, B0T 1W0
(902) 875-4656; (800) 688-2011
e-mail: coopers@ns.sympatico.ca
www3.ns.sypatico.ca/coopers

The Cooper's Inn and Restaurant is a circa 1784 Georgian mansion. The building started as a log cabin in Boston and was brought by the blind British Empire Loyalist, George Gracie, when he moved to Shelburne as a result of the American Revolution. Subsequently the house was expanded to its present configuration. The inn's intimate restaurant is highly recommended in

Where to Eat in Canada. The inn and restaurant have been selected as a favorite by *Frommers* and have been the focus of various travel articles. The Cooper's Inn and Restaurant prides itself on personal contact with the customer. In the restaurant emphasis is placed on exquisitely prepared and presented food. An extensive wine list, a selection of single malt scotch, imported beers and ales, top quality spirits are all served in an intimate and relaxed atmosphere.

Hosts: Joan and Allan Redmond
Rooms: 7 (PB) $75-145
Full Breakfast
Credit Cards: A, B, C
Notes: 4, 7, 11, 12, 14

YARMOUTH

Murray Manor Bed & Breakfast

225 Main Street, B5A 1C6
(902) 742-9625 (phone/FAX)
e-mail: m.manor@auracom.com
www.auracom.com/cts/mmanor

Beautiful Heritage home (circa 1820s) with spacious garden and 100-year-old rhododendrons tucked behind greenhouse. Three attractive bedrooms decorated in period furnishings. Close to ferry, bus, airport, shops, and museums. On historic walking tour. English and French (Acadian) spoken. Canadian personal checks accepted. Pets welcome with prior arrangements.

Hosts: George and Joan Semple
Rooms: 3 (SB) $65
Full Breakfast
Credit Cards: B
Notes: 5, 7, 8, 9, 10, 11, 12, 14

NOTES: Credit cards accepted: A MasterCard; B Visa; C American Express; D Discover; E Diner's Club; F Other; 2 Personal checks accepted; 3 Lunch available; 4 Dinner available; 5 Open all year; 6 Pets welcome;

Prince Edward Island

ALBANY

Carleton Cove Farm Tourist Home

Rural Route 2, C0B 1A0
(902) 855-2795

A warm welcome awaits guests on this beautiful island. This farm home overlooks the Northumberland Strait and the new Confederation Bridge. Trees and flowers surround the house and the lawn includes chairs, a picnic table, and barbecue to enjoy food or a relaxing moment. Two rooms with private bath. Two rooms with shared bath. Cable TV in each room. Join the hosts for a chat and complimentary snack. Full breakfasts are included in price.

Hosts: Gordon and Carol Myers
Rooms: 4 (2 PB; 2 SB) $35-45
Full Breakfast
Credit Cards: B
Notes: 3, 6, 7, 8, 11

CAVENDISH

Kindrezd Spirits Country Inn & Cottages

Memory Lane, Route 6, C0A 1N0
(902) 963-2434 (phone/FAX)
e-mail: info@kindredspirits.pe.ca
www.kindredspirits.pe.ca

A "decidedly country but intentionally quaint" inn that is family owned and specializes in warm hospitality. Spacious rooms and suites are beautifully furnished in country antiques and crafts. Twin, double, queen-, and king-size beds available. Evening tea is served in the cozy parlor-lobby and complimentary breakfast is served in the dining room. Large heated pool; whirlpool. Fireplaces. Air conditioned. Housekeeping cottages available. Pool.

Hosts: Al and Sharon James
Rooms: 27 (PB) $60-185
Continental Breakfast
Credit Cards: A, B
Notes: 7, 8, 9, 10, 11, 12, 15

CHARLOTTETOWN

Barachois Inn

P.O. Box 1022, C1A 7M4
(902) 963-2194
e-mail: BarachoisInn@pei.sympathico.ca
www.metamedia.pe.ca/barachois

Heritage Victorian house, built 1870, recently restored, tastefully decorated, antique furnishings, works of art. Four units with private bath, two suites. Victorian Garden, view of Rustico Bay and rolling landscape. Open May 1 through October 31. Canada Select four-and-one-half-star rating.

Hosts: Judy and Gary MacDonald
Rooms: 4 (PB) $125-145 Canadian
Full Breakfast
Credit Cards: A, B
Notes: 7, 8, 10, 11, 12, 14

Barachois Inn

7 No smoking; 8 Children welcome; 9 Social drinking allowed; 10 Tennis nearby; 11 Swimming nearby; 12 Golf nearby; 13 Skiing nearby; 14 May be booked through a travel agent; 15 Handicapped accessible.

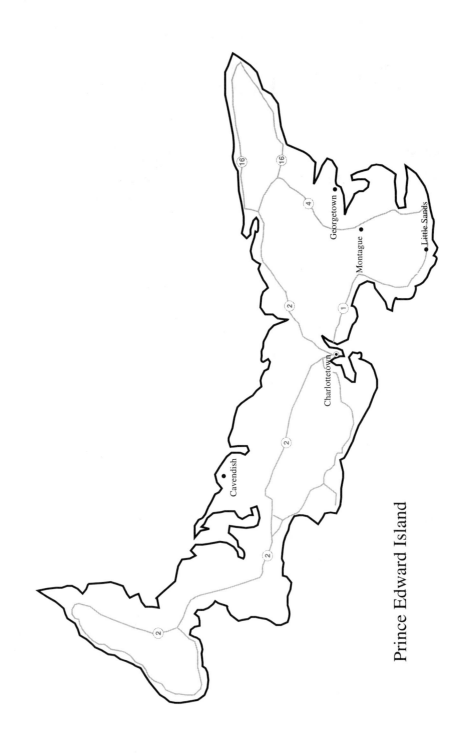

Prince Edward Island

Woodmere

Woodmere Bed & Breakfast

Route 2 East, C1A 7J7
(902) 628-1783; (800) 747-1783

Colonial home built with the guest in mind. Standardbred horses grazing in the fields, with fragrant roses blooming in the gardens. Each spacious room offers a view of the surrounding countryside and features private bath en suite, color TV, individually controlled heat, and attractive interiors. Close to airport, harness racing, theater, fine dining, and central to all attractions. National park beaches and Crow Bush golf course just a short drive of 15 minutes.

Hosts: Doris and Wallace Wood
Rooms: 4 (PB) $65-75
Full Breakfast
Credit Cards: A, B
Notes: 2, 5, 7, 9, 11, 12

GEORGETOWN

The Georgetown Inn

19 Kent Street, P.O. Box 192, C0A 1L0
(902) 652-2511; FAX (902) 652-2544
e-mail: unicorn@pei.sympatico.ca
www3.pei.sympatico.ca/unicorn

The hosts offer comfort with class in this totally remodeled 1840s Heritage home one block from Georgetown Harbour. Seven guest rooms offer queen-size beds and en suite baths. The Ivy and Forget-me-not rroms have deck and harbour views. Scottish Victorian theme

throughout with many accessories and antiques. Only minutes from Brudenell and the new championship Dundarave Golf Course. Thirty-five minutes from Charlottetown.

Hosts: Joan and Ken Taylor
Rooms: 7 (PB) $85-120
Full Breakfast
Credit Cards: B
Notes: 2, 5, 7, 9, 11, 12

LITTLE SANDS

Bayberry Cliff Inn Bed & Breakfast

Rural Route 4, Murray River, C0A 1W0
(902) 962-3395

On the edge of a 40-foot cliff on Northumberland Strait. Turn right at Wood Island Ferry Terminal, 8K on Route 4. Two uniquely decorated post-and-beam barns. Antiques and marine art. Four rooms with private baths and showers. Swimming, seal watching, craft stores, winery, air flights, restaurants handy. Open May 15 through September 30. Fifteen dollars per additional person. Breakfast included. All reservations, one night's deposit. No smoking.

Hosts: Nancy and Don Perkins
Rooms: 4 (PB) $95-135
Full Breakfast
Credit Cards: A, B
Notes: 7, 8, 9, 11, 12, 14

MONTAGUE

Van Dykes Lakeview Bed & Breakfast

Rural Route 3, C0A 1R0

Beautifully decorated bed and breakfast. Four bedrooms in original house and new added touch with three bedrooms with private en suite baths. The original home has 1885 large dining-sitting room with HBO. Collection of Beanie Babies and the noted Anne Figurines. Close to

---

NOTES: Credit cards accepted: A MasterCard; B Visa; C American Express; D Discover; E Diner's Club; F Other; 2 Personal checks accepted; 3 Lunch available; 4 Dinner available; 5 Open all year; 6 Pets welcome; 7 No smoking; 8 Children welcome; 9 Social drinking allowed; 10 Tennis nearby; 11 Swimming nearby; 12 Golf nearby; 13 Skiing nearby; 14 May be booked through a travel agent; 15 Handicapped accessible.

golf, swimming, malls, museum, craft shops, restaurants, and 30 minutes from Anne of Green Gables play. Nice walk on private lake. Prepare one's needs in the gazebo. Coffee, tea, and/or juice in the evening with munchies. One bedroom is handicapped accessible.

Hosts: Lorraine and John Van Dyke
Rooms: 7 (4 PB; 3 SB) $25-85
Continental Breakfast
Credit Cards: None
Notes: 9, 10, 11, 12

VICTORIA _____

Victoria Village Inn

P.O. Box 1, C0A 2G0
(902) 658-2483
e-mail: victoriavillageinn@pei.sympatico.ca

This circa 1880 Victorian home is in beautiful Victoria by the Sea. Within 30 minutes from major attractions and 15 minutes from Confederation Bridge. Enjoy a stroll around the village, explore the beach, and see local crafts. Next door to live theatre, golfing nearby. Enjoy a meal in the Actor's Retreat Café on the premises. Dinner and theatre packages available. Lunch and dinner available seasonally.

Host: Debby MacLean
Rooms: 5 (4 PB; 1SB) $65-100
Continental Breakfast
Credit Cards: A, B
Notes: 5, 7, 11, 12, 13

Québec

BATISCAN

Au Bois Dormant

1521 Rue Principale, G0X 1A0
(418) 362-3182

Au Bois Dormant is on Le Chemin du Roi, 90-minutes' drive from Montréal or 50 minutes from Québec City, and is a bed and breakfast, an antique and art shop, and a charming rural home from yesteryear which offers a warm welcome to guests year-round. The home is surrounded by silver maples and apple trees and includes a promenade that leads to the Batiscan River where it joins the St. Lawrence Seaway.

Hosts: Pierre and Ginette Lajoie
Rooms: 4 (4 SB) $40-45 U.S.
Full Breakfast
Credit Cards: B
Notes: 5, 7, 8, 11

BONAVENTURE/NEW CARLISLE

Bay View Manor

395, Route 132, Bonaventure East, Box 21
New Carlisle, G0C 1Z0
(418) 752-2725; (418) 752-6718

Seaside home beside 18-hole Fauvel golf course, near Bonaventure East lighthouse, on the ruggedly beautiful Gaspé Peninsula of eastern coastal Québec. Once a country store and rural post office, this home now welcomes worldwide guests to this spectacular location. Fresh eggs, fruit, produce from the farm, freshly baked goods, homemade jams at breakfast. Hear the waves, view sunsets, visit museums, caves, bird sanctuary, national parks. Play tennis, canoe, fish, hike, swim, and golf.

Host: Helen Sawyer
Rooms: 5 (1 PB; 4 SB) $35
Full Breakfast
Credit Cards: None
Notes: 5, 7, 8, 10, 11, 12, 13

DESCHAMBAULT

Auberge Chemin Du Roy

106 St. Laurent, G0A 1S0
(418) 286-6958

First step in Québec region, Deschambault invites guests to discover its historic past by staying at this Victorian inn. The antiques evoke a feeling of serenity and romance near the fireplace. Guests can also relax with the murmuring waterfall and the St. Lawrence River breezes in front of the inn.

Hosts: Francine Bouthat and Gilles Laberge
Rooms: 8 (6 PB; 2 SB) $64-99
Full Breakfast
Credit Cards: A, B
Notes: 4, 5, 9, 11, 12

GEORGEVILLE

Auberge Georgeville

71 chemin Channel, J0B 1T0
(819) 843-8683; (888) 843-8686
FAX (819) 843-5045
www.fortune1000.ca/georgeville

A stately Victorian inn, Québec's oldest historic hotel sits majestically overlooking Lake Memphremagog, only 75 minutes east of Montréal and 20 minutes north of the Vermont I-91. Laura Ashley decor with 13 rooms, award-winning cuisine, afternoon tea and

7 No smoking; 8 Children welcome; 9 Social drinking allowed; 10 Tennis nearby; 11 Swimming nearby; 12 Golf nearby; 13 Skiing nearby; 14 May be booked through a travel agent; 15 Handicapped accessible.

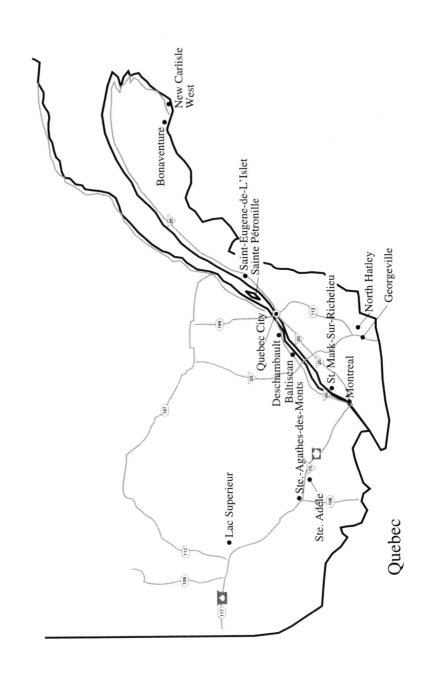

New Carlisle
West

Bonaventure

Saint-Eugene-de-L'Islet
Sainte Pétronille

Quebec City

North Hatley

Georgeville

St Mark-Sur-Richelieu

Deschambault

Baltiscan

Montreal

Ste.-Agathes-des-Monts

Lac Superieur

Ste. Adéle

Quebec

sherry, and many on-site activities. Tour the wine cellar, visit the quaint village with craft shops or stroll to the lake. Recipient: AAA four-diamond culinary award, *Wine Spectator* Award of Excellence. Featured in Fodor's *Great Country Inns* and *Country Inns* magazine. Rates include full country breakfast and five-service gourmet dinner.

Hosts: Steven Beyrouty and Megan Seline
Rooms: 12 (8 PB; 4 SB) $180-275 Canadian
Suite: 1
Full Breakfast
Credit Cards: A, B, C
Notes: 4, 5, 7, 9, 10, 11, 12, 13, 14

LAC SUPÉRIEUR

Auberge Caribou Lodge

141, ch. Tour du Lac, J0T 1P0
(819) 688-5201; FAX (819) 688-2393
e-mail: info@cariboulodge.qc.com
www.cariboulodge.qc.ca

Charming wooden lodge on the shores of splendid Lake Supérieur in the heart of Québec's Laurentian Mountains. In winter enjoy the best alpine and cross-country skiing at Tremblant, "#1 ski resort in eastern North America." In summer discover the beach, the lakefront terrace, and a multitude of outdoor activities at Tremblant Resort and Mont-Tremblant Provincial Park. Bedrooms with private bathrooms and breathtaking lake and mountain view. Lakefront dining room, cosy bar, and central stone fireplace.

Hosts: Jacques Larivière
Rooms: 14 (7 PB; 7 SB) $70-180 Canadian
Full Breakfast
Credit Cards: A, B
Notes: 2, 3, 4, 5, 7, 9, 10, 11, 12

MONTRÉAL

Auberge de la Fontaine

1301 East Rachel Street, H2J 2K1
(514) 597-0166; (800) 597-0597

FAX (514) 597-0496
e-mail: info@aubergedelafontaine.com
www.aubergedelafontaine.com

Nice stone house where guests will be warmly welcomed in this charming bed and breakfast inn in front of Parc la Fontaine, an 84-acre park close to the downtown area. The 21 air-conditioned rooms and suites, some with whirlpool bath, others with terrace or balcony, are beautiful, comfortable, and will make guests feel at home. Enjoy a generous Continental buffet and free access to the kitchen for snacks. Parking is free as well behind the inn and in nearby streets. Eight guest rooms are nonsmoking rooms.

Hosts: Céline Boudreau and Jean Lamothe
Rooms: 21 (PB) $110-222
Continental Breakfast
Credit Cards: A, B, C, E
Notes: 5, 8, 10, 11, 14, 15

Bed & Breakfast à Montréal: A City-wide Network

424 Cherrier, H2L 1G9
(514) 738-9410; (800) 738-4338
e-mail: info@bbmontreal.com
www.bbmontreal.com

In the finest private homes and condo apartments, carefully selected for comfort, cleanliness, and location. Many are within walking distance of Vieux Montréal and the convention center. All of the hosts are fluent in English and will enhance any visit with suggestions, outgoing personalities, and delicious breakfasts. Stay long enough to visit Vieux Montréal, the lively Latin Quarter, the Underground Montréal, Botanical Gardens, Mont-Royal Park, and St. Joseph's Oratory, among others. Visits can also be arranged to Québec City. Coordinator: Marian Kahn

Belvedere Bed and Breakfast. Five large guest rooms, each with private bath, await guests in this sprawling property, adjacent to downtown Montréal. This mansion features beautiful woodwork, a solarium, large grounds

NOTES: Credit cards accepted: A MasterCard; B Visa; C American Express; D Discover; E Diner's Club; F Other; 2 Personal checks accepted; 3 Lunch available; 4 Dinner available; 5 Open all year; 6 Pets welcome; 7 No smoking; 8 Children welcome; 9 Social drinking allowed; 10 Tennis nearby; 11 Swimming nearby; 12 Golf nearby; 13 Skiing nearby; 14 May be booked through a travel agent; 15 Handicapped accessible.

for easy parking and views. The real estate agent/hostess lives here with her two children and Blacky, the dog.

Brigette's Bed and Breakfast. Brigette's love of art and antiques is obvious in this fabulous three-story townhouse. Fireplace, cozy living room, and a view of the city's most historic park all add to the charm of this home. One double with brass bed, duvet, antique pieces, and guests' own bathroom. Experience nearby "bring your own wine" restaurants. $85 Canadian.

Jacky's Bed and Breakfast. This interior designer-hostess has created warmth and charm in this elegant downtown condo, with treasures collected from India and New Mexico. The guest room has a queen-size bed and private bathroom facilities. Sherbrooke Street, the Montréal Museum of Fine Arts, and the city's best shopping are all just two minutes away. $95 Canadian.

Johanna's Bed and Breakfast. This elegant hostess invites guests to this bright, airy, two-story home filled with European style. An avid gardener, she is pleased to share the joys of the garden with guests. This Westmount home is just five minutes from downtown. One double with a private bathroom is offered. $85 Canadian.

Be a guest in **Marian's** downtown triplex, typical of the architecture of that era. In the Latin Quarter, off St. Denis Street and St. Louis Square; subway around the corner. Home features exposed brick walls, high ceilings, lovely flooring, collectibles, and warm decor. Full breakfast. $75-85 Canadian.

Nelson Street Bed and Breakfast. This 15-room Victorian home with three double guest rooms is a real delight. The fashion designer-hostess has brought her artistic flair to the decoration of the house. On a quiet street in a chic neighborhood, where guests can enjoy cafés, restaurants, and elegant shops. Downtown is only 10-15 minutes away. $85-110 Canadian.

A Montréal Oasis Bed & Breakfast

3000 chemin de Breslay, H3Y 2G7
(514) 935-2312

This spacious home is in downtown's select West End, close to the Montréal Museum of Fine Arts, Crescent and St. Catherine Streets. It is decorated with Québec and Swedish furniture, African, Asian, and Swedish art. Breakfast is gourmet. Swedish hostess, in Montréal by choice, has lived in many parts of the world; she also operates a quality bed and breakfast network of homes in downtown, the Latin Quarter, and the Old City. MasterCard and Visa accepted only for reservations.

Host: Lena Blondel
Rooms: 30 (5 PB; 25 SB) $40-90
Full Breakfast
Credit Cards: None
Notes: 5, 7, 9, 13

NORTH HATLEY

Cedar Gables

4080 Magog Road, Box 355, J0B 2C0
(819) 842-4120

Established in 1985 as the area's premier bed and breakfast, Cedar Gables is a large, tastefully decorated home, circa 1890s, at the lakeside on Lake Massawippi in the heart of Québec's eastern townships. Easily accessible, the inn is 10 minutes from the U.S./Canada

Cedar Gables

NOTES: Credit cards accepted: A MasterCard; B Visa; C American Express; D Discover; E Diner's Club; F Other; 2 Personal checks accepted; 3 Lunch available; 4 Dinner available; 5 Open all year; 6 Pets welcome;

I-91/Autoroute 55 northeast corridor. The five guest rooms have private baths en suite. Four rooms have king-size beds and the fifth, a canopied double. It is a five-minute walk to a unique resort village with shopping, browsing, and a full range of dining. Detailed brochure available. Limited smoking. Children over 12 welcome.

Hosts: Ann and Don Fleischer
Rooms: 5 (PB) $80-104
Full Breakfast
Credit Cards: A, B, C
Notes: 2, 5, 6, 9, 10, 11, 12, 13, 14, 15

QUÉBEC CITY

Au Petit Hôtel

3 ruelle des Ursulines, G1R 3Y6
(418) 694-0965; FAX (418) 692-4320

In the heart of Old Québec, Au Petit Hôtel offers quiet surroundings with a warm and hospitable atmosphere. Near major attractions such as the Ursulines convent, the Citadel, and Le Château Frontenac. Discriminating gourmets will have no trouble finding neighborhood restaurants, smart boutiques, and all kinds of entertainment.

Hosts: The Tim Family
Rooms: 16 (PB) $45–70
Continental Breakfast
Credit Cards: A, B
Notes: 5, 8, 9, 11, 13, 14

Au Petit Hôtel

Bed & Breakfast à Montréal: A City-wide Network

424 Cherrier, H2L 1G9
(514) 738-9410; (800) 738-4338
e-mail: info@bbmontreal.com
www.bbmontreal.com

A Québec City Choice. Delight in this restored 17th-century home in Old Québec offering three guest rooms with private bathrooms. Many special architectural features and antique furnishings. This bilingual host couple and their dog welcome guests. $95-110 Canadian.

Hôtel Château de la Terrasse, Inc.

6 Place Terrasse Dufferin, G1R 4N5
(418) 694-9472; FAX (418) 694-0055

Built in 1830, this stately residence is in between the Citadel and Château Frontenac, on the famous Dufferin Terrace overlooking the St. Lawrence River. Its unique inner architecture has been kept with a beautifully sculpted wooden staircase and a few authentic stained-glass windows. The ideal restover to feel the pulse of the oldest city in North America, amid a myriad of activities offered on the boardwalk.

Host: Christiane-Marie Bès
Rooms: 30 (16 PB; 2 SB) $75-120
Continental Breakfast
Credit Cards: A, B, C, E
Notes: 5, 8, 13

Hôtel Marie Rollet

81 rue Sainte-Anne, G1R 3X4
(418) 694-9271
(800) 275-0338

Built in 1876 by the Ursulines order, the Marie-Rollet House offers the ancestral charm of a turn-of-

7 No smoking; 8 Children welcome; 9 Social drinking allowed; 10 Tennis nearby; 11 Swimming nearby; 12 Golf nearby; 13 Skiing nearby; 14 May be booked through a travel agent; 15 Handicapped accessible.

the-century European manor. Guests will be captivated by its warm woodwork and its tranquility and serenity. All area attractions can be reached by foot. Two rooms offer a functional fireplace and most have air conditioning. A rooftop terrace with a garden view gives guests an opportunity to relax in a calm and serene environment.

Hosts: Gerald Giroux and Diane Chouinard
Rooms: 10 (PB) $65-135 Canadian
No Breakfast
Credit Cards: A, B
Notes: 5, 8, 10, 11, 12, 13, 14

La Maison Lafleur

2, re de Laval, G1R 3T9
(418) 692-0685; FAX (418) 694-0551
www.presentix.com/com/lafleur/

A peaceful, residential location in the heart of the old Latin quarter, Old Québec. Surrounded by an exceptional view of 17th-and 18th-century architecture. While this row house was rebuilt in 1950, portions still remain from the 18th century. All of the tourist attractions and services are right at the doorstep. Ten-minute walk to bus and train station. As a long-time resident of Old Québec, the host will gladly suggest many unforgettable places to visit. Cross-country skiing within walking distance. Maximum capacity is six persons. Apartment also available. A healthy breakfast is included in rates.

Host: Gilles Lafleur
Rooms: 3 (1 PB; 2 SB) $60-100
Credit Cards: B
Notes: 5, 7, 8, 10, 11, 13

SAINTE-ADELE

Auberge Beaux Rêves et Spa (Sweet Dreams Inn & Spa)

2310, boul. Ste-Adèle, J8B 2N5
(514) 229-9226; FAX (514) 229-2999
e-mail: welcome@beauxreves.com
www.Beauxreves.com

In Sainte-Adèle midway between Montréal and Mont-Tremblant in the heart of the Laurentians. A unique spa concept with outdoor hot tub, sauna, and relaxation pavilion, open year-round. A riverside nature path brings guests to dozens of natural whirlpools. All rooms have private bathrooms; some overlook the river. A full country breakfast is served fresh every morning. Close to snowmobiling, skiing, golf, cycling, nature walks, etc. Relaxation massages available.

Host: Hannes Lamothe
Rooms: 6 (PB) $80-95 Canadian
Full Breakfast
Credit Cards: A, B
Notes: 5, 7, 8, 9, 10, 11, 12, 13, 14

SAINTE-AGATHE-DES-MONTS

Auberge du Lac des Sables

230 St-Venant, J8C 2Z7
(819) 326-3994; (800) 567-8329
FAX (819) 326-9159
e-mail: info@aubergedulac.com
www.aubergedulac.com

One hour north of Montréal, in the heart of the Laurentians, between St-Sauveur and Mont Tremblant. The warm welcome and the charm of an authentic country inn in an exceptional scenic site on the shores of Lac des Sables. Each of the 23 cozy rooms is equipped with a private bathroom and whirlpool, color TV, and air conditioning. Some rooms include a fireplace and mini-kitchen. Outside heated whirlpool and conference room also available.

Auberge du Lac des Sables

At walking distance from the village and a wide range of summer and winter activities. Many packages available.

Hosts: Dominique Lessard and Luc Menard
Rooms: 23 (PB) $78-136 Canadian (approx. $56-97 U.S.)
Full Breakfast
Credit Cards: A, B, C
Notes: 4, 5, 8, 10, 11, 12, 13, 14

SAINT-EUGENE-DE-L'ISLET _____

Auberge Des Glacis

46, route Tortue, G0R 1X0
(418) 247-7486; (877) 245-2247
FAX (418) 247-7182

This onetime flour mill will seduce guests through its sheer charm, warm ambiance, country decor, and gourmet food. In the heart of beautifully kept grounds, the Auberge is made only more captivating by its exceptional surroundings; a river, small lake for swimming, and bird watching trails. Various packages are also available; golf, biking, cruise, massage, ski, and romance. Continental breakfast is included in the price and guests can have full breakfast (buffet) for an additional price.

Hosts: Micheline and Pierre Watters
Rooms: 10 (PB) $84-129
Continental Breakfast
Credit Cards: A, B, C, F
Notes: 3, 4, 5, 8, 9, 11, 12, 13, 14

SAINT-MARC-SUR-RICHELIEU _____

Hostellerie Les Trois Tilleuls

290 rue Richelieu, J0L 2E0
(450) 856-7787; FAX (450) 584-3146
e-mail: host.3tilleuls@sympatico.ca
www.relaischateaus.sr/tilleuls

A stay at Les Trois Tilleuls means being an eagerly awaited guest in a century-old home.

It's an opportunity to discover a multitude of artworks, acquired over the past 100 years, and to enjoy the labors of craftsmen from bygone days to the present, who put their hearts into creating an incomparable inn. At Les Trois Tilleuls, a colorful garden sparkling in the morning dew, warm oneself in the early morning sun and contemplate the Richelieu River, one of Québec's beautiful and historic rivers. A modern wing contains 24 charming rooms with every modern convenience.

Host: Mr. Michel Aubriot
Rooms: 24 (PB) $115-390 Canadian w/ room only
   $225-530 Candian w/ American plan
Full Breakfast
Credit Cards: A, B, C, D, E
Notes: 3, 4, 5, 8, 9, 10, 11, 12, 13, 14, 15

SAINTE-PETRONILLE _____

Auberge la Goéliche Inn

22 chemin du Quai, G0A 4C0
(418) 828-2248; FAX (418) 828-2745
e-mail: aubergelagoeliche@oricom.ca

The inn is on the west point of the island of Orleans, which offers a wonderful view of both the St. Lawrence River and Québec City. L'Auberge has 18 romantic rooms furnished in heirloom antiques. Two cozy chalets with kitchenettes are also available. All of those units have a view of the river. The main dining room is a glass enclosed terrace. The hosts will serve local products and fine cuisine to guests while watching cruise ships and freighters steaming past. In summer, guests will also enjoy the outdoor terrace and its gardens, the wraparound porch, and the outdoor swimming pool.

Hosts: Mme. Andrée Marchand and Mme. Marie-Andrée Turgeon
Rooms: 18 (PB) $109-194 Canadian
Full Breakfast
Credit Cards: A, B, C, E
Notes: 3, 4, 5, 7, 8, 10, 11, 12, 13, 14, 15

7 No smoking; 8 Children welcome; 9 Social drinking allowed; 10 Tennis nearby; 11 Swimming nearby; 12 Golf nearby; 13 Skiing nearby; 14 May be booked through a travel agent; 15 Handicapped accessible.

RECOMMENDATION FORM

As *The Annual Directory of American and Canadian Bed & Breakfasts* gains approval from the traveling public, more and more bed and breakfast establishments are asking to be included on our mailing list. If you know of another bed and breakfast which may not be on our list, give them a great outreach and advertising opportunity by providing us with the following information:

1) B&B Name _____

Host's Name _____

Address _____

City _____ State _____ Zip Code _____

Telephone _____ FAX _____

2) B&B Name _____

Host's Name _____

Address _____

City _____ State _____ Zip Code _____

Telephone _____ FAX _____

3) B&B Name _____

Host's Name _____

Address _____

City _____ State _____ Zip Code _____

Telephone _____ FAX _____

Please return this form to: Barbour Publishing, Inc.
P.O. Box 719, Uhrichsville, OH 44683
(740) 922-6045; FAX (740) 922-5948

Planning the perfect vacation?

Find all the best lodging in

The Annual Directory of American and Canadian Bed & Breakfasts

Five volumes in the series:

New England (Volume I)—includes Connecticut, Maine, Massachusetts, New Hampshire, Rhode Island, Vermont, New Brunswick, Nova Scotia, Prince Edward Island, and Quebec. 304 pages, $9.95 ($15.50 in Canada), ISBN 1-57748-771-0

Mid-Atlantic Region (Volume II)—includes Delaware, District of Columbia, Maryland, New Jersey, New York, Pennsylvania, Virginia, Ontario. 272 pages, $9.95 ($15.50 in Canada), ISBN 1-57748-772-9

The South (Volume III)—includes Alabama, Arkansas, Florida, Georgia, Kentucky, Louisiana, Mississippi, North Carolina, South Carolina, Tennessee, Texas, Virginia, West Virginia, Puerto Rico, and the Virgin Islands. 288 pages, $9.95 ($15.50 in Canada), ISBN 1-57748-773-7

The Midwest (Volume IV)—includes Illinois, Indiana, Iowa, Kansas, Michigan, Minnesota, Missouri, Nebraska, North Dakota, Ohio, Oklahoma, South Dakota, Wisconsin, Manitoba, and Ontario. 192 pages, $9.95 ($15.50 in Canada), ISBN 1-57748-774-5

The West (Volume V)—includes Alaska, Arizona, California, Colorado, Hawaii, Idaho, Montana, Nevada, New Mexico, Oregon, Texas, Utah, Washington, Wyoming, Alberta, British Columbia, and Saskatchewan. 448 pages, $12.95 ($19.95 in Canada), ISBN 1-57748-775-3

Available wherever books are sold.
Or order from:
Barbour Publishing, Inc.
P.O. Box 719
Uhrichsville, Ohio 44683
http://www.barbourbooks.com

If you order by mail, add $2.00 to your order for shipping.
Prices subject to change without notice.